International Law and International Relations

Events such as the legal arguments surrounding the 2003 Iraq War and the creation of the International Criminal Court highlight the significance of international law in the contemporary world. This new textbook provides an introduction to the relationship between international law and international relations. David Armstrong, Theo Farrell and Hélène Lambert explore the evolution, nature and function of international law in world politics and situate international law in its historical and political context. They propose three interdisciplinary 'lenses' through which to view the role of international law in world politics: realist, liberal and constructivist. These lenses offer different ways of looking at international law in terms of what it is, how it works and how it changes. Topics covered include the use of force, human rights, international crimes, international trade and the environment, and each chapter features discussion questions and guides to further reading.

David Armstrong is Professor of International Relations in the Department of Politics at the University of Exeter.

Theo Farrell is Professor of War in the Modern World in the Department of War Studies at King's College London.

Hélène Lambert is Senior Lecturer in International Law in the School of Law at Brunel University.

Themes in International Relations

This new series of textbooks aims to provide students with authoritative surveys of central topics in the study of International Relations. Intended for upper level undergraduates and graduates, the books will be concise, accessible and comprehensive. Each volume will examine the main theoretical and empirical aspects of the subject concerned, and its relation to wider debates in International Relations, and will also include chapter-by-chapter guides to further reading and discussion questions.

International Law and International Relations

David Armstrong, Theo Farrell and Hélène Lambert

CAMBRIDGE
UNIVERSITY PRESS

CAMBRIDGE UNIVERSITY PRESS
Cambridge, New York, Melbourne, Madrid, Cape Town, Singapore, São Paulo, Delhi

Cambridge University Press
The Edinburgh Building, Cambridge CB2 8RU, UK

Published in the United States of America by Cambridge University Press, New York

www.cambridge.org
Information on this title: www.cambridge.org/9780521605182

© David Armstrong, Theo Farrell and Hélène Lambert 2007

First published 2007
Reprinted 2009

Printed in the United Kingdom at the University Press, Cambridge

A catalogue record for this publication is available from the British Library

Library of Congress Cataloguing in Publication data

ISBN 978-0-521-84410-9 hardback
ISBN 978-0-521-60518-2 paperback

*To Maggie, Eloise, and in memory of
Anne-Marie Lambert.*

Contents

List of tables   *page* viii
Acknowledgments   ix

Introduction   1

Part I   The foundations

1   The nature of international law   9

2   The evolution of international law   34

3   Three lenses: realism, liberalism, constructivism   69

Part II   The law in world politics

4   Use of force   117

5   Human rights   151

6   International crimes   178

7   International trade   222

8   The environment   253

Part III   Conclusions

9   International law in a unipolar age   281

Index   295

Tables

3.1 Interdisciplinary lenses on international law   *page* 106
3.2 Interdisciplinary lenses applied to volume themes   107
7.1 The GATT trade rounds   224
7.2 The structure of the WTO agreements   226
7.3 Developing country coalitions formed at Cancun   243

Acknowledgments

Ranging across history, theory and an expanse of international law, this book has been a long and ambitious journey for us. It has been, at turns, challenging, arduous, exhilarating and fun. We received help from several quarters along the way – help we wish to acknowledge gratefully here. Mike Addo, Maggie Armstrong, Ilias Bantekas, Caroline Fournet, Amrita Narlikar, Iain Hampsher-Monk, Jason Ralph and Javaid Rehman all kindly offered pointed and extremely helpful comments on draft chapters for us. John Haslam at Cambridge University Press has been a 'dream' commissioning editor throughout the project. We are also grateful to our production editor at Cambridge, Elizabeth Davey, and our eagle-eyed copy-editor, Jacqueline French. Finally, we wish to thank the four anonymous reviewers who helped us make critical improvements to the book and one reviewer in particular, who gave us very detailed comments on the whole manuscript.

Introduction

This book is intended to introduce International Relations (IR) students to the complexities of international law. It emphasises the different ways of looking at international law, in terms of what it is, how it works, and how it changes. This book is also intended to introduce International Law (IL) students to the complexities of international relations and, in particular, to the various ways that IR scholars have conceived the dominant structures, main actors and driving forces of world politics. To these ends, we seek to do three things:

(1) to situate international law in its political and historical context
(2) to give students a foundation in the main theories of IR and IL
(3) to enable students to apply those theories to the study of the main empirical areas of IL

It should be immediately obvious that this is not a straightforward, 'blackletter' law book. It does not seek to provide a definitive account of international law. There are a number of excellent books by eminent international lawyers that attempt to do just this.[1] In other words, this book will not provide students with a single perspective on international law, nor will it provide a fully comprehensive guide to all aspects of international law. Rather, it seeks to develop in students a working knowledge of the various perspectives that scholars have taken on international law. Full discussion of the historical, political, and theoretical contexts of international law has necessitated some sacrifices in terms of the breadth of our empirical coverage. Thus, some major topics in black-letter books on international law – such as, the law of the sea, territorial sovereignty, and state responsibility – are not dealt with in this book. However, we do cover those main empirical areas where, in our judgment, international law and world politics most vigorously interact; these being, use of force, human rights, international crimes, international trade, and the environment.

[1] Ian Brownlie, *Principles of Public International Law*, 6th edition (Oxford: Oxford University Press, 2003); Malcolm Shaw, *International Law*, 5th edition (Cambridge: Cambridge University Press, 2003); Antonio Cassese, *International Law*, 2nd edition (Oxford: Oxford University Press, 2005).

To be sure, recent dramas in all these areas have brought into sharp relief the importance of international law in the contemporary world. Domestic and international debate on the US-led war against Iraq in 2003 has centred as much on the legality as on the strategic efficiency of war. Humanitarian law has provided the benchmarks for critical scrutiny, and hence open criticism, of the treatment of detainees by the US government in its self-proclaimed global war on terror, as well as the conduct of military operations by coalition forces in Afghanistan and Iraq. At the same time, the growing culture of human rights provided a central narrative justifying the coalition campaigns against the Taliban in Afghanistan and Saddam Hussein's brutal dictatorship in Iraq. For many states, the management of trade is a bigger concern than the management of armed conflict. Multilateral management of international trade occurs within the legal framework of the World Trade Organization (WTO). Moreover, even this dry and technical area of world politics has attracted much public attention in recent years, as dramatically shown by the anti-globalisation riots in Seattle during the WTO meeting there in 1999. Likewise, highly technical legal regimes to protect the environment, especially the 1997 Kyoto Protocol on climate change, have high salience in public and political debate.

As we shall discuss, the foundation of the modern discipline of IR rested on a rejection by leading scholars such as E. H. Carr and Hans J. Morgenthau of the significance of international law. Writing in the lead-up to and just after World War II (WWII), these 'realist' scholars argued that, when it came to the crunch, international law had no impact on state behaviour. Indeed, for realists, the failure of the League of Nations to prevent the outbreak of WWII vividly demonstrated how foolhardy it was to place much faith in international law. As the discipline of IR developed, so scholars from other perspectives challenged this grim realist reading of the world. Debate continues to this day between realist and liberal scholars concerning the impact of regimes (many legal in foundation) on international relations. However, it is hard to credit the argument that international law has no impact on contemporary world politics and that states can do as they please. In recent decades the legal regimes on use of force, human rights, international crimes, trade, and the environment have all deepened and expanded in scope through evolving state custom and new treaty law. Furthermore, whilst states remain central actors in developing the law in these areas, a number of non-state authoritative bodies now play crucial roles in clarifying state rights and obligations under customary and treaty law; such bodies include the International Court of Justice, the United Nations Security Council, the European Court of Human Rights, the Appellate Body of the WTO, and the new

International Criminal Court. Increasingly, non-governmental organisations (NGOs) are also able to exert influence through national coalitions and transnational networks in getting states to honour existing legal obligations and to create new rules in all of the areas of international law studied in this book.

Given these developments and recent dramas, it is small wonder that there have been a number of books in recent years that have sought to bridge IR and IL.[2] Many of these have been edited volumes which by including IR and IL scholars have facilitated the dialogue between disciplines.[3] It is precisely this dialogue that brought us together for this book. David Armstrong and Theo Farrell are both scholars of IR, and Hélène Lambert is a Law scholar. Dialogue was further aided in the early stages by us all being at the University of Exeter when the project started.

The first two chapters of the book place international law in political and historical context. Chapter 1 provides a general discussion of the nature of international law. In this, we discuss the place and purpose of law in world politics. We introduce students to the main theoretical approach of each discipline – realism in IR and positivism in IL – which we present here as offering rival views of the world (in Chapter 3, we then reveal similarities in their fundamental assumptions about the world). We also situate international law in its normative context by introducing the idea of international society and examining its various political and cultural dimensions.

Chapter 2 discusses the historical evolution of international law. Rules relating to diplomacy and treaties are apparent from ancient times, usually supported by the 'sanction' of divine retribution for oath-breakers. As more extensive commercial and cultural links develop, so do more complex legal systems emerge, although whether a true 'legal order' existed in ancient times is more open to question. It is only with the emergence,

---

[2] Michael Byers, *Custom, Power, and the Power of Rules: International Relations and Customary International Law* (Cambridge: Cambridge University Press, 1999); Shirley V. Scott, *International Law in World Politics: An Introduction* (Boulder, CO: Lynne Rienner Publishers, 2004); Christopher C. Joyner, *International Law in the 21st Century: Rules for Global Governance* (Lanham: Rowan and Littlefield, 2005).

[3] 'Legalization and world politics', special issue of *International Organization* 54 (2000); Michael Byers (ed.), *The Role of Law in International Politics: Essays in International Relations and International Law* (Oxford: Oxford University Press, 2001); Christian Reus-Smit (ed.), *The Politics of International Law* (Cambridge: Cambridge University Press, 2004); David Armstrong, Theo Farrell and Bice Maiguashca (eds.), *Force and Legitimacy in World Politics* (Cambridge: Cambridge University Press, 2005); Thomas J., Biersteker, Peter J. Spiro, Chandra Lekha Sriram, and Veronica Raffo (eds.), *International Law and International Relations: Bridging Theory and Practice* (London: Routledge, 2007). See also the reader by Oona A. Hathaway and Harold Hongju Koh (eds.), *Foundations of International Law and Politics* (New York: Foundation Press, 2005).

from the Middle Ages, of the concept of sovereign equality that something resembling the contemporary international legal system begins to appear.

Chapter 3 introduces the theories and themes that provide the framework for the rest of the book. Our method for bridging the disciplinary divide between IR and IL centres on the use of theoretical 'lenses' through which to view the nature and function of international law in world politics. In so doing, we want students to appreciate how theory frames one's subject of study, illuminating particular problems and processes. In this chapter, we survey the major theoretical approaches to IR and IL and from these we generate three interdisciplinary 'lenses' – realist, liberal and constructivist. We do not set out to 'prove' a particular theoretical approach, but rather to demonstrate what each approach 'tells us'.

Chapter 3 also lays out three substantive themes for our empirical study of international law. The first theme addresses the content of the law. International law is most commonly seen as a system of rules to guide state action. But liberal scholars argue that it must also encompass a common set of progressive values. More recently, some scholars have suggested that international law also provides the discursive resources that enable states to express their identities and engage in meaningful interaction. The second theme concerns why states (and other actors) comply with international law. Understandably, this question is of central concern to IL scholars. Compliance is an explicit aim of law. Moreover, in explaining why states comply, IL scholars also establish the influence of international law.[4] Explanations range from state consent, to notions of fairness, to internalisation of international law in domestic legal systems. The third theme deals with change in international law. Generally speaking, law is more characterised by stasis than change. The stability of law gives it prescriptive force. But ultimately, to function effectively, law must keep up with society. In terms of international society, change has been all too evident in the increasing codification of customary rules, and creation of new treaty-based regimes, since the turn of the twentieth century. In looking at legal change, we focus on the various agents (e.g., states, international judicial bodies and NGOs) and processes (e.g., treaty-negotiation, policy-making, and state learning) involved.

Chapters 4 to 8 deal with international law on, respectively, use of force, human rights, international crimes, international trade and the

[4] Kal Raustiala and Anne-Marie Slaughter, 'International Law, international relations and compliance', in Walter Carlsnaes, Thomas Risse and Beth A. Simmons (eds.), *Handbook of International Relations* (Thousand Oaks, CA: Sage, 2002), p. 538. See also William C. Bradford, 'International Legal Compliance: an annotated bibliography', *North Carolina Journal of International Law and Commercial Regulation* 30 (2004), 379–417.

environment. These chapters are structured around the themes of content, compliance, and change in international law. We use our realist, liberal and constructivist lenses to guide the discussion within each theme. Our goal, therefore, is for students not only to be familiar with the law on crucial matters from armed conflict to trade, but more importantly, to understand the different ways of looking at the nature and functions of international law. The law matters for world politics as never before. We aim to show students the various ways in which this is true.

Part I

The foundations

1 The nature of international law

Two kinds of theoretical perspectives have frequently been employed to cast doubt on the significance of international law. The first, which is located within the branch of legal theory known as 'positivism', argues, in essence, that law as such is distinguished from broader and looser normative structures by its imperative nature. In the most famous version of this, by the nineteenth-century English jurist John Austin, 'law properly so-called' is the command of a sovereign backed by coercive sanctions. Since states in the international system acknowledge no sovereign body other than themselves and since powerful states cannot be forced to take or refrain from taking actions against their will, international law cannot be considered true law. As Austin puts it, the duties which international law imposes do not have the obligatory character of true law because they 'are enforced by moral sanctions, by fear on the part of nations, or by fear on the part of sovereigns, of provoking general hostility, and incurring its probable evils, in case they shall violate maxims generally received and respected'.[1] The second theoretical perspective is drawn from that body of theoretical reflection within International Relations (IR) known as 'realism'.[2] This asserts that states exist in an overall context of international anarchy which impels them towards ceaseless competition in pursuit of their separate interests. In the inevitable struggle for power that ensues, neither moral nor legal principles will significantly constrain states, and co-operation among them will always be limited and short term. The political conditions necessary for an effective legal system to exist are, therefore, absent in international society.

If, however, we move from theoretical discourse to 'real-world' developments, especially since 1945, we are confronted with an apparent paradox. Not only has the number of areas in which international rules appear

---

[1] John Austin, *The Province of Jurisprudence Determined*, ed. Wilfrid E. Rumble (Cambridge: Cambridge University Press, 1995).
[2] To be distinguished from 'realism' in legal theory, a mainly American school of thought which emphasises what judges and other legal actors actually do, rather than legal doctrine, as the essence of law.

to play an important part grown rapidly but an increasing number of those areas are characterised by the emergence of fully fledged legal systems, including various kinds of courts. Moreover, states appear to take these rules seriously. Indeed, 'it is probably the case that almost all nations observe almost all principles of international law and almost all of their obligations almost all of the time'[3] and often, when they do not, they devote significant resources to try to demonstrate that some act deemed 'illegal' by commentators or other states does in fact accord with the relevant rules of international law. Even Austin acknowledges that 'every government defers frequently to those opinions and sentiments which are styled "international law"'.

In this chapter we consider, first, some of the counter-arguments that have been advanced to Austin, especially the most comprehensive of these: the work of Hans Kelsen. Next we consider different perspectives on the larger context within which the politics of international law take place: one which emphasises the key role of power, one focusing on various social, cultural, political and economic factors, and one discussing the societal location of international law, where we discuss the concept of an international society of states. We conclude by further developing the classic IR notion of an international society to take account of the part played by the professional culture of the main participants in international society and the insights of students of communication, human reasoning and linguistic formulation.

The foundations of international law

This central conundrum about the legal nature (or lack of it) of international law has preoccupied thinkers for at least two hundred years. Several distinct lines of argument have been employed in opposition to Austin's thesis. One critique focuses upon his definition of 'law proper', arguing that this oversimplifies and distorts the actual nature of law and legal obligation. For example, in common law systems new rules (or new interpretations of old rules) may emerge from precedents set by important cases or in the course of appeals to higher courts, neither of which processes really qualifies as the command of a sovereign. Similarly, few of the statutes laid down by supreme legislatures – what Austin has in mind when he talks of 'commands' – are so unambiguous or of such timeless validity, however circumstances and opinions may change, as to leave no room for interpretation or even amendment by judges called upon to

---

[3] Louis Henken, *How Nations Behave: Law and Foreign Policy* (New York and London: Praeger, 1968), p. 42.

apply them. A variant of this argument criticises Austin's emphasis on coercion. While this might have some relevance in the case of criminal law, there are numerous regulations, such as the rules relating to valid wills or contracts, which have an undeniably 'legal' quality with little or no coercive character.[4] Moreover, there is room to doubt whether people observe the law primarily because of fear of punishment as against a general acceptance of its legitimacy or a belief that it serves their interests.

Some legal positivists have advanced arguments that derive the 'legality' of international law from essentially positivist principles. They point out, for example, that international law, particularly when created by multilateral treaties, such as the Charter of the United Nations, may become 'law properly so-called' through its 'incorporation' into domestic law via the process of treaty ratification by the domestic legislature.[5] However, the most influential twentieth-century legal positivist, Hans Kelsen, goes beyond this more limited perspective in his advocacy of the case for the fully legal character of international law. Since his thinking continues to be influential, it is worth outlining more fully.

Kelsen's vast literary output spreads over six decades and is not always completely consistent, partly because he himself changed his mind over various matters. However, his writings on international law tend to reaffirm certain basic ideas and, taken in their entirety, retain an underlying coherence throughout. First, in all of his discussions of law (of any kind) he insists upon detaching 'the science of law' from other disciplinary perspectives, such as psychology, sociology, ethics and political theory.[6] In one of his most ambitious works, he attempts to elaborate a 'pure theory of law' that distinguishes law from such other disciplines 'not because it ignores or denies the connection, but because it wishes to avoid the uncritical mixture of methodologically different disciplines . . . which obscures the essence of the science of law and obliterates the limits imposed upon it by the nature of its subject matter'.[7]

Central to Kelsen's theories is the concept of a 'norm', which, in his thought, has the essential meaning that, in the event of an act 'A' occurring, a specific consequence, 'B', is to occur. Hence, norms are

---

[4] H. L. A Hart's famous distinction between someone being obliged (i.e., compelled) to do something and his having an obligation, or duty to do it is important here. This also enables him to see international law as genuine (if primitive) law. H. L. A. Hart, *Concept of Law*, repr. (Oxford: Clarendon Press, 1992), pp. 79–88, 208–31.
[5] For an excellent recent (critical) discussion of legal positivism, see Stephen Hall, 'The persistent spectre: natural law, international order and the limits of legal positivism', *European Journal of International Law* 12 (2001), 269–307.
[6] Hans Kelsen, *The Pure Theory of Law*, trans. Max Knight (Berkeley, Los Angeles and London: University of California Press, 1970), p. 1.
[7] *Ibid.*

propositions that imply that something 'ought to' happen in given cir-cumstances. Kelsen sees norms as having a predominantly prescriptive meaning – i.e., they are commands – but he accepts that they may also empower, permit or derogate.[8] But what distinguishes legal from other norms, such as those located in moral systems, is their coercive nature. Both legal and moral norms may be seen as 'social techniques'[9] for achiev-ing certain ends which may be decided through political processes, such as regulating human behaviour, and both are inherent characteristics of society as such.[10] However, only legal norms employ coercive sanc-tions and, moreover, they function only within their own distinctive and autonomous system, marked by its own institutions, processes and inter-nal rules of procedure, evidence and so forth.

Thus far Kelsen's thinking resembles Austin's but they part company over the issue of whether international law meets these criteria. Kelsen maintains that states may legally engage in various actions against another state in an attempt to secure reparations for a wrong ('delict') commit-ted against them by another state.[11] This right of 'self-help' acts as a functional equivalent of coercive sanctions employed in domestic legal systems so long as certain conditions are fulfilled: the coercive act by the injured state 'is permitted only as a reaction against a delict and the employment of force to any other end is forbidden' and if the coercive act 'can be interpreted as a reaction of the international legal community'.[12]

Having thus, to his own satisfaction, established the essential 'legality' of international law, Kelsen proceeds to develop a number of other argu-ments, of which we may briefly note two that are of relevance to this study. First, he accepts that the international legal system has two characteristics that distinguish it from highly developed domestic systems: it is 'primi-tive' and decentralised. 'Primitive' legal systems, in his view, lack objective organs to determine that a wrong has taken place and to administer sanc-tions. It is left to individuals to avenge wrongs themselves – to kill the mur-derer of their father, for example – but such an individual's actions may still be understood to be executing a legal duty since he is acting in accor-dance with a norm of the community as a whole: 'It is this norm which

---

[8] Hans Kelsen, *General Theory of Norms*, trans. Michael Hartney (Oxford: Clarendon Press, 1991), p. 1.
[9] Hans Kelsen, *The Law of the United Nations* (New York and London: Praeger, 1964), p. xiii.
[10] Kelsen, *General Theory*, pp. 23, 52, 93.
[11] Kelsen, *Pure Theory*, chapter 7. See also Hans Kelsen, *General Theory of Law and State* (Cambridge, MA: Harvard University Press, 1945), pp. 325–63; Hans Kelsen, *Principles of International Law*, rev. and ed. Robert W. Tucker (New York: Holt, Rhinehart and Winston, 1966), pp. 16–87.
[12] Kelsen, *General Theory of Law and State*, p. 328.

empowers him, and him only, under certain circumstances, and under these circumstances only, to kill the suspected murderer.'[13] Self-help performs similar functions in the international community, partly because, like primitive societies, it lacks centralised institutions. Its primary methods of creating law – custom and treaties – are both decentralised, as is the application of the law through the imposition of sanctions. It should be noted, however, that the use by Kelsen (and others) of the word 'primitive' in the context of international relations implies the possibility of the international system evolving to a more 'advanced' form. Indeed, in a work published in 1945, Kelsen optimistically remarked that there was 'a definite tendency' for international law to make such an evolution.[14] In keeping with his belief that advanced legal systems are characterised by the centralisation of the powers of law-making and application, the only direction of such evolutionary processes considered by Kelsen was towards a world state.

Second, Kelsen attempted to reconcile international law with one of his central theoretical arguments: that the validity of any set of norms must always derive from a basic norm (*grundnorm*).[15] It is worth quoting more fully one of his attempts to apply this principle to international law. He starts by considering the decision of an international court ('the lowest norm within international law') and continues:

> If we ask why the norm created by such a decision is valid, the answer is furnished by the international treaty in accordance with which the court was instituted. If, again, we ask why this treaty is valid, we are led back to the general norm which obligates the States to behave in conformity with the treaties they have concluded, a norm commonly expressed by the phrase *pacta sunt servanda*. This is a norm of general international law, and general international law is created by custom, constituted by acts of States. The basic norm of international law, therefore, must be a norm which countenances custom as a norm-creating fact, and might be formulated as follows: "The States ought to behave as they have customarily behaved". Customary international law, developed on the basis of this norm, is the first stage within the international legal order. The next stage is formed by the norms created by international treaties . . . The third stage is formed by norms created by organs which are themselves created by international treaties . . .[16]

Other legal positivists take a far more restrictive view of the 'legality' of international law, arguing that only rules to which states have consented

[13] *Ibid.*, p. 338.   [14] *Ibid.*, p. 341.   [15] Kelsen, *Pure Theory*, p. 31.
[16] Kelsen, *General Theory of Law and State*, pp. 369–70. After holding to this position for more than three decades, Kelsen partly retreated from it in 1960. We should note that Kelsen is also asserting the existence of a hierarchy of sources of legal norms in much the same way as there is a hierarchy of law-creating bodies in the English legal system. See also Jeffrey Brand-Ballard, 'Kelsen's unstable alternative to natural law: recent critiques', *American Journal of Jurisprudence* 41 (1996), 133–64.

can have the force of law. This perspective developed in the eighteenth and nineteenth centuries, partly as a reaction to earlier arguments that located international law within the broader category of natural law: that set of norms deemed universal and eternal either by virtue of its divine origins or because the exercise of reason would inevitably arrive at such norms. There are some obvious problems with consent-based theories of international law, including the logical problem that consent alone cannot be a complete explanation of legal validity since some prior principle is required to explain why consent has this status. A more specific difficulty is the issue of how new states can be considered bound (as they are) by the existing body of international law in areas like diplomacy and the law of the sea when they have not given their explicit consent to such rules. Kelsen, as we have seen, meets such objections by making custom rather than consent the primary or ultimate source of legal obligation, but consent theorists tend to argue that consent may be tacit, as when a state does nothing directly to deny a legal obligation, or implied, as when its conduct is in accordance with the obligation, or indirect, as when a state's acceptance of a particular treaty logically involves also acceptance of other related treaties. Critics of such arguments regard them as stretching the notion of consent rather too far:[17] unnecessarily so since, although, in Henkin's words, there is 'no satisfying jurisprudential explanation as to why a nation cannot totally reject international law',[18] the fact is that no state does so.

To add to the complexity of the problems facing positivists, some international legal obligations have their origin in what appear unmistakeably to be principles of natural law rather than a strict understanding of consent. The most notable of these is the notion of *jus cogens* (literally 'compelling law') in Article 53 of the 1969 Vienna Convention on the Law of Treaties, which invalidates any treaty that conflicts with a 'peremptory norm of international law', defined as 'a norm accepted and recognised by the international community of states as a whole'. This has always been controversial. Seized upon by idealists who would extend it beyond such obvious areas as genocide and war crimes to environmental or feminist issues, it has been criticised for its vagueness and potential for abuse.[19]

---

[17] See, e.g., J. L. Brierley, *The Law of Nations: An Introduction to the International Law of Peace*, 6th Edition (Oxford: Clarendon Press, 1963), pp. 51–6.

[18] Henkin, *How Nations Behave*, p. 85n.

[19] See 'The structure of change in international law or is there a hierarchy of norms in international law?' (Part 2 of a symposium on The Changing Structure of International Law Revisited), *European Journal of International Law* 8 (1997), 545–95 and 'Colloquy on *jus cogens*', *Connecticut Journal of International Law* 3 (1988) 359–71, for a fuller discussion of these issues.

A particular conundrum is whether the *jus cogens* provision binds even states which have not ratified the Vienna Convention, such as France and the United States of America. Nor is it clear how specific *jus cogens* norms might be identified in the event of legal proceedings. Unsurprisingly, perhaps, the International Court of Justice (ICJ) has never cited *jus cogens* in support of any of its decisions, apart from a brief and somewhat vague reference in *Nicaragua* v. *United States* (1986), when it referred to the prohibition on the use of force as 'a conspicuous example of a rule of international law having the character of *jus cogens*'.[20]

Power and politics

During the Berlin Crisis of 1961–2, the American President, John F. Kennedy, considered the possibility of preventing the situation from deteriorating to the point of conflict by offering some concessions to the Soviets. The West German Ambassador to Washington at that time was Wilhelm Grewe, a noted academic authority on international law, who argued with Kennedy that the American proposals violated the Four Power Agreements of 1945 and the Bonn Conventions of 1954 (which Grewe had helped to draw up). As Grewe tells the story years later, the White House 'spread the message that the Ambassador was boring the President with professorial juridical advice and that he was treating a highly political matter with legalistic arguments; that it was tactless to remind the US government of their treaty obligations'.[21]

In a similar vein, former Secretary of State, Dean Acheson, arguing against the view that America's quarantining of Cuba in 1962 was illegal said:

> Much of what is called international law is a body of ethical distillation, and one must take care not to confuse this distillation with law . . . I must conclude that the propriety of the Cuban quarantine is not a legal issue. The power, position and prestige of the United States had been challenged by another state and law simply does not deal with such questions of power . . .[22]

Four decades later, former British Prime Minister, Margaret Thatcher, was to write that she opposed the proposed International Criminal Court in part because it would inhibit the West's ability to exercise its military

---

[20] See Gennady M. Danilenko, 'International *jus cogens*: issues of law making', *European Journal of International Law* 2 (1991), 42–65, for a full discussion of the various issues relating to *jus cogens*.

[21] Wilhelm G. Grewe, 'The role of international law in diplomatic practice', *Journal of the History of International Law* 1 (1999) pp. 28–9.

[22] Henkin, *How Nations Behave*, pp. 265–6n.

power, and partly 'because it is only the latest and most powerful expression of a trend towards the internationalisation of justice, through what is nowadays called "customary international law", that will itself lead to injustice'.[23]

All of these leading political figures were giving unconscious voice to, and indeed providing support for the contentions of IR realist theory. While classical realist thinkers, such as E. H. Carr and Hans Morgenthau were far from dismissing international law out of hand – in fact they accepted it *was* true law – they saw it as having only a very limited role and one always circumscribed by prevailing power realities. Like Kelsen, Carr and Morgenthau both saw international law as, in Carr's words, 'law of an undeveloped, not fully integrated community'[24] and as owing much of its distinctive character to the decentralised nature of international society. Carr pointed to the absence of a judicature, legislature and executive. Morgenthau, who in certain respects may be seen as a disillusioned international lawyer,[25] saw deficiencies in what he regarded as the three main functions of 'an efficient juridical system': compulsory jurisdiction, a hierarchy of judicial decisions and the application of *stare decisis* or the doctrine of precedent (the common law principle by which courts were bound to apply rules developed in previous cases).[26] Both stressed that it was inevitable that international law would reflect the interests of the most powerful states – who were also those least likely to be constrained by it. Carr noted that even the norm that many legal thinkers see as most fundamental to the international legal system – *pacta sunt servanda* (treaties must be observed) – was fundamentally qualified by the principle *rebus sic stantibus* (while circumstances remain the same as they are now), which gives states the freedom to withdraw from treaties, given that they are the sole interpreters of *rebus sic stantibus*.

These and other realist thinkers, especially in the early days of the Cold War, argued against a tendency on the part of Western governments to adopt what they saw as an unduly legalistic approach to world politics. George Kennan saw several problems with this, including the need for the great majority of members of any effective legal regime to have similar values and attitudes to those of the United States, the fact that international law's emphasis on the doctrine of sovereign equality inhibited 'the

---

[23] Margaret Thatcher, *Statecraft: Strategies for a Changing World* (London: Harper Collins, 2003), pp. 262–7.

[24] E. H. Carr, *The Twenty Years Crisis 1919–1939* (London: Macmillan, 1939), p. 219.

[25] Alejandro Lorite Escorihuela, 'Alf Ross: towards a realist critique and reconstruction of international law', *European Journal of International Law* 14 (2003), 703–66.

[26] Hans J. Morgenthau, *Politics Among Nations: The Struggle for Power and Peace*, 3rd edition (New York: Alfred A. Knopf, 1965), p. 285.

process of change by imposing a legal straitjacket upon it', the fact that there were far deeper causes of international instability than the kinds of issues that were capable of legal resolution, and the historical experience that suggested that collective sanctions of the kind envisaged in the UN Charter would inevitably encounter the same problems of military co-ordination evident in any alliance system.[27]

More sceptical – indeed cynical – recent writing has tended to argue that when states employ legal arguments in their international relations, this is evidence, not of their commitment to the relevant legal norm, but simply of their capacity to employ a wide range of weapons in their national interest. For example, Anthony D'Amato points out that, before the United States withdrew from the ICJ proceedings in the case of the complaint brought by Nicaragua, it used primarily legal arguments, including its 'inherent right of self-defence' and its assertion that the political issues involved meant that the case should be considered by the UN Security Council (where the USA had a veto) rather than the ICJ. Afterwards it made it clear that its policy was, in essence, to overthrow the Sandanista Government in Nicaragua: a clear violation of the most basic of international legal norms.[28] Indeed, much recent comment has focused on the increasing American tendency to avoid entering into new legal commitments, for example with regard to the environment and the International Criminal Court, while at the same time (in the view of some critics) disregarding its existing legal obligations under the UN Charter in its invasion of Iraq.

It might, finally, be noted that Realists have also specifically dismissed Kelsen's attempt to offer a Positivist take on the question of the legal nature of international law. John Herz, for example, argues that Kelsen's attempt to apply to interstate relations a theory about law drawn from a purely domestic context 'is in danger of turning fictitious' because 'Kelsen's system requirements presuppose conditions which are, in part at least, idealized; they anticipate developments which are still uncertain and in this way "legalize" (i.e., interpret in terms of legal norms) extralegal phenomena such as international conflict and war.'[29] He adds that international actors lack 'law consciousness' – a clear understanding that their conduct has legal relevance – , that many apparent rules in the area

---

[27] George F. Kennan, *American Diplomacy 1900–1950* (Chicago, IL: University of Chicago Press, 1951), pp. 95–101.

[28] Anthony D'Amato, *International Law and Political Reality*, Collected Papers (The Hague: Kluwer Law International, 1995), vol. I, p. 170.

[29] John Herz, 'The pure theory of law revisited: Hans Kelsen's Doctrine of International Law in the Nuclear Age', in S. Engel and R. A. Metall (eds.), *Law, State and International Legal Order* (Knoxville: University of Tennessee Press, 1964), pp. 108–13.

of conflict merely acknowledge a temporary power arrangement, that far from a 'system' of international law existing, only 'islands', patches of legal material, emerge from time to time as results of a corresponding social intention and that international norms are usually vague and, in the conditions prevailing in the international political system, there can be no guarantee that they will be interpreted and applied uniformly. In a similar vein, Hedley Bull, whose softer version of realism allows for the existence of an international society (including rules of law), questions Kelsen's insistence that international law has the same coercive character as domestic law. He also describes Kelsen's doctrine that the international community has a monopoly control over the legitimate right to use force as 'the product of wishful thinking' and as contrary to the political facts.[30]

Rules and norms

Both positivism and realism utilise a particular conception of law as something separate from political and indeed moral, social, economic and other extraneous factors. In both cases, but especially that of positivism, this reflects the dominance of the notion of the 'rule of law' in Western legal theory. The essential principle underlying the rule of law, which goes back as far as Aristotle in Western thought,[31] is that the only way to protect individuals from the arbitrary exercise of power is to subject all within the state to the ultimate authority of the law. The logical extension of this argument was the view that the legal system in its entirety needed to exist as an autonomous sphere of action in order to prevent it from abuse or corruption. That, in turn, required a professional class of highly trained jurists able to base their deliberations purely on legal considerations, rather than moral, ideological or other factors. It also needed a range of structural requirements to be fulfilled, including sufficient separation of power to ensure the independence of the judiciary. Finally, it needed a number of operational requirements that would help to make the rule of law work in practice: laws should be clear, not retrospective,

---

[30] Hedley Bull, 'Hans Kelsen and international law', in R. Tur and W. Twinning (eds.), *Essays on Kelsen* (Oxford: Clarendon Press, 1986), pp. 320–36.
[31] Among many references, we might note the following from *The Politics of Aristotle*, trans. Ernest Barker (Oxford: Clarendon Press, 1950): 'Rightly constituted laws should be the final sovereign' (III, xi, 19, p. 148); 'He who commands that law should rule may thus be regarded as commanding that God and reason alone should rule' (III, xvi, 5, p. 172); 'This shows that to seek for justice is to seek for a neutral authority; and law is a neutral authority' (III, xvi, 8, p. 173); 'We have to distinguish two senses of the rule of law – one which means obedience to such laws as have been enacted, and another which means that the laws obeyed have also been well enacted' (IV, viii, 6, p. 207).

general and consistent in their application, give rise to stable and pre-
dictable expectations and be interpreted and administered through well-
established and widely understood procedures.

It is this conception of law (which may also be termed 'methodological
formalism'[32]) that underlies the depiction of international law as a 'primitive legal system' that is common to the thought of Kelsen, Hart, Bull
and others, since, clearly, international law lacks many of the characteristics required to qualify as a fully fledged rule-of-law system. However, the
distinction between 'primitive' and 'advanced' legal systems does not tell
us as much as it might about the actual role of law in society. It is commonly used to indicate the difference between the operation of rules in
societies with and without clear and well-developed governmental structures, thus enabling comparisons to be drawn between the 'anarchical'
international society and various pre-state tribal societies.[33] Yet, a great
many contemporary societies are far from 'primitive' in this sense, possessing, as they do, relatively effective central institutions of government,
while, on the other hand, having powers of law-making and legal administration dispersed amongst state, religious and, in some cases, village
authorities. Pakistan, Indonesia and Nigeria, for example, demonstrate
characteristics of this – admittedly ambiguous – arrangement, which does
not quite fit the rule-of-law model but is equally some considerable distance from what is normally implied by the term 'primitive'. It might also
be noted that the United States, Britain and other states normally seen
as exemplars of the rule of law have engaged in a number of practices in
their anti-terrorist policies that do not meet the most rigorous rule-of-
law standards.[34] In both cases, law is less isolated from external social or
political factors than the strict requirements of some legal theories.

This does not mean that we should abandon the pure conception of
law (or the search for such a conception) in our quest for the true nature
of law, and of international law in particular. It does, however, suggest
that we should endeavour to locate law within its larger societal setting. It
also suggests that we should see any legal system in its historical context,
not as some perfect 'end product' of a historical process leading from

---

[32] Alf Ross, *On Law and Justice* (London: Stevens and Sons, 1958), p. 2.
[33] Hedley Bull, *The Anarchical Society: A Study of Order in World Politics*, 3rd edition
(Houndmills: Palgrave, 2002), pp. 57–62, 130.
[34] The wide-ranging speech of Britain's Attorney General, Lord Goldsmith on 10 May
2006 is interesting in this regard, both because of his broad assertion that 'it is essential
to preserve our democratic way of life, our right to freedom of thought and expression
and our commitment to the rule of law; the liberties which have been hard won over the
centuries and which we hold dear' in considering anti-terrorist measures and his specific
criticism of the detention of suspected terrorists at Guantanamo Bay as 'unacceptable'.
The Times, 11 May 2006.

'primitive' to 'advanced' law but as the outcome, at a particular point in an on-going historical evolution, of the interplay among a range of societal factors. It is true that a rule-of-law system may be one outcome of such a process. It may even be the most desirable outcome, in so far as it enables larger communal objectives to be met through methods and institutions that enjoy considerable independence from any particular, transitory power structure. But the legal system should always be viewed in the context of the particular societal conditions that gave rise to it and whose purpose it serves.

Our starting point might be the Roman saying *ubi societas ibi lex* (where there is society there is law). But if we define 'society' and 'law' broadly, this leads to a much larger insight: that any form of social interaction will be rule-governed to some degree.[35] More precisely, all social interaction requires *norms*, or general principles of conduct, and *rules*, or precise delineations of correct behaviour in specific circumstances.[36] If we take one of the simplest forms of social interaction, a conversation between two people, this might take place in accordance with several types of norm: one might enjoin them to try to avoid making hurtful remarks about each other, one might urge them to observe certain basic principles of politeness, a third might suggest that their conversation would be most fruitful if they took turns in presenting their points of view and responded directly to each other's arguments when their turn comes. These might be seen as involving, respectively, norms of morality, etiquette and procedure. Specific rules governing this conversation might range from the necessity of conversing in a mutually comprehensible language and observing the rules of grammar applicable to that language, to a rule that they should not speak simultaneously. If they were adherents of a particular religious code, there might also be rules prohibiting or requiring certain words or verbal formulae.

More complex forms of social interaction are obviously governed by more complex normative structures. A team game has clearly specified rules which have to be observed by both sides as closely as possible: the rules define the game and make it meaningful. A political party or religious group will unite around a common set of values, which in turn will

---

[35] This is not to say that the rules *cause* or *determine* the social interaction but that they form the context within which it takes place and help to give it order and meaning. See the discussion in Nicholas Greenwood Onuf, *World of Our Making: Rules and Rule in Social Theory and International Relations* (Columbia: University of South Carolina Press, 1989), pp. 47–52.

[36] We have been influenced in this distinction by Ronald Dworkin's distinction between 'principles' and 'rules', although our own distinction does not follow his with any precision. Ronald Dworkin, *Taking Rights Seriously* (London: Duckworth, 1991), pp. 22–31.

provide their normative underpinning, while their rules will set out their membership criteria and the procedures through which their common objectives are to be pursued.

All norms and rules may be considered as members of the same conceptual family in the sense that all both derive from and set the conditions for orderly interaction in different forms of association. 'Law', in this sense, is merely a set of norms and rules that have taken a particular form and acquired a particular function in respect of the type of association to which it applies. How it acquired this form and function and, more generally, how any normative structure acquires the content, status, effectiveness and level of development that it possesses is a product of the influence of and interaction amongst various political, social and economic factors. Within a family, for example, the father might have gained the capacity to lay down various rules by virtue of a combination of his superior strength (a crudely 'power-political' factor), his control of the family income (an economic factor) and the paternalistic traditions of the larger society (a social factor). The effectiveness of his regime, as measured by the compliance of family members with his rules, would be a product of several things, including his means of coercion, the degree to which the family was isolated from the larger society within which it existed, and also the sense among family members of the legitimacy and fairness of his authority as well as the extent to which it brought them clear benefits.

Within a larger association such as a nation, such political factors might include the distribution of power and capabilities amongst different classes and other interest groups. They would also include the nature of the outcome at a point in time of the struggle for power amongst these various interests. One outcome might be relative stability, founded either on an overall balance or on the victory and hegemony of one group, or on some kind of agreement amongst all contending parties. All three possibilities would provide some of the conditions for the emergence of a durable set of rules possessing some of the characteristics normally associated with rules of law: they would be obligatory, universally applicable to all members of the society, and increasingly complex, covering ever wider areas of social activity. Most, if not all, contemporary states have experienced such a developmental path.

However, although the resultant legal system would clearly be the outcome of a power struggle, and although one should not ignore the Marxist insight that law is always a reflection of the interests of the most powerful, considerations of power alone are inadequate fully to explain the actual content of the rules, their status in society, their effectiveness or the way in which they evolve over time. For example, a man's compliance with the rules will be influenced by his views of their legitimacy or fairness and of the degree to which they benefit him. These perceptions will, in turn, be affected by various social and economic factors. While the latter are relatively easy to define (a state's absolute level of wealth, the internal distribution of wealth, the nature of the tax system, etc.), the former are more complex and do not fit easily into analytical models that explain human behaviour mainly in terms of the 'rational' pursuit by individuals of selfish objectives. Of these factors, one of the most important, but also one of the most elusive, is the concept of 'culture'.[37] Here we take the term to embrace, amongst other things, the way in which a particular community defines and identifies itself and so gives meaning to its social world, its traditions, customs and moral values, its established attitudes as to what constitutes shameful, honourable and other types of conduct, together with the means through which such ideas and practices are communicated among and internalised by successive generations. We should note also that subgroups within the larger community may develop their own distinctive cultural attributes: a professional subgroup, such as lawyers, will operate within its own professional culture, while the complex bureaucratic structures whose growth has accompanied the emergence of the modern state will have distinct organisational cultures.

Finally, we should take account of the fact that the status, content and effectiveness of rules all change over time. The interplay amongst the sort of political, social and economic factors we have discussed will determine both the nature of the rules at any point in time and the ways in which they will change. For example, all three monotheistic religions frown upon sex before marriage. This moral principle is widely disregarded in practice in many countries, while it is subject to severe punishment under the law of a few countries. In other words, the same moral norm has had a different impact on different countries because of the different ways in which various social and political factors have influenced legal development. Moreover, many of those countries where this norm is currently ignored in previous times subjected offenders against the norm either to legal sanctions or to various forms of social disapproval, which acted as deterrents and sanctions in the same way as the coercive apparatus of the law was designed to do. Once again, this change in the norm's status was a product of the interplay among social, economic and political factors,

---

[37] The Historical School of Legal Philosophy, founded by Friedrich Carl Von Savigny (1779–1861), sees all law as essentially a cultural product. Johan D. van der Vyver, 'Sovereignty and human rights in constitutional and international law', *Emory International Law Review* 5 (1991), 335.

such as industrialisation and urbanisation, the changing role of women and the decline of religion.

Very similar forces are at work in international relations. First, the interaction among states and other international actors takes place in a context of rules and norms. Second, the exact content, status and efficacy of these rules and norms at any point in time will depend upon the precise conjuncture of various political, social and economic factors obtaining at that time. Third, interaction among the same political, social and economic forces will determine the manner and degree of change in international norms and rules.

To illustrate these three points, international society has constitutive norms defining it as a society of sovereign states and rules to uphold that norm, such as the rule of non-intervention by other states in a state's internal affairs. The content of the norms and rules has expanded in recent decades to encompass both broad normative principles relating to human rights and the environment, as well as specific prescriptions in relation to each of these. This has happened as a response to changing political circumstances, such as the collapse of the Cold War power structure and the influence of environmentalist lobbies.

Cultural factors, such as a changing international climate of opinion and the greater availability of information, have also played a part. The status and efficacy of international rules and norms at a particular time will also depend, in part, on basic political factors. For example, after the Napoleonic Wars the great powers were able to construct a relatively durable balance of power that assisted in the development of international law during the nineteenth century.[38] In contrast, by the 1930s, with one major power, the United States, isolating itself from power struggles elsewhere and four of the remaining six great powers all fundamentally opposed to the prevailing order and prepared to use force to overthrow it, the remaining 'status quo' powers, Britain and France, were unable to maintain a balance of power and the era was marked by increasing lawlessness.

Finally, normative change is also a product of the interplay amongst political, social and economic factors. We have already noted the emergence of new human rights and environmental rules and norms. Some discern an even more fundamental change occurring in one of the basic

---

[38] Hedley Bull goes so far as to assert: 'international law depends for its very existence as an operating system of rules on the balance of power' (*Anarchical Society*, p. 104). In this he follows Lassa Oppenheim in his 1905 work *International Law*. See Benedict Kingsbury, 'Legal positivism as normative politics: international society, balance of power and Lassa Oppenheim's positive international law', *European Journal of International Law* 13 (2002), 401–36.

constitutive norms of international society – non-intervention – through the rise to prominence of the principle of humanitarian intervention in recent years. Although not an entirely new phenomenon as an occasional practice, humanitarian intervention has only been able to emerge as a norm because the end of the Cold War produced a radically different power structure in which the United States and its allies were temporarily able to promote this norm. However, the efficacy in practice of the norm was also subject to various short-term political considerations, such as an unwillingness on the part of major powers to commit forces to conflicts where they lacked vital interests. Similarly, the range of economic and political factors encompassed by the term 'globalisation' helped to push the case for a stronger regime in the area of international trade as part of a move by states to provide some regulatory checks and balances to economic liberalisation.

The nature of international society

In Chapter 3 we elaborate three theoretical lenses that may be applied to explain the function and impact of international law. We conclude this chapter by outlining more fully what we have stated to be the social context within which international relations take place and which, therefore, shapes and gives meaning to those rules and norms that govern interaction within international society. For the purposes of this chapter, we shall adopt the understanding of international society defined in Hedley Bull's classic work, *The Anarchical Society*.

Bull's international society is, of course, a society of states, with its 'societal' characteristics comprising common interests, values, rules and institutions. The common interests shared by states, which define their common values, rules and institutions, revolve around states' shared determination to maintain their status as the sole source of legitimate authority and as subject to no external control: the two constituents of 'sovereignty'. For Bull the 'rules' that were central to his conception of international society encompassed informal 'rules of the game' – such as the tacit agreement between the superpowers to respect each other's spheres of interest – as well as more formal rules of international law. Indeed informal rules could be more significant in sustaining order than international law, with the latter's role in international society a limited, if not unimportant, one.[39]

For Bull, the functions of international law are defined and circumscribed by his fairly minimalist conception of international society as an

[39] Bull, *Anarchical Society*, p. 52.

association with the primary aims of legitimising and maintaining state sovereignty. Its three primary functions, therefore, are 'to identify, as the supreme normative principle of the political organisation of mankind, the idea of a society of sovereign states', to 'state the basic rules of coexistence among states and other actors in international society' and 'to help mobilise compliance with the rules of international society'.[40] As with all social interaction, the form and function of the norms and rules of international society are, therefore, determined first by the kind of society to which they apply. Bull distinguishes between rules of coexistence and rules of co-operation. The former are more fundamental, comprising 'rules relating to the restriction of violence among states and other actors; rules relating to agreement among them; and rules relating to sovereignty or independence'.[41] The latter concern the limited (but expanding) range of functional areas where states have been able to develop international regimes, such as trade, sea passage and the ozone layer. As the term 'coexistence' implies, the purpose of international law is not to bind states more closely together in a single political community, such as a world government, but to enable them to pursue their separate interests in ways that protect order without jeopardising sovereignty. This meant, amongst other things, that the main source of international legal obligation was seen as state consent. The precise content, status and efficacy of international law at any point in time will depend upon the interaction among the political, social and economic conditions prevailing at that time. The tendency of any legal system to reflect the interests of the more powerful members of the society to which it applies is inevitably greater in a society with such a strong emphasis on state freedom. Hence, for example, international law governing areas like the acquisition of title to territory, trade, patents, compensation for the expropriation of foreign-owned assets and the freedom of the high seas has tended to cater primarily for the interests of the major powers. The status of international law will also tend to reflect the attitude towards it of the most powerful states. Similarly, state compliance with international law will, in part, depend upon the willingness of the major powers to bring pressure to bear upon law-breakers. States' relative freedom, compared with individuals in domestic legal systems, to choose the degree to which they will abide by particular rules places an even greater premium than is the case in domestic societies on their need to perceive clear benefits for themselves in accepting legal obligations. Robert Keohane and others have devised 'rational choice' theoretical perspectives indicating self-interested reasons why states might choose to

---

[40] *Ibid.*, pp. 134–5.   [41] *Ibid.*, p. 135.

comply with international regimes, including reduced transaction costs, more reliable information and their concern for their reputations.[42]

However, considerations relating to power do not tell the whole story of the content, status and effectiveness of international law, and, in particular, they do not account for significant change in international law over time. Here, various kinds of 'social' factors need to be considered. The model of international society employed by Bull and others tends to present a picture that is at the same time both static and somewhat formal, emphasising the timeless continuities of international relations, which are depicted in terms of the interactions among statesmen, diplomats and armies. If, however, we regard international society more broadly as a context within which many kinds of social interaction occur, we are not only able to see the functioning of international law within a much wider societal perspective but we can also move closer to understanding the reasons for normative change.

Four key facets of this broader context of social interaction are worth stressing. First, states are not the only actors capable of influencing international law. Non-governmental organisations (NGOs) have played a major role in raising international awareness of a wide range of issues, including the environment, human rights, land-mines and other areas. In some cases NGOs have shifted from political activism to quasi-governmental roles in helping to draw up regimes and monitoring compliance with them. What is potentially an even more profound development has been the emergence of 'global policy networks' which bring together actors from governmental and intergovernmental institutions grouped around specific functional areas, broadly divided, according to Anne-Marie Slaughter, into information networks, enforcement networks and harmonisation networks.[43] Taken together, NGOs, other private sector actors, including those in the commercial sector which engage in global self-regulatory activities, and global policy networks contribute to a complex structure of 'global governance' in which the standard functions of legislating, judging and monitoring and enforcing compliance with rules are performed in the much more informal, flexible and decentralised manner appropriate to what remains a society of sovereign states.

Second, states themselves have evolved from what they once were and this evolution has had important consequences for international

---

[42] Robert O. Keohane, *After Hegemony: Cooperation and Discord in the World Political Economy* (Princeton, NJ: Princeton University Press, 1984). See also Beth A. Simmons, 'Compliance with international agreements', in Charlotte Ku and Paul F. Diehl (eds.), *International Law: Classic and Contemporary Readings*, 2nd edition (Boulder, CO: Lynne Rienner, 2003), pp. 181–99.

[43] Anne-Marie Slaughter, *A New World Order* (Princeton, NJ: Princeton University Press, 2004).

relations.[44] Less than one hundred years ago all major states were in their customary posture of permanent readiness for war with each other and were able to carry their societies with them into two world wars. Few would have questioned the assumption that national security was the over-riding objective of state policy and that it should absorb the lion's share of governmental spending. Today, popular expectations revolve around continually improving welfare through national spending on health, education and similar purposes, as well as increasing personal wealth through continuing economic growth – which is again seen as a major governmental responsibility. Today's liberal democracies are kinder, gentler things than they used to be, organised more to provide general benefits for their electorates than to fight foreign wars.

These changes in the nature of states have spilled over into the international arena in a number of ways. First, the major powers constantly observe each other, not, as in the past, out of fear of military threats but because they face the same kinds of economic, social and political problems and are interested in observing how others deal with them. This is another facet of international society's character as a framework within which complex social interaction takes place – most intensively within the major liberal democracies. In the course of such interaction, states are subject to a constant process of socialisation in which they internalise each other's policies and practices across a wide spectrum.

One consequence of this continuing process has been a redefinition in the West of collective understandings of what being a legitimate state entails. Where once legitimacy in international society required primarily the ability to demonstrate control over a specified territorial area and to perform certain limited international obligations, international legitimacy today is coming increasingly to involve considerations that were once deemed to be entirely matters of domestic concern for states, considerations that may be summed up by the term 'good governance': a set of norms embracing democracy, human rights, the rule of law and deregulated economies. With the end of the Cold War, Western states have been less constrained by the perceived need to prop up regimes that fell far short of good governance standards and consequently far readier to press other states to move towards such objectives through attaching political conditions to loans and so forth. They have also perceived it to be in their self-interest to do so. If their own publics impose increasingly high standards on Western governments in areas like the environment or welfare provisions, they risk pricing themselves out of the international marketplace unless they can ensure that such norms spread. Furthermore,

---

[44] The following points are drawn from David Armstrong, 'Law, justice and the idea of a world society', *International Affairs* 75 (1999), 547–61.

there is increasing recognition that capital finds its most secure home in states that are reasonably well governed, with well-educated workforces. Hence, while the most thoroughgoing processes of international sociali-sation operate among the major Western powers, any state participating or aspiring to participate in the international politico/economic order encounters pressures to internalise the norms, institutions and practices that are now believed to characterise the fully legitimate state. The evolving normative basis of statehood has inevitably been reflected in international law to such an extent that some even talk of an emerging legal right to democratic governance.[45]

Third, just as distinct professional and organisational cultures have affected the development of the modern state, including the absorption of rule-of-law principles, so have they played a part in the development of the international legal order.[46] Members of the legal community, for example, work at several different levels in international society: as advisers to their governments, as judges and advocates in international courts and tribunals, as drafters of international treaties and other international documents with some legal relevance and as writers of textbooks on international law. In all of these activities they are influenced not just by consideration of their own state's interests but by the legal culture peculiar to their profession, including all of the principles embedded in the rule-of-law concept. For example, although the Statutes of the International Court of Justice state clearly that previous legal cases are only a 'subsidiary means for the determination of international law', lawyers, especially those brought up within the Anglo-American common law tradition, tend automatically to look for legal precedents set in earlier cases. Similarly, professional diplomats, although perhaps less the embodiment of a common set of values than in the nineteenth century, still share certain attributes of a common professional culture. In one dramatic case on 14, January 1918, the Bolshevik authorities in Moscow arrested the Romanian ambassador to Russia but, faced with a unanimous protest by the entire diplomatic corps on the grounds that this violated rules 'respected for centuries by all governments', they released him on the following day.[47] Such solidarity was, however, less in evidence in the most notorious recent violation of diplomatic immunity, the detention of

---

[45] Thomas Franck, 'The emerging right to democratic governance', *American Journal of International Law* 46 (1992). See also James Crawford, *International Law as an Open System* (London: Cameron May, 2002), pp. 39–68.

[46] Martha Finnemore, 'Are legal norms distinctive?', *New York University Journal of International Law and Politics* 37 (2000), 703–4.

[47] Franciszek Przetacznik, *Protection of Officials of Foreign States According to International Law* (The Hague: Nijhoff Publishers, 1983), p. 25.

American diplomats in Iran in 1979, although there was wide condemnation of Iran.

Finally, we should note the insights (and their application to international law) of students of communication processes, human reasoning and linguistic formulation. This is, of course, a vast and intricate field and we confine ourselves here to noting a few observations with particular relevance to international law. Two caveats are in order: first, we are not arguing that such factors as the nature of reasoning processes in international society *determine* events in the sense that we can derive reliable predictions about state behaviour from them, as realists claim to be able to do with their focus on the pursuit of power. The ways in which states communicate and reason with each other, particularly when these become routinised, are merely one factor that helps to push states towards a particular kind of conduct. They also help to explain normative change in international society. Second, there are obvious limitations in attempting to apply models of social interaction and concepts like socialisation that were developed in the context of small social units such as the family to the vastly greater canvas of international society. However, when the representatives of states make official pronouncements, when they participate in intergovernmental organisations or other meetings and when they sign international conventions and engage in numerous other formal and informal actions (including the networking of which we have already written), they are performing within a context that is sufficiently 'social' for broader hypotheses about social interaction to be applied.[48] Nor should it be forgotten that those acting on behalf of states are not automata but individual human beings who are susceptible to the same kinds of social pressures that help to condition all human behaviour.

A number of theorists have attempted to apply various aspects of discourse theory, especially in the variant developed by Jürgen Habermas, to our understanding of the place of international law in world politics.[49] Habermas's concept of 'communicative action' has been used as the basis for essentially moral arguments about how global politics should move

---

[48] See also David Armstrong, 'Globalisation and the social state', *Review of International Studies* 24 (1998), 461–78.

[49] We should note, in particular, Thomas Risse's presentation of the German academic debate about Habermas in '"Let's argue!": Communicative action in world politics', *International Organization* 54 (2000), 1–39. Other invaluable contributions that have aided the discussion in this section include Friedrich V. Kratochwil, *Rules, Norms and Decisions: On the Conditions of Practical and Legal Reasoning in International Relations and Domestic Affairs* (Cambridge: Cambridge University Press, 1989); Anthony Clark Arend, *Legal Rules and International Society* (Oxford: Oxford University Press, 1999); Onuf, *World of Our Making*; and the contributors to a special section on Habermas and International Relations in *Review of International Studies* 31 (2005).

more in the direction of a community capable of accommodating different voices.[50] Here we are less interested in how his perspective may be used to argue that world politics should change than in the insights his work contains into how all social life works in practice. His central argument is that:

> language can be conceived as the medium of interrelating three worlds; for every successful communicative action there exists a threefold relation between the utterance and (a) 'the external world' as the totality of existing states of affairs, (b) 'our social world' as the totality of all normatively regulated interpersonal relations that count as legitimate in a given society, and (c) 'a particular inner world' (of the speaker) as the totality of his intentional experiences.[51]

Hence, in the course of any discourse, the arguments engaged in by the participants will lead them towards shared understandings of the facts (the 'external world'), the normative issues involved (the 'social world') and their own subjective responses (the 'inner world'). This of course implies that all deliberation has a normative element. In the international context, the 'official language' of interstate relations is frequently the language of international law. This means not only that legal norms increasingly become part of international discourse but that standard forms of legal reasoning creep into international 'conversation'.[52] For example, the debate over the American-led intervention into Iraq did not simply concern the legality of the intervention but whether the right procedures in the UN had been followed. But legal argument and decision-making is not just about the formal application of rules: as Thomas Franck, in particular, has noted, concepts such as 'fairness' and 'legitimacy' have become increasingly important in international discourse.[53] Others have suggested that concern for a state's reputation as a law-abiding and trustworthy actor can also serve as an unseen motivating factor towards legal

---

[50] Andrew Linklater, 'Dialogic politics and the civilising process', *Review of International Studies* 31 (2005), 141–54. But see also Scott Lash, 'Reflexivity and its doubles: structure, aesthetics, community', in Ulrich Beck, Anthony Giddens and Scott Lash (eds.) *Reflexive Modernization: Politics, Tradition, and Aesthetics in the Modern Social Order* (Cambridge: Polity, 1994), pp. 110–73 for an argument that Habermas in fact places more emphasis on power than many of his followers perceive, so that his theories cannot be the basis of an understanding of shared meanings within a community.

[51] Jürgen Habermas, *Communication and the Evolution of Society* (Cambridge: Polity, 1991), p. 67.

[52] Cf. 'the emerging legal regime plays a role in shaping current political policymaking, chiefly by reframing and restructuring the discourse in international affairs in a legalist direction'. Ruti G. Teitel, 'Humanity's law: rule of law for the new global politics', *Cornell International Law Journal* 35 (2002), 365.

[53] Thomas Franck, *The Power of Legitimacy Among Nations* (Oxford: Oxford University Press, 1990) and Franck, *Fairness in International Law and Institutions* (Oxford: Clarendon Press, 1995).

compliance. To repeat, none of this ensures that states will necessarily act in more law-abiding ways, simply that the context within which they operate has a discursive and normative character as well as a material and self-interested one.[54]

Discussion questions

- What do we mean by the word 'law'? Is international law really 'law'? What are the differences between international and domestic law? Why do IR Realists criticise international law?
- Why do states seem to observe international law most of the time? To what extent, if at all, is coercion a factor in states' compliance with international law?
- How valid is Hans Kelsen's description of international law as 'primitive' and 'decentralised'? Is 'self-help' an authentic legal principle?
- Can states be bound by rules to which they have not given their consent? What is the relationship between custom and treaties as sources of international law? Is *jus cogens* an authentic principle of international law?
- What is meant by the term 'international society'? How does the nature of international society influence the content, status and efficacy of international law?

SUGGESTIONS FOR FURTHER READING

Clark Arend, Anthony, *Legal Rules and International Society*, Oxford: Oxford University Press, 1999. An ambitious attempt to argue, using a broadly constructivist perspective, that international rules affect states' interests and even their identity.

Beck, Robert J., Anthony Clark Arend and Robert D. Vander Lugt (eds.), *International Rules: Approaches from International Law and International Relations*, Oxford: Oxford University Press, 1996. One of a number of attempts in the last twenty years to develop an interdisciplinary dialogue between International Law and International Relations. Includes classic contributions by Grotius, Kelsen, Hart and more recent authors.

Bull, Hedley, *The Anarchical Society: A Study of Order in World Politics*, London: Macmillan, 1977. The key text of the so-called 'English School' of International Relations and its central concept of an international society. A more

---

[54] An important recent article argues the case for a broader 'understanding of politics that locates politics at the intersection of idiographic, purposive, ethical and instrumental forms of reason and action'. Christian Reus-Smit, 'Politics and international legal obligation', *European Journal of International Relations* 9 (2003), 591–625. See also the same author's 'The politics of international law', in Christian Reus-Smit (ed.) *The Politics of International Law* (Cambridge: Cambridge University Press, 2004), pp. 14–44.

formalistic approach to international law than several discussed here but still a seminal work.

Byers, Michael, *Custom, Power and the Power of Rules: International Relations and Customary International Law*, Cambridge: Cambridge University Press, 1999. The best recent discussion of the interplay between custom and power in the development of international law.

(ed.) *The Role of Law in International Politics: Essays in International Relations and International Law*, Oxford: Oxford University Press, 2000. Essays by eighteen leading authorities on topics ranging from the concept of international law through the politics of law-making to emerging patterns of governance and international law.

Franck, Thomas, *Fairness in International Law and Institutions*, Oxford: Clarendon Press, 1995. An ambitious attempt to develop a theory of fairness and suggest ways in which a 'fairness discourse' might be applied to several areas of international law.

Joyner, Christopher C., *International Law in the 21ˢᵗ Century: Rules for Global Governance*, Oxford: Rowman and Littlefield, 2005. Attempts to move away from the traditional, case-based textbook of international law by focusing on their application in real-world political situations. Readable and wide-ranging.

Keohane, Robert O., 'International relations and international law: two optics, *Harvard International Law Journal* 38, 2 (Spring 1997), 487–502. A discussion by a leading IR specialist of two perspectives (or 'optics') on international law, one 'instrumentalist', focusing on states' calculations of their self-interest in their approach to international law, the other 'normative', arguing that international rules do have normative power.

Koskenniemi, Martti, (ed.), *International Law*, Aldershot: Dartmouth Press, 1992. A collection, edited by a leading international lawyer, of key articles on some of the central theoretical issues.

Kratochwil, Friedrich, *Rules, Norms and Decisions: On the Conditions of Practical and Legal Reasoning in International Relations*, Cambridge: Cambridge University Press, 1989. A complex and at times dense attempt to argue that rules and norms do influence state choice in world politics.

Ku, Charlotte, and Paul F. Diehl (eds.), *International Law. Classic and Contemporary Readings*, 2nd edition, Boulder, CO: Lynne Rienner, 2003. An excellent collection of several key essays on fundamental questions relating to the sources of international law, participation in the international legal process, compliance and the impact of international law in areas like the environment, the use of force and human rights.

Lynch, Cecelia, and Michael Loriaux (eds.), *Law and Moral Action in World Politics*, Minneapolis: University of Minnesota Press, 2000. Essays by several leading authorities on theoretical, historical and applied aspects of the moral force of international law.

Reus-Smit, Christian, 'Politics and international legal obligation', *European Journal of International Relations* 9, 4 (2003), 591–625. A highly sophisticated discussion of different theoretical approaches to international law that concludes by locating international law within the discursive processes of world politics.

The Politics of International Law, Cambridge: Cambridge University Press, 2004. A valuable collection of essays on specific issues, such as climate change, Kosovo, the International Criminal Court and land-mines that makes use of a broader conception of 'politics' than that embodied in realist thinking.

Scott, Shirley V., *International Law in World Politics*, Boulder, CO: Lynne Rienner, 2004. A useful introduction to a range of key issues in international law, considered from the perspective of world politics.

www.asil.org. This was set up by the American Society of International Law. It provides a great deal of useful information, including primary documents, as well as links to other websites.

www.law2.biz.uwa.edu.au/intlaw/. An Australian University's collection of more than 900 web links relating to international law

2 The evolution of international law

Historians of international law differ over Montesquieu's observation in the *Spirit of Laws* that 'all countries have a law of nations, not excepting the Iroquois themselves, though they devour their prisoners: for they send and receive ambassadors, and understand the rights of war and peace'.[1] One school of thought argues in opposition to Montesquieu that international law is essentially a European invention, although there are different emphases within this school as to whether international law commences with the ancient Greeks,[2] with the Romans,[3] with medieval Christendom,[4] with early modernity,[5] or with the Peace of Westphalia in 1648.[6] Others, who object to the Eurocentrism implicit or explicit in such views, assert that a truly universal system of international law is not apparent until the late nineteenth century.[7] Yet another thesis, with the same starting point of resisting Eurocentric interpretations, maintains that there *was* a universal international legal order roughly from the rise of Islam until the late eighteenth century, but the nineteenth-century doctrine of

---

[1] Cited in Arthur Nussbaum, *A Concise History of the Law of Nations*, rev. edition (New York: Macmillan, 1962), p. 1.
[2] H. Brougham Leech, *An Essay on Ancient International Law* (Dublin: Dublin University Press, 1877), p. 2; C. Phillipson, *The International Law and Customs of Ancient Greece and Rome* (London: Macmillan, 1911), p. 32.
[3] Olga V. Butkevych, 'History of ancient international law: challenges and prospects', *Journal of the History of International Law* 5 (2003), 193.
[4] J. H. W. Verzijl, *International Law in Historical Perspective* (Leyden: A. W. Sijthoff, 1968), vol. I, p. 444.
[5] Wilhelm G. Grewe, *The Epochs of International Law*, trans. and rev. Michael Byers (New York: Walter de Gruyter, 2000), p. 8. See also Henri Legohérel, *Histoire du droit international public* (Paris: Presses universitaires de France, 1996), pp. 17–20; C. G. Roelofson, *Studies in the History of International Law* (Utrecht: Institute of Public International Law, 1991), p. xvi.
[6] Lassa Oppenheim, *International Law* (London: Longmans, Green and Co., 1905), p. 58.
[7] Onuma Yasuaki, 'When was the law of international society born? An inquiry of the history of international law from an intercivilizational perspective', *Journal of the History of International Law* 2 (2000), p. 63. See also the Symposium provoked by this article in *Journal of the History of International Law* 6 (2004), 1–41.

sovereignty and legal positivism, together with European imperialism, involved a shift away from the broad moral principles of natural law that underpinned the universal order towards a self-serving distinction between 'civilised' states, which could have legal obligations towards each other, and the rest, who were outside the legal system.[8] Additional complications are to be found in claims that the true origins of international law are to be found in the ancient Middle East,[9] or China,[10] or India.[11]

The picture of almost complete confusion that is presented by these contradictions becomes a little clearer if we bear in mind that those cited are not necessarily always talking about the same thing. In practice, four key distinctions that are implicitly or explicitly made by the analysts need to be taken into account when considering the history of international law. The first concerns the precise status of the rules and norms under review. As we argued in Chapter 1, all social interaction is governed to some degree by rules and norms, but not all of these qualify as binding obligations: the principal characteristic of law. The relations among ancient societies before the Romans (who had by far the most fully developed legal system) tended to have two kinds of normative underpinnings: religious or moral injunctions and proto-legal rules. Neither, to some authors, quite qualifies as 'law'.[12] Second, to assert that a rule or norm of either kind existed in any ancient society is not the same as establishing the existence of a clear, continuous line of development between it and later international law. This, of course, is crucial if the aim is to identify the origins of the contemporary legal order. Third, some reserve the term 'international law', strictly speaking, for rules and norms governing the relations between *states*, defined as unitary political entities

---

[8] This argument is associated particularly with the work of C. H. Alexandrowitz, but see also R. Ago, 'Pluralism and the origins of the international community', *Italian Yearbook of International Law*, cited in Georges Abi-Saab, 'International law and the international community: the long road to universality', in Ronald St John Macdonald (ed.), *Essays in Honour of Wang Tieva* (Dordrecht: Martinus Nijhoff, 1994), p. 32.

[9] C. Calvo, *Le Droit International Theorique et Pratique*, Libraire nouvelle de Droit et de Jurisprudence, Paris 1896, pp. 2–3; Ammon Altman, 'Tracing the earliest recorded concepts of international law: the early Dynastic Period in Southern Mesopotamia', *Journal of the History of International Law* 6 (2004) 153–72.

[10] Eric Yong-Joong Lee, 'Early development of modern international law in East Asia – with special reference to China, Japan and Korea', *Journal of the History of International Law* 4 (2002), 43.

[11] Jerome A. Thomas, 'History and international law in Asia: a time for review', in Macdonald, *Essays in Honour of Wang Tieva*, pp. 814–15. See also Ved P. Nanda, 'International law in ancient Hindu India', in Mark W. Janis (ed.), *The Influence of Religion on the Development of International Law* (Dordrecht: Martinus Nijhoff, 1991), p. 51.

[12] Julius Stone, *Legal Controls of International Conflict: A Treatise on the Dynamics of Disputes and War-Law* (Sydney: Maitland Publications, 1959), p. 3 n. 2.

exercising sovereignty over a clearly demarcated territorial area: a phenomenon they date from no earlier than the late Middle Ages.[13] There are, of course, several hornets' nests' worth of controversies surrounding this issue and some of the more interesting and important work of recent years has attempted to move away from state-centric perspectives to emphasise transnational forces,[14] 'intersecting networks of social interaction',[15] 'polities' (defined as 'overlapping and interacting political authorities')[16] and 'institutional arrangements'[17]. Each of these types of political organisation will have its own distinctive normative focus and features, but this does not make it impossible to define 'international law' in a more restrictive way, so long as that is made explicit. Finally, some analysts prefer to confine their use of the term 'international law' to cases that demonstrate some of the characteristics of a legal *system* or *order*, as against more random instances where normative elements can be shown to be present in international social interaction. As Wilhelm Grewe defines it, a legal order

can only be assumed to exist if there is a plurality of relatively independent (although not necessarily equal ranking) bodies politic which are linked to each other in political, economic and cultural relationships and which are not subject to a superimposed authority having comprehensive law-making jurisdiction and executive competence. In their mutual relations these bodies politic must observe norms which are deemed to be binding on the basis of a legal consciousness rooted in religious, cultural and other common values.[18]

As these distinctions suggest, 'international law' is a somewhat elastic term, especially where we are talking about pre-literate and ancient societies. However, as the next section shows, various kinds of norms and rules may be discerned in the relations among almost all such societies. We will now consider these without losing sight of the four distinctions we have made.

[13] G. Butler and S. Macoby, *The Development of International Law* (London: Longmans, Green and Co., 1928), pp. 3–9.
[14] The 'foundational' text here is Robert O. Keohane and Joseph Nye, (eds.), *Transnational Relations and World Politics*, (Cambridge, MA: Harvard University Press, 1971). See also Thomas Risse-Kappen (ed.), *Bringing Transnational Relations Back In* (Cambridge: Cambridge University Press, 1995).
[15] Michael Mann, *The Sources of Social Power* (Cambridge: Cambridge University Press, 1986), vol. I, p. 16. See also Anne-Marie Slaughter, *A New World Order*, (Princeton, NJ: Princeton University Press, 2004).
[16] Yale H. Ferguson and Richard W. Mansbach, *Polities: Authority, Identities and Change* (Columbia: University of South Carolina Press, 1996), pp. 33–4.
[17] Hendrik Spruyt, *The Sovereign State and its Competitors* (Princeton, NJ: Princeton University Press, 1994), p. 12.
[18] Grewe, *The Epochs*, p. 7.

'International law' in ancient times

Strangers have been regarded with some suspicion from the earliest times to the present day, as the contemporary European debates about immigration demonstrate. Indeed the ancient Greek and Latin terms for 'stranger' and 'enemy' are the same.[19] It is clear that some ancient societies, notably the Assyrians, maintained a generally fierce attitude towards strangers, seeing them primarily as legitimate targets for theft, enslavement and killing. In other cases, societies developed elementary 'self–other' distinctions, according to which tribes and, later, city states accepted more comprehensive sets of norms and rules for their interactions with members of their own cultural or linguistic group than their relations with 'aliens'. The Israelites, for example, distinguished between three types of relationships: those among the Hebrew tribes, where numerous constraints applied, those with most other tribes and cities, which, in the event of war, were to be allowed the opportunity to surrender peacefully and become tributaries, failing which their women and children would be enslaved, and a small group of sworn enemies, such as the Hittites and other polytheistic tribes, towards whom no mercy should be shown.[20]

It is possible that some pre-literate societies in the Pacific and elsewhere enjoyed relatively peaceful inter-tribal relations,[21] but in general the earliest Mediterranean and Middle Eastern societies of which we have record (as well as the Aztec and other Mesoamerican societies somewhat later) were able to enjoy, at best, an uneasy coexistence, at worst merciless mutual brutality. This, however, did not preclude the possibility of their relations having at least a minimal normative foundation, particularly with regard to two of the most basic aspects of international law: diplomacy and treaties. Although diplomacy today is a highly developed institution, its origins lie in the need for separate communities to be able to communicate about a range of issues – trade, boundaries, peaceful transit, intermarriage, war and peace – with some assurance that the lives, property and freedom of their envoys would not be placed in jeopardy.[22]

---

[19] Henry Wheaton, *History of the Law of Nations in Europe and America* (New York: Gould, Banks and Co, 1845), p. 1.

[20] T. A. Walker, *A History of the Law of Nations* (Cambridge: Cambridge University Press, 1899), vol. I, p. 33; Jacques Bex, *Essai sur l'Evolution du Droit des Gens* (Paris: Librairie de sciences politiques et sociales, 1910), pp. 6–7.

[21] Ragnar Numelin, *The Beginnings of Diplomacy: A Sociological Study of Intertribal and International Relations* (London: Oxford University Press, 1950), pp. 72–4.

[22] Unlike the contemporary institution of diplomatic immunity, however, diplomats in the ancient world could be punished if they violated their host's trust, or even held hostage as a surety against bad faith by their own governments. David J. Bederman, *International Law in Antiquity* (Cambridge: Cambridge University Press, 2001), pp. 91–3.

Similarly, treaties, like contracts, their equivalents in domestic law, originate in the simple requirement (and moral norm) that promises, whether
between individuals, tribes, cities or states, needed to be honoured if
continuing interaction were to proceed on a basis of reliable and stable
expectations. Both treaties and diplomacy needed to be invested with the
most authoritative normative aura, which, at the time, emanated from
religion. Hence, the earliest examples of both of which we have knowledge took place in an atmosphere of oath-taking and other sacred rituals.
In some cases envoys were themselves priests; in parts of the Pacific and
Africa they were obliged to undergo various 'purification' rituals before
being received by their hosts.[23] The fact that diplomacy acquired similar normative underpinnings virtually everywhere in the world, including
North America, indicates that its origins are to be found in simple necessity. The combination of repeated practice (or 'custom') and religious
sanctions gradually gave these norms a law-like quality.

The earliest treaties on record tend to reflect an unequal relationship between the parties, but not one of complete subjection.[24] Their
subject matter ranged from boundaries (treaty of c. 3100 BC between
two Mesopotamian cities)[25] to post-war treaties, such as a famous one
between the Egyptians and the Hittites (c. 1300 BC), which pledged
permanent alliance, freedom of commerce and extradition of criminals, subject to the surprisingly humane provision that neither they
nor their close relatives should be subjected to extreme punishment.[26]
Other treaties of the same period referred to the right of asylum of
refugees.[27] As with diplomatic inviolability, the treaties were accompanied by solemn oaths and other religious rituals, with disasters of various
kinds, such as plagues, sometimes blamed upon one side breaking such a
treaty.[28]

The exact status of these early practices is hard to determine. They were
clearly 'normative' but we know little about the degree to which they were
accepted as general rules by most communities or indeed complied with
by their signatories in the case of treaties. Certainly, any conception that
agreements were being concluded by 'sovereign equals' is still centuries,
if not millennia, away. Nor is there any sign of a true international legal

---

[23] Linda S. Frey and Marsha L. Frey, *The History of Diplomatic Immunity* (Columbus, OH:
Ohio State University Press, 1999), pp. 12–14.
[24] Nussbaum, *Concise History*, pp. 1–5.   [25] *Ibid.*, pp. 1–2.
[26] Calvo, *Le Droit International*, pp. 2–3.   [27] Butkevych, 'History', pp. 198–9.
[28] David J. Bederman, 'Religion and the sources of international law in antiquity', in Mark
W. Janis (ed.), *The Influence of Religion on the Development of International Law* (Dordrecht:
Martinus Nijhoff, 1991), p. 94.

order.[29] What may be argued, however, is the importance of custom in the gradual emergence of an international norm and of treaties in solemnising customary practice and, perhaps, taking it to a higher, more law-like standing. If, as we argued in Chapter 1, rules and norms should be seen as the products of the interplay among a range of political, social and economic factors, inevitably, as such interactive processes become more intense, so do the rules to which they give rise become more complex, wide-ranging and entrenched.

For example, writing around 400 BC, Thucydides suggests that, in earlier times, incessant threats left Greece without a settled population, commerce, safe communications by land or sea, and with no surplus capital and no regular system of agriculture. Among the consequences of this state of affairs was the fact that piracy, 'so far from being regarded as disgraceful, was considered quite honourable'.[30] Clearly, greater stability and prosperity gave rise to a demand for greater security of the person and property: a demand met in part by a shift towards a general denunciation of piracy. By Cicero's time, pirates were seen as falling outside the otherwise universal norm that promises made under oath should be honoured: 'a pirate does not fall within the concept of a lawful enemy, but is the common enemy of all the world; and with a pirate there is no common basis for either faith or oaths'.[31] Fifteen hundred years later, the international legal authority, Gentili, could assert that piracy was a crime against the law of nations, against which what would even later be termed 'universal jurisdiction' could be exercised.[32] As what amounted to semi-officially sanctioned piracy continued for some years in Gentili's adopted country, England, it is impossible to provide an exact date when piracy was explicitly designated as a practice contrary to international law, but we can discern a very clear process during which it moved from enjoying general acceptance, through various stages of social disapproval, to a point when it was seen as one of the most serious of international crimes, against which all civilised countries were obliged to act.

---

[29] However, for an argument that the ancient Near East (1400–1150 BC), the Greek city states (500–338 BC) and the larger Mediterranean before Roman dominance (358–168 BC) all constituted true state systems, see Bederman, *International Law in Antiquity*, passim.

[30] Thucydides, *The Peloponnesian War*, trans. Rex Warner (Harmondsworth: Penguin, 1972), book one, pp. 2, 5.

[31] Cicero, *De Officiis*, cited in J. M. Kelly, *A Short History of Western Legal Theory* (Oxford: Clarendon Press, 1993), p. 77.

[32] Henri Legohérel, *Histoire du droit international public* (Paris: Presses universitaires de France, 1996), p. 15.

With classical antiquity (roughly from 500 BC), we enter an era where social and economic interaction is both more intense and more subject to numerous rules and norms. This is true not only of the Greek city states but of the other great civilisations that flourished at this time, including those in China and India. We should perhaps resist the more exaggerated claims made on behalf of all three civilisations, namely that they constituted distinct international legal orders. This is partly because the status of their various norms ranged from little more than pious injunctions informed by spiritual principles, such as the notion of *dharma* in India, through more precise, but still essentially religious obligations, such as the ancient Greek right of those killed in battle to proper burial, to the elaborate early Roman procedures required before and during declaration of war.[33] In part, also, it is because the notion of a distinctive set of rules governing the relations among equal and independent political communities played a relatively small part in the complex array of norms and rules that have some bearing upon those relations. Even where an apparent equality of status existed, as in the relations between Rome and Carthage until the destruction of the latter, legal issues frequently concerned what would today be termed 'conflict of laws': attempts to determine which of the two sets of domestic laws should apply in contractual arrangements between citizens of two polities.[34] In most other cases rules related to varying degrees of inequality between the parties. In the case of Rome, as its power grew, the increasing emphasis on law in all Roman practice frequently reflected a determination to reinforce its supremacy by endowing it with clear legal formulations. Finally, the degree to which legal norms influenced actual behaviour is highly variable, although this charge has been brought against international law throughout its history.

Nonetheless, rules and norms that have some of the character of international law do become increasingly evident during this period. We cannot yet speak of a single international legal system but, at most, of several elementary regional systems. Rules were clearest in respect of diplomacy, treaties (for which the Greeks had several distinct terms)[35] and warfare. In the case of the last of these, both Greek and especially Roman discourse shows evidence of numerous norms relating to the necessity for war to have a just cause, for clear rituals to be undergone in the commencement and conclusion of war and for the right of neutrality and certain

---

[33] Bex, *Essai*, p. 12; C. H. Alexandrowicz, 'Kautilyan Principles and the Law of Nations', *British Yearbook of International Law*, 1965–66 (Oxford: Oxford University Press, 1968), p. 302; Nanda, 'International law', p. 51.
[34] Sir Paul Vinogradoff, *Historical Types of International Law* (Leiden: Lectures at Leiden University, 1923), p. 24.
[35] Leech, *An Essay*, p. 22.

constraints to be observed in the conduct of war. If the last two of these were honoured more in the breach than the observance, that reflected the inevitable priority that warring parties gave to their military interests.

Other areas where the international relations of both Greeks and Romans were characterised, to some extent at least, by norms and rules, included boundary delineation, maritime transport,[36] trade, intermarriage between individuals from two countries, the position of aliens (where an elementary version of consulates operated[37]), coinage and indeed any area where regular intercourse would have been impossible without some settled and widely understood rules. The 'sources' of these various obligations are to be found, first, in long-established practice – or 'custom' – especially where this was associated with basic moral or religious norms. Specific treaties constituted the second source, and although these bound only the signatories, a body of common jurisprudence emerged over time as to the precise nature and form that legal obligations should assume in similar circumstances. There were even a few attempts to codify the generalised principles that emerged from these treaties, as with the Rhodian sea law.

The degree to which any of this constituted a 'legal order' is still open to question. First, both Greeks and, before they acquired supremacy in Italy, Romans distinguished between relations within their own linguistic group and with those outside it. Even within their own communities, there was no absolute assumption of equality (the Romans formally distinguished between 'equal' and 'unequal' treaties). Finally, there was only the most rudimentary institutional structure to underpin the laws. In the case of the Greeks, this consisted of the Amphyctionic Council and the use of arbitration to settle certain disputes. The Council, however, was essentially a religious institution, whose concern was to provide some protection for shrines such as the oracle at Delphi and to enable Greeks to engage in religious rituals even during times of war.[38] They occasionally played a role in helping to bring wars to an end but were highly constrained in this regard.[39] Resort to third-party arbitration to settle disputes, especially territorial ones, was more common but this practice should be seen as occupying a mid-point between law and politics, rather than as a purely legal institution, since the arbitrators tended to base their decisions on

---

[36] The island of Rhodes had developed an elaborate code of rules relating to the sea by the 3rd century BC. After it was annexed by Rome in 164 BC, the Rhodian code became more widely influential. R. P. Anand, *Origin and Development of the Law of the Sea* (The Hague: Martinus Nijhoff, 1982), p. 11.

[37] Walker, *A History*, p. 40.

[38] Wheaton, *History*. p. 15; Bederman, *International Law in Antiquity*, pp. 168–71.

[39] Walker, *A History*, p. 39.

general principles of justice, rather than specific rules of law.[40] A more lasting Greek contribution to the evolution of law, including international law, may well have been their use of rhetoric and debate in many of their decision-making processes.[41] This may be seen as a precursor to more modern forms of legal reasoning and, more generally, as helping to establish the principle that normative justifications for various actions needed to be found and argued out in public fora.

The Roman emphasis on law and the sophisticated array of legal concepts and procedures they developed – many of which live on today – suggests at first sight that the Romans are likely to have a greater claim to the creation of a true international legal order than the Greeks or any of their other contemporaries, such as the Indians or Chinese. In practice, however (and at the risk of grossly oversimplifying a vast and still hotly disputed topic), two important distinctions need to be borne in mind when evaluating the Roman contribution to international law. First, Roman practice in the early Republican and Hellenistic periods (roughly from 500–150 BC) needs to be distinguished from the later Republican and Imperial periods.[42] During the first period, Rome's international relations were conducted in the context of an approximate (though fluctuating) balance of power, when it dealt with several states on a basis of equality.[43] This enabled agreements to be reached that were characterised by norms of reciprocity and mutual benefit, together with provisions for the use of arbitration.[44] Moreover, the declaration, conduct and termination of war were all considered within a clear legal framework of 'just war' principles, as determined by the College of Fetiales (priests charged with the rituals involved in making war and peace).[45] As Rome's relative power grew, its emphasis on the need for formal legal-religious procedures declined, as did its preparedness to deal with other states on the basis of equality and its use of the Fetiales.

The second distinction is between the meanings and application that Rome's enormous range of legal terminology had at the time and later use of Roman expressions, which sometimes accords Rome's legal practice

[40] Bederman, *International Law in Antiquity*; R. N. Tod, *International Arbitration Among the Greeks* (Oxford: Clarendon Press, 1913). For an interesting discussion of Greek arbitration as a 'discursive norm of procedural justice', see Christian Reus-Smit, 'The Constitutional Structure of International Society and the Nature of Fundamental Institutions', *International Organization* 51 (1997), 555–89.
[41] David J. Bederman, *Classical Canons: Rhetoric, Classicism and Treaty Interpretation* (Aldershot: Ashgate, 2001), pp. 11–15.
[42] Phillipson, *International Law*, p. 103.
[43] Wolfgang Preiser, 'History of the law of nations: ancient times to 1648', in *Encyclopedia of Public International Law* (Amsterdam: Elsevier, 1995), vol. II, pp. 726–7.
[44] Phillipson, *International Law*, pp. 107–8.   [45] Bex, *Essai*, pp. 12–13.

a significance for international law that is not always justified. This is particularly true of what is perhaps the most flourishing period of international legal literature: the work of the 'Publicists' of the sixteenth and seventeenth centuries. The Publicists, as we discuss later, were searching for new legal formulations to define and, hopefully, order to some degree the new international system that was emerging in the wake of the collapse of the medieval order and the discovery of the New World. Roman legal language offered a framework of norms, rules and procedures that could be used for this purpose. However, much of this framework applied in Roman times to municipal law, rather than to international relations. If we may borrow a more modern theoretical perspective, some of the Publicists, in effect, 'constructed' international law from principles that were certainly derived from Roman law but were often employed by the Romans for much narrower purposes that were domestic, not international.

This is, of course, a much larger, and indeed more controversial and hotly debated, topic than we can develop here, but the point may be illustrated by two of the most general terms borrowed by the Publicists. The first is *ius gentium*, normally translated 'law of nations'. The Romans used this in two senses, both deriving from the more accurate present-day rendering of '*gens*' as 'people' or 'race', rather than 'nation', which tends today to be associated with the concept of a state. In the first, and narrowest, usage, the Romans used the term to refer to the legal rights of foreigners living in Roman territory. In the second, they had in mind legal norms that are universal in the sense that they are to be found in every community's legal system. While such norms would certainly have included principles like diplomatic immunity, and while the Romans did occasionally use *ius gentium* in the modern sense of law *between* nations,[46] their understanding of the term was significantly different from the interpretation given by some of the Publicists.[47]

A related point may be made of the Publicists' use of the concept of natural law, which they derived from Greek and Roman Stoic thought, as formulated notably by Cicero, for whom natural law was 'right reason,

---

[46] *Encyclopedia of Public International Law*, p. 728. It should be added that the Publicists were not unaware of these distinctions and tended to opt for *ius gentium* as an all-purpose expression mainly out of convenience. We should also remember that the expression 'international law' was not used until the 1780s, after it was coined by Jeremy Bentham.

[47] A further confusion stems from the fact that many European languages have two distinct terms that are normally both translated as 'law' in English: *nomos* and *themis* in Greek, *lex* and *ius* in Latin, *loi* and *droit* in French, *recht* and *gesetz* in German. The latter of these two words normally denotes something closer to the English terms 'right' or 'justice'. See Wheaton, *History*, pp. 16, 18 n. 7.

conformable to nature, universally diffused, unchanging and eternal'.[48] The Publicists shared Cicero's conviction that natural law had a legal, not merely a moral, significance, in so far as it was at the very least a major source of, if not identical with, international law. Given that natural law was seen as a set of maxims governing the behaviour of all individuals, who were depicted as members of the 'great community' of all mankind, those acting on behalf of states were automatically obliged to observe these maxims in their conduct of international affairs. Here, too, the later employment of the term went somewhat beyond Roman usage. Natural law was not seen by the Romans as a fundamental source of international law (in the sense of rules governing the relations among independent political communities) but as an interlinked set of arguments incorporating such broad assertions as the need for society among human beings and the logical corollary that people living in any society would inevitably have to observe similar rules and norms as they experienced similar requirements and problems. While a certain conception of an 'international society' in terms of natural law's 'great community of mankind' may be fitted into this framework, the more recent notion of international society as consisting of fully sovereign states entering into legal obligations only on a voluntary basis clearly entails a very different idea of 'society'.[49]

None of this is to argue that Rome was without significance for international law. At the most general level, the Roman shift away from the more open-ended Greek rhetoric, conducted within a broad context of religious norms, and towards more precise delineation of fixed rules formulated in legal rather than religious terms inevitably affected that wide range of practices, from diplomacy to alien rights, which had been influenced by norms from the earliest times. This was particularly so in the case of wars. While most early societies had seen war as a solemn undertaking that was subject to divine intervention and direction, and therefore as imbued with moral significance, the Romans went beyond this with their detailed 'just war' principles, which influenced in turn later thinkers such as Augustine and Aquinas.

The Middle Ages

The end of Roman dominance was followed by a complex and multi-faceted international order. We confine ourselves here to Europe and the

[48] A. P. D'Entrèves, *The Notion of the State* (Oxford: Clarendon Press, 1967), p. 77.
[49] Cf. Maine's sceptical discussion of the Publicists' use of Roman legal ideas, especially natural law: H. S. Maine, *Ancient Law* (London: J. M. Dent and Sons, 1954 [orig. publ. 1861]), pp. 56–60.

Islamic world since these are of the greatest importance for the modern international legal system, but this is not to argue that developments elsewhere, such as those in the Chinese tribute system or the maritime relations of South-east Asian nations, are without interest or significance in areas like the law of the sea and treaty law. However, it was the sovereign state system that emerged in Europe that largely determined the character and content of modern international law.

The years between the formal division of the Roman Empire into eastern and western parts in 395 AD and the discovery of the New World in 1492 defy easy classification or generalisation, especially in a section as brief as this. Actors enjoying or claiming different kinds of legal authority were far more varied than they were to become in the modern era, when relations among unitary states exercising sovereignty over a fixed territorial domain became the main focus of international law. In Western Christendom alone, the papacy, the Emperor (after 800 AD[50]), the Hanseatic League and other leagues of mercantile cities, the Knights Templar, the Teutonic Knights and other chivalric orders, together with numerous bishops, barons, dukes, princes and kings all possessed some measure of independent military power and legal authority, as well as being enmeshed in an intricate mosaic of feudal, religious and other obligations and entitlements. Other important international actors, notably Byzantium and the rising forces of Islam, served further to complicate the legal picture. Furthermore, clear distinctions need to be made between theory and practice. The Pope's claim to exercise universal authority was always challenged by the similar claims advanced by the Emperor and the increasing assertions of independence on the party of secular authorities. Moral injunctions regarding the necessity for war to be founded on principles of justice, as advanced by Augustine (354–430), Isidore of Seville (560–636) and Thomas Aquinas (1225–1274), were generally ignored in practice. Similarly, chivalric codes of righteous conduct in war were disregarded not just in the brutality shown towards Muslims during the crusades (often in contrast to the more merciful treatment accorded by Saladin and other Muslim leaders) but even against fellow Christians, as in the brutal sack of Constantinople in 1204.[51] Papal prohibitions against dealing with Muslim states were disregarded in the interests of trade, while the Islamic doctrine that all Muslims formed a single *umma*, or community of believers, did not prevent intra-Islamic conflicts

[50] The expression 'Holy Roman Empire' was not used until 1157. J. Bryce, *The Holy Roman Empire* (London: Macmillan and Co., 1907), p. 196.
[51] G. I. A. D. Draper, 'The Interaction of Christianity and Chivalry in the Development of the Law of War', *International Review of the Red Cross*, January (1965), pp. 3–23.

or alliances between a Muslim and Christian state against another Muslim (or indeed Christian) state.[52]

There was no universal or coherent body of rules and institutions during this period, but in the following subsections, we look at some of the factors that influenced later development of international law.

Moral and ethical doctrines

Both Christendom and the Islamic world developed elaborate doctrines to lay down a normative framework for the conduct of their relations with both co-religionists and infidels. These codes of conduct were most fully developed in the case of war, with, in the case of Christendom, broad conceptualisations of just war together with a host of more narrow injunctions, such as the assertion that Christian prisoners of war should not be enslaved.[53] The Islamic world during this period also had a version of 'just war' theory in its concept of *jihad*. At first, it also maintained that a permanent state of war existed with unbelievers, although truces of up to ten years were permissible. In addition, the 'people of the book' (Jews and Christians) were to be given more favourable treatment than pagans, and a defeated people could continue to practise their religion so long as they paid a poll tax. Islam also adopted a stronger position than Christendom on the necessity of honouring treaty commitments.[54] As with Christendom, although such norms were not without influence, they were disregarded at least as often as they were observed.

State practice

Of rather greater significance was the increasing tendency of the more powerful states to base their commercial and maritime relations with other states on legal principles. Strictly speaking, as with much of Roman imperial law, this was not 'international' but national (or even, sometimes, sub-national or local law) since the rules bound only their polity of origin.[55] However, any state anxious to enjoy the benefits of trade soon found it needed to draw up rules guaranteeing merchants various rights and freedoms. Often these rules were also expressed in bilateral treaties, to such a degree that it is possible to talk in terms of the development of 'customary international law' during this period in the sense of the

---

[52] *Encyclopedia of Public International Law*, p. 811.

[53] Robert Ward, *An Enquiry into the Foundation and History of the Law of Nations in Europe from the Time of the Greeks and Romans to the Age of Grotius* (London, 1795), vol. II, pp. 27–31.

[54] *Encyclopedia of Public International Law*.   [55] Nussbaum, *Concise History*, pp. 27–8.

frequent repetition of similar legal formulae. Although the Church sometimes attempted to argue that a bilateral treaty with a Muslim regime, for
example agreeing to safe passage, was invalid and therefore did not need
to be honoured, such interventions were relatively rare and usually over-
ridden by considerations of commercial interest.[56]

The Church's concept of an international legal order

In support of its claim to exercise a universal jurisdiction over Christendom, the papacy constructed an elaborate legal order, comprising a
system of sanctions, the employment of arbitration, formal legal hear-
ings and the enunciation of specific rules of law in the shape of canon
law. This, at times, exercised considerable influence. The Church's main
sanction – the threat or imposition of excommunication – was taken seriously, as, for example, when King John of England was eventually obliged
to submit to the Pope's authority in 1213.[57] The Church also claimed
the right to appoint and depose kings.[58] Although there were probably as
many occasions when such papal edicts were ignored as when they were
obeyed, the notion of some externally administered system of sanctions
lingered on to the present day. Much the same point may be made of the
other institutional underpinnings of the Church's legal system, such as its
use of law-making councils and of arbitration to settle disputes between
Christian princes.

Diplomacy

As we have seen, diplomatic envoys between rulers have enjoyed some
measure of protection in most societies since ancient times. During the
late Middle Ages, diplomacy became institutionalised and, in the process, acquired a much stronger legal foundation. The Byzantines were
the first to focus upon diplomacy, which they saw as crucial both to the
manipulation of the balance of power for security purposes and to protect and further develop valuable trade.[59] To this end they set up an early
version of an external affairs department. However, diplomacy reached
its most fully developed form in the Italian city-states system, with Venice
issuing the first set of rules specifically relating to diplomacy in the thirteenth century and a system of resident ambassadors throughout Italy in

[56] Grewe, *The Epochs*, pp. 52–3.   [57] Kelly, *Short History*, p. 124.
[58] W. Ullmann, *The Growth of Papal Government in the Middle Ages*, 2nd edition (London:
Methuen and Co., 1962), pp. 281–301.
[59] Nascimento e Silva, *Diplomacy in International Law* (Leiden: A. W. Sijthoff, 1972), p. 18;
H. Nicolson, *The Evolution of Diplomatic Method* (London: Constable, 1954), p. 24.

existence from the middle of the fifteenth century.[60] The medieval period also witnessed a related development under which Christian rulers were also permitted to set up settlements with some extraterritorial privileges in Muslim countries. The heads of these settlements were called 'consuls'.[61]

The origins of sovereignty

The emerging system of resident ambassadors may be taken as an early sign that Europe was moving from the complex structure of overlapping authorities that was so characteristic of the medieval period towards a conception of individual polities as legally independent unitary states. The principles of diplomatic immunity and extraterritoriality, which essentially conferred what would come to be seen as sovereign rights on resident ambassadors, is a clear indication of this and indeed various individuals, such as the French king and the Pope, who still claimed feudal rights over these aspirants to independent status, maintained that such entities had no right to engage in separate diplomacy.[62] However, numerous other developments were pointing in the same direction and it is possible to discern the emergence of a rudimentary system of sovereign states alongside the residual remnants of the feudal order. Princes were increasingly asserting their authority not only over lesser lords in their own domains but against external claimants such as the Pope and Emperor. What is sometimes described as the first treaty in the modern legal sense of an agreement between two equal sovereigns was signed as early as 921 between the first king of Saxony, Henry I, and the Emperor Charles III.[63] Hence, when the fourteenth-century Italian legal commentator, Baldus, laid down one of the founding doctrines of the sovereignty principle, '*Rex in regno suo est Imperator regni sui*' (The king is Emperor in his own kingdom), he was merely confirming what had long been the case in practice.[64] There were even a few instances, such as Venice, where the Doge, as an elected, salaried official, could not be seen as the legal personification of his state, as was the case of the dynastic monarchs, leading, by the sixteenth century, to the modern solution of the Venetian state as such being given a legal personality.[65]

Another legal controversy that may be seen as anticipating modern doctrines of international law occurred at the Council of Constance

---

[60] Nicolson, *Evolution*, p. 24.   [61] Nussbaum, *Concise History*, p. 56.
[62] Nicolson, *Evolution*, p. 29.   [63] *Encyclopedia of Public International Law*, p. 733.
[64] Grewe, *The Epochs*, p. 47.
[65] J. Goebel, *The Equality of States* (New York: Amo Press, 1970), p. 63; D. S. Chambers, *The Imperial Age of Venice, 1380–1580* (London: Thames and Hudson Ltd, 1970), pp. 86–93.

(1414–18). The issue concerned Poland's alliance with the non-Christian state of Lithuania against the Teutonic Order, which had been authorised to spread Christianity by force. The alliance contradicted the prevailing doctrine that pagan communities had no legal rights and war against them was, therefore, justified. The Polish defence of their alliance, led by Paulus Vladimiri, argued that the question whether a community had rights under the law of nations depended entirely on whether they exercised effective jurisdiction over a given territory, not on their religious beliefs.[66]

The legal culture

The later Middle Ages were marked by a growing emphasis on law, with the law of nations simply one beneficiary of this process. First, the many claimants to power and authority sought various means of legitimating their claims, including placing them on some kind of legal foundation, whether this was grounded in natural, Roman, ecclesiastical or local law. Legal justifications and explanations were sought not just for the source of a ruler's power but for its purported consequences, in the form of a well-governed polity: an early version of contractarian and 'rule-of-law' theories of the state.[67] Second, the revival of Roman law from the late eleventh century was also important, not least because it provided a sophisticated vocabulary for the on-going legal discourse. The central Roman concept of *dominium* (lordship), implying, as it did, what J. H. Burns terms 'an absolute and exclusive right of ownership and control', ran counter to the medieval conception of overlapping authority and helped to provide a legal rationalisation for the emergence of monarchical power.[68] International law was never a central element in this evolving legal culture, but it is possible to discern in numerous writings an implicit, if vaguely formulated, assumption that international relations were also subject to legal considerations.[69] The widespread use of treaties is one indication of this, although it should be noted that most treaties in this period still

---

[66] C. H. Alexandrowicz, 'Paulus Vladimiri and the Development of the Doctrine of Coexistence of Christian and Non-Christian countries', *British Yearbook of International Law* (1963), 441–8.

[67] J. R. Strayer, *On the Medieval Origin of the Modern State* (Princeton, NJ: Princeton University Press, 1970), pp. 23–4.

[68] J. H. Burns, *Lordship, Kingship and Empire: The Idea of Monarchy 1400–1525* (Oxford: Clarendon Press, 1992), pp. 18–39.

[69] Dominique Bauer, 'The importance of medieval canon law and the scholastic tradition for the emergence of the early modern international order', in Randall Lesaffer (ed.), *Peace Treaties and International Law in European History. From the Late Middle Ages to World War One* (Cambridge: Cambridge University Press), pp. 198–221.

took the form of personal contracts between rulers, backed by religious oaths and not regarded as binding upon their successors unless expressly stated.[70] Moreover, no real distinction was made in the vast range of international transactions that were, to some degree, regulated by various kinds of legal procedure, between individual, corporate and state subjects of law or between 'private' matters of law, such as inheritance or marriage and 'public' matters, such as war.

The emergence of positive international law 1500–1800

The idea of *ius inter gentes* as opposed to *ius gentium*, or of a system of rules applying to the relations between equal sovereigns, whose consent to the rules is the primary source of their validity, was, as we have seen, foreshadowed in some medieval transactions. It did not, however, take a clear, systematic form until after 1500, a period that also – not coincidentally – witnessed an explosion in scholarly writing on the subject. It should be noted that the Publicists of this period did not 'create' international law; indeed their works had often been commissioned by powerful patrons with a view to providing legal support to some disputed claim, as with the contrasting views of Grotius and Selden on the freedom of the seas. Moreover their underlying theories of law ranged from essentially religious doctrines through natural law to modern legal positivism. However, the combination of state practice and learned commentary justifies the usual depiction of this period as laying down the foundations of contemporary international law.

Three factors in particular contributed to the new impetus to international law from the end of the fifteenth century. First, the discovery of the New World raised the key issues of how occupation and colonisation of these territories could be given legal justification and what legal rights were possessed by the existing inhabitants. Although we should not lose sight of the underlying motive of finding means to rationalise plunder, the fact that international law was the method selected had important consequences (not least in giving rise to continuing Third World objections to international law on the grounds that it is based on unjust foundations).[71] Crucially, law may be seen as helping to formulate and give a particular

---

[70] Randall Lesaffer, 'Peace Treaties from Lodi to Westphalia', in Lesaffer, (ed.), *Peace Treaties*, pp. 20–1.

[71] The *conquistadores* were required to be accompanied by a notary, whose duty was to read out to the Indians a Spanish Proclamation, setting out the legal basis for the Spanish claims. If the Indians refused to acknowledge papal and Imperial authority, war could legally be waged against them. Georg Schwarzenberger, *The Frontiers of International Law* (London: Stevens and Sons, 1962), p. 53.

shape to a further consequence of the discovery of the Americas: a new spatial awareness leading to a much stronger emphasis on territory and strictly defined boundaries. The Pope's famous division of the New World between Spain and Portugal had little legal force but it was a harbinger of a growing interest in matters cartographical and of the ways in which lines on maps might determine political identities.[72]

The new spatial order that began to emerge at this time helped to undermine international actors whose legal authority rested on something other than a clearly defined territorial base. These included the papacy, city leagues such as the Hanseatic League and the chivalric orders.[73] The Pope's authority, which in reality had already declined considerably during the Middle Ages, was further damaged by the two other key developments of this period: the rise of Protestantism and the increasing assertions of monarchical sovereignty against other contenders to power. Although the notion of a Christian republic headed by the Pope lingered on through the sixteenth and seventeenth centuries, particularly in relation to the continuing Ottoman threat, the political reality was one of increasingly acrimonious divisions within Christendom and of a struggle for power amongst monarchs now able to command the ever-growing resources of the emergent modern states. The positivist understanding of international law as the voluntary regulatory structure accepted by states that were sovereign equals did not, of course, emerge overnight. Here we consider briefly the evolving conception which was at the heart of positivism together with some of the treaties that gave formal shape to the new legal order.

Law is always both the product and the servant of a specific political association among human beings. One of the primary concerns, therefore, of the explosion of international legal scholarship in this period was to define the 'society' to which international law belonged, since this had profound implications for the subjects, sources, content, applicability, and efficacy of that law. Broadly speaking, three different conceptualisations of 'international society' may be discerned, although, as we shall see, some of the Publicists believed that two or more types of society could coexist. The first two, which may be characterised as the 'universal society' and the 'great community', each derive ultimately from the long shadow of Rome, in both its secular and religious forms. The third, the

---

[72] Carl Schmitt, *The Nomos of the Earth in the International Law of the Jus Publicum Europaeum*, trans. and annot. G. L. Ulmen, (New York: Telos Press, 2003 [orig. publ. 1950]).
[73] See also Spruyt, *Sovereign State*, p. 200 n. 34.

'society of states', has provided the doctrinal foundation of international law to this day.[74]

Several of the Publicists tried to maintain or revive in a new form the notion that the world was subject to a single legal authority: the essence of the 'universal society' conception. A few still asserted the ultimate authority of the Pope, arguing also that non-Christian 'savages' in the New World held no legal rights, either individually or collectively.[75] However, the first significant Publicist, Francisco de Vitoria, firmly rejected all the numerous legal claims being made on behalf of the *conquista* that derived from the Pope's or Emperor's supposed world authority. Although he retained a conception of the *respublica Christiana*, this, in his view, required a more compassionate approach to the Indians. A more secular version of the 'universal society' was offered more than two hundred years later by Christian Wolff. Although his writings were also influenced by the natural law principles commonly found among the 'great community' thinkers and also by the voluntarism and sovereign equality of the 'society of states' conception, his most original contribution is his assertion that the ultimate source of a state's legal obligation is its membership of a *civitas maxima* – a supreme state. This is essentially an imagined *civitas* that he attempted to derive logically from natural law but he tried to give it substance by arguing that states as a whole have the right of coercion and 'some sovereignty' over individual states, and also by invoking the balance of power as a mechanism 'to protect the common security'.[76]

Most of the Publicists employed a variant of the 'great community of mankind' concept: the idea that the human race as a whole should be seen as a single community governed by fundamental moral norms that all, including monarchs, were obliged to observe. Some, such as Francisco Suarez (1548–1617), started from a religious conception of natural law, as set out most systematically by Aquinas, in elaborating their particular formulation of the 'great community'.[77] In one famous passage, Suarez argues that 'the human race, into however many different peoples and kingdoms it may be divided, always preserves a certain unity, not only as a species, but also a moral and political unity (as it were) enjoined by the natural precept of mutual love and mercy; a precept which applies to

---

[74] These arguments are developed in more detail in David Armstrong, *Revolution and World Order: The Revolutionary State in International Society* (Oxford: Clarendon Press, 1993), pp. 12–41.

[75] Schmitt, *The Nomos*, p. 103.

[76] Christian Wolff, *Jus Gentium Methodo Scientifica Pentractum*, trans. J. H. Drake (Oxford: Clarendon Press, 1934), pp. 14–15, 330.

[77] A full, if sometimes rather eccentric, study of the relation of natural law (especially as expounded by Aquinas) to international society is E. B. F. Midgley, *The Natural Law Tradition and the Theory of International Relations* (London: Paul Elek, 1975).

all, even to strangers of every nation'.[78] However, although he believed natural law to have divine origins, he argued that its spread could be due to custom – 'the habitual conduct of nations' or 'simply as the result of usage and tradition . . . without any special and simultaneous compact or consent on the part of all peoples'.[79] Other natural law thinkers, such as Pufendorf, utilised the earlier, secular version of natural law as elaborated by the Greek Stoics and taken up by Cicero and other Romans.[80]

The most famous of the Publicists, Hugo Grotius, (1583–1645), although himself deeply religious, argued that natural law's precepts would be valid even if there were no God.[81] This, among other things, enabled him to advance an inclusive view of international society.[82] Indeed, the principle that promises should be kept should apply even to such as robbers and pirates.[83] The title that used to be accorded to Grotius of 'father of international law' is unwarranted, partly because he owed much to other writers, such as Gentili, but also because his conception of international society was still closer to the 'great community' idea than to modern international law's emphasis on the 'society of states'. However, he went beyond the understanding of many of his predecessors of international law as essentially natural law by offering what today would be termed a 'cosmopolitan' formulation of international society that incorporates not just states and their rulers but individuals and non-state groups.[84] Moreover, he widened the 'sources' of international law beyond 'nature and divine command' to include 'custom and tacit command'.[85] He even, in discussing the rules applicable to diplomatic immunity, came close to a consent-based conception of international law by arguing 'this law of nations is not like Natural Law, which flows in a sure way from certain reasons; but this takes its measure from the will of nations'.[86]

In the eighteenth century, Emerich de Vattel (1714–67) came closest to the first systematic presentation of modern international law. Although he claimed to be working from principles of natural law, his starting point

[78] Francisco Suarez, *Selections from Three Works* (Oxford: Oxford University Press, 1944), vol. II, p. 348.

[79] *Ibid.*, pp. 349, 351.

[80] P. E. Corbett, *Law and Society in the Relations of States* (New York: Harcourt, Brace and Co., 1951), pp. 11–12.

[81] Nussbaum, *Concise History*, p. 108.

[82] Hedley Bull, 'The importance of Grotius in the study of international relations', in Hedley Bull, Benedict Kingsbury, and Adam Roberts (eds.), *Hugo Grotius and International Relations* (Oxford: Clarendon Press, 1992), p. 80.

[83] Hugo Grotius, *De Juri Belli et Pacis*, ed. William Whewell, (Cambridge: Cambridge University Press, 1853), vol. III, p. 306.

[84] Bull, 'The importance of Grotius . . .', pp. 83–7.

[85] Grotius, *Prologomena* to *De Juri*, p. xxxvii.   [86] *Ibid.*, vol II, p. 206.

was the fact that, while individuals of necessity had to surrender some of their freedom to a superior authority, 'nothing of this kind can be conceived or supposed to subsist between nations. Each sovereign state claims, and actually possesses an absolute independence on all others.'[87] This independence, he emphasised, was not something to be deplored but was beneficial because it enabled each state to 'govern herself in the manner best suited to her own circumstances'.[88] States were, therefore, akin to individuals living in the complete freedom of a state of nature but whereas individuals could be ruled by emotion, states were able to act with 'more deliberation and circumspection' and to arrive at agreed arrangements to promote order within their own society.[89] In particular, the rules applicable to the society of states could be deduced 'from the natural liberty of nations, from the attention due to their common safety, from the nature of their mutual correspondence, their reciprocal duties, and the distinctions of their various rights, internal and external, perfect and imperfect'.[90] This meant, especially, that international law consisted of 'voluntary' maxims as well as the injunctions of natural law. In other words, while the simple requirements of living in society imposed a general obligation on states to seek to live in harmony with other states, more specific obligations needed the consent of states through treaties.[91] States were equal in this respect and in their entitlement to enjoy their freedom without interference from other states.[92] This principle of non-intervention in a state's internal affairs was repeatedly stressed by Vattel, who gave it a very broad interpretation, encompassing not just a state's freedom to choose its own government and religion but to be free from 'manoeuvres' by other states 'tending to create disturbance . . . to foment discord, to corrupt its citizens, to alienate its allies, to raise enemies against it, to tarnish its glory, and to deprive it of its natural advantages'.[93] A determination to avoid further religious wars was obviously a major motivating factor for Vattel, apparent also in his emphatic dismissal of the notion that alliances should not be made with non-Christians: 'Different people treat with each other in the quality of men, and not under the character of Christians and Mahommedans. Their common safety requires that they should be capable of treating with each other, and treating with security.'[94] His only exception here was where advocates of a religion wanted to promote it by violence. In this case, 'the common safety of mankind' invited states to 'enter into an

---

[87] Emerich de Vattel, *The Law of Nations or Principles of the Law of Nature Applied to the Conduct and Affairs of Nations and Sovereigns*, ed. J. Chitty, (London, 1834), p. xiii.
[88] *Ibid.*, p. xiv.   [89] *Ibid.*   [90] *Ibid.*, pp. xiv–xv.   [91] *Ibid.*, pp. lv–lx.
[92] *Ibid.*, pp. lx–lxi.   [93] *Ibid.*, p. 141. See also pp. 154–6.   [94] *Ibid.*, pp. 195–6.

alliance against such a people – to repress such outrageous fanatics, who disturb the public repose and threaten all nations'.[95]

In view of his emphasis on the freedom of states, Vattel rejected 'universal society' ideas, such as Wolff's *civitas maxima*. He argued instead that the only permissible institutional underpinnings to maintain order in a society of states were diplomacy and the balance of power. The former should be seen as an obligation on all states since, without it, states would not be able to 'cultivate the society that nature has established among them, to keep up a mutual correspondence, to treat of their affairs or to adjust their differences'.[96] Given this, ambassadors needed to 'be held sacred and inviolable', with violence against them regarded as an attack against 'the common safety and well being of nations'.[97]

What Vattel does here is to enshrine diplomacy more completely in international law: to make it an obligatory and protected practice. He achieved this end through his conception of international society as one united not by moral obligations but by one essential common interest shared by all states: preserving their sovereign status. Much the same is true of his discussion of the balance of power, which, in a notable passage, he made the central institution of his international society:

Europe forms a political system, an integral body, closely connected by the relations and different interests of the nations inhabiting this part of the world. It is not, as formerly, a confused heap of detached pieces, each of which thought herself very little concerned in the fate of the others, and seldom regarded things which did not immediately concern her. The continual attention of sovereigns to every occurrence, the constant residence of ministers, and the perpetual negotiations, make modern Europe a kind of republic, of which the members – each independent but all linked together by the ties of common interest – unite for the maintenance of order and liberty. Hence arose that famous scheme of the political balance, or the equilibrium of power; by which is understood such a disposition of things, as that no one potentate be able absolutely to predominate, and prescribe laws to the others.[98]

Vattel's enormously influential book did not 'create' international law but essentially set out systematically what was emerging as the prevailing understanding of post-medieval international relations. Different aspects of the new order may be discerned in numerous treaties during this period: a shift away from religious to more legalistic language, an increasing emphasis on sovereign equality and the principle of non-intervention, references to the importance of the balance of power as 'the best and most solid basis of mutual friendship and durable harmony',[99] agreements to

---

[95] *Ibid.*   [96] *Ibid.*, p. 470.   [97] *Ibid.*, p. 464.   [98] *Ibid.*, pp. 311–12.
[99] Treaty of Utrecht, 1713, cited in E. V. Gulick, *Europe's Classical Balance of Power* (Ithaca, NY: Cornell University Press, 1955), p. 35.

accept permanent embassies together with a continual development of the rules and procedures relating to diplomacy[100] and a growing concern to ensure, if necessary by underwriting them with great-power guarantees, the stability of existing territorial possessions.[101] The most famous of these treaties were the two that made up the Peace of Westphalia, which ended Europe's last great religious war in 1648. In fact, although these had crucial clauses ensuring the 'exact and reciprocal equality' of the members of the Empire,[102] explicitly referred to as their *'droit de souverainité'* by the French delegation,[103] Westphalia does not really deserve the reputation it has acquired in the International Relations community as the virtual 'constitution' of the new international system.[104] Much earlier treaties, such as Augsberg in 1555, had lain down the principle that it was the right of the rulers of a given territory to determine the official religion of that territory, while key principles such as the balance of power were not formally introduced until later treaties, notably Utrecht in 1713. Nonetheless, Westphalia may still be seen as marking the symbolic origin of the modern European international society in the sense that it crystallised and gave legal weight to developments that had been taking place in a random and unfocused way over many years. It was the first major congress of its kind, attended by almost all European states, and it assumed a collective right to confer various entitlements on individual rulers, as in the case of Alsace, to insist that states adhere to certain general practices of religious toleration and, most important of all, formally to admit new members to the society of states (the United Provinces and the Swiss Confederation).[105] Although the many months of wrangling over precedence that took place showed that the delegates had not entirely abandoned medieval notions of a hierarchical international order, the reality of Westphalia was that a decisive shift had been made towards the positivist principle that international law was what a society of sovereign states consented to.

---

[100] G. Butler and S. Maccoby, *The Development of International Law* (London: Longmans, Green and Co., 1928), pp. 76–102.

[101] Laurens Winkel, 'The peace treaties of Westphalia as an instance of the reception of Roman law', in Lesaffer (ed.), *Peace Treaties*, pp. 229–36.

[102] Treaty of Osnabruck, 24 October 1648, in Clive Parry (ed.), *Consolidated Treaty Series*, i, (New York: Oceana, Dobbs Ferry, 1969), pp. 198–270.

[103] Ronald G. Asch, 'The *ius foederis* re-examined: the Peace of Westphalia and the constitution of the Holy Roman Empire', in Lesaffer (ed.), *Peace Treaties*, p. 331.

[104] Armstrong, *Revolution*, pp. 32–3; see also Andreas Osiander, 'Sovereignty, international relations and the Westphalian myth', *International Organization* 55 (2001), 251–87 and Stephen Krasner, 'Westphalia and all that', in Judith Goldstein and Robert O. Keohane (eds.), *Ideas and Foreign Policy: Beliefs, Institutions and Political Change* (Ithaca, NY: Cornell University Press, 1993), pp. 235–64.

[105] Armstrong, *Revolution*, p. 35.

From the French Revolution to the League of Nations

The new emphasis on consent had important implications for the key issue of the sources of international legal obligation as well as for specific rules of law. Previously these had derived either from a real (Roman Empire) or putative (Catholic Church) hegemony or from 'custom', which meant, essentially, the cumulative effect of numerous states adopting similar norms in conducting their international affairs. Natural law and various religious doctrines were perceived by many analysts and some practitioners as providing an ultimate intellectual or ideological foundation for the resultant loose, vague, and frequently disputed array of rules, norms and practices that made up the 'law of nations' – itself an ambiguous and contested term. With the rise of the doctrine of sovereignty, states increasingly sought to base their legal obligations on clearer, more precise, more formal and, most of all, more consensual foundations. This had several consequences. First, there was much greater use of written agreements: by one estimate some 16,000 treaties were signed during the period 1814–1924.[106] Second, since treaties, formally, bound only their signatories, major international conferences became much more frequent as means of securing broad agreement on new rules of law. These may be seen as exercising quasi-legislative functions. The pattern was set by the major conferences and congresses held between 1814 and 1821 and less frequently thereafter, which together constituted what came to be known as the 'Concert of Europe'. Thirdly, in issue areas that did not impinge upon key national interests but which involved rapidly growing levels of interstate contact (and potential friction), states increasingly resorted to various means of institutionalising their legal obligations. During the nineteenth century, many 'public international unions' were established to regulate areas like postal communications, international rivers and railways, telegraphy and sanitation. These not only laid down rules for their specific functional area but also set up permanent secretariats and procedures for amending the rules and settling disputes. A further step towards a fully fledged international legal system was the use of arbitration to settle disputes between states, often in more politically sensitive areas than those covered by the public international unions. From 1794, when the Jay Treaty between Britain and the United States inaugurated the new era of arbitration, until 1900, there were at least 177 arbitrations.[107] Although these were not always successful, and indeed sometimes served to increase tensions between the two parties, they were deemed sufficiently valuable for the first Hague Conference of 1899 to establish a

---

[106] Nussbaum, *Concise History*, p. 196.   [107] Butler and Maccoby, *Development*, p. 303.

Permanent Court of Arbitration (in reality little more than a list of possible arbitrators).[108]

Four further developments that impinged upon international law in crucial ways may be noted. First, by the end of the Napoleonic Wars a distinct category of 'great powers' had emerged who, on the occasions when they were broadly in agreement, were able, in effect, to lay down the law to the smaller states. This privileged position was institutionalised in the League of Nations and United Nations in the form of permanent membership of the main decision-making bodies, the Council and Security Council, although the principle was somewhat diluted from its Concert of Europe origins by the inclusion of non-permanent members. Second, the society of states gradually became more universal. For much of the nineteenth century, world politics were dominated by the frequently selfish interests of the major European powers. Where once 'international law' in reality comprised coexisting European, Islamic, Indian, Chinese and other systems, now the only significant non-European power was the United States, which had unilaterally excluded Europe from the Americas in the 1823 Monroe Doctrine. This state of affairs began to change after the Crimean War, when the (now seriously weakened) Ottoman Empire was admitted to the Concert and when Japan began the rapid rise to great power status that culminated in the defeat of Russia in the war of 1904–5. One sign of these changing circumstances was the fact that the second Hague Conference of 1907 was attended by delegates from North and South America and Asia as well as Europe.

The third development is more complex and revolves around a partial shift away from a strict application of the principle of non-intervention in states' internal affairs. In a sense, this process had begun with the French Revolution.[109] The most basic principle of the Revolution was that sovereignty was vested in the nation not the ruler. This, in essence, advanced a novel principle of international legitimacy based upon national self-determination rather than dynastic rights, which meant that a people not happy with its lot within one sovereignty could join another. The principle was used to support the French annexations of Alsace, Avignon and Savoy, which were at the time under the auspices of the Empire, the Holy See and Sardinia respectively. The ideological basis for such policies included a belief that all peoples were part of one great society governed by natural law, which justified French interventions to 'overthrow all thrones, crush all kings and render universal the

---

[108] David Armstrong, Lorna Lloyd and John Redmond, *From Versailles to Maastricht: International Organisation in the Twentieth Century* (Houndmills: Macmillan, 1996), p. 11.
[109] The following section draws upon Armstrong, *Revolution*, pp. 84–111, 204–19.

triumphs of liberty and reason'.[110] The Peace of Westphalia was frequently denounced by name: it had guaranteed liberty for princes alone,
the Revolution would now guarantee liberty for peoples.[111]

Ironically, one impact of the Revolution was to provoke a counter-
revolutionary interventionism in the few decades following the defeat of
Napoleon. This was sometimes justified by appeals to 'the public law
of Europe' and standards of 'legitimacy', which, in this interpretation,
upheld the rights of existing monarchs. The British, however, maintained
that the Concert should uphold 'all correct notions of internal sovereign
authority'[112] and therefore that non-intervention remained the true international legal norm. In the longer term, however, the impulse given by
the French and American revolutions to national self-determination and
democracy was to have a more enduring impact on the underlying principles of international law.

The fourth development was in the area of war. Many thinkers, working
from Christian, Hindu, Islamic, natural law and other perspectives, had
sought to lay down general principles designed to limit the incidence,
conduct and consequences of war. Their common starting point was,
as Grotius put it, 'War is not one of the acts of life. On the contrary,
it is a thing so horrible that nothing but the highest necessity or the
deepest charity can make it right.'[113] However, the large gap between
such often very elaborate writings on 'just war' and related topics and the
actual conduct of states during war suggests that war remained effectively
outside the remit of international law. This situation began to change on
the margins in the fifty years leading up to World War I. While there were
still few legal constraints on a state's right to go to war, the establishment
of the Red Cross movement and the subsequent Geneva Conventions on
the laws of war brought humanitarian principles to bear upon such issues
as the treatment of the wounded and of prisoners of war.[114]

Legal constraints on a state's freedom to go to war did not appear
until the League of Nations was established in 1919. Neither the League

---

[110] Instruction of Committee of Public Safety to Ministry of Foreign Affairs, cited in F.
Masson, *Le Département des affaires étrangères pendant la revolution*, 1787–1804 (Paris,
1877), p. 288.

[111] S. S. Biro, *The German Policy of Revolutionary France* (Cambridge, MA: Harvard University Press, 1957), vol. I, p. 63.

[112] Castlereagh, speaking on the proposed interventionist Protocol of the Congress of Trop-
pau, quoted in L. S. Woolf, *International Government*, London: Allen and Unwin, 1916,
p. 24.

[113] Grotius, *Prologomena to De Juri*, vol. II, p. 442.

[114] The best general account of these developments is Geoffrey Best, *Humanity in Warfare:
The Modern History of the International Law of Armed Conflicts* (London: Methuen,
1983).

Covenant nor the more stringent conditions of the UN Charter had much effect in that crucial area, which is considered in a later chapter. However, the League did constitute a highly significant step in the progressive legalisation of international affairs that had been taking place in a gradual and piecemeal fashion since 1815.[115] At the most general level, the League Covenant was part of international law and its central theme was that states should be guided by rules of conduct. So, whenever the League attempted to carry out its peace treaty obligations to minorities by organising plebiscites or investigating disputes; when it tried to decide rules and guidelines to govern international economic relations or such matters as the post-war refugee problem; when it drew up international conventions on environmental or ecological questions, such as the regulation of whaling or controlling the pollution of the seas by oil; when it devised more comprehensive international regimes in areas like communications and transit, preventing the spread of epidemic disease or controlling the drug trade: in all such work it was undertaking tasks which, at the very least, had important implications for international law.

The League's most direct involvement with international law was the creation of the Permanent Court of International Justice (PCIJ). This consisted of eleven (later fifteen) judges selected so as to 'represent the main forms of civilisation and the principal legal systems of the world'.[116] The Court had the capacity to make judgments on disputes brought before it and to give 'advisory opinions' when requested by the League. These opinions were not formally binding upon states but (as with the PCIJ's successor, the International Court of Justice (ICJ)) they acquired considerable legal significance. The Court heard sixty-six cases between 1922–1939, of which twenty-eight were requests for advisory opinions. States had the option (as with the ICJ) of declaring in advance their acceptance of the Court's jurisdiction of certain classes of dispute, an option taken up with various reservations by forty governments, with jurisdiction otherwise being voluntary.

Other aspects of the League's work had important implications for international law. The 120 international conventions concluded by it continued and extended the practice of submitting important international issues to major international conferences.[117] There was an ambitious attempt to begin the codification of international law in such areas

---

[115] The following discussion is drawn from David Armstrong, *The Rise of the International Organisation* (Houndmills: Macmillan, 1982), Chapter 2.

[116] Article 9 of the Statute of the Court.

[117] R. P. Dhokalia, *The Codification of Public International Law* (Manchester: Manchester University Press, 1970), p. 115.

as nationality, territorial waters and the rights of aliens.[118] Although this attempt was eventually abandoned, it is not without significance as the first effort to derive precise, universally applicable rules from customary international law as well as numerous bilateral treaties.[119] The League's involvement in the international administration of the Saar Territory and the city of Danzig, as well as its insistence on having a (mostly formal) role in overseeing the system under which former enemy colonies were mandated among the victors of the war, may all be seen as embodiments of the key principle that the international community as a whole had the right to concern itself with areas that might otherwise have been left to the great powers to divide among themselves. Finally, although obviously a failure in its central function of providing collective security, the League had a more lasting significance in the growing range of economic and social functions it undertook. By 1939 more than 60 per cent of its budget went to support such work[120] with numerous institutions such as the Health Organisation, the International Labour Organisation, and committees on the drugs trade, refugees, the traffic in women and children and intellectual co-operation all sufficiently well established to continue in similar forms in the United Nations.

The contemporary era

We consider several specific aspects of contemporary international law in later chapters. Here we briefly discuss the six facets of the post-war international order that are of most general significance. The first is that the United Nations (UN) gave institutional form to a legal order that was, for the first time, genuinely universal. This was particularly the case after many European colonies won their independence during the two decades following the war. This meant, inevitably, that the concerns of what was now a majority in the UN with issues such as decolonisation, racism and development came increasingly to dominate UN debates. In all three areas the Third World sought, with some success, to lay down general legal norms.

Second, the post-war period witnessed continuing expansion and development of the areas of international life that were subject to

[118] S. Rosenne (ed.), *The League of Nations Committee for the Progressive Codification of International Law (1925–1928)* (Dobbs Ferry, NY: Oceana Publications, 1972), vol. I, Introduction, pp. xxx–xxxi.

[119] Sir Hersch Lauterpacht, *The Development of International Law by the International Court* (London: Stevens and Stevens, 1958), p. 7.

[120] *The Bruce Report on the Technical Work of the League* (Special Supplement to the Monthly Summary of the League of Nations, September 1939), p. 7.

international law. As well as the subjects we examine in detail in this volume, this expansion embraced communications and transit, outer space, civil aviation, intellectual property, the Antarctic and terrorism. Particular emphasis may be given to the new law of the sea regime that was elaborated at three UN conferences, especially the last of these which took from 1973–1982 to develop a comprehensive body of law on matters ranging from an agreed territorial sea, through the new concept of an 'exclusive economic zone' to a completely novel regime for deep sea-bed mining. Maritime issues have been subject to some measure of international legal regulation for more than 2,000 years but this was the first time the entire international community had been able to agree such an all-embracing regime.

Third, as well as an expansion in the content of international law, the period also saw a far deeper process of legalisation of world politics than anything that had previously occurred. This process had several aspects. At one level, the UN was given an explicit responsibility in the Charter for the codification and progressive development of international law. As we saw, the League's efforts in this regard came nowhere, so it was significant that the UN's founders showed a desire to return to a task that, at the least, demonstrated a symbolic commitment to the need to place increasing areas of international relations on an agreed and more precise legal foundation. More fundamentally, legal and quasi-legal institutions, procedures and language came to play an increasing role in world politics. This was most marked in the case of Europe, with the European Union's (EU) Court able to take binding decisions and the Council of Europe's human rights court, with a much larger membership than the EU, acquiring an ever-increasing case-load and authority. But other regional organisations have also created (sometimes limited) legal and quasi-legal institutions, while the Word Trade Organization (WTO) has established more formal and compulsory dispute settlement procedures than its predecessor, the General Agreement on Tariffs and Trade (GATT). The ICJ's jurisdiction remains limited by its lack of sanctions and also the need for states to consent to submit cases to it. However, international tribunals to put war criminals on trial, first in respect of the defeated powers in 1945, then following the conflicts in Rwanda and former Yugoslavia, were able to indict and punish a number of key individuals. The more far-reaching possibilities of the new International Criminal Court (ICC) are constrained by strong American opposition to it. The fullest recent discussion of legalisation uses three criteria to evaluate degrees of legalisation in different areas: the levels of obligation, precision and delegation to third parties. They identify a range of economic and political factors influencing legalisation, including domestic pressures in favour of it in the powerful capitalist economies, but also, pointing to areas like international monetary relations where legalisation has diminished since 1970 and others where more flexible, less institutionalised arrangements have suited states better, argue that it is neither an inevitable nor, necessarily, an automatically desirable process.[121]

Fourth, several writers distinguish between 'hard' and 'soft' law to make the point that rules and norms that create some sense of obligation among states may emerge in more ways than through treaties and custom: the traditional sources of 'true' international law. For example, General Assembly resolutions adopted by all or even most UN members are sometimes seen as having a limited 'quasi-legislative' competence.[122] In a strict legal sense, General Assembly resolutions are not binding upon states but in practice they may acquire legal significance if they come to be seen as evidence of what states regard as customary international law or as providing an authoritative interpretation of a particular rule.[123] They may also be seen as part of the constant interplay between politics and law that has served to construct the normative underpinnings of international relations since ancient times through a process in which legal language and reasoning techniques are drawn upon by international actors to communicate their arguments in mutually comprehensible forms. Indeed, in recent years, such 'discourse' has itself, in effect, been given a certain legal standing as states in international law-making conferences have moved from 'consent' to 'consensus' as the basis of their legal obligations. The classic case here was the third law of the sea conference, which adopted the *modus operandi* of seeking to arrive through a bargaining process at a consensus in which no state had any remaining formal objections to a specific part of the treaty.[124] The definition of consensus as 'the absence of any formal objection' was actually written into Article 161 of the 1982 Convention as the basis on which certain future decisions would be taken.

Fifth, the nature of the international society that international law serves has been affected to some extent by the various phenomena collectively subsumed under the term 'globalisation'. The structures and processes of international society have become globalised and transnational as well as interstate, and states are no longer the only international

---

[121] 'Legalization in world politics', special issue of *International Organization* 55 (2000).
[122] Richard Falk, 'On the quasi-legislative competence of the General Assembly', in his *The Status of Law in International Society* (Princeton, NJ: Princeton University Press, 1970), pp. 174–84.
[123] Ingrid Detter, *The International Legal Order* (Aldershot: Dartmouth Publishers, 1994), pp. 212–51, provides a very thorough discussion of this and other aspects of 'soft law'.
[124] Barry Buzan, 'Negotiating by consensus: developments in technique at the United Nations Conference on the Law of the Sea', *American Journal of International Law* 75 (1981), 324–48.

actors of significance. The international community had already begun to recognise this last development as long ago as 1945, when the UN Charter formally gave non-governmental organizations consultative rights in the Economic and Social Council. Since then non-state entities ranging from giant transnational corporations to single issue advocacy groups have had an increasing input into new legal norms including those relating to trade law, human rights and environmental regulation. Some would go so far as to argue that globalisation has produced a new 'global civil society', able to engage in instant and cheap communication via the Internet, with the land-mines convention sometimes cited as a paradigm of how this new phenomenon was able to lead to changes in international law.[125]

Sixth, while international society remained firmly based on the principle of state sovereignty, it also displayed a far greater concern with states' internal affairs than ever before. This was, initially, a consequence of the general horror that greeted the revelations about Nazi atrocities: a major driving force behind the seven references to human rights in the UN Charter, the Universal Declaration of Human Rights in 1948, the two International Covenants on Civil and Political and Economic and Social Rights, the numerous other UN declarations on the rights of specific groups and the various regional agreements on human rights, especially the Council of Europe's influential Human Rights Court. However, none of these instruments was provided with really effective sanctions to enforce its provisions. Even the European Court, whose decisions are taken seriously by states, relies essentially on its members' regard for human rights. Its only real sanction is the threat to expel a member, as might have happened to Greece when it was under military government, had it not forestalled this by voluntarily withdrawing. Human rights institutions with real teeth, including the capacity to punish individual violators, did not appear until the war crimes tribunals of the 1990s and the International Criminal Court, which commenced activities in 2003. The post-Cold War humanitarian interventions as well as the increasing tendency of the World Bank and International Monetary Fund (IMF) to insist on progress towards 'good governance' as a condition of their loans may also be seen as evidence of a shift away from an undiluted emphasis on sovereignty.

Some would argue that developments like globalisation, the growing significance of global civil society, legalisation and interventionism, taken together, amount to the first signs of the emergence of a fundamentally different legal order, founded on cosmopolitan principles, whose

---

[125] See David Armstrong, Lorna Lloyd and John Redmond, *International Organisation in World Politics* (Houndmills: Palgrave, 2004), pp. 251–65, for a fuller discussion of this.

origin is to be found in the ideas of a 'great community of mankind' and natural law. Cosmopolitanism sees moral obligations and rights as possessed equally by all rather than as dependent upon the specific political community to which an individual belongs. The leading cosmopolitanist thinker, David Held, discerns signs of cosmopolitan ideas in many post-war treaties and customary rules of international law, especially those relating to human rights and the environment, and goes so far as to claim that 'cosmopolitan ideas are, in short, at the centre of significant post-World War II legal and political developments'.[126]

As Held himself recognises, the use of cosmopolitanist language in some legal documents (e.g., the 'common heritage of mankind' in the law of the sea convention and the assertion that all have 'equal and inalienable rights' in the Universal Declaration of Human Rights) does not signify a decisive shift either in the actual practice of states or in the continuing emphasis on sovereignty in international law. Indeed there are other reasons for resisting claims that a fundamental change in the nature of international society is under way. Most of the 'cosmopolitan' ideas that are supposedly at the heart of this emerging new agenda of world politics – especially those revolving around the notion of individual freedom – are, in fact, Western rather than universal concepts. As such they have been resisted by other countries on numerous grounds: that they constitute a disguised form of Western imperialism, or that they are incompatible with 'Asian values' or Islam, or that they conflict with the requirements of development. In addition, global or regional power structures have always been a major determinant of the content and efficacy of international law in the past, and there are no signs of this ceasing to be the case. Since the end of the Cold War, the American attitude to international law has been governed in large part by a careful calculation of its own interests, although it should be noted that this has, at times, led it as often to support initiatives (the WTO, war crimes tribunals) as to resist them (the International Criminal Court, the Land-mines Convention). Similarly, the Western emphasis in recent years on promoting 'good governance' is, if successful, more likely to lead to a legal order founded even more strongly on effective, independent states than to a breakdown of that order. Hence, while there have been many important developments in international law since 1945, these should not be seen as having produced, or being about to produce, a substantially different international legal system.

---

[126] David Held, 'Cosmopolitanism: ideas, realities and deficits', in David Held and Anthony McGrew (eds.), *Governing Globalization: Power, Authority and Global Governance* (Cambridge: Polity, 2002), p. 316.

Discussion questions

- Why is there so much disagreement about the origins of international law?
- Does international law reflect primarily European values? Does it matter if it does? Is a system of international law based on universal norms possible?
- To what extent was there a true international legal order in ancient times? What were the main contributions of Greece and Rome to the development of international law?
- Why was natural law so influential in pre-modern conceptions of international law?
- To what extent did Christendom and the Islamic world constitute distinct systems of international law in the medieval period?
- Why was there such an explosion of legal scholarship in the sixteenth and seventeenth centuries? What lasting ideas may be found in these writings?
- What was the significance of the Peace of Westphalia for the later development of international law?
- Did the League of Nations mark a significant turning point in the evolution of international law?
- Why have international organisations played a greater role in international law since 1945?

SUGGESTIONS FOR FURTHER READING

Alexandrowicz, C. H., *An Introduction to the History of the Law of Nations in the East Indies*, London: Oxford University Press, 1967. Alexandrowicz was, for years, almost the only Western writer attempting to shift international law away from its Eurocentric assumptions by showing how European states derived international legal principles from the Asian states during the period up to the nineteenth century (i.e. when they dealt with such states on a basis of relative equality).

Anand, R. P., *Origin and Development of the Law of the Sea*, The Hague: Martinus Nijhoff, 1982. A useful account utilising Asian as well as Western sources of this key aspect of international law.

Development of Modern International Law and India, Baden-Baden: Nomos, 2005. A thoroughly researched and interesting contribution by a leading Indian authority to the revisionist refutation of Eurocentric accounts of the origins of international law.

Anghie, Anthony, *Imperialism, Sovereignty and the Making of International Law*, Cambridge: Cambridge University Press, 2004. Part of an influential body of recent academic literature with a critical, revisionist perspective on the ways in which the legal history of encounters between the West and the non-Western world was one in which law was used to legitimise relations of domination and subordination.

Bederman, David J., *International Law in Antiquity*, Cambridge: Cambridge University Press, 2001. An elegant and thought-provoking account by the leading authority on ancient international law.

Best, Geoffrey, *Humanity in Warfare: The Modern History of the International Law of Armed Conflicts*, London: Methuen, 1983. A highly readable account by the leading British authority on this subject.

Cohen, Raymond, and Raymond Westbrook (eds.), *Amarna Diplomacy: The Beginnings of International Relations*, Baltimore and London: Johns Hopkins University Press, 2000. A fascinating set of essays on what may have been the earliest international system: in ancient Near East, with one chapter specifically on international law.

Harris, E. M., and L. Rubinstein (eds.), *The Law and the Courts in Ancient Greece*, London: Duckworth, 2004. Mostly on internal law but has an interesting chapter by Angelos Chaniotis entitled 'Justifying territorial claims in classical and Hellenistic Greece: the beginnings of international law'.

Grewe, Wilhelm G., *The Epochs of International Law*, trans. and rev. Michael Byers, New York: Walter de Gruyter, 2000. Grewe was both an international lawyer and a diplomat and this is an updated version of a book he wrote during World War II. Dogmatically realist in its conceptualisation of historical 'epochs' each dominated by a single power (Spain, France, Britain and America) and highly controversial because of its tendency towards apologism of Germany during the Hitler period, it contains some interesting material on earlier periods.

Janis, Mark W. (ed), *The Influence of Religion on the Development of International Law*, Dordrecht: Martinus Nijhoff, 1991. Essays on the impact of several religions on international law. This helps to fill a gap in a key aspect of the history of international legal norms, particularly with its chapters on various non-Western religions.

Journal of the History of International Law. The foundation of this journal in 1999 was evidence of the growing interest in the history of international law, as was the ever-increasing body of writings in France and Germany on the subject. The articles are of uneven quality but most display substantial scholarship.

Koskenniemi, Martti, *The Gentle Civiliser of Nations: The Rise and Fall of International Law 1870–1960*, Cambridge: Cambridge University Press, 2001. A magisterial and thought-provoking set of essays by a leading international lawyer on the rise and fall of liberal internationalist attitudes. The story is told in part through the history of key institutions, in part through consideration of the lives of leading legal authorities, such as Hersch Lauterpacht, Hans Kelsen, Earl Schmitt and Hans Morgenthau.

Lesaffer Randall, (ed.), *Peace Treaties and International Law in European History: From the Late Middle Ages to World War One*, Cambridge: Cambridge University Press, 2004. An excellent collection of scholarly articles with many insights into the gradual changes in the normative underpinnings and assumptions of peace treaties.

Neff, Stephen C., *War and the Law of Nations: A General History*, Cambridge: Cambridge University Press, 2005. A fascinating and wide-ranging account using perspectives from several cultures on this crucial aspect of the history of international law.

Nussbaum, Arthur, *A Concise History of the Law of Nations* (rev. edition), New York: Macmillan, 1962. The best general history of international law in English, if now somewhat dated and Eurocentric.

Roelofsen, C. G., *Studies in the History of International Law*, Utrecht: Institute of Public International Law, 1991. Written mainly from a Dutch perspective and with a primary focus on the law of the sea, but insightful and interesting.

Verzijl, J. H. W., *International Law in Historical Perspective*, Leyden: A. W. Sijthoff (12 vols., commencing in 1968 and continued after Verzijl's death in 1987). Sometimes dense and idiosyncratic but nonetheless the most ambitious and detailed account of its subject.

3 Three lenses: realism, liberalism, and constructivism

There is a certain irony in the mutual antipathy displayed by the disciplines of International Relations (IR) and International Law (IL). For as it happens, both disciplines are (and have been) united by common theoretical divisions. That is to say, the dominant paradigms in both disciplines are similar in their core ontological assumptions about the world; the main challengers in each discipline also share remarkably similar worldviews. The dominance of realism in IR is matched by the dominance of positivism in IL. Both realism and positivism offer structural approaches to their subject that prioritise the role of states and instrumental action and downplay the significance of domestic politics, norms and ethics. Just as liberal institutionalism developed to challenge the dominance of realism in IR from the 1950s onwards, so legal positivism was challenged by an emerging liberal approach to IL from the 1940s onwards. These liberal challengers offer agent-centric approaches that highlight a plurality of actors in addition to states, as well as the role of domestic processes, normative action and ethical considerations in world politics.

As we noted in the introduction, there is growing appreciation among some IR and IL scholars that there is much to learn from each other's discipline. But this appreciation is confined to liberal scholars in IR and IL; realists still have little time for law, and legal positivists still consider politics and policy to be none of their concern.[1] To be sure, liberalism in IR should be naturally inclined to take law seriously, given its focus on norms, regimes and institutions. Equally, the liberal approach to IL explicitly seeks to situate the law in broader sociopolitical contexts. At the same time, given realism's and legal positivism's shared world-views, an engagement between these two disciplinary giants is long overdue.

More recently, realism and positivism have faced challenges from less-conventional quarters – namely, critical theory in IR and New Stream

---

[1] This is noted in Onuma Yasuaki, 'International law in and with international politics: the functions of international law in international society,' *European Journal of International Law* 14 (2003), 109–10.

scholarship in IL, both of which emerged in the 1980s. Both share a common epistemological critique respectively of realism and positivism, one that questions the objective status accorded to knowledge systems like law and thereby seeks to uncover the power relations that underpin and are reinforced by the current international legal order. Our main concern, however, is with constructivism in IR. Constructivism has enjoyed a spectacular rise since the early 1990s and arguably is not far behind liberal institutionalism in its appeal within the discipline. Mainstream constructivists accept the realism epistemology – we can 'know' things about the world – but they use it to launch a fundamental assault on realist onotology. For constructivists, the *material* world of states and rational action (the world of realists) only makes sense when located in a *social* world that gives meaning to states as actors and defines what is rational in given circumstances. Constructivists are beginning to turn their attention to international law. And given that it accepts that objective knowledge of international law is possible, we consider constructivism to provide a more promising line of engagement with positivism than critical theory.

In this chapter, we draw on the literatures above in order to propose three interdisciplinary lenses for the study of international law – a realist, a liberal and a constructivist lens. In generating each lens, we first distil the core principles of the respective theoretical approaches in IR and IL and from these identify the points of agreement that form that interdisciplinary world-view.[2] Our aim is for each lens to be logically coherent, in terms of these shared core principles, and to offer a world-view that is distinct from the other two lenses.[3] This methodology, centred on identifying core principles in rival theoretical approaches, is commonly employed in IR to wage theory wars.[4] However, we do not seek to demonstrate

---

[2] In so doing, we are not claiming that there is an exclusive readership between these respective approaches to IR and IL. For instance, we recognise that legal positivism, with its emphases on states and rules, informs neoliberalism in IR. Rather, our claim is that these respective approaches to IR and IL do share common principles which form the basis of an interdisciplinary lens that is distinct from other interdisciplinary perspectives on the subject, On legal positivism and neoliberalism, see 'Legalization and world politics', Special issue of *International Organization* 54 (2000).

[3] The coherence and distinctiveness criteria for rival paradigms in IR are emphasised in Jeffrey W. Legro and Andrew Moravcsik, 'Is anybody still a realist?' *International Security* 24 (1999), 9–10.

[4] This method of testing (or, properly speaking, 'falsifying') rival schools of theory in the social sciences was developed by Imre Lakatos. See Lakatos, 'Falsification and the methodology of social science research programs', in Lakatos and Alan Musgrave (eds.), *Criticism and the Growth of Knowledge* (Cambridge: Cambridge University Press, 1970), pp. 91–195. For examples of its application in IR, see John A. Vasquez, 'The realist paradigm and degenerative versus progressive research programs: an appraisal of neo-traditional research on waltz's balancing proposition', *American Political Science Review* 91 (1997), 899–912; Theo Farrell, 'Constructivist security studies: portrait of a research

the superiority of any particular lens. Rather, we highlight theoretical differences in order to equip students to make sense of the many ways that international law exists, works and evolves.

The first three sections of this chapter take each lens in turn. We start by surveying realism in IR and legal positivism. We show how they share four core principles which form the basis for our realist lens. Next we survey liberal IR theory and legal process theory and again extract four core principles which underpin our liberal lens. Finally, we present constructivist theory in IR. IL scholars are beginning to draw on IR constructivist theory, but this IL literature is embryonic. Accordingly, we apply constructivism to international law in order to generate four principles that inform our constructivist lens. In the fourth section of this chapter we discuss how these three lenses apply to our three volume themes of content, compliance and change in international law.

Realism

Realism and positivism are commonly considered to be natural opposites – with realists dismissing the importance of law in world politics and positivists declaring law to transcend the everyday world of politics. But actually, as Gerry Simpson puts it, they are 'quite compatible'. Looking at how each paradigm developed, Simpson points out: 'Each was state-fixed, each found temporary solace in the facts of international life such as state practice or national interest, and each took a conservative approach to change.'[5]

Realism in IR

The realist world-view of states and power politics has been well rehearsed elsewhere.[6] The story of the roots and rise of realism will be familiar to any student of IR. Nonetheless, some pointers are in order for the non-IR reader. Realism pre-dates the modern state system in the writings of

program', *International Studies Review* 4 (2002), 49–72; Edward A. Kolodziej, *Security and International Relations* (Cambridge: Cambridge University Press, 2005).

[5] Gerry Simpson, 'The situation on the international legal front: the power of rules and the rule of power,' *European Journal of International Law* 11 (2000), 452.

[6] For intellectual histories and paradigm surveys of realism, see Michael J. Smith, *Realist Thought from Weber to Kissinger* (Baton Rouge: Louisanna State University Press, 1986); Brian Schmidt, *The Political Discourse of Anarchy: A Disciplinary History of International Relations* (New York: State University of New York Press, 1998); John Vasquez, *The Power of Power Politics: From Classical Realism to Neotraditionalism* (Cambridge: Cambridge University Press, 1998); Jack Donnelly, *Realism in International Relations* (Cambridge: Cambridge University Press, 2000).

Thomas Hobbs and Niccolo Machiavelli in the fifteenth and sixteenth centuries, and further back. Indeed, the founding text of modern realism is commonly recognised to be Thucydides' contemporary account of the Peloponnesian War in ancient Greece. Put another way by David Welch, 'Realists univocally embrace Thucydides as their founder and inspiration.'[7] Hobbes, Machiavelli and Thucydides all stressed the ever-present risk of war and the raw exercise of power in statecraft. Thus, Hobbes is famous for portraying life as 'brutish and short' (a fair portrayal of life in Civil War England), and Machiavelli is renowned for recommending that princes use all means at their disposal (however underhand) to advance the interests of state.

Arguably more significant, however, because their work coincided with the founding of IR as a discipline, have been E. H. Carr and Hans J. Morgenthau. Carr was a former Foreign Office official who was to occupy the first Chair in IR in the world (at the University of Aberystwyth), named after the great liberal US President, Woodrow Wilson. This was ironic both because Carr was a staunch critic of Wilsonian liberalism and because he was openly hostile to the development of IR as a discipline. In *The Twenty Years' Crisis*, his famous critical history of the interwar period that was first published in 1939, Carr attacked the 'utopian' musings of liberals that had led to a dangerously flawed post-war settlement in 1919. For Carr, misplaced liberalism was to blame for the collapse of the world economy in 1929 and the rise of fascism in Europe shortly thereafter. Carr contrasted this philosophical 'utopianism' or 'idealism', with a more empirical 'realism' that saw the world as it truly was: a place where there was little harmony of interests and much powerplay between states. *The Twenty Years' Crisis* was to have an enormous impact, both (much to Carr's disapproval) in launching IR as a discipline and (more to Carr's pleasure) in giving the discipline a realist mould.[8]

Even more influential on the early development of IR was Morgenthau's realist tract, published in 1948, *Politics Among Nations: The Struggle for Power and Peace*. Morgenthau was a German émigré to the United States and former scholar of international law. But he lost his faith in the law when it failed to stop the Nazis seizing power in Germany

---

[7] David A. Welch, 'Why IR theorists should stop reading Thucydidies', *Review of International Studies* 29 (2003), 304. As the title suggests, Welch thinks that realists have been misguided.

[8] For a brief history on Carr's work, see Michael Cox's excellent introductory essay to E. H. Carr, *The Twenty Years' Crisis: An Introduction to the Study of International Relations* (Basingstoke: Palgrave, 2001[1939]). For more thorough studies on Carr, see Charles Jones, *E. H. Carr and International Relations: A Duty to Lie* (Cambridge: Cambridge University Press, 1998); and Jonathan Haslam, *The Vices of Integrity: E. H. Carr, 1892–1982* (London: Verso, 1999).

and plunging the world into war. Morgenthau's realist creed was aptly summed up in the subtitle of his new book: international politics was about the struggle for power, and only through balancing power would peace prevail. *Politics Among Nations* was written as a textbook and therein lay its appeal. With concepts such as national power and the balance of power carefully dissected for the reader, it was a far less challenging read than *Twenty Years' Crisis*. In it, Morgenthau breaks realism down into six easy principles, at the heart of which is the 'concept of interest defined in terms of power'. Moreover, unlike Carr, Morgenthau was supportive of the development of IR as a science of politics. Indeed, his first principle of realism is that politics 'is governed by objective laws' that may be captured in 'a rational theory.'[9]

The third major work in the realist school is Kenneth Waltz's *Theory of International Politics*. Realism faced challenges from liberal and institutionalist theory in the 1950s–1970s. The nuclear stalemate followed by détente between the superpowers, America's failure in the Vietnam War and the rise of international economic issues with the currency and oil crises all called into question the primacy of military power in world affairs. Published in 1979, *Theory of International Politics* coincided with the renewal of Cold War tension, the massive building-up of US military forces, and so a return to realism in world affairs. Developing realism as a social scientific paradigm was central to Waltz's purpose. To this end, he drew on microeconomic theory in his account of international politics: states were likened to firms exposed to a competitive marketplace. Where Morgenthau recommended rational action to policy-makers, Waltz took states to be rational actors. For Waltz, it was unnecesssary to inquire into the domestic conditions of rational state action; states are conditioned by international 'market forces' – i.e., military competition and the threat of war – to be rational; those that are not get wiped out. Therefore Waltz focused in his neorealist theory on the structure of the international system which was determined by the number of great powers. Taking his lead from the lack of open war between the superpowers, Waltz argued that bipolar orders are more stable than multipolar ones.[10] This systemic emphasis is the key characteristic of neorealist theory. It also makes for a parsimonious theory, which neorealists identify as a major strength of their theoretical explanation of world politics.

While realist thought contains much variety from Thucydides to Waltz, certain core principles can be identified. First, that states are the only

---

[9] Hans J. Morgenthau, *Politics Among Nations: The Struggle for Power and Peace* (New York: McGraw-Hill, 1993 [1948]), pp. 4–5.
[10] Kenneth Waltz, *Theory of International Politics* (Reading, MA: Addison-Wesley, 1979).

significant actors in world politics. Second, that the international system – which is anarchic – is fiercely competitive.[11] Third, that the material factors, such as military resources and the balance of power, matter far more than non-material factors, such as, norms, institutions and international law. Fourth, given the points above, states are rational actors and rational action ultimately depends on self-help. Following on from Waltz, a fifth principle may be added, which is that realism has a systemic focus. Since the mid-1990s, some realist scholars have tried to recover the richness of classical realism. But the default for these neoclassical realists is still systemic: only when structural factors are unable to explain state behaviour do they look inside the state to see what's going on.[12]

Legal positivism

In the last chapter we noted how international law was dominated by natural law thinking up to early modern times. We also discussed how embryonic positive law emerged from 1500–1800 within the natural law tradition. Thus the Publicists of the period, Vittoria, Wolff, Suarez, Grotius, and Vattel, all derived their legal theories from natural law principles, either religious or secular in origin. Moreover, while Grotius and Vattel introduced the elements that were to dominate modern international law – state choice, custom and convention – legal theory far outpaced state practice at this time. As Stephen Hall notes: 'Whereas positive international law was relatively sparse, European thought had spent almost two millennia building up a mature body of jurisprudence corresponding to natural law.'[13] In this context, the dominance of positivism and rejection of naturalism in modern international law is really quite remarkable.

Natural law fell out of favour in the nineteenth century for a number of reasons. For starters, natural law was discredited when it took an ideological turn and was used to justify the annexation of territory by revolutionary France. As we noted in Chapter 2, the novel idea of 'national self-determination', which suggested French conquest by popular invitation, was based on the belief that all peoples were part of a

---

[11] This point is emphasised in the work of 'offensive realists', who seek aggression by powerful states compounding the dangers of interstate competition. See Randall L. Schweller, *Deadly Imbalances: Tripolarity and Hitler's Strategy of World Conquest* (New York: Columbia University Press, 1998); John Mearsheimer, *The Tragedy of Great Power Politics* (New York: Norton, 2001).

[12] Stephen G. Brooks, 'Dueling realisms', *International Organization* 51 (1997), 445–77. Core propositions of realism are also discussed in Jeffrey W. Legro and Andrew Moravscik, 'Is anybody still a realist?' *International Security* 24 (1999), 5–55.

[13] Stephen Hall, 'The persistent spectre: natural law, international order and the limits of legal positivism,' *European Journal of International Law* 12 (2001), 270.

single great society governed by natural law. Positivism countered this dangerous ideology by asserting the sovereign will of states, as opposed to that of humanity. In addition, the early nineteenth century also saw the development of a new way of thinking about the natural and social world. Philosophy gave way to science, and with it abstract reasoning yielded to evidence-based analysis. Accordingly, as Hall points out: 'the path to scholarly respectability lay in the transformation of one's field of study into a "proper" science, i.e., a science in the likeness and image of the natural sciences'.[14] Jurisprudence was no exception. Positivism conformed to this new fetish of science. Central to positivism is the idea that jurisprudence should be concerned with the empirical study of existing law, as opposed to the moral theorising about the possibilities of law which was characteristic of naturalism.

This latter theme dominates the work of the Utilitarians – the social reformers and positivist jurists of Victorian England in the early nineteenth century – especially the work of Jeremy Bentham and John Austin. As one leading scholar of positivism notes, 'Bentham and Austin constantly insisted on the need to distinguish, firmly and with maximum clarity, law as it is from law as it ought to be. This theme haunts their work, and they condemned natural-law thinkers precisely because they had blurred this apparently simply but vital distinction.'[15] Underpinning this 'separability thesis' was the Utilitarian's 'command theory'; i.e., a theory of law that facilitated scientific study. Austin's starting point was the view that 'Law, simply and strictly so called [is] law set by political superiors to political inferiors.' Thus it took the form of a command from a sovereign to a subject. For Bentham, this meant that law had to be reducible to a verbal command; Austin allowed for some commands to be expressive. Both agreed that to be law, a command had to be general in nature (i.e., directed towards a public subject), had to come from a sovereign source that was superior to the subject, and had to be backed by sanctions.[16] Viewed thus, international law is not really law. The conditions for a command – a sovereign source and sanctions – do not exist. The subjects of international law (i.e., states) are themselves sovereign. Moreover, as sovereigns, states are above legal sanction (this was true in the nineteenth century but is less so today). Therefore, for Austin, international law was no more law than the 'law of honor' or the 'law of fashion' since it was based on 'general opinion' among nations and not

---

[14] Hall, 'The persistent spectre', 277.
[15] H. L. A. Hart, 'Positivism and the separation of law and morals,' *Harvard Law Review* 71 (1958), 594.
[16] Anthony J. Sebok, 'Misunderstanding positivism,' *Michigan Law Review* 93 (1995), 2063–5.

the command of sovereign will.[17] Thus, positivism began as an approach to domestic law and was actually antipathetic to international law.

Victorian positivism attracted much attention in Germany, and in the late nineteenth to mid-twentieth centuries German jurists suggested revisions to Austin's fundamentalist positivism that would allow for international law to be classified as law. Georg Jellinek proposed the idea of 'auto-limitation of sovereignty', whereby states could subject themselves to legal obligations by self-imposing limitations on their own sovereignty. However, in order to preserve the notion of state sovereignty, Jellinek also (and indeed had to) argue that auto-limitation was reversible, thereby allowing states to withdraw from obligations under international law. Herein lay the problem from a positivist perspective: for how can a law be truly binding if the subject is able to release himself at will? For this reason, Heinrich Triepel rejected the idea of auto-limitation of sovereignty. Instead he proposed that law-making agreements constituted the 'common will' of states. Triepel argued that this act of common will, expressed explicitly in treaties and implicitly in custom, bound states to international law. In other words, states could not re-assert their sovereign right to withdraw from obligations under international law. This move by Triepel is very significant, for it introduces a more passive concept of sovereign will whereby consent replaces command.[18] The Austrian jurist Hans Kelsen suggests an alternative revision of Austinian positivism. We discussed Kelsen's theory in Chapter 1, but a brief recap is in order here. Kelsen accepted the Utilitarian premise of law as a command, but he suggested that sanctions are not always necessary for law to function. Central to Kelsen's contribution is his rejection of the dualistic view that separates the sovereign and the law, and indeed international and domestic law. Instead, Kelsen argued there to be a single 'world of law' at the top of which is international law and from which delegate domestic legal systems. However, Kelsen built his legal world-view on a weak foundation – namely, on a *grundnorm* of legal obligation, the existence of which he maintained must be presumed but could not be proven. This was a crucial failing for an approach to law that aspired to be scientific.

While these Germanic revisions were significant, the most influential legal positivist of the twentieth century was the Professor of Jurisprudence at Oxford University, H. L. A. Hart. Hart fully accepted the need to separate law and morals. But he is critical of Austin's command theory of law

---

[17] Robert J. Beck, Anthony Clark Arend and Robert D. Vander Lugt, *International Rules: Approaches from International Law and International Relations* (Oxford: Oxford University Press, 1996), 57.
[18] Hall, 'The persistent spectre,' pp. 282–3.

because of its emphasis on the role of sanctions in enforcing sovereign will on subjects. For Hart, this confuses the difference between being obliged and having an obligation to do something – the former rests on coercion the latter on legal duty. In his most important work, *The Concept of Law*, published in 1961, Hart proposes a rules-based theory of law. For him, developed legal systems are characterised by primary rules that specify substantive obligations, and secondary rules that empower actors to interpret, apply and revise primary rules. This rules-based theory enables Hart to argue that there is such a thing as international law. From this perspective, the lack of legal sanctions against states is not so significant. As Hart elaborates, 'To argue that international law is not binding because of its lack of organised sanctions is tacitly to accept the analysis of obligation contained in [Austin's] theory that law is essentially a matter of orders backed by threats.' Hart is quick to reiterate that such a theory fails to distinguish between coercion and duty. While Hart recognises international law to be law proper, he does not consider it to be a legal system. This is because it lacks 'secondary rules of change and adjudication which provide for legislature and courts'. Hart concludes that 'the absence of these institutions means that the rules of states resemble that simple form of social structure, consisting only of primary rules of obligation'.[19]

From our brief survey we may identify two main principles of the positivist school of international law. First is the 'separability thesis': that law is separate from morality and, as such, can and should be subject to empirical study. Thus, for positivists, legal scholarship is about figuring out what is international law as opposed to what it should be. Second is the concept of international law as binding rules to which states have consented. This second principle requires a bit of unpacking. We have seen how the dual role of states as sovereigns and subjects of international law created problems for positivists and indeed led Austin to reject the very existence of international law. Proposed remedies included the ideas of reversible auto-limitation of state sovereignty, and of law as expressing the common will of states. In the end, positivists were able to break out of the Austinian trap by replacing the concept of law as 'command' backed by 'sanctions' with that of law as expressing state 'consent' (Triepel) and thereafter being supported by a 'sense of obligation' (Hart). Positivists have also followed Hart in conceiving of international law in terms of a collection of rules as opposed to some kind of system. This can be seen, for instance, in the work of Anthony Clark Arend – one of the most interesting contemporary positivist scholars of international law. Thus, Arend

[19] H. L. A. Hart, *The Concept of Law*, 2nd edition (Oxford: Oxford University Press, 1998), p. 214.

conceives of international law as 'a set of binding rules'. Moreover, Arend makes plain that 'it is the perception of legitimacy that makes the rule law and not the guarantee of sanction'.[20]

States, rules and the balance of power

There is little love lost between realism and legal positivism. Each developed with the purpose of excluding one another's disciplines. Carr, Morgenthau, as well as realist-practioners like George Kennan and Dean Acheson, explicitly warned of the dangers of 'legalistic-moralistic' approaches to world politics.[21] Positivists, likewise, sought to separate law from everyday politics and moral debate. Despite this, there is much common ground between these apparent rivals. First off, both are committed to the scientific study of the social world. Developing the science of international relations has occupied realists from Morgenthau on.[22] Developing a science of jurisprudence was a driving imperative for positivists right from the beginning.

Second, both purged moral considerations from their respective theories. Conventional wisdom has it that classical realists considered the world to be too dangerous for states to pay much heed to moral concerns; that states had to focus on doing whatever was necessary to survive. New scholarship is questioning this conventional reading of classical realism – both in terms of the hazards of reading Thucydides through modern eyes, and in terms of suggesting that Hobbes, Carr and Morgenthau did recognise that statecraft ought to have some moral purpose.[23] But there can be no mistaking the absence of moral considerations from Waltz's worldview. Notwithstanding the new scholarship mentioned above, Waltzian scepticism is well entrenched in contemporary neorealism and neoclassical realism. This is not to say that modern realists are immoral; rather, they believe that states make the world safer by focusing on balancing

---

[20] Anthony Clark Arend, 'Toward an understanding of international legal rules,' in Beck, Arend and Vander Lugt (eds.), *International Rules*, p. 292. See also Anthony Clark Arend, *Legal Rules and International Society* (Oxford: Oxford University Press, 1999).

[21] Beck, Arend and Vander Lugt (eds.) *International Rules*, pp. 94–109.

[22] Carr recognised the emergence of political science in the early twentieth century, but he expressed doubt that this new discipline would mature beyond its utopian phrase, to be able to study objectivity the real world of power politics. Carr, *Twenty Years' Crisis*, pp. 3–11.

[23] Welch, 'Why IR theorists'; Michael C. Williams, 'Hobbes and international relations: a reconsideration', *International Organization* 50, 2 (1996), 213–36; Ken Booth, 'Security in anarchy: utopian realism in theory and practice', *International Affairs* 67 (1991), 527–45; Michael C. Williams, 'Why ideas matter in international relations: Hans Morgenthau, classical realism, and the moral construction of power politics', *International Organization* 58 (2004), 633–65.

power and this serves the larger human good.[24] There is no doubting the positivist view on the relationship between moral concerns and law – that the two are and should be completely separate. Indeed, this is necessary in order to advance the science of jurisprudence. But, as with realists, this is not to say that legal positivists are unconcerned about morality in public life. In fact, the work of Austin and Bentham was focused on issues of social reform in Victorian England. Nor did they deny the influence of moral standards on the development of law. Rather, they sought to emphasise the distinction between law and morality – that a rule does not have to be moral to be legal, and that legal rules have a force that moral rules do not.[25] Put even more bluntly by Hart: 'The rules of international law, like those of municipal law, are often morally quite indifferent.'[26]

Third, both approaches are state-centric. Realism is well noted for its treatment of states as 'black boxes' or 'billiard balls'; in other words, entities whose internal workings do not require study. This is more true of neorealism than classical realism. Domestic politics did also matter for Carr and Morgenthau. For Carr, the internal characteristics of states – especially in terms of economic organisation and public opinion – were crucial elements of the balance of power.[27] Equally, Morgenthau introduced all manner of domestic variables – including, national leadership, ideology, character, and morale – in his estimation of the balance of power.[28] As we noted above, Waltz did away with domestic politics altogether. He did not enquire into the units of world politics (i.e., states) which he took to be undifferentiated in function and form. Moreover, the competitive pressures of the international system made it safe for him to assume that states do (and must) act rationally. As we noted above, even neoclassical realists accept this neorealist assumption. Hence, neoclassical realists only look inside states when they encounter deviant cases, i.e., states acting irrationally.[29] States are also central to the legal positivist view of international law – i.e., law by states and for states. For positivists then, international law comprises those rules to which states have consented, either explicitly in law-making treaties or implicitly through customary practice. And states are the principle subjects of international law. Obviously, contemporary international law does confer rights and duties

---

[24] Michael Desch, 'It is kind to be cruel: the humanity of American realism,' *Review of International Studies*, 29 (2003), 415–26.
[25] Hart, 'Positivism,' pp. 598–9.   [26] Hart, *Concept*, pp. 228–9.
[27] Carr, *Twenty Years' Crisis*, pp. 97–134.
[28] Morgenthau, *Politics Among Nations*, pp. 99–111, 138–66.
[29] See, for example, Jack Snyder, *Myths of Empire* (Ithaca, NY: Cornell University Press, 1991).

on other actors – especially, numerous intergovernmental organisations (IGOs) (most importantly, the United Nations (UN) and the European Union (EU)), peoples (in the form of self-determination movements), and individuals (especially in terms of human rights and international criminal law). Some IGOs may also create legal rules (e.g., binding UN Security Council resolutions and EU directives). But here positivists argue that IGOs only have such powers because 'states have vested this authority in the organization' and hence, IGOs are 'not truly *independent* actors in the law-creating process'.[30]

Finally, realism and positivism both offer structural approaches, respectively to IR and IL. The classical realism of Carr and Morgenthau was already tending towards structuralism with its focus on the balance of power. Waltz offered an entirely structural realist approach (hence, neorealism is also known as 'structural realism').[31] For Waltz, the structure of international politics contains three main elements. Two are unchanging: the units and the ordering principle, which are states and anarchy respectively. So all the explanatory action occurs in the third element, which is the distribution of capabilities among the units, or put another way, the number of great powers. Waltz did not foresee a unipolar system – rather he compared the relative stability of Cold War bipolarity with the instability of previous multipolar orders. Stability here means prevalence of great-power war. Contemporary neorealist and neoclassical realist work is concerned with the theoretical and policy implications of the current concentration of US power; with exploring whether this constitutes a unipolar order, whether it will be long lasting and peaceful, and what it means for US leadership on the global stage.[32] Legal positivism is also structural in approach. International law is constituted by rules that are *binding* on states. The binding quality of law is central to the positivist approach, for it is this characteristic that distinguishes legal rules from moral rules. Thus, while states have some agency in creating law in the first place through treaties and customary practice, thereafter state action is bound by the contours of international law. For positivists,

---

[30] Arend, 'Toward', p. 295.
[31] Thus Waltz's approach is called structural realism in Beck, Arend and Vander Lugt (eds.), *International Rules*, pp. 144–6. We prefer the term neorealism as some structural realist scholarship is actually much closer in content to neoclassical realism. See Barry Buzan, Charles Jones and Richard Little, *The Logic of Anarchy: Neorealism to Structural Realism* (New York: Columbia University Press, 1993).
[32] Christopher Layne, 'The unipolar illusion: why new great powers will arise,' *International Security* 17 (1993), 5–51; Michael Mastanduno, 'Preserving the Unipolar Moment: 'Realist theories and US grand strategy after the Cold War', *International Security* 21 (1997), 44–98; William C. Wohlforth, 'The stability of a unipolar world', *International Security* 24 (1999), 5–41.

a sense of obligation, supported by the prospect (if not application) of sanction, produces state compliance with legal rules.

The suggestion that there may be common ground between realists and positivists on the structures of world politics might strike the reader as odd. But the fact is that these two concepts of structure – the balance of power and rules of international law – provided the one area of common conceptual ground where realists and positivists *did* meet in the past. As it happens, classical realists were not as opposed to international law as they were subsequently made out to be. Stanley Hoffman notes that when it came out, *Politics Among Nations* was read to be a 'declaration of war' against legal approaches to world politics.[33] In fact, Morgenthau was much more measured in his critique of international law. Indeed, he explicitly warned against an all-or-nothing approach to international law. This can hardly be surprising given his legal background. For Morgenthau, we cannot deny the existence of international law, but equally we should not rely too much on it. Likewise for Carr, 'politics and law are indissolubly intertwined' though 'the ultimate authority of law derives from politics'.[34] Moreover, both Morgenthau and Carr adhered to the positivist approach to international law. Carr equated naturalism with discredited idealism, and positivism with more reliable realism. Indeed, Carr even noted that it was Hobbes who first came up with the concept of law as command.[35] Interestingly Morgenthau was initially critical of positivism for seeking to, as he saw it, divorce law from politics.[36] But later on, in *Politics Among Nations*, he conceptualised international law in terms of legal rules to which states have consented.[37] For Morgenthau, the crucial weakness in international law was the lack of effective enforcement. He readily conceded that this did not matter for 'the great majority of rules in international law' that are voluntarily complied with. But in 'a minority of important and generally spectacular cases', as he put it: 'considerations of power rather than law determine compliance and enforcement'.[38] Ultimately, for both Carr and Morgenthau,

---

[33] Cited in Beck, Arend and Vander Lugt (eds.), *International Rules*, p. 95.
[34] Carr, *Twenty Years' Crisis*, pp. 165, 176.   [35] Ibid., p. 163.
[36] Hans J. Morgenthau, 'Positivism, functionalism, and international law', *American Journal of International Law* 34 (1940), 260–84.
[37] Here there was a difference between Morgenthau, who ignored customary law altogether and defines state consent in terms of treaty law, and Carr, who recognised the importance of customary law and the hazards of presuming that treaties expressed state consent (given that states may be forced to sign treaties). See Morgenthau, *Politics Among Nations*, p. 257; Carr, *Twenty Years' Crisis*, pp. 160, 168–77. As we noted above, for positivists, state consent may be expressed both in the rules of customary state practice as well as rules codified in treaty law.
[38] Morgenthau, *Politics Among Nations*, pp. 256–9, quotes from pp. 267–8.

international law could only do so much. The mistake of the 'idealist' or 'legal-moralist' approaches of the past was to ask too much of international law. Crucially, while international law is efficient in regulating everyday relations between states, it cannot deal with power politics. Thus, both Carr and Morgenthau argued that international law required a balance of power to function.[39] On this point, Morgenthau cited the leading legal positivist, Lassa Oppenheim, who declared the balance of power to be 'an indispensable condition of the very existence of International Law.'[40]

This mutual appreciation by realists and positivists of the structures of law and power politics has been lost. Following Waltz, law is ignored in most contemporary realist approaches to world politics. An exception is the 'English School' of realism, which continues the classical realist tradition of producing historically grounded scholarship that is sensitive to, among other things, the presence of international law.[41] The key concept of the English School is that of states existing in an 'international society', where the exercise of power occurs within a normative context. However, the historically sensitive methodology of the English School has limited global reach given the dominance of American-style, social science approaches to IR.[42] Positivists have also lost sight of the balance of power. Oppenheim advanced the moral necessity of the balance of power for international law in his hugely influential two-volume textbook *International Law*, first published in 1905–1906. Posthumous updated versions of this textbook were published under successive editors (and indeed continue to be), and it was in the 1935 later addition of the book that reference to the balance of power was dropped. As Benedict Kingsbury notes, 'ever since, the notion that balance of power principles might

---

[39] Carr, *Twenty Years' Crisis*, p. 176.
[40] Cited in Morgenthau, *Politics Among Nations*, p. 256.
[41] Timothy Dunne, *Inventing Tradition: A History of the English School* (Basingstoke: Macmillan, 1998); Richard Little, 'The English School's contribution to the study of international relations', *European Journal of International Relations* 6 (2000), 395–422; Andrew Linklater and Hidemi Suganami, *The English School of International Relations* (Cambridge: Cambridge University Press, 2006).
[42] Martha Finnemore, 'Exporting the English School?' *Review of International Studies* 27 (2001), 510, Dale C. Copeland, 'A realist critique of the English School', *Review of International Studies* 29 (2003), 428. As we suggested in Chapter 1 in our discussion on Hedley Bull, there is much mileage in this approach to understanding world politics precisely because it integrates the balance of power, normative concerns and the social structure of international law. However, we do not adopt an English School approach in this book because, as we elaborate in this chapter, we want to separate out these variables into our realist, liberal and constructivist lenses so as to distinguish between the different ways of analysing international law and world politics.

be relevant to international law has been virtually unutterable among members of the "invisible college of international lawyers".[43]

In short, realists and positivists have more in common than they appreciate (or perhaps will admit). For all their differences, realism and positivism agree, in principle, on the scientific study of the social world, the separation of morality from the mechanisms for ordering world politics, the primacy of states, and the twin structures of the balance of power and the rules of international law.

Liberalism

Liberalism in IR and legal process theory in IL form an obvious interdisciplinary pairing.[44] For starters, each is sensitive to the other's discipline. Liberals are predisposed to recognising the importance of law in promoting international co-operation. Equally, legal process theory explicitly recognises the importance of policy in creating the conditions whereby law can serve humanity.[45] Liberal approaches to IR and IL also share the same basic concerns and assumptions. Both offer critiques of the power-obsessed, state-centric, approaches taken by realists and positivists. Instead, liberalism in IR and IL highlights the normative imperatives and multitude of actors in world politics. This provides the basis for a progressive vision of law-enabled global governance. At the same time, the liberal critique of the amoral universe of realism and positivism contains within it a dangerous moral relativism, one that prioritises liberal values over world order.

Liberalism in IR

Liberals have a far more optimistic view of human nature than realists, one where harmony and not war is the natural state of things. The basic liberal

---

[43] Benedict Kingsbury, 'Legal positivism as normative politics: international society, balance of power and Lassa Oppenheim's positive international law', *European Journal of International Law* 13, 2 (2002), 420.

[44] Among liberalism in IL, we include the New Haven school (Lasswell, McDougal, Reisman), legal process theory (Falk, Chayes, Koh) and new liberal theory (Slaughter, Teson, Franck).

[45] See also the emphasis on liberal scholarship in IR and IL in the following prominent interdisciplinary surveys: Anne-Marie Slaughter, 'International law and international relations: a dual agenda', *American Journal of International Law* 87 (1993), 205–39; Robert O. Keohane, 'International Relations and International Law: Two Optics', *Harvard International Law Journal* 38, 2 (1997), 487–502; Anne-Marie Slaughter, Andrew S. Tulumello and Stepan Wood, 'International law and international relations theory: a new generation of interdisciplinary scholarship', *American Journal of International Law* 92 (1998), 367–87.

position was laid out by John Locke (a contemporary of Thomas Hobbes) in his famous *Two Treatises of Government* (1690). Locke argued that all men are born free and equal, with the capacity to reason and hence to co-operate. Thus a harmony of interests in self-preservation and material wellbeing may be said to exist among all people. From this perspective, people are not naturally inclined to war – since it threatens lives and livelihoods. Rather, war is the product of militaristic and undemocratic government. War serves the ends of state not people. Indeed, throughout history war has been an important engine for the growth in state power through the internal mobilisation and the external acquisition of resources. The beneficiaries of war are the governing oligarchies and military class. In short, contrary to the realist position, state power is the problem for liberals. Locke advocated a social contract between people and government, one that reduced government interference in individual liberty and permitted ordinary people to get on with realising their natural harmony of interests. Locke also argued for a strengthened legislature, as a means to ensure majority rule and hold the executive to account.[46]

Locke was primarily concerned with internal political organisation. But these themes of state accountability and individual liberty also form two basic liberal prescriptions for a more peaceful international order – one involving peace between publicly accountable states, and another involving strengthening the ties between peoples of different nations through increased trade and trans-border contacts. The first, most clearly presented by Immanuel Kant in his famous manifesto *Perpetual Peace* (1795), depended on co-operation between republican states. The great virtue of republican states, for Kant, is executive accountability to a strong independent legislature. The idea was for republican states to form a 'pacific federation' to abolish war between them. The second prescription rested on increased transnational commerce and contact between peoples. Put thus by John Stuart Mill in 1848: 'it is commerce which is rapidly rendering war obsolete, by strengthening and multiplying the personal interests which act in natural opposition to it'.[47] Thus for liberal free-traders such as Adam Smith and Richard Cobden, the increased movement of goods, services and labour promised peace as well as prosperity.

Both republican and commercial liberalism were discredited by the world wars of 1914–1918 and 1939–1945. Commerce, specifically increased trade in the late nineteenth and early twentieth centuries, did

---

[46] John Locke, *Two Treatises of Government*, 2nd edition, ed. Peter Laslett (Cambridge: Cambridge University Press, 1967).
[47] Michael Howard, *War and Liberal Conscience* (Oxford: Oxford University Press, 1978), p. 37.

nothing to halt the descent into World War I. Likewise democracy did not deliver a lasting post-war peace: German democracy elected Adolf Hitler into power, and the other great democracies did little to stop Nazi aggression. As we discussed, the abject failure of the League of Nations (and other schemes to reduce war) gave cause to realists such as Carr and Morgenthau. Liberals were dismissed as a bunch of 'utopian' dreamers. Perhaps not surprisingly then, questions of institutional design, purpose and effectiveness were to occupy liberals following World War II (WWII). The post-WWII period also saw a boom in international institutions – such as the United Nations and its specialised agencies, various international economic regimes, the North Atlantic Treaty Organisation and the embryonic institutions of the European Economic Community. Liberal institutionalism (in its various guises of functionalist, neofunctionalist and interdependence theory) explored how these institutions promoted interstate co-operation and even supplanted the state in certain policy areas.[48] Interdependence theory, in particular, presented an immensely complex and inter-linked policy world, where non-state actors and state bureaucracies operated through transnational networks and international institutions.[49]

Liberal institutionalism reflected world developments, with the post-war institutional building of the 1940s–1960s, and dominance of economic issues (such as the oil crises, trade liberalisation, and 'Third World' debt) in the 1970s. But, as we noted earlier, the world became much more realist in appearance with the collapse of détente and renewal of Cold War tensions in the early 1980s. Once again, states and military security came to dominate the international agenda. Liberal theorists responded by surrendering ground to neorealists. A new liberal institutionalism emerged in the mid 1980s that recognised the primacy of the state and accepted a more limited role for institutions, as mechanisms for reducing barriers to state co-operation (by increasing transparency and building trust). Crucially, neoliberals no longer looked inside states, at how they are politically organised, but rather followed neorealists in treating states as rational actors. Neoliberal institutionalists also conceded that their approach was best suited to explaining non-security policy areas, such as institutionalised co-operation in trade, monetary

---

[48] Ernst B. Haas, *Uniting for Europe: Politics, Economic, and Social Forces* (Stanford, CA: Stanford University Press, 1958); Ernst B. Haas, *Beyond the Nation-State: Functionalism and International Organization* (Stanford, CA: Stanford University Press, 1964); David Mitrany, *A Working Peace System* (Chicago: Quadrangle Press, 1966).

[49] Robert O. Keohane and Joseph S. Nye, Jr., *Power and Interdependence: World Politics in Transition* (Boston, MA: Little, Brown, 1977).

policy, and environmental protection; thus, state security was left to neorealism.[50]

Neoliberal institutionalism has proven hugely influential in the United States, for it has provided a way for liberals to challenge neorealism on its own terms – with a social scientific, parsimonious, and structural theory of world politics. But critics argue that it has conceded too much to neorealism; that instead of debate we have a 'neo-neo synthesis' on the centrality of state action and anarchy in world politics. Neoliberal institutionalists openly recognise their proximity to neorealists. As two leading neoliberal theorists admit: 'for better or worse, institutional theory is a half-sibling of neorealism'.[51] Traditional liberal assumptions about the importance of how states are politically organised, and of the progressive role of transnational activity between non-state actors, were lost in this neoliberal move towards realism.

In the 1990s, liberals once again began to look inside the state. In what has been a recovery of republican liberalism, a new literature has emerged seeking to explain the absence of war between liberal democracies. To be sure, realists have tried to show that liberal democracies have been too few in number across history for there to be any statistical significance in the absence of war between them.[52] But the historical evidence, especially of the twentieth century, suggests that there is something about liberal democracies that prevents them from fighting each other.[53] Liberals have offered several, reinforcing, explanations for this. Some emphasise domestic norms of 'bounded competition' and non-violent dispute resolution that are externalised by liberal democracies when they encounter one another on the world stage.[54] Other liberals point to the role of domestic and international institutions. Democratic institutions make it difficult for political leaders to mobilise their populaces for wars against

---

[50] Robert Axelrod, *The Evolution of Cooperation* (New York: Basic Books, 1984); Robert Keohane, *After Hegemony: Cooperation and Discord in the World Political Economy* (Princeton, NJ: Princeton University Press, 1984); David Baldwin (ed.), *Neorealism and Neoliberalism: The Contemporary Debate* (New York: Columbia University Press, 1993).

[51] Robert O. Keohane and Lisa Martin, 1999 conference paper, cited in Robert Jervis, 'Realism, neoliberalism, and cooperation', *International Security* 24 (1999), 43. By 'institutional theory', Keohane and Martin mean 'neoliberal institutionalism'.

[52] Christopher Layne, 'Kant or can't: the myth of the democratic peace', and David Spiro, 'The insignificance of the liberal peace', both in *International Security* 19 (1994), 5–49 and 50–86.

[53] For a liberal response to realist scepticism, see Zeev Maoz, 'The controversy over the democratic peace: rearguard action or cracks in the wall', *International Security* 22 (1997), 162–98.

[54] William J. Dixon, 'Democracy and the peaceful settlement of disputes', *American Political Science Quarterly* 88 (1993), 14–32.

fellow democracies.[55] At the international level, democracies are more likely than non-democracies to work through institutional structures to settle differences peacefully.[56] Shared identity also matters. Peaceful compromise and institutionalised co-operation are prevalent between liberal democracies because, at a fundamental level, they trust each other.[57] Equally, war is almost unthinkable between liberal democracies because of mutual empathy.[58] Finally, the liberal democratic peace benefits from a virtuous dynamic whereby the shared expectation and common experience of peaceful relations reinforce one another.[59]

Liberalism, like realism, is a broad church. Nonetheless, we may distil from the above discussion three core principles that are applicable to most liberal theory (with the exception of the 'realist leaning' neoliberal institutionalism). First, states are not the only or even main actors in world politics. Liberals take a 'bottom-up' view of politics and emphasise the role of individuals and groups in domestic and transnational civil society. Second, the internal make-up of states does matter to how they act externally. In this sense, states are not rational actors but rather a vehicle for preference advancement by domestic constituencies. As republican liberalism emphasises, government accountability – expressing liberal norms and institutionalised in democratic structures – is therefore crucial to ensuring that state policy reflects the preferences of the majority. It is this that prevents liberal democracies from fighting one another. Third, states can form interdependent ties, through trade and institutionalised co-operation, which in turn can shape state preferences and policy. Commercial liberalism points to the power of transnational trade in reducing conflict between states, and liberal institutionalism highlights the role of institutions in international politics.[60] State interdependence, in turn, promotes peace.

---

[55] Zeev Maoz and Bruce Russett, 'Normative and structural causes of democratic peace' *American Political Science Review* 87 (1993), 624–38.

[56] Bruce Russett and John Oneal, *Triangulating Peace: Democracy, Interdependence, and International Organizations* (New York: W. W. Norton, 2001).

[57] Charles Lipson, *Reliable Partners: How Democracies Have Made a Separate Peace* (Princeton, NJ: Princeton University Press, 2005).

[58] John M. Owen, *Liberal Peace, Liberal War: American Politics and International Security* (Ithaca, NY: Cornell University Press, 1997).

[59] The interplay of experiences and expectations of peaceful relations is explored in Ido Oren, 'The subjectivity of the democratic peace: changing US perceptions of Imperial Germany', *International Security* 20 (1995), 147–84.

[60] These core principles of liberalism are discussed in Andrew Moravcsik, 'Taking preferences seriously: a liberal theory of international politics', *International Organization* 51 (1997), 516–21.

Liberalism in IL

Legal process theory challenges the core principle of positivism, namely, that law is and should be separate from morality. For liberal IL scholars, this position robs law of its purpose, which is to serve progressive social ends. Legal process theory also seeks to situate law in the political context within which it is created and operates. Thus, law is not simply a system of rules to regulate state behaviour, but rather it is part and parcel of international policy-making processes. As Rosalyn Higgins, formerly of the London School of Economics and now judge at the International Court of Justice, puts it: 'This view rejects the notion of law merely as the impartial application of rules. International law is the entire decision-making process.'[61]

This interdisciplinary perspective on international law was developed by a team at Yale University – Myres McDougal (a law professor) and Harold Lasswell (a professor of political science and law).[62] In the early 1940s, McDougal and Lasswell made the case for legal training in the United States to prepare lawyers to be domestic policy-makers.[63] For McDougal and Lasswell this policy-orientated approach to domestic law was equally applicable to international law. Their idea was for international lawyers, trained in the methods of policy sciences, to develop progressive law – law that would help fashion a world public order that advanced human dignity. This is a *prescriptive* approach to international law, quite unlike the *descriptive* approach of legal positivism. From the point of view of scholarship, therefore, the job is not to ascertain the content of law but to advocate law that promotes core community values. Indeed, McDougal and Lasswell were highly critical of the 'make-believe universalism' of traditional international law, i.e., the notion that international law comprises only those rules to which all states have consented. This perspective, they argued, cloaks the tough moral choices that need to be faced in developing a functioning world order. These choices necessarily reflect conflicting values. The values that serve the interests of most community members – in particular, human dignity – must take priority so as to develop a stable and sustainable world public order. As things stood, in the 1950s, the value-free position of legal positivism gave equal recognition to democratic and totalitarian systems of public order. This simply did not make sense to McDougal and Lasswell in the context of

---

[61] Rosalyn Higgins, 'Policy, consideration and the international judicial process', *International and Comparative Law Quarterly* 17 (1968), 58.

[62] This liberal approach to IL is commonly known as the New Haven school.

[63] Harold D. Lasswell and Myres S. McDougal, 'Legal education and public policy: professional training in the public interest', *Yale Law Journal* 52 (1943), 203–95.

the Cold War ideological struggle between the Western democracies and Eastern dictatorships.[64]

The development of this New Haven school was spurred on by the challenge from realism in IR. As we saw, Morgenthau's *Politics Among Nations* was read as a frontal assault on international law. We also noted earlier how Morgenthau and Carr offered more nuanced critiques of international law, to the effect that international law should be confined to regulating the humdrum everyday business of states as it was incapable of dealing with power politics. Recall also that ethics was subservient to considerations of power politics in the realist scheme of things. Liberal IL scholars responded to the realist challenge by placing people, law and ethics at the centre of world order. Human agency was conceived as operating through authoritative decision-making processes, defined and legitimated by international law, and by which individuals and institutions exercise power, deploy resources and realise values[65] This is an agent-centred view of things that recognises the mutually constitutive functions of power and law in social order, as well as the political struggle over values and possibilities for progressive social development.

Later versions of legal process theory developed along the two core ideas of law as expressing fundamental values and law as a process. The former was developed by Richard Falk and his associates on the World Order Models (WOM) project in the 1960s. For Falk, world peace was as important a value as human dignity to be advanced by international law. By the 1960s, both superpowers had acquired large arsenals of thermonuclear weapons and the ballistic missiles to deliver them rapidly. The 1962 Cuban Missile Crisis, commonly considered to be the closest the world came to all-out nuclear war, vividly demonstrated the dangers of this period in the Cold War. In this context, world peace served the most fundamental value of all: the survival of humanity. From this perspective, the purpose of law was to ensure the stability and smooth running of this extremely dangerous international system by providing agreed rules and common expectations for state conduct, and a process for states to communicate in crises and co-operate on technical matters.[66] By the mid-1970s, when the dangers of nuclear war appeared to have receded, Falk

---

[64] Myres S. McDougal and Harold D. Lasswell, 'The identification and appraisal of diverse systems of public order', *American Journal of International Law* 53 (1959), 1–29; Myres S. McDougal, 'Some basic concepts about international law: a policy-orientated approach', *Journal of Conflict Resolution* 4 (1960), 337–54.
[65] McDougal and Lasswell, 'Identification'.
[66] Richard A. Falk, 'New approaches to the study of international law', *American Journal of International Law* 61 (1967), 477–95; Falk, *The Status of Law in International Society* (Princeton, NJ: Princeton University Press, 1970).

and his colleagues in the WOM project advocated transformative change in the world, away from a state-based system, as the means to promote both peace and human dignity.[67]

The concept of law as an international legal process was developed in the late 1960s and 1970s. Here the purpose was to ascertain the causal impact of international law. Where McDougal, Lasswell and Falk responded to the realist challenge by locating law within broader political and strategic processes, a new breed of scholarship sought to respond to the realists by empirically showing that law matters. This was an *explanatory* approach to international law – one that set out to show how (and how much) law affects international relations. To this end, the American Society of International Law commissioned a series of studies on the role of law in international crises. Thus, Abram Chayes showed that international law affected decision-making even during the Cuban Missile Crisis, when power politics was at its most intense during the Cold War.[68] An explanatory approach is also taken in Louis Henkin's hugely influential book *How Nations Behave* (1968). Henkin explicitly set out to show that 'law *is* a major force in world affairs', by operating in numerous ways (as previously identified by liberal IL scholars) to ease, regulate and enable international relations.[69] Underpinning this explanatory work by legal process scholars is recognition of the importance of law in contributing to system stability, and thereby the liberal value of world peace.

Since the 1990s, liberal IL scholars have returned to their ideological roots and prescriptive purpose. Drawing on republican liberalism, a handful of prominent US law scholars – Fernando Teson, Thomas Frank and Anne-Marie Slaughter – have resurrected the notion of a moral asymmetry in the world between democracies and non-democracies. Teson does not beat around the bush: 'tyrannical governments are outlaws'. He argues that liberal international law should seek to protect individuals from tyrannies, and that force may be legitimately used for this purpose. Indeed, he maintains that sovereignty rests on internal legitimacy, and since tyrannies lack this, they also lack the 'proper foundation' of state sovereignty. The conclusion is a subversive one from the perspective of traditional international law: 'Sovereignty is to be respected only when it is justly exercised.' In practical terms, Teson would have the democracies boot the non-democracies out of the United Nations, suspend their right to make treaties, remove their diplomatic privileges and refuse

---

[67] David Wilkinson, 'World order models project: first fruits,' *Political Science Quarterly* 91 (1976), 329–35.

[68] Abram Chayes, *The Cuban Missile Crisis* (Oxford: Oxford University Press, 1974).

[69] Louis Henkin, *How Nations Behave: Law and Foreign Policy* (New York: Columbia University Press, 1979).

to recognise them as legitimate.[70] Thus this new liberal theory seeks to harness international law for the purpose of promoting core values. Interestingly, where Falk juxtaposed human dignity and strategic stability as competing values – arguing that the world could not afford moral relativism given the risk of nuclear war – the new liberal theorists of IL see no such tension. In 1992, Franck argued that democracy had evolved 'from moral prescription to international legal obligation'. This finding was based on 'various texts' and on 'the practice of global and regional organisations' which Franck argues specify in remarkable detail the content of this new legal norm, especially 'the requirement for free and open elections'.[71] Slaughter emphasises the political benefits and strategic imperatives for distinguishing between democracies and non-democracies in international law. She argues that liberal democracies are more likely to honour obligations undertaken in treaties.[72] She also maintains that they can be more trusted with weapons of mass destruction (WMD) than non-democracies; indeed, she argues that democracies have a 'duty' to use force to prevent non-democracies from acquiring WMD in order to protect international peace and security.[73]

Critics have noted that liberal democracies are not necessarily more compliant with international law. Public opinion and judicial interpretation may prevent democratic governments from following through on their treaty commitments.[74] Critics also point to a contradiction of purpose in this new liberal theory. Slaughter seeks to both explain and prescribe a new transnational liberal order. The former enterprise requires her to pursue a 'value-free' scientific study of the current legal order as its stands, while the latter involves promoting a particular set of values.[75] As it happens, Slaughter attempts to distinguish the new liberal theory of IL from early liberal IL scholarship on the grounds that the former is explanatory and the latter prescriptive.[76] This is odd because, as we noted above, there is a branch of earlier liberal IL scholarship (i.e., the legal process approach) that does seek to explain rather than prescribe

---

[70] Fernando R. Teson, 'The Kantian theory of international law', *Columbia Law Review* 92 (1992), 89, 92, 100.

[71] Thomas M. Franck, 'The emerging right to democratic governance', *American Journal of International Law* 86 (1992), 47, 90.

[72] Anne-Marie Slaughter, 'International law in a world of liberal states', *European Journal of International Law* 6 (1995), 503–38.

[73] Lee Feinstein and Anne-Marie Slaughter, 'A duty to prevent', *Foreign Affairs* (Jan. Feb. 2004).

[74] José E. Alvarez, 'Do liberal states behave better? A critique of Slaughter's liberal theory,' *European Journal of International Law* 12 (2001), 183–246.

[75] Christian Reus-Smit, 'The strange death of liberal international theory', *European Journal of International Law* 12 (2001), 573–93.

[76] Slaughter, 'International law', p. 235 n. 143.

international law. But more importantly, it would seem that, if anything, explanation takes second place to prescription in this new liberal theory of IL. This is perfectly clear in Teson's work, and even in Franck's creative take on the global entitlement to democracy. It is also evident in Slaughter's claim that her theory does not recognise liberal democracies to be morally superior to non-liberal and non-democratic states, when it is abundantly clear that it does precisely this.[77] These scholars are seeking to promote liberal values in international law and, as such, their work falls within the traditional liberal IL school.

Three core principles of the liberal IL school may be identified from the above discussion. First is the notion that international law includes more than rules codified in treaties and embedded in custom. Crucially, international law is conceived as authoritative decision-making processes that sustain and are sustained by systems of social, political, and strategic order.[78] Second is the principle that law should be directed to promoting core community values. As we saw there was some difference within the liberal IL school as to which values – human dignity, world peace or liberal democracy – are most essential to world public order. Only those liberal IL scholars that take an explanatory approach (such as Henkin and Francis Boyle) reject this principle on the grounds that prescribing law is inconsistent with the normative neutrality required for the scientific study of its causal effect.[79] Third, is the view that international law performs a broad range of functions. Whereas positivists take a narrow view of law as rules that regulate and constrain state behaviour, all legal process scholars see law as facilitating and enabling international relations by providing modes of communication, legitimation, reassurance, co-operation and habituation.[80]

Liberal values and global governance

Liberals in IR and IL have a shared vision of world order – one in which community values take centre stage, which is populated by a multitude of policy actors, and where law and institutions serve a broad range of

---

[77] Feinstein and Slaughter, 'Duty'. This is also noted in Alvarez, 'Do liberal states behave better?', pp. 189–90.

[78] Critics have responded that by including policy processes in international law, legal process theory is unable to distinguish law from politics. Michael Byers, *Custom, Power and the Power of Rules: International Relations and Customary International Law* (Cambridge: Cambridge University Press, 1999), p. 210; Arend, *Legal Rules*, p. 26.

[79] Henkin, *How Nations Behave*, p. 40; Francis Boyle, *World Politics and International Law* (Durham, NC: Duke University Press, 1985).

[80] Anne-Marie Slaughter Burley, 'International law and international relations theory: a dual agenda,' *American Journal of International Law* 87 (1993), 209.

functions. In this vision, there are substantial levels of global governance provided through transnational policy networks, supranational organisations and international institutions. Let us take these common points in turn.

First is the focus on values. Liberalism in IL emphasises community values in direct challenge to the amorality of realism and 'separability thesis' of positivism. Contrary to realism, it holds that world order must be built on the foundation of core values – identified at various times as human dignity, strategic stability and liberal democracy – in order to be sustainable. And contrary to positivism, it submits that law must promote such values if it is to have purpose. Liberalism has a somewhat different take on values. Man is rational for liberals. Thus, co-operation is based on the enlightened rationality of mutual gain. But nonetheless, such social action is achieved through value-laden institutions – namely, the liberal democratic state and free trade. It is liberal values that ensure that these institutions serve the interests and preferences of the majority for peace and prosperity over war and ruin. As we saw, one stream of liberal thinking – republican liberalism and new liberal theory in IL – argues for the promotion of liberal values even at the cost of war. To be sure, the spread of democracy promises a peaceful and just order, but the path to this liberal order invariably involves taking on totalitarian states. This presents a profound challenge to realism and positivism which both privilege stability over justice in world ordering. Indeed, placing ideological conditionality on state sovereignty is an anathema to modern positivist international law. In place of the current universalist legal order codified in the UN Charter, the new liberal theory of IL would have a relativist liberal legal order.[81]

Second is the challenge to the state-centrism of realism and positivism. For liberals, the most important actors in world politics are not states but individuals and groups in civil society. Commercial liberalism highlights the importance of transnational trade and social relations in circumventing state control of world politics. Republican liberalism, especially in its modern guise of liberal democratic peace theory, critiques the whole notion of the state as a rational actor: domestic political ideology and structures are crucial in empowering a range of agents to determine what their state wants and accordingly how it should act in the world. Liberalism directs our attention to actors that operate above as well as below the level of the state. Liberal institutionalism, in particular, explores the

---

[81] Gerry Simpson, 'Two liberalisms', *European Journal of International Law* 12, 3 (2001), 537–71.

role of transnational networks and institutions in binding states together and in supplanting states in some policy areas.

Third is a prioritising of agency. Indeed, the plurality of actors discussed above is suggestive of the more agent-centric approach to IR and IL.[82] Certainly, recovering agency is fundamental to liberalism in IL. As we noted, positivism takes a structural approach to international law. To be sure, positivists have fretted over the methodology of determining state consent. But essentially, they have concerned themselves with describing the rules that already exist to structure relations between states. In contrast, liberalism in IL promotes the role of lawyers, retrained in the policy sciences, as progressive agents in world politics. Agency is also recovered by expanding the purview of international law to include decision-making processes that constitute world public order. Recent work by Anne-Marie Slaughter in the liberal IL school argues that the state has become 'disaggregated' as legislators, regulators and judges increasingly work with counterparts in other states and supranational organisations. Thus, seemingly national policy is often actually informed, harmonised and enforced by these transnational legislative, regulative and judicial networks.[83]

Fourth is the common concept of international law and institutions as playing a broad range of functions. For realists, institutions play a minimal role in facilitating state co-operation. Crucially, institutions will only be effective, even at this minimal level, when they serve and hence are supported by powerful states.[84] Liberals see institutions as playing a more independent role in promoting co-operation between states. In time, states may be bound together in patterns of institutionalised co-operation. Liberals recognise that institutions do benefit from the support of powerful states, but institutions can outlive powerful patrons and such support is not dependent on the institution serving the interests of the powerful. Indeed, great powers often bear a disproportionate share of the costs for international institutions because they recognise institutionalised co-operation as providing long-term system-wide benefits.[85] Liberals also present institutions as having the potential to supplant state action in some policy areas, such as trade and the environment. Positivists see more force in law than do most realists. But to sustain this

---

[82] Cecelia Lynch, 'E. H. Carr, international relations theory, and the societal origins of international legal norms,' *Millennium* 23 (1994), 589–619.

[83] Anne-Marie Slaughter, *A New World Order* (Princeton, NJ: Princeton University Press, 2004); see also Eric Stein, 'Lawyers, judges, and the making of a transnational constitution', *American Journal of International Law* 75 (1981), 1–27.

[84] John Mearsheimer, 'The false promise of institutions', *International Security* 19 (1994/95), 5–49.

[85] G. John Ikenberry, *After Victory: Institutions, Strategic Restraint, and the Rebuilding of Order After Major Wars* (Princeton, NJ: Princeton University Press, 2001).

position they narrowly define law as only those rules to which states have bound themselves in treaty and custom. Liberalism in IL recognises the important role of legal rules in regulating state activity. But law is also seen to play a far broader range of functions in enabling states and other actors to communicate, co-operate, reassure and ultimately live with one another. Hence, liberals recognise the role of 'soft law' in world politics; i.e., quasi-legal technical and policy agreements that prescribe behaviour for states, bureaucracies and private actors, but which are not, strictly speaking, binding.[86]

Constructivism

Realism and liberalism provide rationalist accounts of world politics: for realism, such rationality is informed by the distribution of power, for liberalism it is informed by the distribution of interests. In the 1990s, a new literature emerged in IR to challenge these rationalist theories. This rapidly growing literature examines how the world, and what goes on in it, is socially constructed – i.e., constructed by the very ideas that actors share with themselves and others about the world they live in, and (given these 'things') what they can and should do. Some rationalist scholars (i.e., neoliberalists) have conceded a minimal role for ideas as 'roadmaps' and rules that guide state action.[87] But constructivism gives ideas a more fundamental role, arguing that ideas operate 'all the way down' to shape actors and action in world politics.[88] Constructivism highlights the role of non-instrumental action, of social structures comprised of identities and norms, and of a broad range of normative actors in world politics. As such, it offers a fresh perspective on the formation and workings of international law.

Constructivism in IR

Constructivism in IR draws on social and sociological theory for its philosophical foundation. Arguably, most influential has been the sociology of Emile Durkheim and Max Weber. In his writings of the 1890s and early 1900s, Durkheim comes to grips with the role of ideas in social life. Thus, his concern is not with ideas residing inside people's heads but ideas that

---

[86] Dinah Shelton (ed.), *Commitment and Compliance: The Role of Non-Binding Norms in the International Legal System* (Oxford: Oxford University Press, 2000).

[87] Judith Goldstein and Robert O. Keohane (eds.), *Ideas and Foreign Policy: Beliefs, Institutions and Political Change* (Ithaca, NY: Cornell University Press, 1993).

[88] Alexander Wendt, *Social Theory of International Politics* (Cambridge: Cambridge University Press, 1999), pp. 92–138.

exist out there in the social world. Durkheim's starting point was that ideational factors are real and not reducible to other factors: thus, it was possible and necessary to subject them to scientific study. He argued that ideas become transformed through social interaction into 'social facts' – such as language, religious beliefs and ethical norms – and that once so established, these social facts influence behaviour. The question of *how* ideas influence behaviour was tackled by Weber in the late 1940s. Weber's causal theory required first uncovering the meaning of social facts for the actors concerned, and from this perspective locating action in its social context. Between them, Durkheim and Weber establish the philosophical underpinnings of constructivism – namely, that ideas provide the social context for, and hence make possible, meaningful action, and that the influence of such social facts on behaviour may, and indeed must be, subject to scientific study.[89]

Constructivists hold that who we think we are in large part determines what we want. Thus, states that perceive of themselves as great powers want to act and be recognised as such regardless of their actual relative material capabilities. Arguably, it was for this reason that small Sweden entered the Thirty Years' War against the mighty Habsburg Empire: this war did not serve Swedish interests but it did validate Swedish identity as a power to be reckoned with in seventeenth-century Europe.[90] Rationalists in IR take the interests of states (and other actors) as given: namely, to increase security and prosperity through (for realists) self-help and (for liberals) mutual-help activities. Constructivists problematise interests, arguing that they flow from identities. As Ted Hopf puts it: 'In telling you who you are, identities strongly imply a particular set of interests or preferences with respect to choices of action in particular domains, and with respect to particular actors.'[91] Thus, while realism and liberalism offer explanations for why states, given their interests and material capabilities, choose to fight or co-operate with one another, such rationalist theories cannot account for 'the content and source of state interests and the social fabric of world politics'.[92]

---

[89] This discussion of Durkheim and Weber is based on John Gerard Ruggie, 'What makes the world hang together? Neo-utilitarianism and the social constructivist challenge', *International Organization* 52 (1998), 857–61. For one of the first applications of Durkheim by a constructivist in IR, see Friedrich Kratochwil, 'The force of prescriptions', *International Organization* 38 (1984), 699–703.

[90] Erik Ringmar, *Identity, Interest and Action: A Cultural Explanation of Sweden's Intervention in the Thirty Years' War* (Cambridge: Cambridge University Press, 1996).

[91] Ted Hopf, 'The promise of constructivism in international relations theory', *International Security* 23, 1 (1998), 175.

[92] Jeffrey Checkel, 'The constructivist turn in international relations theory', *World Politics* 50 (1998), 324. On this point, see also Paul A. Kowert, 'National identity: inside and out', *Security Studies* 8 (1998/99), 2.

The social fabric of world politics contains norms as well as identities. Norms are inter-subjective beliefs about the social and material world that tell actors what they can and should do in given circumstances. These beliefs are inter-subjective in that they are shared by people and communities (hence they are 'social facts'). They are beliefs not only about social rules and conventions, but also about the physical world and the laws of science.[93] Thus, norms include both beliefs about what is right and proper (e.g., the belief that use of nuclear weapons is immoral),[94] and beliefs about what is doable and effective (e.g., beliefs about how nuclear weapons cause damage).[95] Norms encompass both thoughts and things, in that shared beliefs are enacted in social practice, embedded in institutions and embodied in artefacts. For instance, beliefs about the morality and effectiveness of different forms of warfare (such as strategic bombing, aircraft carrier warfare and armoured warfare) are embodied in military technologies, embedded in military doctrines and organisations, and enacted in military planning, training, and operations.[96] In this way norms do far more than simply regulate action, they operate at a deeper level to constitute and thereby enable meaningful action.[97]

Actors follow norms for a number of reasons. Norms often express the dominant ideas in a society and so they may be backed by sanctions – this is most obviously the case with domestic laws. Hence actors may act in conformity with norms so as to avoid such sanctions.[98] Norms may also be followed in order to realise self-interest. In short, actors may want to realise the stability and security afforded by a norm-governed order. But much of constructivist analysis is directed towards explaining that which rationalists cannot explain; namely, norm-compliant behaviour in the absence of incentives (be they sticks or carrots). Constructivists point to the process whereby actors are socialised into following norms. This socialisation process may involve elite learning of new norms, institution-alisation of norms in official policy, community laws and organisational

---

[93] Friedrich Kratochwil, *Rules, Norms and Decisions: On the Conditions of Practical and Legal Reasoning in International Relations and Domestic Affairs* (Cambridge: Cambridge University Press, 1989); Jan Golinski, *Making Natural Knowledge: Constructivism and the History of Science* (Cambridge: Cambridge University Press, 1998).

[94] Nina Tannenwald, *The Nuclear Taboo* (Cambridge: Cambridge University Press, forthcoming).

[95] Lynn Eden, *Whole World on Fire: Organizations, Knowledge and Nuclear Weapons Devastation* (Ithaca, NY: Cornell University Press, 2004).

[96] On the development of these forms of warfare, see Williamson Murray and Allan R. Millett (eds.), *Military Innovation in the Interwar Period* (Cambridge: Cambridge University Press, 1996).

[97] David Dessler, 'What's at stake in the agent-structure debate', *International Organization* 43 (1989), 454–6.

[98] G. John Ikenberry and Charles A. Kupchan, 'Socialization and hegemonic power', *International Organization* 44 (1990), 283–315.

structures, and internalisation of norms in community discourse and culture. Elite learning may be driven by sanctions or self-interest and so occur at a fairly shallow level. Institutionalisation is crucial because it embeds and empowers norms in community practice. Internalisation involves a deep learning process whereby actors accept the new norms as legitimate and appropriate. Of course, even shallow learning can, over time, lead to internalisation. Once internalised, norms are enacted automatically by actors. Indeed, norms may be followed even at the cost of self-interests because actors cannot imagine acting otherwise.[99]

Constructivism aspires to recognise the role of both structure and agency in world politics. It draws on structuration theory, which sees structures and agents as being mutually constituted.[100] Social structures comprise identities and norms that constitute actors, their social situation and range of social action. By engaging in action consistent with these identities and norms, actors validate and reproduce the social structure in question. Thus, just as human rights norms impact on and are codified in domestic laws and policy, they are also reaffirmed by the same said legislative, judicial and regulative practices. However, often constructivism comes across as a mostly structural theory of world politics. This is certainly the case when one is dealing with established normative systems, where the identities and norms in question have been internalised by actors. When norm-following is automatic, there is little room for agency.

Even as a mostly structural theory constructivism has much to offer. Indeed, Alexander Wendt's *Social Theory of International Politics* (1999), widely considered to be the most important work in constructivism in IR, is intended to be a critical response to the structural neorealism of Waltz's *Theory of International Politics*. The title of Wendt's book does rather give this away. Neorealism focuses solely on the material structure of world politics – i.e., the distribution of power – in accounting for state action. As suggested above, constructivism highlights the importance of prior social structures that give meaning to material things and relations. As Wendt notes, 'constructivists argue that material resources only acquire meaning for human action through the structure of shared knowledge in which they are embedded'. He goes on to give the example of the

---

[99] Joseph S. Nye, Jr., 'Nuclear learning and US–soviet security regimes', *International Organization* 41 (1987), 371–402; Martha Finnemore, *National Interests in International Society* (Ithaca, NY: Cornell University Press, 1996), pp. 22–31; Martha Finnemore and Kathryn Sikkink, 'International norm dynamics and political change', *International Organization* 52 (1998), 887–917.

[100] Alexander Wendt, 'The agent-structure problem in international relations theory', *International Organization* 41 (1987), 335–70.

United States fretting about North Korea having a nuclear weapon but not being bothered at all by Britain's large nuclear arsenal because 'the British are friends of the United States and the North Koreans are not'.[101] Wendt argues that the very thing that realists take for granted – that power politics is an inherent feature of an anarchical system – is the product of social structure. For Wendt 'there is no "logic" of anarchy apart from the practices that create and instantiate one structure of identities and interests rather than other'.[102] Instead, he suggests that 'anarchy can have at least three distinct cultures, Hobbesian, Lockean and Kantian, which are based on different role relationships, enemy, rival and friend'. These cultures acquire 'logics' over time through the social practices (war, co-operation and community building) they produce and are reproduced by.[103]

Agency does come back into constructivist theory when it comes to normative change. Most constructivist accounts of normative change involve norm entrepreneurs. These may be visionary leaders in policy communities, or powerful states in the world system – in other words, actors with the material resources to force through normative change. Sometimes normative change is needed to realign norm systems with new material realities. Here the trigger is often some kind of external shock to the normative system, and this external condition may also empower norm entrepreneurs.[104] The adoption of anti-militarist strategic cultures in Germany and Japan following the utter defeat of these states in WWII is one such example.[105] These accounts involving powerful leaders and external shock involve essentially instrumental processes. Normative change also involves social processes – argumentation, and discursive interventions in normative debate.[106] Here norm entrepreneurs draw on social resources – expertise and/or moral authority – to persuade

[101] Alexander Wendt, 'Constructing international politics', *International Security* 20 (1995), 73.

[102] Alexander Wendt, 'Anarchy is what states make of it: the social construction of power politics', *International Organization* 46 (1992), 395.

[103] Wendt, *Social Theory*, p. 309.

[104] Theo Farrell, *The Norms of War: Cultural Norms and Modern Conflict* (Boulder, CO: Lynne Rienner, 2005), pp. 13–14, 174; Jeffrey W. Legro, *Rethinking the World: Great Power Strategies and International Order* (Ithaca, NY: Cornell University Press, 2005).

[105] Peter J. Katzenstein, *Cultural Norms and National Security: Police and Military in Postwar Japan* (Ithaca, NY: Cornell University Press, 1996); Thomas U. Berger, *Cultures of Antimilitarism: National Security in Germany and Japan* (Baltimore, MD: Johns Hopkins, 1998).

[106] Thomas Risse, '"Let's Argue!": communicative action in world politics', *International Organization* 54 (2000), 1–30; Antje Wiener, 'Contested compliance: interventions in the normative structure of world politics', *European Journal of International Relations* 10 (2004), 189–234.

the community at large to accept new norms.[107] Thus, constructivist accounts of global normative change in the area of human rights and the environment highlight the role of socially empowered actors in transnational civil society (activist leaders and non-governmental organisations), as well as that of materially powerful progressive states.[108]

Most constructivists, certainly most American constructivists and all of those discussed above, are committed to the social scientific study of world politics. Following on from Durkheim and Weber, these 'conventional constructivists' seek to explore the causal impact of identities and norms on behaviour. However, we should note in closing that some 'critical constructivists' (mostly European scholars) take their cue from critical theories of IR. Critical theorists reject the whole enterprise of social science because it is based on the notion that scholars may objectively study social entities; for critical theorists, scholars project their own perspective on any social thing they study thus rendering impossible objective knowledge of that social thing. Critical theorists also seek to uncover the power relations that underpin and are reproduced by social relations, including knowledge-creating and knowledge-laden relations. A critical perspective on international law, as a knowledge-laden form of social relations, might note how it privileges some actors (sovereign states) over others (non-state actors). Academic disciplines, such as IR and IL, also reproduce social hierarchies in the so-called objective categories they propagate. In this sense, for critical theorists, knowledge is also 'for someone'. Conventional constructivists, in contrast, are less concerned with archaeology of power in social systems. They recognise that power plays a role in social practice, but equally they argue that norms (especially those that have been internalised) influence behaviour even in the absence of incentives. Finally, critical theorists tend to want to change the world, to somehow make it a better place. Conventional constructivists, again in contrast, have a normative focus but not a normative mission: because they are engaged in a social science of IR, constructivists take ethical and

[107] Peter M. Haas, 'Introduction: epistemic communities and international policy coordination', *International Organization* 46 (1992), 1–35; Rodney Bruce Hall, 'Moral authority as a power resource', *International Organization* 51 (1997), 591–622.
[108] Ethan A. Nadelmann, 'Global prohibition regimes: the evolution of norms in international society', *International Organization* 44 (1990), 479–526; Audie Klotz, *Norms in International Relations: The Struggle Against Apartheid* (Ithaca, NY: Cornell University Press, 1995); Margaret E. Keck and Kathryn Sikkink, *Activists Beyond Borders: Advocacy Networks in International Relations* (Ithaca, NY: Cornell University Press, 1998); Thomas Risse, Stephen C. Ropp and Kathryn Sikkink (eds.), *The Power of Human Rights* (Cambridge: Cambridge University Press, 1999); Richard Price, 'Reversing the gun sights: transnational civil society targets land mines', *International Organization* 52 (1998), 613–44.

emotional distance from their object of study (the norms themselves). In sum, while critical constructivists also 'aim to "denaturalize" the social world', in so doing they differ considerably in approach and purpose from conventional constructivists.[109]

Constructing international law

There is an emerging constructivist literature in IL. IL scholars have mostly taken a critical constructivist approach. At the same time, conventional constructivists in IR are beginning to turn their attention to the matter of international law.

In their survey of the two disciplines for the *American Journal of International Law*, Slaughter *et al.* do discuss the constructivist approach to IL. They correctly note that fundamental to such an approach is the notion that legal norms 'play a *constitutive* role in the formation of actors' identities and interests and in the structure of the international system itself'. Marti Koskenniemi and Shirley Scott are both presented as constructivists in this discussion because they examine how legitimating discourses underpin power relations in world politics. For example, how discourses of security and aggression empower some states (the Western powers) and marginalise others ('rogue states').[110] However, if they are constructivists, then Koskenniemi and Scott belong in the 'critical' rather than the 'conventional' camp. Much like critical constructivists in IR, both are critical of the positivist project to objectify international law, and both seek to uncover the power relations embedded in and reproduced by the legal structure of world politics. Indeed, strictly speaking, they belong to the critical legal studies approach to IL (also known as New Stream scholarship). As David Kennedy (a leading scholar of this approach) notes, critical legal studies aims to interrogate deeply international law, to 'concentrate upon discourse and upon the hidden ideologies, attitudes and structures which lie behind discourse, rather than the subject matter of legal talk'.[111] Thus, Kennedy explores the supposed division of labour and actual tension between doctrines that define participation and jurisdiction in international law, and doctrines that define

---

[109] Hopf, 'Promise of constructivism,' p. 182. See also Richard Price and Christian Reus-Smit, 'Dangerous liaisons? Critical international theory and constructivism', *European Journal of International Relations* 4 (1998), 259–94.

[110] Slaughter, Tulumello and Wood, 'International law', p. 382.

[111] Cited in Robert J. Beck, Anthony Clark Arend, and Robert D. Vander Lugt, *International Rules: Approaches from International Law and International Relations* (Oxford: Oxford University Press, 1996), p. 227.

the sources and substance of international law.[112] As it happens, Koskenniemi's first major book on international law conceived of it in terms of a structure of 'argumentative moves and positions'.[113] This was reasonably consistent with the structural normative approach of conventional constructivism. But in his latest book, *The Gentle Civilizer of Nations*, Koskenniemi moves away from any suggestion that the normative content and processes of international law might be fixed for the purpose of causal analysis. Thus, international law is reconceived as 'a particular sensibility, or set of attitudes and preconceptions about matters international'. He describes an international sensibility that is historically contingent and directed towards international reform on the model of Western 'civilisation' and institutional modernity. Koskenniemi prefers the concept of 'sensibility' to that of 'ideas' (or 'norms') because sensibility suggests a more fluid inter-subjective world – one more easily able to accommodate contradiction and change.[114]

Less well developed is the conventional constructivist approach to IL.[115] And yet, this approach has much to offer.[116] Indeed, we would argue that it offers a more promising line of engagement with positivism and the legal process theory than do critical legal studies, because it accepts the epistemology of traditional and liberal approaches to international law. In other words, conventional constructivism seeks to develop objective knowledge of the social world and workings of international law. We would suggest the following as four key contributions and core principles of an emerging conventional constructivism of IL.

First is the focus on norms – ethical, political and legal – as explanatory variables in world politics. This contrasts with the purging of normative considerations from legal positivism and realism. It also differs significantly from liberal approaches to IR and IL. Norms are important to

---

[112] David Kennedy, 'A New Stream of International Law Scholarship', *Wisconsin International Law Journal* 7 (1988), reproduced in Beck, Arend and Vander Lugt (eds.), *International Rules*, pp. 244–7.

[113] Martti Koskenniemi, *From Apology to Utopia: The Structure of International Legal Argument* (Helsinki: Lakimiesliiton kustannus, 1989).

[114] Martti Koskenniemi, *The Gentle Civilizer of Nations: The Rise and Fall of International Law, 1870–1960* (Cambridge: Cambridge University Press, 2005), pp. 1–3.

[115] Important exceptions include the work of Ryan Goodman, Derek Jinks and Oona A. Hathaway. See Goodman and Jinks, 'How to influence states: socialisation and international human rights law', *Duke Law Journal* 54 (2004), 621–703; and Hathaway, 'Between power and principle: an integrated theory of international law', *University of Chicago Law Review* 72 (469), 469–536.

[116] Indeed, this is noted in Kenneth W. Abbot, 'Toward a richer institutionalism for international law and policy', *Journal of International Law and International Relations* 1 (2005), 9–34.

liberal IR theory, but these norms are considered to be rational in origin and operation: thus, norms of co-operation and of 'bounded competition' come from situations where the logic of mutual gain applies. Where this logic is absent, such as in situations of intense militarised competition, liberals readily concede ground to realist power politics. Constructivists take a very different view. Norms define social situations: the roles of actors and 'rules of the game'. As Wendt argues, interstate relations do have logics (Hobbesian, Lockean and Kantian), but these are defined by the distribution of identities and interests and not by the distribution of interests and power between actors. Norms are central to legal process theory, but this is a very different notion of norms – norms as core values to be promoted within a sustainable world public order. In contrast, constructivists seek to recover the meaning of norms for those communities that practise them. So although both approaches attribute social power to norms, liberal IL scholars seek to harness that power while constructivists seek to explain it.

Second is a concept of structure that differs significantly from that offered by realism and positivism. The only structure that matters for realists is that created by the distribution of power in the world system – hence the realist obsession with the number of great powers and with balancing dynamics in international relations. Positivism conceives of international law as a system of legal rules that structure relations between states. Material power also matters to this positivist concept of structure in that legal rules depend on state support (i.e., state consent), if not on sanctions, to work. We discussed above how constructivists examine the *social* structures of world politics. As one leading constructivist, Martha Finnemore, has pointed out, customary international law is one such obvious social structure in that it 'exists only when there is a norm', in other words when there is *opinio juris* and state practice.[117] The most thorough constructivist treatment of international law as a social structure is provided by Christian Reus-Smit. Reus-Smit presents international law and multilateralism as 'fundamental institutions' that structure interstate relations. These institutions are 'generic structural elements of international society' in that the practice of them transcends the distribution of power and interests in the world system. These fundamental institutions in turn rest on three metavalues, or 'constitutional structures', that constitute international society: the moral purpose of the state, the norm of sovereignty and the norm of pure procedural justice. This perspective on the normative structure of the international system enables Reus-Smit to

[117] Finnemore, *National Interests in International Society*, p. 139.

uncover the 'deeper intersubjective values that define legitimate agency and action'; values that precede and are reflected in the international law.[118]

Third is a conception of agency that recognises the social foundations of state primacy but also the role of non-state actors in influencing normative change. Realist and positivist state-centrism rests on material power: for realists, states have the power to ignore international law (and other non-state forces in world politics); for positivists, only states have the power to make and break international law. Several constructivists have pointed to the crucial role of the norm of sovereignty in empowering states. This constructivist work highlights the social power of states by denaturalising the power that states (and IR and IL scholars) take for granted: the power to tax citizens, to control domestic markets and to use force at home and aboard. The norm of sovereignty legitimates these activities and thereby enables states to have these seemingly material powers.[119] At the same time, constructivists have pointed to the role of non-state actors in leading and supporting normative change. As we noted earlier, this is most evident in constructivist studies on evolving norms of human rights, where the agents for change come from domestic and transnational civil society. In highlighting the role of non-state actors, especially in promoting human rights, constructivism shares a common focus of the liberal IL school. But not a common cause: constructivists seek to explain the process of progressive normative change whereas liberal IL scholars seek to affect such a process.

Finally is appreciation not only of the broad functions but also the deep constitutive effect of international law. Constructivism reveals world politics to involve the interplay of rational and social action: what counts as rational action is socially determined, by norms and identity, and norms are in turn often deployed rationally by 'skilled users of culture'.[120] This is certainly true with international law. As Stephen Toope argues, there is invariably some competition between beliefs and interests in the process of determining norms. Thus, norm construction, enactment and

---

[118] Christian Reus-Smit, 'The constitutional structure of international society and the nature of fundamental institutions', *International Organization* 51 (1997), 555–6, 585.

[119] Wendt, 'Anarchy is what states make of it', p. 413; J. Samuel Barkin and Bruce Cronin, 'The state and the nation: changing norms and the rules of sovereignty in international relations', *International Organization* 48 (1994): 107–30; Ian Hurd, 'Legitimacy and authority in international politics', *International Organization* 53 (1999), 397–9.

[120] Ann Swidler, 'Culture in action', *American Sociological Review* 51, 2 (1986), 273–86; Theo Farrell, 'World culture and military power', *Security Studies* 14 (2005), 448–88.

change involves politics.[121] Reus-Smit suggests that politics involves four forms of reason and action – idiographic, purposive, ethical and instrumental – which express and replicate, respectively, social identities, actor interests, shared moral principles and preferred means of action. All are involved in the politics of international law. And accordingly, international law serves to define and validate state sovereignty and jurisdiction, to protect the core interests of most states and humankind, to advance those core values shared by all states and to enable states to co-operate.

International law does these things through the broad range of functions identified by liberal IL scholars, by providing modes of legitimation, communication, reassurance and co-operation. To this list constructivists would add 'mode of argumentation'. But legal process scholars underplay the constitutive effect of these various modes of action: progressive advancement of human rights and/or peaceful relations between states is to be achieved by manipulating state interests – through increased transborder trade, institutionalised co-operation or liberal imposed order – to increase the incentives for supporting these values.[122] For constructivists, these activities and other forms of social interaction have the power to transform the identities of states and other actors in world politics. This is nicely illustrated by the work of Harold Koh.[123] Consistent with liberalism in IL, Koh conceives of international law in terms of a process involving transnational networks of governmental and non-governmental actors. But consistent with constructivism, this 'transnational legal process is normative, dynamic and constitutive'. Koh presents a process with three stages: first 'interaction' between transnational actors, leading to 'interpretation' of an international norm, and finally 'internalisation' of that norm in the domestic legal system of applicable states. Thus, in seeking to explain why states obey international law, Koh argues that it is mostly due to 'internalized obedience' rather than 'enforced compliance'.[124] In other words, international law operates at a deep level to shape how states and other actors see themselves, their social situations, and the possibilities of action.

---

[121] Stephen J. Toope, 'Emerging patterns of governance and international law', in Michael Byers (ed.), *The Role of Law in International Politics* (Oxford: Oxford University Press, 2000), p. 102.

[122] The rationalism of liberal approaches to IL is also evident in the special issue of *International Organization* on 'Legalization and world politics', See *International Organization* 54 (2000).

[123] To be fair to Slaughter *et al.*, they correctly identify Koh as a constructivist. See Slaughter, Tulumello and Wood, 'International law' p. 381.

[124] Harold Hongju Koh, 'Why do nations obey international law', *Yale Law Journal* 106 (1997), 2598–9.

Table 3.1 *Interdisciplinary lenses on international law*

Realist	Liberal	Constructivist
– descriptive theory	– prescriptive theory	– explanatory theory
– value-free approach	– promotion of core values	– norms as explanatory variables
– state-centric	– plurality of actors	– state primacy and civil society
– structural (material)	– emphasis on agency	– structural (social)
– law as rules	– law serving range of functions	– law as constituting world politics

Volume themes

The literatures discussed above provide three interdisciplinary lenses through which to view our themes of content, compliance and change in international law. Table 3.1 summarises what each interdisciplinary lens says about international law and thereby illustrates the differences between them. We can see that each serves a different purpose. In essence, realists seek to descript international law, liberals seek to prescribe it and constructivists seek to explain it. Each lens has a different approach to values. Realists seek to banish values from the law, liberals seek to promote core values and constructivists look upon values, and norms more generally, as explanatory variables. Each lens has a different take on state primacy in international law. Realists take state primacy as an empirical fact based on state power and state sovereignty. Liberals emphasise the plurality of actors in world politics – including individuals, non-governmental organisations, multinational corporations and international and inter-governmental organisations. Some liberals also disaggregate the state into domestic constituencies and inter-linking transnational networks. Constructivists take a midway approach. Some recognise the primacy of the state as a social fact that needs to be explained. In interrogating the evolution of state sovereignty the inference is that the social world may change and become less state-centric.[125] Other constructivists explore the role of socially resourceful non-state actors, mostly from transnational civil society, in influencing domestic and international normative change. Each lens differs on the structure of world politics. Realism offers a material structural account of international law – law comprises state-empowered rules underpinned more generally by a functioning balance of power. Liberalism emphasises agency in international law – both in terms of the range of agents and also in terms of the power of agency

---

[125] Alexander Wendt, 'Why a world state is inevitable', *European Journal of International Relations* 4, 9 (2003), 491–542.

Table 3.2 *Interdisciplinary lenses applied to volume themes*

	Interdisciplinary lens		
Theme	Realist	Liberal	Constructivist
Content	Rules	Values	Discourse
Compliance	Coercion and consent	Self-interest and fairness	Persuasion, congruence and habit
Change	Formal process	Policy process	Social process

to affect progressive change in international law. Constructivism tends towards structural theory, but in so doing emphasises social structure, both in terms of the social foundations of international law, and of the legal constitution of world politics. Finally, each lens attributes different functions to international law. For realists, law amounts to rules that regulate interstate relations. For liberals, law fulfils a broader range of functions, permitting states and other actors to communicate and co-operate with one another. Constructivists also see international law as carrying out a broad array of instrumental functions which more than facilitating co-operation actually constitute actors and action in world politics.

In the rest of this section, we discuss how these three interdisciplinary lenses apply to our three volume themes. At this stage, we only want to sketch out these applications; we leave it to the empirical chapters to explore them in greater detail. Table 3.2 illustrates how our lenses map onto our themes.

The content of international law

Determining the content of international law is the major concern of realism. As we noted, realists take a minimalist view of law as binding rules to which states have explicitly consented in treaties and tacitly consented in customary practice. In stark contrast, liberals have an enlarged view of international law, as encompassing core community values. Finally, constructivists see international law as a discourse of identity representation and norm enactment. Here we mean discourse in the broadest sense as encompassing all forms of expressive social practice – communication, argumentation, deliberation and action.

We shall look for particular evidence of each of these forms of content in the chapters that follow on substantive areas of international law. For rules, we shall concentrate on treaty law, as this provides the clearest evidence of law to which states have consented. That said, in some areas, such as use of force, we shall also consider customary law. Next we shall examine whether any of the three core liberal values – human dignity, world peace (via strategic stability) or liberal democracy – are present in the law on use of force, human rights, international crime, trade and the environment. Finally, in examining the law as discourse, we shall focus on the shared principles underlying state use of, and deliberation about, the law in each of these areas.

Compliance with international law

This theme is about how the law works and has causal impact on world politics. Each of our lenses accounts offers multiple reasons for state compliance. As we noted, legal positivism is more concerned with describing what international law is than with explaining how it works. Nonetheless, the realist lens does point to two reasons for compliance – coercion and consent. Coercion is central to command theory whereby legal rules depend on sanctions to be effective. Realism also suggests that where powerful states have an interest in a particular legal rule or regime, they may coerce other weaker states into compliance.[126] Consent is central to the modern positivist move from the concept of law as command to law as expressing the free will of states. The notion of consent is codified in modern international law. Under article 52 of the 1969 Vienna Convention on the Law of Treaties, a 'treaty shall be void if its conclusion has been procured by the threat or use of force'. However, coercion is not ruled out altogether. The Vienna Conference did issue a Declaration on the Prohibition of Military, Political or Economic Coercion in the Conclusion of Treaties, but because this broader definition was not incorporated in the convention itself, use of political and economic coercion to get a state to sign up to a treaty may not be illegal.[127] Coercion operates more generally in that many legal rules *are* backed by the threat of sanctions. These rules may be contained in treaties that states have become a party to or in customary law. It is true that states may avoid being bound by rules of customary law if they persistently object, but this is provided that the rules do not express peremptory norms of international law from which derogation is not permitted (such as war crimes norms), and in

---

[126] This is noted in Oona A. Hathaway who incorrectly identifies the coincidence of great-power interests and legal rule as the caused factor. Such coincidence is a *correlative* factor but compliance is *caused* by the ability and willingless of great powers to coerce weaker states. Hathaway, 'Do human rights treaties make a difference', *Yale Law Journal* III (2002), 1944–5.

[127] Antonio Cassese, *International Law* (Oxford: Oxford University Press, 2003), p. 127.

any case the social and political pressures to conform to new customary law usually overwhelm objectors.[128]

Explaining the workings of international law also comes second in liberalism in IL to the task of prescribing law. Those liberal IL scholars that do focus on state compliance with international law identify two reasons – self-interest and fairness. Self-interest lies at the heart of Henkin's account of why states obey international law. For Henkin, states are rational actors who carefully weigh up the benefits of compliance and costs of non-compliance. He concludes that 'barring an infrequent non-rational act, nations will observe international obligations unless violation promises an important balance of advantage over cost'.[129] Of course, the advantages of compliance include the general benefits of legal order beyond any immediate benefits from a particular treaty. Hence Higgins notes: 'It is rarely in the national interest to violate international law, even though there might be short-term advantages in doing so.'[130] Self-interest is also central to liberal institutionalism, whereby co-operation serves state interests and is facilitated by legal regimes. Franck argues that states comply with legal rules they perceive to be fair both in substance (by providing distributive justice) and in procedure (by providing right process). The McDougal–Lasswell legacy is evident in Franck's approach. Thus, for Franck 'distributive justice is rooted in the moral values of the community in which the legal system operates'. Right process is a function both of the attributes of specific rules (e.g., compliance will be greater for rules that are clear and consistently applied) and of the procedural regularity and legitimacy of the whole system of international law. Obviously, there can be a tension between these two aspects – especially as distributive justice often demands progressive change while right process rests on stable order.[131]

Constructivism, which is very much concerned with explaining the social world, suggests three possible reasons for state compliance with international law – persuasion, congruence and habit. The role of persuasion in getting states to abide by legal norms is highlighted especially in constructivist studies on human rights and environmental protection. As we noted earlier, often it has been non-state actors who have been promoting these causes (such as Human Rights Watch, the International Committee of the Red Cross (ICRC) and Greenpeace) and usually persuasion is the only tool at their disposal. Persuasion rests on the expertise

---

[128] Byers, *Custom*, pp.102–5.
[129] Henkin, *How Nations Behave*, as cited in Koh, 'Why do nations obey?' p. 2621.
[130] Higgins, *Problems and Process*, p. 16.
[131] Thomas M. Franck, *Fairness in International Law and Institutions* (Oxford: Oxford University Press, 1997), pp.1–46, quote from p. 8.

and/or moral standing of non-state actors. Obviously, states may also rely on persuasion to induce peers to comply when material power is unavailable or inapplicable. Constructivists also point to the importance of congruence between the norm in question and the normative system of the compliant or non-compliant state. The proposition is fairly obvious but well made nonetheless in constructivist studies, namely, when there is congruence, norm-following behaviour (compliance in our terms) is more likely than when there is not. Congruence is not an exact measure; rather, constructivists suggest plotting congruence on a sliding scale running from norm match to norm clash.[132] Finally, as we discussed earlier, much norm-following for constructivists is routine, everyday and automatic. In other words, it occurs habitually.[133] Koh suggests that when international law has been internalised in the domestic legal system 'through executive action, judicial interpretation, legislative action, or some combination of the three', it produces 'institutional habits that lead nations into default patterns of compliance'.[134] Thus, compliance becomes a matter of habit.

These reasons for compliance have been differentiated for the purposes of analytical clarity. In the real world, any actual instance of compliance is likely to involve a mix of these reasons. Moreover, there is some overlap between the reasons themselves. For instance, consent comes into Franck's theory as a key pillar of procedural legitimacy in international law (namely, the principle that state sovereignty may only be restricted by consent).[135] Equally, as we saw, legitimacy (an aspect of fairness) comes into Arend's theory of why states consent to legal rules and is suggested by Hart's theory that states comply out of a sense of obligation. Our job, therefore, is to determine which reasons best capture the bulk of state compliance in the various areas of law we examine in this volume.

Change in international law

Legal change is under-theorised in IL. This is hardly surprising since law is slow to change by nature. Treaties are laborious to produce, sometimes agonisingly so for those involved. In principle, customary law can appear overnight provided there is consistency and general conformity among

---

[132] Jeffrey T. Checkel, 'Norms, institutions, and national identity in contemporary europe', *International Studies Quarterly* 43 (1999), 86–7; Andrew P. Cortell and James W. Davis, 'Understanding the domestic impact of international norms: a research agenda', *International Studies Review* 2 (2000), 70–2.

[133] Habitual norm-following is most effectively explored in Ted Hopf, *Social Construction of International Politics: Identities and Foreign Policies, Moscow, 1955 and 1999* (Ithaca, NY: Cornell University Press, 2002).

[134] Koh, 'Why do nations obey?' pp. 2655, 2657.   [135] Franck, *Fairness*, p. 29.

states in the new practice. But in reality, it is generally recognised that all states that may be bound by the new customary norm must be given the opportunity to protest against its creation, and this takes time.[136] An exception is judicial interpretation, by a domestic or international court, which can produce rapid legal change.

Given the dearth of theorising about change in international law, we shall explore this theme inductively in our substantive chapters. Notwithstanding, we may use our three lenses to outline, in broad terms, three processes of change: formal, policy and social. The notion of international law as a process is closely associated with liberal approaches, but change is a process and as such may be described by the realist lens. This lens would suggest a formal process with two key characteristics: first, the agents of change are sovereign states; second, change requires state consent. Legal change is not possible from the realist perspective in the absence of state consent. Change and process are both integral to the liberal lens. Liberals seek progressive change in international law to advance core community values. Liberals combine this normative agenda with a view of law as an authoritative decision-making process. We suggest that these two characteristics – ends and means – amount to a conception of legal change as a policy process. Hence, McDougal and Lasswell's original project to retrain lawyers as policy specialists. From the liberal perspective, this policy process involves executive, legislative and judicial action, especially by authoritative decision-making bodies, and a plurality of actors including activist groups, trans-governmental networks and international organisations. Constructivists have been accused of neglecting change in their theories of social action.[137] This is understandable, since constructivists have concentrated on explaining how we almost automatically enact social roles and norms. As constructivism suggests, once norms have become internalised, change becomes very difficult. After all, habits are hard to break. But constructivism does account for change. Indeed, there are plenty of constructivist studies on norm evolution, and these all point to this as a social process involving elite learning, community socialisation, and/or internalisation of new norms. As discussed earlier, both norm entrepreneurs (both socially empowered and materially powerful) and external shock figure prominently in constructivists, accounts of more rapid, non-evolutionary, forms of normative

[136] H. Meijers, 'How is international law made? The stages of growth in international law and the use of its customary rules', *Netherlands Yearbook of International Law* 9 (1978), 23–4.

[137] Paul Kowert and Jeffrey Legro, 'Norms, identity and their limits: a theoretical reprise', in Peter J. Katzenstein (ed.), *The Culture of National Security* (New York: Columbia University Press, 1996), pp. 488–90.

change. A recent study has suggested that these factors are also important in affecting change in international law.[138]

Discussion questions

- What are the core principles of realism? What distinguishes neorealism from classical realism? Is international law irrelevant for realists?
- What are the core principles of legal positivism in international law? Why did it replace natural law in the nineteenth century? How did legal positivists reconcile the notion of states as sovereigns and as subjects of international law? What place does the balance of power occupy in positivist thinking about the international legal system?
- What are the four principles of our interdisciplinary *realist lens*? What are the points of disagreement between realists and legal positivists?
- What are the core principles of liberalism? What distinguishes republican liberalism from commercial liberalism? What distinguishes liberal from neoliberal institutionalism? What is argued in liberal democratic peace theory?
- What are the core principles of legal process theory? How did McDougal and Lasswell seek to respond to the challenge from realism in IR? How did legal process theory develop in the 1960s–70s? What is argued in the new liberalism of IL (by Franck, Teson and Slaughter)?
- What are the four principles of our interdisciplinary *liberal lens*? What are the points of disagreement between liberalism and legal process scholars?
- For constructivists, how do identities and norms function to shape actors and action in world politics? How is agency returned to the mostly structural constructivist world-view? What is the distinction between critical and conventional constructivism?
- What are the three principles of our interdisciplinary *constructivist lens*? How is this lens distinct from critical legal scholarship?
- What do the realist, liberal and constructivist lenses say about the content of, compliance with, and change in international law?

SUGGESTIONS FOR FURTHER READING

For readings on each of the various schools of theory examined in this chapter, you are directed to the sources cited in the footnotes. Below we list a number of scholarly works that seek to bridge IR and IL.

---

[138] Paul F. Diehl, Charlotte Ku and Daniel Zamora, 'The dynamics of international law: the interaction of normative and operating systems', *International Organization* 57 (2003), 57–61.

Armstrong, David, Theo Farrell and Bice Maiguashca (eds.), *Force and Legitimacy in World Politics*, Cambridge: Cambridge University Press, 2005.

Beck, Robert J., Anthony Clark Arend and Robert D. Vander Lugt, *International Rules: Approaches from International Law and International Relations*, Oxford: Oxford University Press, 1996.

Biersteker, Thomas J., Peter J. Spiro, Chandra Lekha Sriram and Veronica Raffo (eds.), *International Law and International Relations: Bridging Theory and Practice*, London: Routledge, 2007.

Byers, Michael, *Custom, Power, and the Power of Rules: International Relations and Customary International Law*, Cambridge: Cambridge University Press, 1999.

(ed.), *The Role of Law in International Politics: Essays in International Relations and International Law*, Oxford: Oxford University Press, 2001.

Finnemore, Martha, and Stephen J. Toope, 'Alternatives to "legalization": richer views of law and politics', *International Organization* 55, 3 (2001), pp. 743–58.

Hathaway, Oona A., 'Between power and principle, an integrated theory of international law'. *University of Chicago Law Review* 72 (469), 469–536.

Hathaway, Oona A. and Harold Hongju Koh (eds.), *Foundations of International Law and Politics*, New York: Foundation Press, 2005.

Joyner, Christopher C., *International Law in the 21st Century: Rules for Global Governance*, Lanham: Rowan and Littlefield, 2005.

Koh, Harold Hongju, 'Why Do Nations Obey?' *Yale Law Journal* 106 (1997), 2599–659.

'Legalization and World Politics', special issue of *International Organization* 54, 3 (2000).

Reus-Smit, Christian (ed.), *The Politics of International Law*, Cambridge: Cambridge University Press, 2004.

Scott, Shirley V., *International Law in World Politics: An Introduction*, Boulder, CO: Lynne Rienner, 2004.

Simpson, Gerry, *Great Powers and Outlaw States: Unequal Sovereigns in the International Legal Order*, Cambridge: Cambridge University Press, 2004.

Slaughter, Anne-Marie, Andrew S. Tulumello and Stepan Wood, 'International Law and International Relations Theory: A New Generation of Interdisciplinary Scholarship', *American Journal of International Law* 92 (1998), 367–97.

Slaughter Burley, Anne-Marie, 'International law and international relations theory: a dual agenda', *American Journal of International Law* 87 (1993), 205–39.

Yasuaki, Onuma, 'International law in and with international politics: functions of international law in international society', *European Journal of International Law* 14, 1 (2005), 105–39.

Part II

The law in world politics

4 Use of force

The power of international law is severely tested when it comes to the use of force by states. The development of modern international law was spurred on by the quest to eliminate war from world politics. War in the industrial age promised to be more awful than ever before experienced by humankind. And indeed the two world wars of the twentieth century claimed countless millions of lives and left whole continents in tatters. Hence, the use of force was prohibited in the new United Nations system. This prohibition is further supported by a larger corpus of treaty and customary international law. The only exceptions permitted under the UN Charter are the use of force in self-defence, and when authorised by the United Nations Security Council (UNSC) for the purpose of protecting international peace and security. Notwithstanding this, states have continued to use force not in self-defence and without UNSC authorisation.

It is clear that law, in itself, is a poor restraint on the use of force by states. This is recognised in the realist lens by the emphasis placed on a functioning balance of power as a necessary enabler for international law to function. Viewed from a narrow perspective, therefore, international law is weak in the face of state power. But viewed more broadly, international law on the use of force clearly captures values in the international community and provides a discourse on the legitimacy of using force. The first section examines the content of the law in this area as rules, values and discourse, and gives detailed consideration to the evolving law on use of force in self-defence and for humanitarian purposes. The second section discusses why states comply, when they do, with the legal prohibition on using force. The formal, policy and social process of change in law on the use of force are examined in the third section. We conclude by considering the impact of increasing legalisation on the occurrence of war in the contemporary world.

The law on use of force

Use of force is clearly regulated by rules of treaty and customary international law. Use of force is prohibited under Article 2(4) of the UN Charter, which declares that '[a]ll members shall refrain in their international relations from the threat or use of force against the territorial integrity or political independence of any state, or in any other manner inconsistent with the purposes of the United Nations.'[1] This prohibition is widely taken to refer to 'armed force', as opposed to non-military forms of coercion. At the same time, by referring to force, this prohibition covers the use of armed force below the threshold of war proper. Also covered is the threat of use of force. This point was clarified by the International Court of Justice (ICJ) in its 1996 opinion on the *Legality of the Threat or Use of Nuclear Weapons*, where the Court noted that 'if the use of force in a given case is illegal – the threat to use force will likewise be illegal'.[2] As noted above, the UN Charter recognises two exceptions to the prohibition on the use of force: Article 51 recognises 'the inherent right of individual or collective self-defence'; and Chapter VII provides that the UNSC may authorise the use of force to protect or restore international peace and security.

A number of other treaties sustain the normative prohibition on state use of force. Most significant is the 1928 General Treaty for the Renunciation of War (also known as the Kellogg–Briand Pact). Under Article 1, the parties undertake to 'condemn recourse to war for the solution of international controversies, and renounce it as an instrument of national policy'. Notwithstanding the obvious recourse to aggressive war by the fascist states during World War II, the Kellogg–Briand Pact carries considerable normative weight since all but four states in the interwar period signed up for it. Moreover, in addition to informing Article 2(4) of the UN Charter, the Kellogg–Briand Pact remains in force today with sixty-three states being party to it.[3] Also significant is the 1970 Declaration on Principles of International Law Concerning Friendly Relations which elaborates the prohibition on the use of force by:
- declaring war of aggression to be a war crime
- prohibiting states from using force to change borders, resolve disputes or in reprisal

---

[1] UN Charter available at www.un.org/aboutun/charter/.
[2] International Court of Justice (ICJ), 'Legality of the threat or use of nuclear weapons', General List no. 95, 8 July 1996, para. 47 [hereafter *Nuclear Weapons* Opinion], at www.icj-cij.org/icjwww/icases/iunan/iunanframe.htm.
[3] Ian Brownlie, *Principles of Public International Law*, 6th edition (Oxford: Oxford University Press, 2003), pp. 698–9.

- prohibiting the use of force to oppress people seeking self-determination
- prohibiting states from supporting terrorist acts or insurgency in another state.

The Declaration is not binding and so, strictly speaking, has no force in law. But it does provide an authoritative interpretation of Article 2(4) of the UN Charter.[4]

Equally important is customary law which comprises the values held by the international community regarding the legitimacy of recourse to force. The Kellogg–Briand Pact has been taken as evidence of a customary norm prohibiting the use of force. But customary law may be traced much further back to natural law, which recognises the sovereign right of states to use force in given circumstances. In the 1986 *Nicaragua* case, the ICJ found that the UN Charter did not, as some commentators had suggested, replace customary law on the use of force. Since Article 51 referred to an 'inherent' right of self-defence, the ICJ reasoned that 'it is hard to see how this [right] can be other than of a customary nature, even if its present content has been confirmed and influenced by the [UN] Charter'.[5]

Traditionally, distinction is drawn in customary international law between *jus ad bellum* (law on recourse to war) and *jus in bello* (law on the conduct of war). Natural law on both originates in the 'just war' tradition. This tradition, which combines Christian theology, secular moral philosophy, and medieval military and diplomatic practice, provides the resources for practical ethical reasoning about the legitimacy of using force. These philosophical resources centre on an evolving set of criteria for when and how force may be used justly. Whilst this is a Western tradition of thought, many of the principles contained within just war thinking may also be found in Islamic religious doctrine and political thought.[6] This chapter focuses on *jus ad bellum*; we shall leave *jus in bello* to the next chapter when we discuss international humanitarian law. However, we do need to be mindful of the considerable overlap in the principles of *jus ad bellum* and *jus in bello*. For instance, the principle of proportionality applies to both, whereby the recourse to and conduct of military action must do more good than harm.

The notion of just war (and its inverse, unjust war) was recognised as far back as ancient Rome. As we noted in Chapter 2, under Roman

---

[4] Malcolm Shaw, *International Law*, 5th edition (Cambridge: Cambridge University Press, 2005), p. 1018.

[5] ICJ, 'Case concerning military and paramilitary activities in and against Nicaragua', Merits, 27 June 1986, para. 176, at www.icj-cij.org/icjwww/icases/inus/inusframe.htm.

[6] John Kelsay, 'Al-Shaybani and the Islamic law of war', *Journal of Military Ethics* 2 (2003), 63–75.

law the state could wage war only once an opponent had declined the opportunity to satisfy Rome's demands. Moreover, a college of priests were charged with determining whether there were sufficient grounds, in terms of the offences committed by the opponent, for justifying war. These legal requirements have symbolic importance for thinking about just war, even if they are unlikely to have operated actually to restrain Roman leaders at the time. Christian theology was originally opposed to all forms of war when Rome was ruled by pagans. But when Christianity became the official religion of the Holy Roman Empire, Christian theologians had to find some way of reconciling the evil of war with the moral necessity of using force to protect the empire. The key philosopher here was St Augustine, who in the fifth century suggested that war could be justly waged to protect the faithful. The principles of just war were elaborated by St Aquinas in the thirteenth century. Aquinas argued that 'just cause' for war was to be found in righting wrongs – to remedy wrongful acts and/or punish wrongdoers. Aquinas also proposed two additional principles: the principle of 'rightful authority' whereby war was not a private matter but had to be conducted under the authority of a prince; and the principle of 'rightful intent', whereby those using force had to do so with the intent of doing good and avoiding evil. International law, as it developed from the late Middle Ages on, was substantially concerned with regulating relations between newly emerging nation-states, and between European states and the extra-European world. The idea that only just war was permissible was widely accepted by jurists of this period who, accordingly, focused on elucidating lists of just causes for recourse of force. Often political concerns – such as legitimating the forceful acquisition of resources in Asia and the Americas – coloured these lists.[7]

Just war principles applied to individuals as they exercised public duties – namely, the duty of war. And while just war tradition provided moral guidance that applied beyond as well as within the Christian world (unlike Islamic injunctions on war which only applied in the 'house of Islam'), it was not concerned with promoting human dignity (nor, obviously, world peace). Thus, just wars should be waged in a manner that protected innocents but (contrary to the modern practice of humanitarian intervention) not for the purpose of protecting innocents.[8] The just

---

[7] James Turner Johnson, *Just War Tradition and the Restraint of War: A Moral and Historical Inquiry* (Princeton, NJ: Princeton University Press, 1981); Yoram Dinstein, *War, Aggression and Self-Defence*, 2nd edition, repr. (Cambridge: Cambridge University Press, 1995), pp. 61–5; Stephen C. Neff, *War and the Law of Nations: A General History* (Cambridge: Cambridge University Press, 2005), pp. 39–82.

[8] This limitation in the just war tradition is explored in Ian Holliday, 'When is a cause just?' *Review of International Studies* 28 (2002), 557–76.

war tradition ran into trouble when it was deployed by opposing sides in the intra-faith religious wars of early modern Europe. This created a contradiction in that only one side could have a just claim to war under just war thinking. Just war thinking was also discredited by its association with religious wars that were so destructive as to have threatened the viability of the emerging European state-system.

Thus, a concern with system stability led to the development of a more secular natural law, one based on the 'law of nations' as opposed to religious ethics. This new law of nations, most famously elaborated in Hugo Grotius, *On the Law of War and Peace* (1625) and Emmerich de Vattel, *The Law of Nations* (1758), contained a number of crucial innovations. Most crucial of all was the notion of state practice as a source of law – law was what states did as opposed to what God dictated. Hence, law on war (unlike the just war tradition) was a matter of state responsibility not personal morality. This new natural law recognised the possibility that both sides in a dispute might (from their own perspective) have just cause. Accordingly, it shifted emphasis from justifying war to following correct formal procedures in declaring, conducting and ending war. The move to a more secular law of nations needs to be seen in the context of the Peace of Westphalia in 1648, which ended some eighty years of brutal warfare between the Catholic and Protestant powers in Europe, and which established the concept of state sovereignty. By formalising relations between these new sovereign states, the law of nations contributed to the stability of the new European states system.[9]

This emphasis on system stability, and with it international peace over other values such as human dignity, continued into positivist international law. It is evident in the use of force prohibition in Article 2(4) of the UN Charter, and also the prohibition in Article 2(7) against intervention in the internal affairs of sovereign states; as we discuss later in this chapter, these norms have retarded the use of force for humanitarian purposes. It is also contained in the recognition of the lawful right of self-defence (in Article 51) and in the UN's role in authorising force to protect international peace and security (as provided under Chapter VII). Both these functions are consistent with systemic stability as they provide restrictive grounds for recourse to force that are consistent with necessary rebalancing of the international system to stop rising aggressors.[10] As we discuss in this chapter, a state practice of humanitarian

---

[9] Shaw, *International Law*, pp. 1014–15; Neff, *War and the Law of Nations*, pp. 85–158.

[10] On the necessity for such rebalancing, see Randall Schweller, *Deadly Imbalances: Tripolarity, and Hitler's Strategy of World Conquest* (New York: Columbia University Press, 1998). On rebalancing dynamics, see Dale C. Copeland, *The Origins of Major War* (Ithaca, NY: Cornell University Press, 2001).

intervention has developed in the post-Cold War period. Humanitarian intervention presents a direct challenge to the norm of state sovereignty and the non-use of force norm. It suggests a reprioritisation of human dignity over system stability. However, as we shall see, state concerns with system stability have inhibited state recognition of a *legal* norm permitting forcible humanitarian intervention.[11]

International law also provides states with the vocabulary, concepts and terms to debate the legitimacy of using force in world politics. Through this mode of communication, deliberation and argumentation, states enact their identities as responsible and rightful sovereign entities. This function of international law as discourse is clearly evident in the claims states make for lawful use of force in self-defence, and the deliberation that often ensues at the international level as to whether such use of force was indeed lawful.[12]

The right of self-defence is subject to the two key principles of customary law on the use of force – necessity and proportionality. The principle of necessity comes from the just war principle of 'last resort'; in essence, states may only resort to force when peaceful alternatives have been exhausted. As we noted, this principle stretches back to Roman times. The early modern law of nations placed considerable restrictions along these lines on the use of force short of war – such as reprisal. But provided states followed correct procedure in declaring war, and a state of war was thus deemed to exist, these restrictions did not apply. Thus, it was important for states to declare the necessity of war, in order to remove themselves from the rules that normally regulated interstate relations. Modern international law places even greater restrictions on unilateral use of force by limiting it to self-defence. Predictably, the principle of necessity is central to the right of self-defence. Indeed, as we shall see, arguments for a more expansive right of self-defence are based on necessity claims attached to particular and exceptionally demanding strategic circumstances. Notions of necessity also underpin the new unilateral and UN practice of humanitarian intervention (again shown below). In both cases, the general rule of non-use of force is being affirmed whilst claims are advanced for necessary exceptions to this rule.[13]

---

[11] Nicholas J. Wheeler, 'The humanitarian responsibilities of sovereignty: explaining the development of a new norm of military intervention for humanitarian purposes in international society', in Jennifer M. Welsh (ed.), *Humanitarian Intervention and International Relations* (Oxford: Oxford University Press, 2004), pp. 29–51.

[12] This is explored in some detail in David Armstrong, Theo Farrell and Bice Maiguashca (eds.), *Force and Legitimacy in World Politics* (Cambridge: Cambridge University Press, 2006).

[13] Dino Kritsiotis, 'When states use armed force', in Christian Reus-Smit (ed.), *The Politics of International Law* (Cambridge: Cambridge University Press, 2004), pp. 45–79.

The principle of proportionality, as noted earlier, also comes from the just war tradition. This principle is not codified in the UN Charter, and so there is no requirement for states to estimate whether use of force in self-defence would do more good than harm. Nonetheless, it is generally accepted that use of force must be proportionate to be lawful. Proportionality does not mean that use of force must be of the same scale or nature as the armed attack, but rather must be of a scale and nature as required to repel the attack.[14] As we shall see, claims to proportionality also inform state discourse regarding the legitimacy of use of force in particular circumstances.

Use of force in self-defence

The interplay of international law as rules, values and discourse is evident when it comes to use of force in self-defence. As we noted, both Charter and customary rules of international law recognise the right of self-defence. However, the scope of this right, both in content and application, is open to debate. Most noteworthy have been attempts by some states in recent years to expand the right of self-defence on two grounds in particular, use of force in response to terrorist attacks and anticipatory self-defence. The value of system-stability is a restraining influence in the international community's response to expansion of the right of self-defence, for expansion along these or any other lines risks fatally undermining the normative power of the non-use of force rule. Against this, there is general recognition by states of the increasing problem of attacks by terrorist groups and of the strategic logic of pre-emptive action, especially given weapons of mass destruction (WMD). Accordingly, states have tended to take a case-by-case approach in deliberating on the legitimacy of using force in such circumstances, with each case being considered in light of the principles of necessity and proportionality.

Use of force against terrorists and state sponsors of terrorism raises the question of what constitutes 'armed attack' under article 51. An agreed definition of terrorism has proven elusive. However, various terrorist acts – such as hijacking, hostage-taking and bombing – are banned under twelve UN Conventions adopted between 1963 and 1999. The UN General Assembly (UNGA) also declared in 1994 'all acts, methods and practices of terrorism' to be 'criminal and unjustifiable'. Moreover,

---

[14] Judith Gardam, *Necessity, Proportionality and the Use of Force by States* (Cambridge: Cambridge University Press, 2004), pp. 4–13. The requirement for lawful use of force to be both necessary and proportionate was confirmed by the ICJ in the *Nuclear Weapons* Opinion (para. 41).

in 1992 the UNSC recognised terrorism to constitute a threat to international peace and security (leaving open the option of forceful action in response to terrorist acts under Chapter VII of the UN Charter).[15] In 1965 the UNGA also held state support for terrorist attacks on another state to be a violation of the UN Charter.[16] Thus, state sponsorship of terrorism is clearly prohibited. But that is not to say that it constitutes an 'armed attack' under international law, which would permit the state undergoing terrorist attack to use force in self-defence against the state sponsoring the terrorists. This matter was considered by the ICJ in the *Nicaragua* case (1986). In a majority judgment, the Court found that 'armed attack' could include use of force by irregulars (including terrorists) sent by another state, provided that the use of force is of sufficient gravity to be equivalent to an armed attack by the regular forces of a state. However, the Court concluded that the provision of support to irregular armed groups by a state did not itself amount to 'armed attack'.[17]

Many of the cases where use of force was justified in response to a terrorist attack have involved two states – Israel and the United States – with the terrorist attacks mostly emanating from the Middle East. The UNSC condemned Israel for breaching international law in its counter-terrorist operations in Beirut in 1968 and Tunis in 1985. Obviously the US veto prevented UNSC condemnation of US counter-terrorist strikes. Britain and France also vetoed a UNSC resolution condemning the US bombing of Libya in 1986, in response to Libyan-sponsored terrorism against US targets in Europe. There was more sympathy for the US cruise missile attacks on Baghdad in 1993, in response to an alleged assassination attempt against former US President George W. Bush. But only Russia and the United Kingdom accepted the US legal case for self-defence in this instance. Finally, when the United States responded to terrorist attacks on its embassies in Kenya and Tanzania with cruise missile strikes against terrorist facilitates in Afghanistan and Sudan in 1998, this was condemned by Russia, Pakistan and most Arab states. The problem for Israel and the United States was that in each of the cases above, force was used after the terrorist attack had passed. For this reason, most states concluded that force was used punitively and not defensively. In pre-Charter days armed reprisal was permitted and practised, but as made clear by General Assembly declarations in 1965 and 1970, it is now held by all states to be contrary to Article 2(4) and therefore illegal under

---

[15] General Assembly resolution 49/50 and UNSC resolution 731, both cited in Shaw, *International Law*, pp. 1049–50.
[16] General Assembly resolution 2131, cited in Higgins, *Problems*, p. 249.
[17] Rosalyn Higgins, *Problems and Process: International Law and How we use it* (Oxford: Clarendon Press, 1994), pp. 250–1; Dinstein, *War*, pp. 192–3.

international law. The UNSC also declared in 1964 that reprisal was incompatible with the UN Charter.[18] The one exception here may be if armed reprisal is forward-looking and intended for the purpose of deterring further attack. Counter-terrorist operations often take this character. In such cases, reprisal may be legal as a form of self-defence.[19] Critiques see this as amounting to 'half-hearted attempts to extend the doctrine of self-defence.'[20] However, state discourse and practice shows no consensus on this. Where reprisal has been justified on grounds of self-defence, states have tended to condemn or accept the action on the basis of their own assessment of the necessity and proportionality of the action taken. Thus, Israel's occupation of Southern Lebanon in 1982 was widely condemned as a disproportionate response to terrorist attacks, whereas brief incursions by Senegal forces into Guinea-Bissau (1992 and 1995), Tajiki forces into Afghanistan (1993) and Turkish forces into Kurdistan (1995) were all accepted as proportionate and necessary to counter terrorist attacks.[21]

The US invasion of Afghanistan in 2001 (with British military assistance) further shows that the issue for states is one of necessity and proportionality, not scale, of response. US military action was in response to the September 11 (9/11) terrorist attacks that destroyed New York's Twin Towers, badly damaged the Pentagon, and killed over 2,800 people. Immediately following September 11, the UNSC passed a number of resolutions strongly condemning the terrorist attacks and providing new measures to combat international terrorism. Moreover, the UNSC declared international terrorism 'to constitute one of the most serious threats to international peace and security in the twenty-first century'.[22] American use of force was directed against al-Qaeda, the terrorist organisation responsible for the 9/11 attacks, and the Taliban regime that was playing host to al-Qaeda in Afghanistan. The United States justified its actions in response to the 'on-going' threat from al-Qaeda, and the Taliban's refusal to take action to remove this threat.[23]

---

[18] Christine Gray, *International Law and the Use of Force* (Oxford: Oxford University Press, 2001), pp. 115–19.

[19] Dinstein, *War*, p. 222; Shaw, *International Law*, pp. 1023–4.

[20] Hilaire McCoubrey and Nigel D. White, *International Law and Armed Conflict* (Aldershot: Dartmouth, 1992), p. 113.

[21] Thomas M. Franck, *Recourse to Force: State Action Against Threats and Armed Attacks* (Cambridge: Cambridge University Press, 2002), pp. 65–6.

[22] S/RES/1377 (2001), at www.un.org/Docs/sc/unsc_resolutions.htm.

[23] Letter from US Ambassador John Negroponte to the UNSC President, 7 October 2001, cited in Christopher Greenwood, 'International law and the "war against terrorism"', *International Affairs* 78 (2002), 310.

The fact that US military operations against al-Qaeda and the Taliban happened almost a month after the 9/11 attacks is strongly suggestive of armed reprisal. Indeed, Bush told his nation on the night of September 11 that the United States intended 'to punish whoever harbors terrorists, not just the perpetrators'.[24] As noted above, the lawfulness of armed reprisal is contested in general. The legality in particular cases depends on the necessity and proportionality of use of force. In this case, necessity is possible to demonstrate. Al-Qaeda had a track record of attacking American targets, from the first World Trade Center bombing in 1993, to the attacks on the US embassies in 1998 and on a US warship in Yemen in 2000. It was reasonable for American policy-makers to conclude from this that more attacks were likely to come if military action was not taken against al-Qaeda. Some have argued that taking over a whole country in response to the destruction of some buildings in New York and Washington DC amounted to disproportionate use of force.[25] But, as noted earlier, proportionality should not be thought of in terms of 'an eye for an eye' but rather whatever force is required to repel an armed attack and prevent further attacks. Lobbing some cruise missiles at al-Qaeda facilities in Afghanistan and Sudan in 1998 had not deterred the terrorists, nor had it retarded their capabilities. Clearly, in this case, more drastic action was required and proportionate to the threat. Hence, the US invasion of Afghanistan enjoyed broad international support even though it was clearly directed at replacing the Taliban regime.

Even more controversial than the expansion of self-defence to include use of force against terrorists and state sponsors of terrorism, and potentially subversive to modern international law, is the notion of anticipatory self-defence. Article 51 does not provide for anticipatory self-defence. The wording is clear: there is a right of self-defence '*if* an armed attack occurs'. This is also how the overwhelming majority of states read the UN Charter.[26] The legality of anticipatory self-defence must be found, if it may be found at all, in customary international law. Customary law on this dates back to the *Caroline* case. In 1837 British troops attacked and destroyed a ship found in American waters that had been supplying Canadian rebels. In a now famous diplomatic note sent to the British Ambassador to Washington in April 1841, US Secretary of State Daniel Webster provided an authoritative definition of anticipatory self-defence. He wrote that such use of force was legal when the necessity is 'instant,

---

[24] Cited in Bob Woodward, *Bush at War* (London: Pocket Books, 2003), p. 31.
[25] Eric P. J. Myjer and Nigel D. White, 'Twin Towers attack: an unlimited right of self-defence', *Journal of Conflict and Security Law* 7 (2002), 8.
[26] Antonio Cassese, *International Law*, 2nd edition (Oxford: Oxford University Press, 2005), p. 361.

overwhelming, and leaving no choice of means, and no moment for deliberation'.[27] This is taken to mean that anticipatory self-defence is only legal when a state is facing imminent and overpowering attack. The imperative for pre-emption in such cases flows from a powerful strategic logic: the advantage is often with the state that strikes first. This is particularly (though not exclusively) true of war between nuclear armed opponents. As Judge Rosalyn Higgins noted, 'in a nuclear age, common sense cannot require . . . a state passively to accept its fate before it can defend itself'.[28] And, indeed, the ICJ refused to rule out anticipatory self-defence in its *Nuclear Weapons* Opinion.

State practice shows some sympathy for anticipatory self-defence when, as in the Webster formula, the defending state is facing a threat of imminent and overpowering attack. Thus, Israel's pre-emptive air-strike against the Egyptian air force in 1967 was generally recognised as justified (if not strictly legal) by the UNSC and UNGA, given Egypt's hostile intent and Israel's vulnerability to conventional attack. In contrast, Israel's bombing of an Iraqi nuclear reactor in 1981, designed to forestall an Iraqi nuclear threat, was strongly condemned both by the UNSC and UNGA because the threat from Iraq was not clear and immediate.[29] Against this conditional support among the international community for pre-emptive use of force is evidence of a deep reluctance on the part of states that engage in such action to invoke a right of anticipatory self-defence. States prefer to claim that force was used in response to an on-going or prior attack, and only if this claim cannot be made or sustained will anticipatory self-defence be invoked. Thus, Israel started off claiming that it had been attacked first in 1967, and only after this claim was shown to be false did it switch to one of anticipatory self-defence. In another striking case, the shooting down of an Iranian passenger airliner by an American warship in 1988, the United States declared that it had acted in self-defence against an on-going attack even though its warship was operating under rules of engagement that explicitly permitted pre-emptive use of force.[30]

In sum, state opinion is undecided over the legality of anticipatory self-defence. Nor has the ICJ been prepared to rule it in or rule it out. The wording of Article 51, combined with the overall purpose of the Charter to promote international peace and security, suggests that it may not be legal. But pre-Charter customary law suggests that it may be so. To be sure, debate on this matter has been clouded by confusion over pre-emptive and preventive use of force. This confusion has been

---

[27] Caroline Case, *British and Foreign State Papers* 29 (1836), 1137–8, and 30 (1837), 195–6.
[28] Higgins, *Problems*, p. 242.   [29] Franck, *Recourse*, pp. 101–7.
[30] Gray, *International Law*, pp. 111–13.

compounded by the ICJ's ambivalence in the *Nicaragua* case on the legality of anticipatory self-defence, as well as by the shifting justifications
(moving from anticipatory self-defence to humanitarian intervention)
given by the US and UK governments for the use of force against Iraq in
2003.[31] Nonetheless, as we noted, state practice shows some acceptance
of anticipatory self-defence where the threat is imminent and overwhelming, turning to general condemnation when it is not.[32]

Notwithstanding state consensus on this, it would appear that the
United States has been trying to change the self-defence norm in order
to provide a more permissive legal environment for the exercise of its preponderant military power. Where in the past America shied away from
claiming a right of anticipatory self-defence, even when its actions suggested otherwise, the Bush administration has made such a right central
to its 2002 *National Security Strategy*: 'To forestall or prevent such hostile
acts by our adversaries, the United States will, if necessary, act preemp-
tively.'[33] Note that 'prevent' and 'pre-empt' are being used interchange-
ably. In reality they are very different. The US Department of Defense
defines pre-emption as 'an attack initiated on the basis of incontrovert-
ible evidence that an enemy attack is *imminent*'. In contrast, preventive
war is 'a war initiated in the belief that military conflict, while *not imminent*, is inevitable, and that to delay would involve great risk'. Pre-emptive
war meets the *Caroline* criteria and may be legal; preventive war plainly
does not and is illegal.[34] The *National Security Strategy* is trying to affect
legal change, by arguing that the *Caroline* criteria need to be updated to
tackle the new threat of 'rogue states' and 'terrorists' acquiring WMD.
Following its publication, the US State Department's legal adviser clarified that the *National Security Strategy* imagines pre-emptive use of force
only 'in the face of overwhelming evidence of an imminent threat'. However, the US National Security Adviser subsequently noted that 'new
technology requires new thinking about when a threat actually becomes
"imminent"'; suggesting a blurring of a boundary between imminent and
emerging threats.[35]

---

[31] Dino Kritsiotis, 'Arguments of mass confusion', *European Journal of International Law*
15 (2004), 233–78.
[32] Shaw, *International Law*, p. 1030.
[33] *The National Security Strategy of the United States of America* (Washington DC, 2002),
p. 15. See also *The National Security Strategy of the United States of America* (Washington
DC, 2006), p. 18.
[34] DOD definitions and argument from Jeffrey Record, 'The Bush Doctrine and
War with Iraq', *Parameters* (Spring 2003), at http://carlisle-www.army.mil/usawc/
Parameters/03spring/record.htm, pp. 3–4.
[35] Miriam Sapiro, 'Iraq: the shifting sands of preemptive self-defense', *American Journal of
International Law* 97 (2003), 602, 604.

Only Russia, Israel and Australia have supported this new formulation of the self-defence norm. The rest of the international community has refused to endorse it, with many states expressing outright scepticism.[36] Scepticism is well founded in this case: any state locked in a long-term adversarial relationship could justifiably use force on the grounds that war was inevitable. At a more profound level, states are concerned with the impact of this new doctrine which risks returning the world to an earlier era of power politics where might makes right.[37] The issues at stake were dramatically rehearsed in the 2003 Iraq War.

In November 2002, the UNSC passed resolution 1441, finding Iraq in material breach of its obligations under past resolutions, especially resolution 687. UNSC resolution 687 established the conditions for the cease-fire at the end of the 1991 war against Iraq. These included Iraqi co-operation in destroying its existing weapons of mass destruction and long-range missiles, and in dismantling the programmes to produce such weapons. Despite strong lobbying from the US and UK governments, the Security Council was not prepared to authorise use of force in resolution 1441. Instead Iraq was given 'a final opportunity to comply with its dis-armament obligations' and threatened with 'serious consequences' if full compliance was not forthcoming.[38] In early 2003, the United States and the United Kingdom once again tried to get Security Council support for war against Iraq. However, when they pushed ahead and tabled a draft resolution for this purpose on 24 February, Russia and France threatened to veto it. One month later, the USA and UK went to war against Iraq regardless.

The USA and UK did articulate the legal case for military action. It centred on the claim that consent for use of force was implied in previ-ous UNSC resolutions. This rather convoluted argument involves tracing such authorisation back to resolution 678, which was passed by the Secu-rity Council in November 1990 and authorised use of force to eject Iraq from Kuwait and 'restore international peace and security to the area'. The argument goes that resolution 687 did not repeal this authorisation but rather put it on hold while Iraq complied with the UN's demands to disarm (among other things). The USA and UK asserted (in the words of a UK brief) that 'a material breach of resolution 687 revives the author-ity to use force under resolution 678'. They also argued that had it been necessary to secure further UNSC authorisation for use of force, that

---

[36] Cassese, *International Law*, p. 361.
[37] Thomas Franck, 'What happens now? The United Nations after Iraq', *American Journal of International Law* 97 (2003), 607–20.
[38] S/RES/1441 (2002), pp. 3, 5.

this would have been expressly stated in resolution 1441. Instead 'all that resolution 1441 requires is reporting to and discussion by the Security Council of Iraq's failures, but not an express further decision to authorise force'.[39]

The legal grounds for war advanced by the USA and UK had precedents. The 'implied' authorisation for use of force in resolution 687 was claimed by the USA and UK when they intervened to protect the Kurds in 1991 and when they launched bombing raids against Iraqi air-defence installations in 1998 and 2001. The international community let this claim slide in 1991, but in 1998 and 2001 it was rejected by most states including Russia, China and France.[40] The UK and USA also claimed, in trying to rally international support for the 2003 war against Iraq, that a French (and later Russian) veto would be 'unreasonable'.[41] This echoed the argument in Kosovo, namely that NATO had to act because the UNSC was unable to do so. Indeed, the former British Solicitor-General argued 'that actions by states to enforce UN resolutions and contain threats to the peace might be lawful, as the Kosovo action showed'.[42] However, if anything the international response to Kosovo showed the opposite; that, unilateral action to enforce UNSC resolutions was illegal. Finally, the United States tagged on a claim of acting in self-defence. The US State Department's senior legal adviser declared that in addition to the other reasons above, 'The President may also, of course, always use force under international law in self-defence.'[43] This was an appeal to the new doctrine of pre-emptive/preventive self-defence. As the Arab League Secretary-General wryly noted: 'I don't think America is coming under attack from Iraq.' In his public address to the nation days before the war, President Bush declared: 'Terrorists and terror states do not reveal these threats with fair notice, in formal declarations; and responding to such enemies only after they have struck first is not self-defense, it

---

[39] 10 Downing Street, 'Legal basis for use of force against Iraq', at www.pm.gov.uk/output/Page3287.asp. For a more lengthy brief provided by the Foreign and Commonwealth Office see, British Embassy Berlin, 'Iraq: legal basis for the use of force', A Statement by the FCO, 17 March 2003, at www.britischebotschaft.de/en/news/items/030317a.htm/.

[40] Christine Gray, 'From unity to polarization: international law and the use of force against Iraq', *European Journal of International Relations* 13 (2002), 9–13.

[41] Richard Norton-Taylor, 'Law unto themselves', *Guardian*, 14 March 2003. Downloaded from Global Policy Forum website, www.globalpolicy.org/security/issues/iraq/attack/law/2003/0314themselves.htm.

[42] Michael White, 'Publish advice on legality of war, opposition urges No. 10', *Guardian*, 13 March 2003, www.guardian.co.uk/Iraq/Story/0,2763,913128,00.html.

[43] Peter Slevin, 'US says war has legal basis', *Washington Post*, 21 March 2003, p. A14, at www.washingtonpost.com/.

is suicide.'[44] America's Afghan War revealed that the international community was prepared to support a right of pre-emptive self-defence, especially against terrorists. But it also showed little support among states for a right of preventive self-defence, and it provided no basis for the development of a legal right to use force against states that support terrorism. The problem faced by the Bush administration (and Blair government for that matter) is that it did not present convincing evidence of an imminent threat from Iraq, or of a link between Baghdad and any terrorist group that presents such a threat.[45] In other words, this was preventive not pre-emptive use of force, and therefore illegal. Some allied states – such as Spain, Italy and Poland – accepted the necessity for war against Iraq. But many states recognised this for what it was: namely preventive use of force and so illegal. Echoing the concerns of many states, and in a thinly veiled critique of US action, the UN Secretary-General warned that the logic of preventive use of force 'represents a fundamental challenge to the principles on which, however imperfectly, world peace and stability have rested for fifty years'.[46]

Humanitarian intervention

Humanitarian intervention involves the use of force to support aid and reconstruction operations in failed states and stop massive human rights abuses by murderous states. Each state's right to sovereignty, territorial integrity and political independence is guaranteed by a general prohibition on intervention in the affairs of any state. This norm is codified in Article 2(7) of the UN Charter, and it has been reiterated in numerous UNGA resolutions. Where intervention involves use of force, it is also prohibited by Article 2(4) of the UN Charter. So how can humanitarian intervention be reconciled with the non-intervention and non-use of force norms? The UN Charter aspires to promote fundamental human rights, but it does not contain any concrete and enforcement provisions for this purpose. A right of humanitarian intervention was discussed but not adopted at the San Francisco conference on the draft UN Charter

---

[44] Peter Ford, 'As attack on iraq begins, question remains: is it legal?', *Christian Science Monitor*, 21 March 2003. Downloaded from Global Policy Forum website, www.globalpolicy.org/security/issues/iraq/attack/law/2003/0321question.htm.
[45] Peter Gould, 'War with Iraq "could be illegal"', *BBC News*, 10 March 2003, www.news.bbc.co.uk/.
[46] 'The Secretary-General: Address to the General Assembly', New York, 23 September 2003, p. 2, at www.un.org/webcast/ga/58/statements/sgeng030923.htm.

in 1945.[47] On the face of it, then, there is no provision in Charter law for humanitarian intervention. The legal basis for humanitarian intervention, if it exists at all, must be found in customary law. Here we find state discourse and practice being pulled in opposite directions by competing values of system stability and human dignity. States have practised humanitarian intervention for decades, but they are reluctant to recognise the legality of such practice for fear that it could destabilise the Charter system. As we shall see, the principle of necessity has also guided use of force by intervening states and the response of the international community to particular cases of humanitarian intervention.

Humanitarian intervention occurred four times during the Cold War: Indian intervention in East Pakistan (1971), Tanzanian intervention in Uganda (1978) Vietnamese intervention in Kampuchea (1978), and French intervention in the Central African Empire (1979). The first three of these armed interventions actually amounted to full-blown invasions resulting in regime change. But in each of these cases there was a compelling humanitarian necessity for the intervention; brutal government repression had killed a million people in East Pakistan and in Kampuchea, and 300,000 people in Uganda. In the Central African Empire, the French intervention was more discrete and supported a bloodless coup against a dictator who had killed hundreds of his own people. What is most striking is the reluctance of the intervening states to justify their use of force on humanitarian grounds: India, Tanzania and Vietnam all claimed to be acting in self-defence even though none had suffered anything more than minor border incursions.[48] Peter Hilpold rightly observes: 'The fact that both Vietnam and Tanzania have tried to justify their actions by allegations that do not withstand an even rudimentary scrutiny while the humanitarian argument would have been at hand speaks volumes for the legal quality both states have attributed to this concept.'[49] The reaction of the international community was mixed to these interventions. The interventions in East Pakistan, Uganda and

---

[47] Franck, *Recourse*, p. 136; Thomas M. Franck, 'Interpretation and change in the law of humanitarian intervention', in J. L. Holzgrefe and Robert O. Keohane (eds.), *Humanitarian Intervention: Ethical, Legal and Political Dilemmas* (Cambridge: Cambridge University Press, 2003), p. 207.

[48] For analysis of these case studies, Supplementary Volume to the Report Commission on Intervention and State Sovereignty (ICISS), *The Responsibility to Protect: Research, Bibliography, Background* (Ottawa, ON: International Development Research Centre, 2001), pp. 49–67, at www.iciss.ca/report-en.asp; Nicholas J. Wheeler, *Saving Strangers: Humanitarian Intervention in International Society* (Oxford: Oxford University Press, 2000), pp. 55–138.

[49] Peter Hilpold, 'Humanitarian intervention: is there a need for a legal reappraisal?' *European Journal of International Law* 12 (2001), 443.

the Central African Empire were quietly condoned, or at least accepted. In contrast, Vietnam's intervention was condemned by most developing countries and most Western states. In part this was because of Cold War politics – Vietnam was an ally of the Soviet Union. Vietnam's humanitarian motives were also suspect because it stayed on for years in Kampuchea. But there was also a matter of legal principle, expressed thus by the French representative to the UNSC: 'The notion that because a regime is detestable foreign intervention is justified and forcible overthrow is legitimate is extremely dangerous. That could ultimately jeopardize the very maintenance of international law and order and make the continued existence of various regimes dependent on the judgment of their neighbours.'[50] This view captures the mood, then and still now, of the international community: unilateral intervention for humanitarian purposes may be excusable, but to make it legal would undermine Articles 2(4) and 2(7) of the UN Charter.

The 1990s saw a dramatic explosion in collective humanitarian interventions (i.e., UNSC-authorised interventions). The end of the Cold War broke the veto log-jam in the UNSC. Conflicts around the world were no longer viewed as extensions of East–West rivalry, and this enabled the Security Council to authorise armed intervention in humanitarian crises in Somalia (1992), Bosnia (1992), Kosovo (1999) and East Timor (1999).[51] Nobody disputes the Security Council's right to do this. Under Chapter VII of the UN Charter, it is empowered to determine that the humanitarian crisis (caused by a failed or murderous state) constitutes a threat to international peace and security (Article 39) and accordingly to authorise the use of force in response (Article 42). Moreover, it is evident from the Dumbarton Oaks and San Francisco conferences on the draft UN Charter, that the UNSC was intended to have wide discretion in determining threats to peace and security.[52]

However, there is a problem in so far as the UNSC has tended not to provide legal reasoning to justify the characterisation of a humanitarian crisis as a threat to international peace. This was evident right from the first time that the UNSC invoked Chapter VII for a humanitarian operation, when it authorised intervention by a US-led force in the failed state of Somalia. Antonio Cassese puts this lack of reasoning by the Security Council down to expediency: 'The SC is eager to retain discretionary power in this matter and tends to avoid explaining the nature of the link

---

[50] Franck, *Recourse*, p. 148.
[51] For details on these interventions, see ICISS, *Responsbility*, pp. 79–126.
[52] J. L. Holzgrefe, 'The humanitarian intervention debate', in Holzgrefe and Keohane (eds.), *Humanitarian Intervention*, p. 41.

[between humanitarian crises and international peace] and the reasons for its action.'[53] The Security Council has also sought to maximise its discretion in this matter by repeatedly declaring those humanitarian crises that it deems warrant action under Chapter VII to be unique in some way, thereby suggesting that these cases do not set precedent. Accordingly, Security Council resolutions recognised 'the unique character of the situation in Somalia', as well as the 'unique character' of the Haiti crisis, and again declared that the crisis in Rwanda was 'a unique case which demands an urgent response by the international community'.[54] Thus, it is difficult to read a legal right of humanitarian intervention in UNSC action.

There have also been a number of cases of intervention by coalitions of states and regional organisations that proceeded without clear UNSC authorisation. Indeed, the very first of the post-Cold War humanitarian interventions, the US-led intervention in Northern Iraq in 1991 to protect Kurds against brutal repression, was not directly authorised by the UNSC. Instead, the intervening powers argued that consent was implied in UNSC resolution 688 which recognised the crisis to be a threat to international peace and security. There have also been a number of collective interventions by regional organisations that went ahead without UNSC authorisation. There is provision for action by regional organisations in the UN Charter. Article 52 gives regional organisations a role in dealing with international peace and security at a regional level. Article 53 also permits the Security Council to use regional organisations for enforcement action, but at the same time, it specifies that regional organisations may not engage in such action without UNSC authorisation. As with the new interventionism in general, this mechanism was rarely invoked prior to 1989. But post 1991, there has also been an explosion of activity by regional organisations in conflict prevention and resolution. Many such missions have proceeded with explicit UNSC authorisation, but some have not. Military interventions by the Commonwealth of Independent States (CIS) in the internal conflicts in Tajikistan in 1993 and Georgia in 1992 were cautiously welcomed by the Security Council, but neither was actually authorised under Chapter VII. Equally, forcible interventions by the Economic Community of West African States (ECOWAS) in the civil wars in Liberia in 1990 and Sierra Leone in 1997 were both retrospectively authorised by the Security Council, even though neither was legal to begin with.[55]

---

[53] Cassese, *International Law*, p. 347.   [54] Hilpold, 'Humanitarian', pp. 445–7.
[55] Gray, *International*, pp. 212–14, 200, 224–7.

NATO's intervention in the Kosovo crisis in March 1999 provided the test case for the legality of humanitarian intervention in the post-Cold War system. NATO use of force (in the form of precision bombing) was aimed at stopping violent Serb repression of ethnic Albanians in the Yugoslav province of Kosovo. This intervention by NATO was widely seen as responding to dire humanitarian need and hence legitimate. But serious doubts were expressed about its legality. Two UNSC resolutions (1160 and 1199) did provide the triggers for military action by identifying the situation in the province as a threat to international peace and security. But neither resolution actually authorised use of force, precisely because Russia and China would not agree to it. Given this, it was incumbent on NATO to lay out the legal case for war. This NATO did not do.[56] In part this was because NATO governments were divided and uncertain as to what legal case to make. Drawing on precedent from the intervention in Iraq in 1991, the US and UK governments suggested that consent for use of force could be implied from resolutions 1160 and 1199 (with the French, Canadian and Dutch adopting a similar line). Such an argument had little credibility, however, as Russia and China both attached declaratory statements to their votes stating that these resolutions should not be interpreted as authorising use of force. Significantly, whilst NATO states declared to be acting on the grounds of overwhelming humanitarian necessity, only Belgium claimed a *legal* right to intervene forcibly in Kosovo on humanitarian grounds.[57]

The international community was divided in its response to NATO's humanitarian war. Russia and China sponsored (and Namibia supported) a UNSC resolution condemning the NATO bombing, but this resolution was opposed by the other twelve council members.[58] Most states in and out of the Security Council accepted the humanitarian necessity for use of force in this case.[59] However, there was no mood among states to infer a general rule from this specific case. Hence, the G77 group of 133 non-industrialised states issued a statement in April 2000 declaring: 'We reject the so-called "right" of humanitarian intervention, which has no legal basis in the United Nations Charter or in the general principles of international law.'[60] Nor was NATO trying to generalise from the Kosovo

---

[56] Jonathan I. Charney, 'Anticipatory humanitarian intervention in Kosovo', *American Journal of International Law* 93 (1999), 836–7.
[57] Catherine Guicher, 'International law and the war in Kosovo', *Survival* 41 (1999), 25–9; Wheeler, *Saving*, pp. 275–7.
[58] Wheeler, *Saving*, pp. 278–80; Frank, *Recourse*, 167–70.
[59] Antonio Cassese, 'A follow-up: forcible humanitarian countermeasures and *opinio nessitatis*', *European Journal of International Law* 10 (1999), 791–9.
[60] Declaration of the Group of 77 South Summit, Havana, Cuba, 10–14 April 2000, at www.g77.org/Declaration_G77Summit.htm.

case; indeed, it was declared to be an 'exceptional case'.[61] In short, states are increasingly using force to protect human dignity, but their overriding concern with system stability is preventing states from recognising the practice of humanitarian intervention in law.

Compliance with the law on use of force

It is widely believed, especially by realist scholars in IR, that when it comes to war, states pay no heed to international law. Of all areas of state activity, war involves the highest stakes. Therefore, states cannot afford to get hung up on legal niceties. They must do whatever is necessary to secure the national interest.[62] At the same time, it is an empirical fact that the growth of international rules restraining recourse to force by states has coincided with the decline of interstate war (even though wars continue to rage within states). This decline is most pronounced in the post-World War II period, following the creation of the UN system.[63] Of course, correlation is not causation. It would be extremely difficult, as an analytical exercise, to demonstrate that the growing force of law is responsible for states abandoning war as a means for settling their disputes. In any case, we would argue that this is a crude understanding of how the law works. International law expresses the values and interests of the most (including the most powerful) states at a particular moment in time. Compliance, therefore, primarily rests on state consensus, consent and congruence: self-interest and coercion are secondary drivers, especially in the area of use of force. In addition, since much of the law in this area is under-specified in terms of its application (e.g., in cases of terrorist attacks and pre-emption), compliance is often not a straightforward matter. The principles of necessity and proportionality invoke notions of fairness in state deliberation about whether the use of force in particular cases has complied with international law.

State disenchantment with war preceded the creation of the UN system. The American Civil War and Wars of German Unification in the mid to late nineteenth century demonstrated the horrors and scale of mass industrialised warfare.[64] The development of modern international law was very much driven by the conviction that war had become too

---

[61] Michael Byers and Simon Chesterman, 'Changing the rules about the rules? Unilateral humanitarian intervention and the future of international law', in Holzgrefe and Keohane (eds.), *Humanitarian Intervention*, p. 199.

[62] John Mearsheimer, 'The false promise of institutions', *International Security* 19 (1994/5), 5–49; Michael Desch, 'It is kind to be cruel: the humanity of American realism', *Review of International Studies* 29 (2003), 415–26.

[63] John Mueller, *The Remnants of War* (Ithaca, NY: Cornell University Press, 2004).

[64] Stig Forster and Jorg Nagler (eds.), *On the Road to Total War: The American Civil War and the German Wars of Unification, 1861–1871* (Cambridge: Cambridge University Press, 1997).

destructive in the industrial age to remain a rational tool of statecraft.[65] World War I, which devastated a whole continent and consumed a European generation, underlined the imperative to restrain war. It caused a profound shift in European culture, away from the romantic ideal of war, and galvanised public support for the anti-war movement.[66] Hence the Covenant of the League of Nations (1919) required state parties to submit disputes for arbitration, and only following a three-month 'cooling-off' period could they resort to force to settle matters. Greater restraints were also placed in this period on the use of force short of war. Thus, the 1907 Hague Convention II outlawed the state practice of using military force to recover debt on behalf of nationals.[67] These treaties were followed by the Kellogg–Briand Pact (1928) which, as we have already noted, sought to do away altogether with recourse to force. A second world war even more destructive than the first, made the moral and prudential case for renouncing war overwhelming. The Charter prohibition on use of force should be viewed in this context – that is 'the steady erosion of force's normative value in international politics'.[68] The onset of the nuclear age gave added reason to suppress war. With the creation of hydrogen weapons in the 1950s (which were up to 1,000 times more powerful that the atomic bombs dropped on Japan in 1945) and long-range ballistic missiles in the 1960s, war became unthinkable between nuclear armed powers.[69] To be sure, there were wars between and involving states after 1945, fuelled by decolonisation as well as by Cold War politics. But what is remarkable is that the consensus supporting the UN system did not shatter as the Cold War worsened. East and West, and the non-aligned states, all accepted the legal order created by the UN Charter. This consensus underpins international consent for Charter law.

This is not to say that coercion is irrelevant to the functioning of modern international law. The UNSC, established under Chapter V of the UN Charter, provides the mechanisms, so sorely missing from the League of Nations, to enforce compliance with Charter rules. Chapter VI requires disputes to be resolved peacefully and gives the UNSC a role in investigating disputes and making recommendations for settlement. Chapter VII empowers the UNSC to find threats or breaches of the peace

---

[65] Martti Koskenniemi, *The Gentle Civilizer of Nations: The Rise and Fall of International Law, 1870–1960* (Cambridge: Cambridge University Press, 2001).

[66] Paul Fussell, *The Great War and Modern Memory* (Oxford University Press, 1975); John Mueller, 'Changing attitudes towards war: the impact of the First World War', *British Journal of Political Science* 21 (1991), 1–28.

[67] Shaw, *International Law*, p. 1016.

[68] Martha Finnemore, *The Purpose of Intervention: Changing Beliefs about the Use of Force* (Ithaca, NY: Cornell University Press, 2003), p. 19.

[69] Robert Jervis, *The Meaning of the Nuclear Revolution* (Ithaca, NY: Cornell University Press, 1989).

(Article 39) and, where such threats or breaches are found, to use sanctions (Article 41) and/or military force (Article 42) to restore international peace and security. Most often the UNSC relies on calling for the cessation of hostilities and the withdrawal of military forces. On occasion it has condemned one or both sides of a conflict for serious violations of Article 2(4); Israel was so condemned in 1985 for its attack on the PLO headquarters in Tunisia, and both Ethiopia and Eritrea were condemned in 1999 for their war.[70] When the UNSC has needed to resort to sanctions, these have taken the form of cutting communications, removing diplomatic privileges, seizing financial assets in foreign territory, halting arms sales and military supplies, and stopping the flow of economic goods. Sanctions were rarely used by the UNSC during the Cold War. The first occasion was in 1966, when UN economic sanctions were imposed on Rhodesia, which had declared independence under white minority rule. With the end of the Cold War, the UNSC has made more comprehensive use of sanctions in response to acts of aggression – against Iraq for its invasion of Kuwait (1990–1), Libya for its sponsorship of terrorism (1992–9), Yugoslavia for its part in the Balkan Wars (1992–5), and both Ethiopia and Eritrea for their war (2000–1). Most widely applied (as in all cases above) are arms embargos, both to coerce aggressors and reduce their capacity for further aggression. In the Libya case, diplomatic sanctions involved a reduction of diplomatic missions to Libya and an embargo on all air travel to the country, to isolate the regime. Most severe of all, and hence applied most reluctantly by the UNSC, are economic sanctions. These were applied both to Iraq and to Yugoslavia.[71] The problem with economic sanctions is that they tend to hurt the weakest and most vulnerable in the target state, rather than the ruling elite. Thus the regime of Slobodan Milosevic in Yugoslavia was able to defy sanctions that were imposed during the Kosovo crisis.[72] In the case of Iraq, sanctions imposed between 1992–2003, to force the regime to comply with UNSC demands for disarmament and non-sponsorship of terrorism, were a major contributing factor to the deaths of up to one million infants through preventable disease and malnutrition.[73] The effectiveness of sanctions is best considered on a case-by-case basis. On some occasions, as in Libya and Yugoslavia, diplomatic, arms and/or economic sanctions did eventually work in coercing the target regime to comply with international law. But in the case of Yugoslavia, other factors also

---

[70] Cassese, *International Law*, p. 342.   [71] Shaw, *International Law*, pp. 1124–30.
[72] 'Yugoslav sanctions failing', *BBC News*, 10 July 2000, at www.news.bbc.co.uk/1/hi/world/europe/827836.stm.
[73] Eric Herring, 'Between Iraq and a hard place: a critique of the British government's narrative on UN economic sanctions', *Review of International Studies* 28 (2002): 39–56.

affected the outcome – including, the promise of eventual integration in the West European institutions.

Self-interest also has a place in compliance with law on the use of force. All states have an interest in the long-term stability afforded by rule-governed relations. The non-intervention and non-use of force norms are especially important for the smaller states to protect them against aggression by more powerful states. The great powers also have an interest in maintaining the current international legal system. The victorious powers of World War II – the United States, Soviet Union (now Russia), Britain, France and China – hold special positions as the permanent five members of the UNSC. The right of veto that each permanent member enjoys on the UNSC (under Article 27) ensures that they cannot be made to bow to Charter rules. To be sure, international law does not always serve the immediate interests of the most powerful states, especially when it hinders a preferred course of action. But, against this, rule-following by the great powers brings two general benefits. First, it reinforces the fairness and hence legitimacy of the international legal system – a system which regulates interstate relations to the benefit of all states, great and small. Second, it legitimates the exercise of great power influence in the authoritative decision-making bodies provided by international law, such as the UNSC. In short, it is easier for big states to wield soft power through international institutions than to do so unilaterally.[74] In contrast, the disdain for international law demonstrated by the United States under George W. Bush – by attempting to block the International Criminal Court, withdrawing from the Comprehensive Test Ban Treaty and using force against Iraq without clear UNSC authorisation – has galvanised international opposition to the US role in world affairs and made it more difficult for the United States to persuade other states to follow its lead.[75]

Most important, after consent, is congruence in explaining state compliance with international law on the use of force. We would suggest that there is a mutually constitutive relationship between the evolution of legal restraints on recourse to force by states and the spread of liberal democracy. Indeed, the architects of the UN system were liberal democracies – the United States and Britain. Critics would point out that both states have used forced aggressively since the founding of the UN.[76] In some of these cases, an expanded concept of self-defence or humanitarian purpose

---

[74] G. John Ikenberry, *After Victory: Institutions, Strategic Restraint, and Rebuilding of Order After Major Wars* (Princeton, NJ: Princeton University Press, 2001).
[75] Christian Reus-Smit, *American Power and World Order* (Cambridge: Polity, 2004).
[76] Noam Chomsky, *Deterring Democracy* (London: Verso, 1991).

can explain US and British use of force – and whilst this does not necessarily make military action legal, it does lend some legitimacy to it. Other
cases, such as the British-led seizure of the Suez Canal (1956) and the
US bombing of Cambodia (1970–3), lacked both legality and legitimacy.
But, the restraint exercised by liberal democracies in the twentieth century is still favourable in comparison to the violent record of illiberal and
non-democratic states, such as the Soviet Union, China, South Africa,
Indonesia, Iraq and Syria. Liberal theorists argue that liberal democracies externalise in their foreign policy internal norms of compromise
and non-violent dispute resolution. The security dilemma and crusading
liberalism retard this external expression of internal values when liberal
democracies encounter autocratic and dictatorial states.[77] Of course, liberal democracies have no right in law to be violent towards any state,
regardless of its domestic make-up or ideology. But given that those large
swathes of the planet that are populated by liberal democracies happen
to be the most peaceful, there is something to the liberal hypothesis that
liberal democracies are *inclined* to be more law-abiding when it comes
to restraints on the use of force.[78] The constructivist lens helps us to
understand how the zone of liberal democratic peace in the world is
also a zone of law-following. Constructivists emphasise the importance
of identity in producing the liberal democratic peace – this is a peace
between states that consider each other to be like-minded and trustworthy when it comes to pursuing non-violent relations.[79] This identity is
internalised in national discourses, policies and laws. Sometimes such
internalisation might actually facilitate offensive war with illiberal and
undemocratic states – hence, the Bush administration had little trouble
mobilising the US polity for war with Iraq in 2003. But equally, sometimes such internalisation can make it difficult for a liberal democracy to
fight an illegal war against even the most dictatorial regimes – again, as

[77] Zeev Maoz and Bruce Russett, 'Normative and structural causes of democratic peace',
American Political Science Review 87 (1993), 624–38; William J. Dixon, 'Democracy
and the peaceful settlement of disputes', *American Political Science Quarterly* 88 (1993),
14–32.
[78] However, there is some debate as to whether or not liberal democracies have a general tendency to be more law-abiding in all areas of international law. See Anne-Marie
Slaughter, 'International law in a world of liberal states', *European Journal of International
Law* 6 (1995), 503–38; and José E. Alvarez, 'Do liberal states behave better? a critique
of slaughter's liberal theory', *European Journal of International Law* 12 (2001), 183–246.
[79] Ido Oren, 'The subjectivity of the democratic peace: changing US perceptions of Imperial Germany', *International Security* 20 (1995), 147–84; Thomas Risse, 'Collective identity in a democratic community', in Peter J. Katzenstein (ed.), *The Culture of National
Security: Norms and Identity in World Politics* (New York: Columbia University Press,
1996), pp. 357–99.

demonstrated in the problems experienced by the British government in gaining political and public support for the 2003 Iraq War.[80]

Change in the law on use of force

Change in the law on use of force has involved all three processes – formal, policy and social – identified in chapter 3. The formal process, involving states as agents of change and resting on state consent, is evident in a succession of major treaties progressively outlawing the use of force. Already noted in this chapter have been the 1907 Hague Convention II outlawing use of force to recover debts, the 1919 Covenant of the League of Nations restraining recourse to force by states and the Kellogg–Briand Pact of 1928 renouncing war. Obviously, most significant for the current legal order is the UN Charter, especially the prohibition against use of force contained in Article 2(4). We noted that whilst states have frequently breached this prohibition, no state has withdrawn its consent to be bound by Charter rules and, indeed, that states reaffirmed the non-use of force rule in the 1970 Declaration on Principles of International Law Concerning Friendly Relations.

Also significant has been the progressive outlawing of the means available to states to employ military force through a succession of treaties. States have consented not to acquire or use certain weapons systems and technologies that are deemed to be particularly brutal in how they injure and kill, or are deemed to carry a disproportionate risk of collateral damage.[81] Hence, biological and chemical weapons are banned under the 1972 Biological Weapons Convention (BWC) and 1993 Chemical Weapons Convention (CWC) respectively. Both conventions build on the 1925 Geneva Protocol which bans the use of bacteriological agents and poison gas in war.[82] Arguably these weapon technologies are no more barbaric than conventional weapons, which injure and kill by ripping apart human bodies. Indeed, it could be said that those biological and chemical agents that kill instantly are more humane than conventional weapons that cause combatants to die slowly through their painful injuries. However, biological and chemical weapons developed a certain normative quality in the public consciousness and this, combined with their uncertain military utility, pushed states to codify a general ban.[83] A

---

[80] Clare Taylor and Tim Youngs, *The Conflict in Iraq*, House of Commons Library Research Paper 03/50, 23 May 2003, pp. 10–16.
[81] Collateral damage is unintended damage to civilians and civilian structures.
[82] BWC at www.opbw.org/; CWC at www.opcw.org/.
[83] Richard M. Price, *The Chemical Weapons Taboo* (Ithaca, NY: Cornell University Press, 1997).

range of conventional weapons considered 'to be excessively injurious or to have indiscriminate effects' are also banned under the 1980 Convention on Certain Conventional Weapons (CCW); included here are booby traps, incendiary weapons and blinding laser weapons. Though it has to be noted that the CCW is only binding on those states that are party to it, of which there are only 79.[84] This is in contrast to the BWC and CWC, which have 169 and 178 state parties respectively, and which also derives force in customary international law from the traditional norm against the use of 'plague and poison' in war.

The development and acquisition of nuclear weapons is also restrained by a range of treaties, including the 1963 Partial Test Ban Treaty the 1996 Comprehensive Test Ban Treaty, and treaties creating of nuclear-weapons-free zones in South-east Asia (1995) and Africa (1996). Of course, most significant is the 1968 Nuclear Non-Proliferation Treaty (NPT) to which 187 states are party, and which was renewed in 1995. The NPT recognises the right of five states to have nuclear weapons (who also happen to be the permanent five members of the UNSC: the United States, Russia, Britain, France and China) and commits the other parties to renounce ownership of nuclear weapons. However, three states – Israel, India and Pakistan – have refused to sign this treaty; Israel is known to have a sizeable nuclear arsenal, and India publicly tested a nuclear weapon in 1974 with Pakistan following suit in 1998. Moreover, North Korea withdrew from the NPT in 2003 in order to pursue its nuclear weapons programme.[85] In its *Nuclear Weapons* Opinion, the ICJ noted that none of the above treaties explicitly included or implicitly provided for a prohibition against nuclear use.[86] The five recognised nuclear weapons states did commit themselves to not using nuclear weapons against non-nuclear parties of the NPT, but this commitment was not formally included in the treaty. The permanent five renewed this commitment before the UNSC in 1995, however, the United States, the United Kingdom, France and Russia have all since renounced it by invoking the possibility of nuclear retaliation against non-nuclear attacks by rogue states.[87]

Law on the use of force has also changed through a policy process involving a plurality of actors. Central to this policy process is the UNSC

---

[84] CCW at www.un.org/millennium/law/xxvi-18-19.htm.
[85] NPT at www.iaea.org/Publications/Documents/Treaties/npt.html.
[86] ICJ, *Legality*, para. 62, at www.icj-cij.org/icjwww/icases/iunan/iunanframe.htm.
[87] S/RES/984 (1995) at www.un.org/documents/scres.htm; Nicholas Kralev, 'US drops pledge on nukes', *Washington Times*, 22 February 2002; Stephen Pullinger, *Military Action Against Iraq: The Nuclear Option*, ISIS policy paper 83, April 2002, p. 3; 'The future of nuclear deterrence: perversely indispensible?' *IISS Strategic Comments* 12, 1 (2006), 1; Nikolai Sokov, 'Russia's nuclear doctrine', *NTI Issue Brief* at www.nti.org/e_research/e3_55a.html.

as the authoritative decision-making body in this area. By defining particular events and acts as constituting threats to international peace and security, the UNSC has expanded the legal scope for use of force. The UNSC has done this in a succession of cases involving humanitarian disasters, though as we noted, it took care to avoid setting precedent by declaring each case to be unique. Nonetheless, Western states on the UNSC are cautiously pushing forward the humanitarian intervention agenda. Hence, the UNSC passed resolution 1296 in 2000 establishing that 'the targeting of civilians in armed conflict and the denial of humanitarian access to civilian populations affected by war may themselves constitute threats to international peace and security and thus be triggers for Security Council action'. In responding to humanitarian crises, the UNSC has acted as an executive agent in interpreting its duties under Chapter VII of the Charter. But in its response to terrorism in the wake of 9/11, the UNSC has arguably taken legislative action. It has done so through a number of resolutions, starting with Resolution 1373 (2001), by authoritatively and without reservation defining terrorism as constituting a general threat to international peace and security, and in placing obligations on states to respond to this threat appropriately. Indeed, UN member states have openly recognised Resolution 1373 as being 'groundbreaking' and 'historic' for this reason.[88]

The role of states remains pre-eminent in this policy process. But international courts, international organisations, non-governmental actors and transnational networks are also involved. The ICJ is charged with interpreting the law and, in principle, could through this function change how states understand and apply the use of force. In the *Nicaragua* case, the ICJ defended its competency to deal with unlawful use of force, but it equally recognised the 'primacy' of the UNSC in this domain of high politics. To be sure, states are increasingly bringing cases to the ICJ on use of force issues. But the ICJ continues to show reluctance to adjudicate on matters that it considers to be the purview of the UNSC. In practice, therefore, the ICJ has played a limited role in this area of law.[89] International organisations have played a secondary role, in spurring the UNSC, UNGA and ICJ to action. Hence, it was the World Health Organization that originally requested an advisory opinion from the ICJ on the legality of nuclear weapons use, and this request was subsequently

[88] Stefan Talmon, 'The Security Council as world legislature', *American Journal of International Law* 99 (2005), 175–93.
[89] Christine Gray, 'The use and abuse of the international court of justice: cases concerning the use of force after *Nicaragua*', *European Journal of International Law* 14 (2003), 867–905.

supported by the UNGA.[90] Some international organisations may also give testimony before the UNSC, as the United Nations High Commissioner for Refugees did in September 1998 concerning the Kosovo crisis, and this has helped push forward the humanitarian intervention agenda. Non-governmental actors also influence UNSC deliberations, through informal contacts with the New York missions of member states.[91] In addition, transnational NGO networks have been important in mobilising states to outlaw certain means and methods of warfare. The 1997 Mine Ban Treaty (MBT) – which outlaws the production, stockpiling, transfer and use of anti-personnel land-mines – provides a dramatic example of non-state-led change: some 1,000 non-governmental organisations from sixty countries joined the International Campaign to Ban Land-mines (ICBL). Supported by the International Committee for the Red Cross, and various UN agencies which demonstrated the indiscriminate effect of land-mines on civilians in war zones, the ICBL got a partial mine ban integrated in amendments to the CCW in 1996 and thereafter pushed for a treaty completing banning anti-personnel mines. The ICBL were able to exert social pressure on states because they were able to frame land-mines as taboo weapons (much like chemical and biological weapons) in the public mind. At March 2006, 154 states were party to the MBT.[92]

Finally, the law on the use of force has changed through a social process involving social learning and internalisation. Central to this process was the development of international law as a transnational profession. In the late nineteenth and early twentieth centuries, institutes and societies on international law were established, and gradually universities began offering courses on international law, in Europe and North America. Hence professional knowledge was created, codified and diffused through legal conferences, journals and training. Social learning of the new discipline of international law occurred both nationally and transnationally (as many institutes and societies had transnational membership).[93] Internalisation of new professional knowledge also occurred through the

---

[90] The WHO was indeed found to lack competence to request an advisory opinion on an issue falling outside the scope of its activities.

[91] Adam Roberts, 'The United Nations and humanitarian intervention', in Jennifer Welsh (ed.), *Humanitarian Intervention and International Relations* (Oxford: Oxford University Press, 2004), pp. 91–2; Ian Johnston, 'The power of interpretive communities', in Michael Barnett and Raymond Duvall (eds.), *Power in Global Governance* (Cambridge: Cambridge University Press, 2005), p. 196.

[92] ICBL at www.icbl.org/; Richard Price, 'Reversing the gun sights: transnational civil society targets land mines', *International Organization* 52 (1998), 613–44.

[93] Frederic L. Kirgis, 'The formative years of the american society of international law', *American Journal of International Law* 90 (1996), 559–89; Koskenniemi, *The Gentle Civilizer of Nations*.

influx of trained lawyers into the diplomatic services of the great powers. Martha Finnemore argues that this transformed the way that states looked at the problem of war. Increasingly the problem became framed in legal terms for which statesmen sought legal solutions. Finnemore notes that whereas at the Geneva Congress of 1864 (which produced the first Geneva Conventions on the laws of war) almost all delegates were military or medical personnel, at the 1907 Hague Peace Conference (where states agreed to outlaw use of force to recover debt) more than half the delegates were lawyers. Moreover, the heads of the US, British, German and French delegations all had extensive law backgrounds.[94] This is not, of course, to overstate the influence of lawyers on state policy. Foreign policy reflects state interests and values, as well as domestic politics. Indeed, in this regard, there are distinct limits to the internalisation of the law on the use of force. Even in established democracies there is tremendous variation in the mechanisms for legislative involvement in executive authorisation of state use of force. Moreover, these mechanisms concern political accountability; invariably, the executives self-certify conformity with international law.[95] Nonetheless, the internalisation of international law in the diplomatic services of states has facilitated the search for legal means to restrain use of force.

External shock and norm entrepreneurs have also been important in this enterprise. The wars that occasioned unification of both the United States and Germany in the middle of the nineteenth century, which, as noted earlier, vividly demonstrated the destructive scale of war in the mass industrialised age, prompted the interest of legal scholars in war. This triggered the development of international law as a profession. Successive shocks caused by the first and second world wars, led states to fashion post-war legal orders that promised peace. US leaders acted as norm entrepreneurs for all these major legal innovations: Secretary of State Elihu Root led the campaign to ban use of force for debt-collection at the 1907 Hague Convention, President Woodrow Wilson provided the blueprint for the League of Nations, and President Franklin D. Roosevelt was the main architect for the United Nations. Shock and entrepreneurs continue to play important roles in affecting change in the law on the use of force. The genocide in Rwanda in 1994, when the world failed to intervene to stop the slaughter of 1 million civilians, shocked key Western policy-makers into recognising the imperative of humanitarian cause for use of force. This cause is being advanced by the UN Secretary-General,

---

[94] Finnemore, *The Purpose of Intervention*, pp. 39–46.
[95] Charlotte Ku and Harold K. Jacobson (eds.), *Democratic Accountability and the Use of Force in International Law* (Cambridge: Cambridge University Press, 2003).

Kofi Annan, and the British Prime Minister, Tony Blair. Blair has tried to advance the notion of humanitarian intervention as new 'doctrine of the international community'.[96] In fact, as we discussed, states are not yet prepared to accept the legality of unilateral humanitarian intervention because of the threat this presents to system stability. Annan has led the effort to get states to codify humanitarian criteria for the collective use of force.[97] More recently still, the 9/11 attacks shocked the world into appreciating the scale of the threat from international terrorism. The result, as we noted, was a true legal innovation in UNSC resolution 1373.

Conclusion

Consistent with the realist lens, law on the use of force is codified in formal rules that are binding on states. Through a series of treaties – the 1907 Hague Convention, the Kellogg–Briand Pact and, most important of all, the UN Charter – states have progressively outlawed the use of force. States have also agreed a number of multilateral treaties – the BWC, CWC, CCW and MBT – to outlaw certain forms of force. The general prohibition on the use of force is now considered to have become state custom, which gives it added force in law. Other treaty rules, such as the prohibition against the use of chemical and biological weapons, are widely considered to be rooted in prior customary law, and this too adds to their binding effect. The realist lens also highlights consent as a vital driver of state compliance with law rules on the use of force. Such consent has been based on state recognition of the increasing destructiveness of war and hence the need to suppress it. Finally, the formal process of legal change is evident in the succession of treaties noted above. The crucial thing to note, from the realist perspective, is that none of these treaties would have been concluded without the sponsorship of powerful states, and none would have come into force without the consent of most states in the system.

The liberal lens points us towards the values that underpin law on the use of force. The just war tradition provided a rich pre-modern heritage on the use of force. However, this tradition gave way in the modern period to a secular 'law of nations' which focuses on a single value: system stability. The primacy of this value, over all others, remains in modern customary and treaty law concerning the use of force and can

---

[96] Tony Blair, 'Doctrine of the international community', Economic Club of Chicago, 24 April 1999, at www.pm.gov.uk/output/Page1297.asp.

[97] Report of the Secretary-General's High-Level Panel on Threats, Challenges and Change, *A More Secure World: Our Shared Responsibility* (New York: United Nations, 2004), para. 203, p. 66, at www.un.org/secureworld/.

be seen in widespread state scepticism towards notions of preventive self-defence and humanitarian intervention. The liberal lens is less useful in explaining compliance and change in this area of law. Liberalism points to self-interest as a motive for state compliance: the legal prohibition on use of force protects small states against aggression and legitimates the peaceful exercise of influence by the great powers. But, at an individual level, states may be pushed by powerful countervailing self-interests to violate the non-use of force rule. Arguably, the US-led war against Iraq in 2003 is one such example – in that many in the US and UK polities genuinely overestimated the threat from Iraq's WMD programmes, and this led them to support preventive use of force. Countervailing values – such as human rights versus system stability – may also push states to use force illegally. One such example is NATO's forcible intervention in the Kosovo crisis in 1999. The policy process of legal change is most evident in the central role of the UNSC as the prime authoritative body in this area of law. Crucially, from the liberal perspective, the UNSC is a political not a legal body, and yet it has the capacity through its resolutions to legislate on matters of international security. Beyond this, liberals would point to the role of various non-state actors in the process of legal change. Certainly a plurality of actors is involved – including the ICJ, international organisations (IOs), and transnational networks of NGOs – but these affect legal change by mobilising states to accept further restraints on the use of force. In other words, non-state actors play a secondary role, in triggering and informing change, but change depends on state support.

The paradox is that the increasing legalisation of the use of force from the late nineteenth century on did little to stop the ravages of war. The world wars of the twentieth century dwarfed those of the century before in their scale and destructiveness. Indeed, arguably war 'degenerated' as the twentieth century wore on with the deliberate destruction of homelands and entire civilian populations in World War II, in the post-colonial wars of the late 1940s to 1970s, and the ethnic conflicts of the 1990s.[98] The constructivist lens explains the role of international law in such a violent world. As a discourse, law gives states a common language and set of principles with which to engage in meaningful debate with one another about the legitimacy of using force. Two principles are central to such debate: those of necessity and proportionality. Both principles underpin the legality of self-defence, as a general norm and in consideration by the international community of specific cases of claimed self-defence. Both principles also guide state deliberation over humanitarian intervention,

[98] Martin Shaw, *War and Genocide* (Cambridge: Polity, 2003).

as an imperative in specific cases and as a potential new exception to the non-use of force norm. The constructivist lens also gives a powerful account of the general pattern of state compliance with legal restraints on the use of force. The fact is the world could be a far more violent place. Western Europe has enjoyed an unprecedented period of peace and, for all their relative power, Western states are remarkably war-shy. Liberals highlight the role of liberal democracy in producing zones of peace in the world. And indeed, liberal democracies designed the UN order. Constructivism adds another layer to this liberal account, but locating this effect in shared identities that promote rule-governed and peaceful relations between liberal democracies. Constructivism also completes our picture of change in this area of law. It helps us understand why states struggled to create legal structures to restrain war, all the while waging ever-more destructive wars. The cause of international law was promoted by an emerging profession in the twentieth century, and the ranks of diplomats were increasingly filled by lawyers. Thus a process of social learning and internalisation occurred, leading states to frame the problem, and hence solution, of war in terms of law. Shock – and what is more shocking than major war? – and a succession of mostly American norm entrepreneurs have pushed along the quest to outlaw aggressive war and, more recently, to legalise humanitarian war.

Discussion questions

- What does the UN Charter say about the use of force? What are the other major treaties outlawing the use of force? Is it legal for states to merely threaten to use force?
- What are the roots and core principles of the just war tradition? Why did this tradition falter in early modern Europe? What rose in its place? Which liberal value – system stability or human dignity – has priority in modern positivist international law?
- What are the two key principles of customary law on the use of force? Where do these principles originate? How are they manifest in the right of self-defence?
- What is the definition of 'armed attack' and why is it important to the law on self-defence? In what way do the principles of necessity and proportionality guide states' consideration of the lawfulness of use of force in self-defence? Can a state lawfully use force in response to a terrorist attack? How lawful is anticipatory self-defence? Was the US-led invasion of Iraq in 2003 lawful?
- Is there any basis for humanitarian intervention in treaty law? Why have states been reluctant to recognise the legality of humanitarian

intervention? On what grounds has the UNSC authorised forcible intervention in post-Cold War humanitarian crises? What does the Kosovo crisis reveal about the lawfulness of humanitarian intervention?

- To what extent does the UN Charter reflect the normative de-valuing of war? What mechanisms does the UN Charter provide for enforcing state compliance with the prohibition against use of force? Does this prohibition serve the self-interests of states? Indeed, why should the most powerful states bother at all with international law? Are liberal states more compliant with the rules prohibiting use of force and, if so, why?

- Is there much evidence to suggest a formal process of change in the law on use of force? What role have the UNSC and ICJ played as agents of legal change? Have NGOs had any role in affecting change in this area of law? How have states learned about and internalised legal solutions to the scourge of war? How important have external shock and norm entrepreneurs been in pushing along this socialisation process?

SUGGESTIONS FOR FURTHER READING

Armstrong, David, Theo Farrell and Bice Maiguashca (eds.), *Force and Legitimacy in World Politics*, Cambridge: Cambridge University Press, 2005. An interdisciplinary volume, with contributions from leading IL and IR scholars on the evolving nature and complex relationships of legitimacy, legality and force.

Byers, Michael, *War Law: International Law and Armed Conflict*, London: Atlantic Books, 2005. A highly readable introduction to the subject.

Desch, Michael. 'It's kind to be cruel: the humanity of American realism', *Review of International Studies*, 29, 3 (2003), 415–26. A strident statement of the realist position on the minimal role of norms and law in a world where the risks of conflict are ever-present.

Dinstein, Yoram, *War, Aggression and Self-Defence*, Cambridge: Cambridge University Press, 1994. A standard reference work in the field.

Farrell, Theo, *The Norms of War: Cultural Beliefs and Modern Conflict*, Boulder, CO: Lynne Rienner, 2005. An interdisciplinary study on the normative fabric of force in the modern world.

Finnemore, Martha, *The Purpose of Intervention: Changing Beliefs About the Use of Force*, Ithaca, NY: Cornell University Press, 2003. An important constructivist study on the erosion of the normative value of force in world politics.

Franck, Thomas M., *Recourse to Force: State Action Against Threats and Armed Attacks*, Cambridge: Cambridge University Press, 2002. A provocative book, based on a series of lectures delivered at Cambridge, by a leading US liberal professor of international law.

Gardam, Judith, *Necessity, Proportionality and the Use of Force by States*, Cambridge: Cambridge University Press, 2004. A comprehensive analysis of these two key principles underpinning international law on use of force.

Gray, Christine, *International Law and the Use of Force*, Oxford: Oxford University Press, 2001. A thorough and carefully argued book that provides a British perspective on the subject by a Cambridge professor of international law.

International Commission on Intervention and State Sovereignty (ICISS), *The Responsibility to Protect*, 2 vols., Ottawa, ON: International Development Research Centre, 2001, at www.iciss.ca/report-en.asp. A high-profile report making the case for humanitarian intervention through a thorough analysis of the political, military, ethical and legal dimensions of the subject.

Johnson, James Turner, *Just War Tradition and the Restraint of War: A Moral and Historical Inquiry*, Princeton, NJ: Princeton University Press, 1981. An accessible introduction by a leading scholar on the just war tradition.

Kritsiotis, Dino, 'When states use armed force', in Christian Reus-Smit (ed.), *The Politics of International Law*, Cambridge: Cambridge University Press, 2004. An exploration of the constitutive impact of international law – as a system of expression, identity, argument and persuasion – on the politics of use of force.

Neff, Stephen C., *War and the Law of Nations: A General History*, Cambridge: Cambridge University Press, 2005. A highly readable history of war from the perspective of international law, ranging from the beginning of history to the present day.

The White House, *The National Security Strategy of the United States of America*, Washington DC, 2002, at www.whitehouse.gov/nsc/nss.html. Received much attention for making the US government's case for pre-emptive use of force (see Chapter 5).

Wheeler, Nicholas J., *Saving Strangers: Humanitarian Intervention and International Society*, Oxford: Oxford University Press, 2000. An important book, combining normative theory and multiple case study analysis, on the changing legitimacy of humanitarian intervention.

5   Human rights

International human rights law is mainly treaty law (a characteristic of modern international law) with some human rights principles having passed into customary international law and some having acquired the status of general principles of law. Prior to the development of international human rights treaties, a relatively small number of states provided protection of human rights through their constitutions or specific domestic laws, but even fewer provided an effective legal system of remedies. There has been a parallel growth in domestic provision and international instruments for the promotion and protection of human rights, with important cross-over between the domestic and international.[1] The focus of this chapter is on the international law of human rights. Nonetheless, some consideration is given to domestic law as a source of law in this area and also, crucially, as a source of remedy. Indeed, a principle common to all human rights treaties is that they may only be invoked by individuals when domestic instruments have failed to provide remedy for breaches of human rights.

In the first section we consider the content of international human rights law as rules, liberal or community values, and discourse. The next section explores the reasons for state compliance with human rights law. Here we might note the curious irony of this area of international law, namely, that individual states have nothing to gain by it. Unlike use of force and trade, where legal regulation promises mutual benefit for states – peace and prosperity – human rights law restricts the sovereign right of states to do as they please in their own domain. Moreover, with few exceptions, states of all creed, from liberal democracies to dictatorships, have signed up for human rights law. Raising the question why? Also noteworthy is the growing breadth and depth of international human rights law. The final section examines the formal, policy and social processes of change in this area of international law.

[1] Henry J. Steiner and Philip Steiner, *International Human Rights in Context: Law, Politics, Morals* (Oxford: Oxford University Press, 2000), Chapter 12.

The content of international human rights law

There exist today more than 100 international treaties on the protection of human rights, some of a multilateral character others of a bilateral character. In addition, the International Court of Justice (ICJ) has recognised that all United Nations member states have a legal obligation to respect human rights under the United Nations Charter and under general international law.[2] It further held that some universally recognised human rights constitute not only individual rights but also generally held obligations on all governments.[3] Even though the ICJ itself has not yet defined the extent to which human rights also limit the actions of the United Nations (e.g., the Security Council) and of its specialised agencies,[4] a general consensus in law exists that such actions are indeed required to respect peremptory norms of general international law, such as inalienable core human rights. This section discusses the content of human rights as being either rules (i.e., a minimal set of rules that states have clearly signed for), community values (such as universal principles or ethics) or a discourse (i.e., processes of communication, argumentation and legitimation).

Human rights clearly encompass values but some lawyers tend to conceptualise human rights in terms of rules and principles. This view is best illustrated by the work of Ian Brownlie, Emeritus Professor of Public International Law at Oxford. In his writing for the Académie of International Law on 'International Law at the Fiftieth Anniversary of the United Nations', Brownlie considered the nature of international law in terms of 'the actual use of rules described as rules in international law by Governments'. For Brownlie, these 'rules are essentially principles of self-delimitation and, for Governments, they are immanent and not external'.[5] Not surprisingly, therefore, his discussion relating to 'the protection of human rights' concentrates on those 'rules' as they appear in the League Covenant of 1919, the UN Charter of 1945, the Universal Declaration of Human Rights (UDHR) of 1948, the Helsinki Act of 1975 and the Paris Charter of 1990. Brownlie further notes that '[t]here can

---

[2] *Barcelona Traction* (ICJ judgment, ICJ Reports 1970, 32) and *Nicaragua v. USA* (ICJ judgment, ICJ Reports 1986, 114).

[3] *Ibid.*

[4] Petersmann, 'Human rights and the law of the World Trade Organization', *Journal of World Trade* 37, 2 (2003), 245–6.

[5] I. Brownlie, 'International law at the fiftieth anniversary of the United Nations', *Académie de droit international, Recueil des cours* 1995, Tome 255 (Dordrecht, the Netherlands: Martinus Nijhoff, 1996), p. 32. Brownlie further considers that 'the rules applicable should be reasonably ascertainable and reflect the normal expectations of States'. *Ibid.*, p. 36.

be no doubt that the main corpus of human rights standards consists of an accumulated code of multilateral standard-setting conventions'. These can be listed as being the two International Covenants on Civil and Political Rights and on Economic, Social and Cultural Rights adopted in 1966, the European Convention on Human Rights of 1950, the American Convention on Human Rights (ACHR) of 1969, the African Charter on Human and Peoples' Rights of 1981, and finally the conventions dealing with specific wrongs (genocide, torture, racial discrimination) and the protection of specific categories of people (refugees, women, children, migrant workers).

Brownlie recognises that the rules contained within these treaties flow from and contribute to principles of customary international law.[6] Indeed, it is generally recognised that the growing corpus of human rights law is increasingly applicable to all states regardless of what treaties they have signed up for. Arguably, however, states still take centre stage in human rights law. Indeed, international law codifies a 'state-centric' conception of human rights: hence breaches of human rights involve state action (or inaction) and are distinct from domestic crime. We also noted that the state is first port of call for individuals seeking remedial action under human rights treaties. This is consistent with a positivist perspective on the primacy of the state in international law. Liberals would argue that individuals have become subjects of modern international law under human rights treaties which grant rights to individuals that they may enforce directly before an international body.[7] But this is only after the state in question has failed to provide effective remedy. Moreover, positivists would point out that these rights conferred by treaties are provided by state consent and that includes the right to appeal directly to an international body for remedy.[8]

As values, the immediate post-World War II human rights instruments reflect Western liberal conceptions of rights – emphasising civil and political over economic, social and cultural rights, and individual rights over the rights of the community. The main rights protected in international law include the right to life, liberty and security, as well as the right to expression, non-discrimination and association. Fundamental human

---

[6] *Ibid.*, pp. 83–4.
[7] Rosalyn Higgins, 'The European Convention on Human Rights', in T. Meron (ed.), *Human Rights in International Law: Legal and Policy Issues* (Oxford: Clarendon Press, 1984), p. 537. Mark Janis, 'Individuals as Subjects of International Law', *Cornell International Law Journal* 17 (1984), 61.
[8] Louis Henkin, 'Compliance with international law in an inter-state system', *Académie de droit international, Recueil des cours* 1989, Tome 216 (Dordrecht, the Netherlands: Martinus Nijhoff, 1990), 227.

rights are also protected via the prohibitions against slavery, genocide and torture under international law. Over time, however, the whole notion of universal rights has been undermined by the development of ideals of cultural relativism.[9] This relativist position is mostly advanced by those non-liberal states seeking to prevent international interference in their domestic affairs. It has little credence in the face of the growth of the global human rights culture.[10]

Relevant here is the concept of *erga omnes* obligations; these are obligations that apply to the international community as a whole and not just individual states. This concept was introduced by the ICJ in the *Barcelona Traction* case (1970). The court held that some rights by their very 'nature' and 'importance' are rights that 'all States can be held to have a legal interest in their protection; they are obligations *erga omnes*.' By way of illustration, it further noted that '[s]uch obligation derives, for example, in contemporary international law, from the outlawing of acts of aggression, and of genocide, as also from the principles and rules concerning the basic rights of the human person, including protection from slavery and racial discrimination'.[11] Thus, in the *East Timor* case (1995), the ICJ recognised the nature of the right of self-determination to be *erga omnes*[12]. In a similar vein of argument, the European Court of Human Rights in Strasbourg has recognised the European Convention of Human Rights as constituting much more than a treaty of international law; it is also an instrument of European public order (*order public*) for the protection of individual human beings.[13]

Human rights law is concerned with all three core liberal values: human dignity, system stability and peace, and liberal democracy. Judge Rosalyn Higgins (President of the ICJ 2006–9) argues that human rights are 'part and parcel of the integrity and dignity of the human being'. Thus, she notes, while such rights are most effectively protected within domestic legal systems, they 'cannot be given or withdrawn' by domestic law.[14]

---

[9] The African system, for instance, emphasises greatly the concept of 'duties' as well as 'rights, and its Charter (the African Charter on Human and Peoples' Rights) is grounded in regional cultural distinctiveness. Makau wa Mutua, 'The Banjul Charter and the African cultural fingerprint: an evaluation of the language of duties', *Virginia Journal of International Law* 35 (1995), 339–80; Mutua, 'The ideology of human rights', *Virginia Journal of International Law* 36 (1996), 598–657.

[10] Rosalyn Higgins, *Problems and Prospects: International Law and How We Use It* (Oxford: Clarendon Press, 1994), p. 96; Jack Donnelly, *Universal Human Rights in Theory and Practice* (Ithaca, NY: Cornell University Press, 1989), p. 118.

[11] *Barcelona Traction* case, ICJ Reports 1970, p. 3 at p. 32, paras. 33–4.

[12] ICJ Reports 1995, p. 90 at p. 102, para 29.   [13] *Loizidou* v. *Turkey* (1995), para. 75.

[14] Rosalyn Higgins, *Problems and Process: International Law and How We Use It* (Oxford: Clarendon Press, 1994), p. 96; see also Myres S. McDougal, Harold D. Lasswell and Lung-chu Chen, *Human Rights and World Public Order: The Basic Policies of an International Law of Human Dignity* (New Haven and London: Yale University Press, 1980).

But equally, the origins of modern human rights law in the construction of the United Nations system is rooted in a concern for the stability of the international system. Following World War II, the victorious powers (and especially the United States) came to appreciate, as Antonio Cassese notes, 'that the Nazi aggression and the atrocities perpetrated during the war had been fruits of a vicious philosophy based on utter disregard for the dignity of human beings'.[15] Proclaiming basic standards in human rights was thus viewed as integral to post-war peace and security. And, as David Forsythe points out, '[i]t is not by accident' that Article 55, in which the United Nations commits itself to promoting 'universal respect for, and observance of, human rights and fundamental freedoms', begins by noting that it shall do so: 'With a view to the creation of conditions of stability and well-being which are necessary for peaceful and friendly relations among nations.'[16] Some liberal scholars maintain that there is an emerging right to democracy. A key element of this is the right to freedom of expression, which is recognised in the Universal Declaration of Human Rights as well as a raft of other human rights treaties. More directly, the right of individuals to partake in genuine and periodic elections, resulting in representative and accountable government, is provided in Article 3, Protocol 1 of the European Convention on Human Rights (1950), Article 23 of the American Convention of Human Rights (1969) and Article 25 of the International Covenant on Civil and Political Rights (1966). There has been some disagreement by states as to the precise meaning of these rights – hence socialist states felt able to argue during the Cold War that their citizens enjoyed these rights when they manifestly did not.[17]

Finally, as a discourse, human rights law provides the vocabulary, concepts and terms of debate over the relationship between the state and individuals. In this sense, it does much more than regulate this relationship. It actually constitutes it. As Donnelly argues, '[h]uman rights constitute individuals as a particular kind of political subject: free and equal rights-bearing citizens. And by establishing the requirements and limits of legitimate government, human rights seek to constitute states of a particular kind.'[18] This is very much a debate between states, but non-state actors (especially, human rights international non-governmental organisations (INGOs)) are also powerful voices in this discourse. Courts and tribunals,

---

[15] Antonio Cassese, *International Law*, 2nd edition (Oxford: Oxford University Press, 2005), p. 377.

[16] David P. Forsythe, *Human Rights in International Relations* (Cambridge: Cambridge University Press, 2000), p. 35.

[17] Thomas M. Franck, 'The emerging right to democratic governance,' *American Journal of International Law* 86 (1992), 46–91; Cassese, *International Law*, p. 395; Alastair Mowbray, 'The promotion of democracy by the European Court of Human Rights: recent cases', *Human Rights Law Review* 4 (1999), 16–23.

[18] Donnelly, *Universal Human Rights*, p. 16.

at the national, regional and international levels, are equally important agents in interpreting and applying (and thereby also 're-reading') legal norms of human rights.

This discourse is rooted in the past whilst also looking to the future. Modern international human rights law owes its origins to customary law on the treatment of alien visitors and their assets – but also to treaty law on the treatment of minorities and international humanitarian law on the treatment of individuals leading to humanitarian intervention (such as the French intervention in Lebanon in 1861). The law relating to aliens developed in the context of the expansion of Western capital into the extra-European world. Much of this law concerns enunciating international minimum standards of treatment for aliens and equality of treatment under national law.[19] While the law of aliens continues to be applicable, human rights law has created a higher bar for states regarding the minimum standards of treatment for both nationals and aliens.

Human rights law as a visionary and aspirational discourse is illustrated in the UN Charter and the Universal Declaration of Human Rights. The Preamble to the UN Charter proclaims that member states 'reaffirm faith in fundamental human rights, in the equal rights of men and women'. Also, Article I includes amongst the purposes of the United Nations, 'international co-operation . . . in promoting and encouraging respect for human rights and for fundamental freedoms for all without distinction as to race, sex, language, or religion'. We have already noted that Article 55 commits the United Nations to promoting human rights and fundamental freedoms. In even stronger terms, Article 56 states that 'All Members pledge themselves to take joint and separate action in co-operation with the Organization for the achievement of the purposes set forth in Article 55.' In spite of its historical importance, it is generally recognised that the legal obligation to respect and observe human rights for all in the UN Charter is too general in provenance. Thus, as soon as it was established (1947), the UN Commission on Human Rights drafted the Universal Declaration of Human Rights (1948) as an authoritative guide to the interpretation of the UN Charter. In spite of its non-binding legal status, the Universal Declaration of Human Rights has had considerable normative impact, affecting the content of national laws and being expressly invoked by domestic as well as international courts. Many of its provisions indeed are now binding through customary law, and are reflected in national constitutions.

---

[19] Ian Brownlie, *Principles of Public International Law*, 6th edition (Oxford: Oxford University of Press, 2003), pp. 497–527.

There was obviously a gap between aspiration and reality in the human rights discourse of the early Cold War period. Many states were far from meeting their commitments under the United Nations Charter to promote and protect human rights. Nonetheless, human rights law has increasingly functioned to regulate and constitute relations between states and their citizens. Human rights law provides an alternative discourse on the moral purpose of the state to the traditional realist discourse of national interest (*raison d'Etat*). It provides new standards for judging the ethics and efficiency of state action. Often it is non-state actors – non-governmental organisations like Human Rights Watch and Amnesty International, and international organisations like the Organization for Security and Cooperation in Europe (OSCE) and the Council of Europe – that do the judging and hold states to account when they fail in their duties to their citizens. And yet human rights law is also a discourse between states – especially between progressive liberal democracies and more conservative illiberal and non-democratic states, but also between liberal democracies – about the rights of individuals and the role of states in providing for these rights.[20] Through this discourse, states communicate and affirm settled norms of state–society relations (e.g., the norm against torture), deliberate over the scope and effect of norms (e.g., the norm of self-determination which prohibits the violent oppression of minority groups) and argue over emerging norms (e.g., the norm of democratic government).

Compliance with international human rights law

Notwithstanding an expanding body of treaty law, there has not been universal compliance with human rights. Instead, it varies greatly across space and time. The general trend since 1948 has been one of growing numbers of states committing to human rights treaties. But, we should be cautious in inferring increasing compliance from increasing rhetorical commitment to human rights.[21] A transnational human rights movement gained increasing voice from the 1970s onwards. In the late 1980s and 1990s, state compliance with these treaties significantly increased worldwide. Empirical evidence suggests a correlative relationship between the end of the Cold War and the growing global culture of human

---

[20] Thomas Risse, Stephen C. Ropp and Kathryn Sikkink (eds.), *The Power of Human Rights* (Cambridge: Cambridge University Press, 1999).

[21] Hans Peter Schmitz and Kathryn Sikkink, 'International human rights', in Walter Carlsnaes, Thomas Risse and Beth A. Simmons. (eds.), *Handbook of International Relations* (Thousand Oaks, CA: Sage, 2002), p. 529.

rights;[22] a causal relationship may be inferred from the post-Cold War wave of democratisation, both in Europe and Asia but also in Latin America and Africa.[23] Yet even today, there is great variation in the promotion and implementation of human rights. In part, this is because many human rights treaties, especially at the international level, do not contain enforcement mechanisms.[24] States are merely obliged to self-validate compliance with these treaties through period reports, and even this reporting obligation is poorly complied with. States can have a clear interest in complying with human rights law, as in the case of the refugee protection regime. But in this area of international law, more so than in the law on the use of force and trade, persuasion, congruence and habit are key motives for compliance with human rights.

There are three principal agencies in the United Nations that are charged with monitoring state compliance with human rights law: the Commission on Human Rights (now the Human Rights Council), the Human Rights Committee and the Office of the High Commissioner for Human Rights. From 1946–2006, the UN Commission on Human Rights was the main forum for negotiating international human rights standards (such as the UDHR and the Covenants). It also gained some very modest monitoring powers. The Economic and Social Council (ECOSOC) Resolution 1503 (1970) authorised the Commission on Human Rights to investigate complaints (communications) that 'appear to reveal a consistent pattern of gross and reliably attested violations of human rights'. Practice shows that the 1503 procedure was by no means an efficient or timely implementation procedure; the admissibility threshold (e.g., only situations of gross and systematic violations are covered) was very high, the entire procedure was confidential, delays were frequent and political considerations were very strong due to the fact that the Commission was composed of states' representatives, and not of independent experts.[25] This led Jack Donnelly to describe the procedure as 'largely a

---

[22] Jack Donnelly, 'International human rights: a regime analysis', *International Organization* 40 (1986), 599–642.

[23] Samuel P. Huntington, *The Third Wave: Democratization in the Late Twentieth Century* (Norman: University of Oklahoma Press, 1991).

[24] Internal accountability measures may operate as surrogate enforcement mechanisms in liberal democracies. But non-democratic states may commit to human rights treaties with little fear of actually having to make good on the legal obligations that flow from such commitments. This has triggered some debate among IL scholars about what, if anything, one can infer from the growth in numbers and membership of human rights treaties. Oona A. Hathaway, 'Do human rights treaties make a difference', *Yale Law Journal* 111 (2002), 1944–5; Ryan Goodman and Derek Jinks, 'Measuring the effects of human rights treaties', *European Journal of International Law* 14 (2003), 171–83.

[25] Donnelly, *Universal Human Rights*, p. 129 and p. 132.

promotional device involving weak, sporadic, and limited monitoring'.[26] An additional problem with the UN Commission on Human Rights was that it was constituted by a rotating membership and thus any United Nations member, regardless of their human rights record, could sit on the Commission (or even chair it). Thus, in 2006 Cuba, Saudi Arabia and Sudan – all serious human rights abusers – were members of the Commission.[27] The Commission on Human Rights ceased to exist in April 2006 and was replaced by the Human Rights Council. It is planned that this Council will meet more often and for longer periods of time than the Commission did but that membership will continue to be drawn from the list of United Nations members.[28]

The second UN body competent to promote human rights at the international level is the Human Rights Committee which was created under the International Covenant on Civil and Political Rights (ICCPR) (1966) to monitor compliance with the Covenant. This is a treaty-based body and not a UN Charter-mandated body. Unlike the Commission on Human Rights / Human Rights Council, the Human Rights Committee is composed of independent experts whose primary function is to review reports submitted periodically by the states parties to the ICCPR. However, in many cases, states remain unco-operative: reports are often incomplete and submitted late, if at all. A more interesting mechanism, also provided under the ICCPR, allows states to consent to the Committee receiving communications from other states parties concerning alleged violations. But this mechanism has proved to have limited effect because states are reluctant to bring formal complaints against one another for fear of political and economic retaliation, or counter-allegations of human rights violations. Finally, the Human Rights Committee also has jurisdiction over petitions brought by individuals but this enforcement procedure is only optional; the state against which a petition is being brought must be a party to the First Optional Protocol to the ICCPR. This system illustrates the reluctance of states to accept a worldwide system of human rights 'supervision' let alone 'enforcement'.[29] But, as highlighted by Henry Steiner, there is much more to the dispute-resolution function of the Human Rights Committee, particularly in its key role in engaging in an on-going, fruitful dialogue with states parties, non

---

[26] *Ibid.*, p. 132.
[27] Hence, David Harris described the Commission as 'a highly political animal, with its initiatives and priorities reflecting bloc interests as well as the human rights merits of each case'. D. J. Harris, *Cases and Materials on International Law*, 6th edition (London: Sweet and Maxwell, 2004), p. 628.
[28] UN General Assembly Resolution 60/251, 3rd April 2006.
[29] Richard Gardiner, *International Law* (Harlow, England: Longman, 2003), p. 276.

governmental and intergorvernmental institutions, advocates, scholars and students.[30]

The third United Nations body competent to promote and protect human rights at the international level is the Office of the UN High Commissioner for Human Rights (UNHCHR, 1993). The UNHCHR has a rolling mandate, under the authority of the UN Secretary-General, to promote and protect human rights, principally through naming and shaming human rights violators. The UNHCHR has been successful in drawing attention to gross violations of human rights though, as the on-going crisis in Sudan suggests, often effective enforcement action does not follow on from this.

The United Nations has also sponsored several other human rights treaties: the International Covenant on Economic, Social and Cultural Rights (ICESCR), the Conventions on the Elimination of All Forms of Racial Discrimination (1966) and Discrimination Against Women (1979), the Convention Against Torture (CAT) and Other Cruel, Inhuman or Degrading Treatment or Punishment (1984) and the Convention on the Rights of the Child (1989). Each has its own monitoring system and its own success rate in terms of compliance, but generally it is poor. For example, the system of supervision under the ICESCR is very loose (even looser than under the ICCPR and Optional Protocol) because as far as these rights are concerned, states' compliance is dependent on having the necessary resources. Equally, the Convention on the Elimination of All Forms of Racial Discrimination establishes a Committee on the Elimination of Racial Discrimination but this Committee has adopted a very narrow interpretation of its powers and depends on self-reporting by contracting parties.[31]

Human rights treaties at the regional level developed in parallel with United Nations treaties. Of the three regions providing human rights treaties (i.e., Europe, the Americas and Africa), Europe is by far the most advanced in its system of protection, thanks largely to state consent for an effective mechanism of enforcement. The European Convention on Human Rights and Fundamental Freedoms (ECHR), adopted under the auspices of the Council of Europe (Strasbourg) in 1950, favours a system of enforcement over a reporting requirement.[32] This system is

[30] Henry Steiner, 'Individual claims in a world of massive violations: what role for the Human Rights Committee?', in Philip Alston and James Crawford (eds.), *The Future of UN Human Rights Treaty Monitoring* (Cambridge: Cambridge University Press, 2000), pp. 15–53.

[31] On the work of each of these UN monitoring systems, see Philip Alston and James Crawford, *The Future of UN Human Rights Treaty Monitoring* (Cambridge: Cambridge University Press, 2000), pp. 15–198.

[32] Economic, social and cultural rights are protected by the Council of Europe (albeit less robustly) under the 1961 European Social Charter.

generally regarded as being very effective. The principle of subsidiarity still operates (under Art. 1 of ECHR), which places primary responsibility for the protection of human rights on state authorities.[33] It is when the state fails, that the Strasbourg Court steps in. The Court may go beyond individual redress for a breach of human rights and require a contracting party to change its law or practice. However, as a general rule, the Court's judgments are declaratory of violation, leaving it to the member states how best to address the violation. Since 1998, the jurisdiction of the Court is compulsory for contracting parties, and individuals within these states have a right of direct petition to the Court. Enforcement depends on the state in question taking remedial action. Recalcitrant states face pressure from the Committee of Ministers of the Council of Europe but its punitive powers are limited – ultimately it may threaten to expel a recalcitrant member from the organisation of the Council of Europe. But in the vast bulk of cases, states do comply with Court judgments, even if only after some time.[34] The Council of Europe also established a Commissioner for Human Rights in 1999. The Commissioner deals directly with governments and issues opinions, reports and recommendations regarding human rights. In short, the effectiveness of this regional regime rests more on consent than coercion. This point is underlined by Jack Donnelly, who puts the success of the European regime down to state consent and a strong collective commitment to effective monitoring and enforcement. Indeed, he sees these enforcement measures as 'less a cause than a reflection of the regime's strength'.[35]

In the Americas, the human rights system comprises of two main treaties. The American Declaration of the Rights and Duties of Man (1948), adopted at the founding of the Organization of American States (OAS), presents a list of human rights very similar to that of the UDHR. The American Convention of Human Rights of 1969 recognises personal, legal, civil and political rights, and the right to property.[36] The latter establishes the Inter-American Court of Human Rights (1979, San Jose, Costa Rica), which has both an advisory and a dispute settlement function, but since its jurisdiction is optional on contracting parties, it

---

[33] Paul Mahoney, 'Marvelous richness of diversity or invidious cultural relativism', *Human Rights Law Journal* 19 (1998), 1.

[34] R. R. Churchill and J. R. Young, 'Compliance with judgments of the European Court of Human Rights and decisions of the Committee of Ministers: the experience of the United Kingdom, 1975–1987', *British Yearbook of International Law* 62 (1991), 283.

[35] Donnelly, *Universal Human Rights*, p. 141. The limitations, in general, of coercive measures in inducing compliance with international law is explored in Andrew T. Guzman, 'A compliance-based theory of international law', *California Law Review* 90 (2002), 1823–87.

[36] Economic, social and cultural rights came to be recognised by the 1988 Protocol of San Salvadore which came into force in 1999.

has had limited effectiveness. In addition, the Inter-American Commission on Human Rights was established in 1959 to protect rights under both the OAS Charter and the ACHR. When dealing with states parties to both the Charter and the ACHR, it has powers of enforcement through a system of complaint similar to that provided originally under the European Convention on Human Rights. But its powers are more limited, to making recommendations for effective compliance, when it comes to states that are only party to the Charter.[37] Overall, the Inter-American system has been less successful than its European counterpart, especially in its impact on the domestic legal systems of contracting parties. Nonetheless, the Commission, rather than the Court, has exercised a broad range of powers and thereby has been more effective in protecting human rights. Here coercion, especially as exercised by the United States, has been a motive in state compliance; this empirical finding is consistent with the realist emphasis on the role of hegemonic power in ensuring regimes effectiveness. At the same time, as suggested above, progressive democratisation in the region has led to increasing voluntary acceptance of (and consent to) the human rights system largely replacing external coercion.[38]

The African Charter on Human and Peoples' Rights or Banjul Charter (1981), unlike its other regional counterparts, seeks to protect community (i.e., collective or peoples) as well as individual rights, and to impose duties. Furthermore, it contains no derogation clauses comparable to Article 15 of the ECHR (i.e., war or other public emergency) – having said that it allows for so-called 'claw-backs' clauses.[39] Thus from a normative perspective, the African Charter offers considerable innovations over its counterparts in Europe and the Americas. However, its monitoring system is weak. It provides a reporting system similar to international human rights treaties, as well as a largely ineffective (and underused) Commission to hear complaints. The system can be described as mostly conciliatory.[40] In 1998, a Protocol for the Establishment of an African Court

---

[37] Cecilia Medina, 'The Inter-American Commission on Human Rights and the Inter-American Court of Human Rights: reflections on a joint venture', *Human Rights Quarterly* 12 (1990), 439–64.

[38] Thomas Risse, Stephen C. Ropp and Kathryn Sikkink (eds.), *The Power of Human Rights: International Norms and Domestic Change* (Cambridge: Cambridge University Press, 1999).

[39] Rose M. D'Sa, 'Human and peoples' rights: distinctive features of the African Charter', *Journal of African Law* 29 (1985), 72–81.

[40] Ian Brownlie, *Principles of Public International Law*, 6th edition (Oxford University Press, 2003), p. 545. For a more optimistic account of the work of the Commission, see, Chidi Anselm Odinkalu, 'The individual complaints procedure of the African Commission on Human and Peoples' Rights: a preliminary assessment', *Transnational Law and*

of Human and Peoples' Rights was signed. The new African Court has advisory, conciliatory and contentious jurisdiction. The latter is unusually broad in extending to any relevant human rights treaties, and not only the African Charter and the Court is Protocol. However, only states parties to the Protocol, the African Commission and African intergovernmental organisations have direct access to the Court; not individuals, nor non-governmental organisations (NGOs). In short, of all the regional systems, the African one has been the least successful in shaping state compliance with human rights.[41] This is mainly the result of institutions that still need time to develop.

Finally, in Asia there are neither regional norms nor monitoring procedures. The 1996 Asian Human Rights Charter was drafted by NGOs and has attracted no state support. In the Middle East, the League of Arab States established a Permanent Arab Commission on Human Rights in 1968, but it has been famously inactive, except on the issue of the human rights situation in the Israeli-occupied territories. As far as the normative framework is concerned, it is equally weak. The Arab Charter of Human Rights, which was drafted in 1971, was only adopted by the Council of the League in 1994 and remains largely ignored.[42]

Consent goes some way to explaining this variation in the effectiveness of regional human rights regimes, and the limitation of international instruments. But we would argue that congruence, internalisation and habit are equally, if not more, important motives.[43] Most obvious is congruence between norms of liberal democracy and human rights. The European human rights regime is so effective because of the concentration of liberal democracies in this region. Indeed, a state must be democratic to join the Council of Europe. Moreover, we may note a virtuous circle whereby newly democratic states use the ECHR to lock in newly imported Liberal democratic norms in their internal political systems.[44] One of the stated purposes of the OAS is 'to promote and consolidate representative democracy'. However, many of the twenty-one founding members have

---

Contemporary Problems 8 (1998), 359 (most of this article is reproduced in Steiner and Alston, *International Human Rights*, pp. 923–9).

[41] Donnelly, *Universal Human Rights*, p. 144; Malcolm N. Shaw, *International Law*, 5th edition (Cambridge: Cambridge University Press, 2003), pp. 363–5. Ann Pieter van der Mei, 'The new African Court on Human and Peoples' Rights: towards an effective human rights protection mechanism for Africa?', *Leiden Journal of International Law* 18 (2005), 113–29.

[42] Donnelly, *Universal Human Rights*, pp. 144–5.

[43] Harold Hongju Koh, 'Why do nations obey international law?', *Yale Law Journal* 106 (1997), 2598–9.

[44] Andrew Moravcsik, 'The origins of human, rights regimes, democratic delegation in postwar Europe', *International Organization* 54 (2000), 228.

not been democracies for most of the organisation's history: included here are Argentina, Brazil, Chile, Colombia, Cuba, El Salvador, Guatemala, Nicaragua and Peru. Not surprisingly, democracies have a far better track record when it comes to protecting and promoting human rights than non-democracies. Democratic governments may be held to account for human rights violations whereas non-democratic governments often rely on systematic abuses of human rights to stay in power. Liberalism is also important. As we noted in Chapter 3, restraints on the internal use of state violence is a core liberal value. Again, Europe has a far higher concentration of liberal countries than other regions. Indeed, the human rights regime that has emerged in Europe very much reflects the liberal values and aspirations of these states.[45] The extension of the Council of Europe to new democracies in Eastern Europe and the former Soviet Union presents a challenge to the regime, in that there is less congruence between the political culture of these states and human rights law than in Western Europe. This goes to underline the importance of the Council of Europe as an agent of socialisation in driving the eastward expansion of the European human rights regime.[46]

Compliance with human rights law ultimately depends on internationalisation of international rules in domestic legal systems. In this respect, Henkin argues that the international law of human rights differs greatly from international law in general because 'compliance with international human rights law [. . .] is wholly internal'.[47] Indeed, there cannot be a violation of international human rights law unless state authorities fail to provide adequate remedies. The remedy in question may have its source in the international law of human rights (e.g., the UN Convention Against Torture requires states to 'ensure that all acts of torture are offences under its criminal law') but equally a remedy may be found in domestic law and state practice (e.g., the granting of asylum to refugees is not provided under the 1951 Refugee Convention but has evolved as practice in many states). David Forsythe also emphasises the importance of internationalisation to compliance. He argues that one of the basic functions of all law, including international law, is 'to educate in an informal sense'. By informing foreign policy, military doctrine and training, and the action of private groups (corporations and NGOs), international human rights law takes persuasive effect. In this sense, conformity and compliance with international human rights law does

---

[45] Moravcsik, 'The origins of human rights regimes' 217–52.
[46] Jeffrey T. Checkel, 'Norms, institutions, and national identity in contemporary Europe,' *International Studies Quarterly* 43 (1999), 83–114. Mahoney, 'Marvelous richness of diversity', p. 1.
[47] Henkin, 'Compliance with international law', p. 250.

not depend on judicial enforcement. Indeed, for Forsythe, 'the optimum situation is for legal standards to be internalized by individuals to such an extent that court cases are unnecessary'.[48]

Of course, this perspective raises the issue of the process of internalisation and, in particular, variation in the willingness and capacity of states to internalise international rules on human rights. Congruence between domestic culture and international rules can ease the process of internalisation. This is true for domestic political culture, as noted earlier, but also for legal culture. Some legal cultures are more prepared to adapt in line with international regimes. The legal cultures of the European Union member states are noteworthy in this respect. The decades-long process of European integration has socialised these states into accepting the primacy of the European Union. This has produced a habit of internalisation among European Union states that makes them more ready to internalise international human rights law. Domestic legal culture matters also in terms of variation in state capacity to internalise international law. Even among European Union states there is some variation. For instance, international law is generally given priority over domestic law in civil law systems (e.g., France, Germany, Spain and Poland), whereas in common law systems (such as the United Kingdom and Ireland) the judiciary need only recognise international rules that have been incorporated in domestic legislation. There is even more pronounced variation between the established and emerging democracies of Europe, in terms of the capacity of domestic legal systems to absorb international human rights law.[49] In general, international and regional human rights law requires profound and wide-ranging change to the legal and law-enforcement systems of new democracies seeking to catch up with their Western neighbours. Such profound internal change may occur in any democratising state (or even non-democracy) as part of a broader process of 'acculturation' into human rights.[50] Thus, as we discuss in the next section, internalisation often actually involves socialisation by states into the norms and rules codified in human rights regimes.

The refugee protection regime provides a good example of where state compliance may be motivated by self-interest. That is not to say that other reasons – such as congruence – do not operate here. Thus, the norm of providing refuge for those fleeing persecution is arguably constitutive

---

[48] Forsythe, *Human Rights in International Relations*, p. 14.

[49] Mark Janis, 'Russia and the 'legality' of Strasbourg Law', *European Journal of International Law* 8 (1997), 93–9.

[50] Ryan Goodman and Derek Jinks, 'How to influence states: socialization and human rights law', *Duke Law Journal* 54 (2004), 621–703. See also Koh, 'Why do nations obey?'

of modern liberal democracy.[51] At the same time, states have a strong interest in regulating the cross-border flow of refugees.[52] Historically, the refugee protection regime originated in the need to give some stability to post-colonial and post-war spurts of state building. Thus, Bruce Cronin argues 'the [international protection regime] IPR for refugees was not created to assist those displaced from war. Rather states constructed the system to address post-war political developments that were related to the construction of new states and new political orders.'[53] Fairness was also relevant, in that state leaders shared a common sense of responsibility for the welfare of refugees.[54] State interest took a new twist during the Cold War, as Western states used the Refugee Convention as a political tool to embarrass the Soviet bloc and sweep up defectors.[55] The European Union committed itself to creating a common asylum regime for the Union at the turn of new millennium. Underlying this new regime is a liberal vision promising expanded rights to refugees and other persons in need of protection. But driving the process is self-interest: the need for the European Union to harmonise and improve efficiency in this policy area. Indeed, national self-interests, and some dispute about the fair distribution of costs among European Union members, is compromising the original liberal vision.[56]

Change in international human rights law

States have played a central role in the evolution of international human rights law. This body of law rests on a raft of major treaties at the

[51] Matthew J. Gibney, *The Ethics and Politics of Asylum: Liberal Democracy and the Response of Refugees* (Cambridge: Cambridge University Press, 2004).
[52] James C. Hathaway, 'Framing refugee protection in the new world disorder', *Cornell International Law Journal* 34/, 2 (2001), 257–320.
[53] Bruce Cronin, *Institutions for the Common Good: International Protection Regimes in International Society* (Cambridge: Cambridge University Press, 2003), p. 156.
[54] John Garvey, 'Towards a reformulation of international refugee law', *Harvard International Law Journal* 26 (1985), 483–502; Paul Weis, 'The 1967 Protocol Relating to the Status of Refugees and some questions of the Law of Treaties', *British Yearbook of International Law* (1967), p. 61; Vera Gowlland-Debbas, 'La Charte des Nations Unies et la Convention de Genève du 28 juillet 1951 relative au statut des réfugiés', in *La Convention de Genève du 28 juillet 1951 Relative au Statut des Réfugiés 50 ans après: Bilan et Perspectives* (Brussels: Bruylant, 2001), pp. 207–8.
[55] Gil Loescher and J. A. Scanlan, *Calculated Kindness: Refugees and America's Half-Open Door, 1945 to the Present* (New York: Free Press, 1986). Loescher *Beyond Charity: International Cooperation and the Global Refugee Crisis* (Oxford: Oxford University Press, 1993); Gil Loescher, *The UNHCR and World Politics: A Perilous Path* (Oxford: Oxford University Press, 2001).
[56] Hélène Lambert, 'The EU Asylum Qualification Directive: its impact on the jurisprudence of the United Kingdom and international law', *International and Comparative Law Quarterly* 55 (2006), 161–92.

international level (e.g., ICCPR, ICESCR, CAT, and the Refugee Convention) and regional level (especially the ECHR and ACHR). Some fundamental human rights principles, such as the prohibition of torture, genocide and slavery, and the principle of racial non-discrimination, exist in customary international law. Arguably state consent is less central to customary law than treaty law, because customary law may be said to express the collective will of states – that is, the will of most states, especially the most powerful states – and, in any case, does not require explicit state consent. Thus, unlike treaties where states must actively give consent, inaction or silence by a state is taken to mean that it has consented to new customary law. It may be possible for a state through persistent objection not to be bound by an emerging rule of customary law (this possibility does not exist for established customary rules). But where that rule expresses a peremptory norm, derogation by individual states is not permitted. We have already noted that many of the principles of human rights law are peremptory in nature. Of course, states exercise some leeway in interpreting the precise meaning of many human rights norms; for example, on whether abortion violates the right to life. Another very controversial and current example is state disagreement over what constitutes torture and degrading treatment (which we discuss in the conclusion to this chapter in the context of the US 'global war on terror'). These issues of interpretation aside, the peremptory character of human rights norms is further expressed in international human rights treaties to which almost all states have consented. Accordingly, it may be said that international human rights law has evolved through a formal process where states have been the major agents of law-creation and change, and so state consent has played a central role.

At the same time, it is abundantly clear that change in international human rights law involves a plurality of actors, including transnational policy networks, INGOs/NGOs and judiciaries. Policy networks embedded in intergovernmental organisations (IGOs) play an essential role in formulating new rules of human rights law. Hence, the UN Commission on Human Rights spent twenty years preparing the ICCPR and the ICESCR, in order to put flesh on the bones of the UDHR. This can be read through the realist lens as illustrating state action. But equally, transnational policy coalitions can emerge within IGOs to pressure home governments to adopt particular policies.[57] Transnational policy networks also play a crucial role in elaborating human rights standards, and

---

[57] This is illustrated in the context of security policy in Thomas Risse-Kappen, *Cooperation Among Democracies: The European Influence on US Foreign Policy* (Princeton, NJ: Princeton University Press, 1995).

co-ordinating implementation of human rights rules.[58] For instance, EU harmonisation on standards of refugee protection is being advanced by a transnational network of policy-makers based in member states (empowered through the Council of the EU) and in the EU Commission. EU Directives on asylum, as on other matters, are a source of EU law. But, at the same time, this process of law-making is essentially one of policy elaboration and co-ordination between EU member states.[59]

NGOs operating at the national and transnational level have also played a crucial role, both in creating a general climate conducive to the advancement of human rights law, and in influencing change in specific areas through informing public and policy debate. INGOs/NGOs wield such influence through their expert knowledge of and moral standing on human rights issues. INGOs often lead international campaigns to evolve human rights law. This effort usually involves mobilising political support in host (liberal) states to exert pressure for change in human rights law, as well as working directly with NGOs and opposition groups to resist oppression in non-Western states.[60] A classic example of NGO-led change in this area of law is the abolition of slavery, which was outlawed following a campaign by British abolitionist groups in the nineteenth century to pressure the British government to deploy the Royal Navy to close down slave trading routes.[61] More recently, an umbrella of human rights and health NGOs, working with progressive Western states, led the campaign to create the CAT.[62] NGOs may also indirectly influence the evolution of human rights law through informal and occasionally formal channels of policy consultation. Thus, some NGOs (such as the AIRE Centre) have recognised 'participatory status' at the Council of Europe.[63]

Another important way that international law can change is through the interpretation given by international courts or other quasi-legislative bodies such as the United Nations General Assembly. The difficulty here,

[58] Anne-Marie Slaughter, *A New World Order* (Princeton, NJ: Princeton University Press, 2004), p. 24.
[59] Lambert, 'EU Qualification Directive'.
[60] Audie Klotz, *Norms in International Relations* (Ithaca, NY: Cornell University Press, 1995); Margret Keck and Kathryn Sikkink, *Activists Across Borders: Transnational Advocacy Networks in International Politics* (Ithaca, NY: Cornell University, 1998); Risse *et al.* (eds.), *The Power of Human Rights*.
[61] Ethan A. Nadelmann, 'Global prohibition regimes: the evolution of norms in international society,' *International Organization* 44 (1990), 491–8.
[62] Preslava Stoeva, 'Norm development and knowledge creation in the world system: protecting people, intellectual property and the environment', PhD thesis, University of Exeter, 2006, Chapter 2.
[63] 'Discours de Daniel Zielinski, Président sortant de la Commission de Liaison des OING', at www.coe.int/T/e/Com/Files/Events/2004-01-NGO/news_zielinski.asp.

in terms of establishing change, is well summarised by Oscar Schachter: 'the line between interpretation and new law is often blurred. Whenever a general rule is construed to apply to a new set of facts, an element of novelty is introduced; in effect new content is added to the existing rule. This is even clearer when an authoritative body re-defines and makes more precise an existing rule or principle.'[64] An obvious example is the role played by the European Court of Human Rights in the development of the principles guaranteed in the ECHR. For instance, in the context of the norm prohibiting torture (Article 3), the Strasbourg Court lowered the threshold for what constitutes torture in recognition of 'the increasingly high standard being required in the area of the protection of human rights', which demands 'greater firmness in assessing breaches of the fundamental values of democratic societies'.[65] The Court further requires states not only to refrain from torture, but also to enforce this prohibition in their own legal systems. Thus, change here was to the effect of significantly strengthening the rule against torture, both in its substantive and procedural scope.[66] Unlike in common law systems, there is no rule of precedent at the Strasbourg Court, nor at the ICJ or European Court of Justice. Thus decisions by these courts, while binding on the parties to the dispute, are not strictly binding on the courts themselves. However, these decisions are commonly taken to be statements of existing law and are used as benchmarks in future cases.[67] Hence states accept these interpretations of law, even when it works against them in future cases. As Rasmussen observes, 'even governments overtly hostile to the Court's authority do not seek to ask the [ECJ] to overturn a previous ruling but rather use it as a statement of the law and use it as a point of departure for making arguments in subsequent cases'.[68] Anne-Marie Slaughter locates the Strasbourg Court at the centre of a transnational legal network and emerging 'global jurisprudence' on human rights. In addition to a 'vertical dialogue' within Europe between the Strasbourg Court and domestic courts, she points to the 'persuasive authority' of the Strasbourg Court's decisions beyond Europe. Hence, the highest courts in Israel, Jamaica, South Africa and Zimbabwe, as well as the Inter-American Court of

---

[64] Oscar Schachter, *International Law in Theory and Practice* (The Hague: Martin Nijhoff, 1991), p. 87.

[65] *Selmouni v. France*, judgment of 28 July 1999, para.101.

[66] Hélène Lambert, *The Position of Aliens in Relation to the European Convention on Human Rights* (Strasbourg: Council of Europe, 2006), p. 29.

[67] Anne-Marie Burley and Walter Mattli, 'Europe before the court: a political theory of legal integration', *International Organization* 47 (1993), 67.

[68] Hjalte Rasmussen, *On Law and Policy in the European Court of Justice*, pp. 275–81, quoted in Anne-Marie Slaughter-Burley and Walter Mattli, 'Europe before the Court: a political theory of legal integration', *International Organisations* 41 (1993), 67.

Human Rights, and the UN Human Rights Committee have all cited judgments of the Strasbourg Court.[69] It may also be noted that the traffic in persuasive decisions is two-way between international courts and quasi-judicial bodies: hence the Committee Against Torture has cited the Strasbourg Court and vice versa.[70]

Finally, human rights law has changed through a social process involving elite learning, community socialisation, and internalisation of new norms. This is well illustrated in the Helsinki Final Act of the Conference on Security and Co-operation in Europe, adopted in 1975, which included a 'basket' on human rights. Like the UDHR (which was used as a standard when drafting the Final Act), the Final Act is a non-binding instrument which has had considerable normative impact, especially in validating the universal applicability (i.e., in the Soviet bloc) of Western conceptions of human rights.[71] It facilitated learning of Western human rights norms by Soviet political elites and gave support to norm entrepreneurs within the Soviet Union that were seeking to promote political liberalisation.[72] The political class in post-Soviet Russia has become socialised into accepting political human rights and people expect to exercise the right to vote, to free expression and free association. However, it is too early to judge whether these norms have become internalised in functioning institutions and are habitually practised. Indeed, some argue that democracy has become de-railed in Russia, under the corrupting influence of rapid economic liberalisation and in the face of an authoritarian executive inadequately held to account by a weak legislature.[73] The social process of normative change is much more complete in Western Europe, with elite learning of new human rights rules leading, for the most part smoothly, to internalisation in domestic policy and law. As already suggested, this easy path to internalisation is understandable given the congruence between Western political and legal culture and evolving international human rights law. Congruence may also explain variation in the levels of internalisation of international human rights

---

[69] Slaughter, *New World Order*, pp. 79–81.

[70] Hélène Lambert, 'The influence of the European Court of Human Rights judgments on other international treaty bodies – Keynote presentation', in *Second Colloquy on the European Convention on Human Rights and the Protection of Refugees, Asylum-Seekers and Displaced Persons* (Strasbourg: Council of Europe, 2000), pp. 124–7.

[71] ICJ, *Nicaragua v. USA* (1986) para.189 and para. 264.

[72] Thomas Risse-Kappen, 'Ideas do not float freely: transnational coalitions, domestic structures, and the end of the Cold War', *International Organization* 48 (1994), 185–214; Matthew Evangelista, *Unarmed Forces: The Transnational Movement to End the Cold War* (Ithaca, NY: Cornell University Press, 1999).

[73] Michael McFaul, *Russia's Unfinished Revolution: Political Change from Gorbachev to Putin* (Ithaca, NY: Cornell University Press, 2001); M. Steven Fish, *Democracy Derailed in Russia: The Failure of Open Politics* (Cambridge: Cambridge University Press, 2005).

law elsewhere around the world, both across and within regions. Hence the poor provision for political and civil rights in the Middle East may be explained in terms of an Arab political culture that is antipathetic to Western-style democracy.[74] Equally, the stark contrast between the breadth and depth of internalisation of human rights law in China and Japan is down to an East–West divide within this region between authoritarian Confucian China and democratic Westernised Japan.

Norm entrepreneurs have been instrumental in developing international human rights law and in diffusing these rules around the world. We have already noted the prominent role played by NGOs in this regard – such as the anti-slavery movement in Victorian Britain (and the United States), and the human rights and medical groups that lobbied for a ban on torture. In refugee law, the United Nations High Commissioner for Refugees (UNHCR) has and continues to play a vital role in elaborating law in this area, and in educating new and democratising states in their obligations under the 1951 Refugee Convention.[75] External shock has also been important to the recent development of refugee law. Conventionally, protection under the Refugee Convention is only offered to those who can demonstrate an individual fear of persecution. The shock of the wars in the former Yugoslavia in the 1990s, generating mass flight of populations from Balkan war zones, caused the conventional refugee regime to collapse. In response, some Western governments offered refugee status to whole categories of those fleeing war. Other Western states offered temporary asylum on a non-legal basis but, again, this was to whole groups of people. A new EU Asylum Directive gives legal force to the provision of temporary protection in law in all EU states.[76]

Notwithstanding the growing strength of international human rights law, human rights continue to be abused by many states around the world. Most of these cases involve violations of international law. Massive abuses of human rights in the 'ethnic conflicts' of the 1990s have triggered changes in international criminal law (e.g., with the extension of humanitarian law to civil wars) and law on the use of force (e.g., with the evolving state practice of forcible humanitarian intervention). These

---

[74] Arab political culture does create space for some democratic practices but arguably these do not allow for the institutionalised protection of human rights. See Larbi Sadiki, *The Search for Arab Democracy* (New York: Columbia University Press, 2001).

[75] Guy S. Goodwin-Gill and Jane McAdam, *The Refugee in International Law* (Oxford: Oxford University Press, 2007), pp. 215–32. James C. Hathaway, *The Rights of Refugees Under International Law* (Cambridge: Cambridge University Press, 2005), pp. 112–18.

[76] Council Directive 2001/55/EC of 20 July 2001 on minimum standards for giving temporary protection in the event of a mass influx of displaced persons and on measures promoting a balance of efforts between member states in receiving such persons and in bearing the consequences thereof.

changes will be dealt with in Chapters 6 and 4 respectively. More minor violations of international human rights law can also lead to legal change where such violations are caused by lack of clarity in the substance and/or application of the law (as opposed to where the law is clear and the state is plainly violating it). In such cases, where there is judicial oversight (e.g., by the Strasbourg Court), this may also involve judicial interpretation which, as we noted earlier, can produce change in international law.

Conclusion

All three lenses provide useful perspectives on international human rights law. This area of law is characteristic of modern international law given that it is mostly treaty law. Consistent with the realist lens, this points to the role of state consent as reason for compliance, and to legal change as a formal process. At the same time, international human rights law expresses core values of the international community. Human rights rest on the dignity of the individual, and the protection of human rights serves system stability. Arguably, democratic rights are also increasingly being recognised by the international community. The liberal lens has less use when it comes to explaining state compliance with international human rights law. Self-interest is not a powerful motive for compliance as international law in this area generally serves to restrain state freedom of action.[77] One exception may be refugee law, where states do have a mutual interest in managing the movement of people across their borders. However, the liberal notion of legal change as a policy process has considerable explanatory power in the area of human rights, especially in terms of the plurality of actors involved. The authoritative decision-making process in human rights substantially involves international organisations, courts and other quasi-legal bodies. NGOs operating through transnational coalitions led campaigns to advance international human rights law. Much of the law in this area is elaborated and implemented through transnational policy networks. Judicial interpretation is also an important method of change in international human rights law, and here too there is much transnational traffic of those judicial decisions that carry 'persuasive authority'. Finally, the constructivist lens draws our attention to the role of international human rights law as a discourse – as constituting

---

[77] In this sense there is a cost in committing to human rights treaties, though this cost is greater for liberal democracies then non-democracies, since the latter can more easily evade their legal obligations under such treaties. Oona A. Hathaway, 'The cost of commitment', *Stanford Law Review* 55 (2003), 1821–62.

the relationship between state and citizens, and as providing a vocabulary and moral purpose for judging state action. Congruence and internalisation emerge as powerful and reinforcing reasons for compliance with international human rights law – thus, explaining significant national and regional variation in compliance. Change in international human rights law – especially in terms of its spreading influence – may be explained in terms of a social process centred on elite learning and state socialisation. Key actors – NGOs and progressive states – have also played the vital role of norm entrepreneurs in pushing forward the boundaries of international human rights law.

Empirically, the overall picture is one of the growing normative strength (both in breadth and depth) of international human rights law. As we noted, many norms of human rights law are peremptory in character from which no derogation is permitted, such as the prohibition against slavery, genocide, racial discrimination and torture. Moreover, the new 'doctrine of human rights' has also brought changes in many other areas of traditional international law; included here are the recognition of individuals as subjects of international law, the expansion of international organisations, international monitoring of compliance with law, the notion of *jus cogens*, the development of the international criminal justice system, and the expanding scope of humanitarian law. It might even be argued that in recent decades there has been a shift from a slowly evolving consent-based international law of human rights to a more dynamic doctrine that expresses community values.[78]

This conclusion might appear odd to some in the context of the challenge presented by the United States to some aspects of human rights. The redefinition of torture by the administration of George W. Bush to make lawful interrogation techniques, and the non-recognition of rights and detention without trial of terrorists and other 'unlawful combatants' held in Guantanamo Bay, dramatically illustrate the limits of international human rights law. Here is the most powerful state in the world apparently trampling over the rules in its treatment of detainees.[79] US action, which offends core liberal values and defies condemnation by a host of international and non-governmental human rights organisations, is hard to understand from a liberal perspective. A realist lens offers one explanation – namely, as the world hegemon, the United States has the power to introduce more permissive human rights standards for the treatment of unlawful combatants, and in the context of the new threat from

---

[78] Cassese, *International Law*, p. 393.
[79] Philippe Sands, *Lawless World: America and the Making and Breaking of Global Rules* (London: Allen Lane, 2005), pp. 143–73.

catastrophic terrorism, it claims the right to do so. But this is an impov-
erished account. A richer account is provided by the constructivist lens.
It points to the role of international human rights law as providing the
moral resources to debate and judge what the United States is doing
in its self-proclaimed 'war on terror'. From the US point of view, it is
consciously acting as a norm entrepreneur in seeking to revise human
rights and humanitarian law to permit extraordinary measures against
what it portrays as an extraordinarily dangerous and unusually barbaric
enemy. The terrorist attacks of September 11 on the US homeland provide the shock for normative change within the United States, in terms of
both permitting law-enforcement measures that restrict civil liberties and
mobilising support for those calling for a more forceful military unilateralism in US foreign policy. Congruence is also significant. It is true that the
United States considers itself to be a champion of human rights around
the world, though its record on human rights is mixed. But more significant is a legal culture that is more punitive in nature than in Europe, in
terms of the treatment of prisoners in the criminal justice system (a treatment that includes lawful execution which is banned in the European
Union). Also significant is a legal culture that permits the 'purposive'
reading of international law to serve vital national policy.[80] Here we may
see the New Haven School as a manifestation of US legal culture. From
the perspective of US legal culture, therefore, its treatment of detainees
in Guantanamo is not as bad as the Europeans make out and represents a
necessary and acceptable re-interpretation of international law given the
threat to US security.[81]

The international discourse on this indicates a general scepticism in
the international community regarding the lawfulness, and hence legitimacy, of this new US practice. This, in turn, generated some disquiet
in the US polity about the prudence, if not ethics, of the attempt by
the Bush administration to redefine international norms on the detention and treatment of prisoners.[82] In early 2006, the UN Commission
on Human Rights produced a damning report on Guantanamo. It found
that the interrogation methods used amounted to degrading treatment in

[80] This constructivist reading of the US war on terror draws on Theo Farrell, 'Strategic
culture and american empire,' *SAIS Review* 25 (2005), 9–10, 13–14. See also, chapters
by Helen Kinsella and Michael Sherry in David Armstrong, Theo Farrell and Bice
Maiguashca, *Force and Legitimacy in World Politics* (Cambridge: Cambridge University
Press, 2005).
[81] 'Guantanamo regime defended by US', *BBC News*, 14 February 2004, at
www.news.bbc.co.uk/.
[82] Jeffrey Smith and Dan Eggen, 'Justice expands "torture" definition: earlier policy drew
criticism', *Washington Post*, 31 December 2004, p. A01, at www.washingtonpost.com/.

violation of Article 7 of the ICCPR and Article 16 of the CAT. Furthermore, it expressed considerable alarm at the failure to permit detainees to challenge their detention legally as provided in Article 9 of the ICCPR. Finally, it concluded that the use of military commissions to try detainees amounted to violations of Article 14 of the ICCPR which provides for the right to a fair trial before an impartial tribunal.[83] The military commissions were subsequently struck down by the US Supreme Court in June, in *Hamden* v. *Runmsfeld*, for violating US domestic law, in that they were not authorised by the US Congress. In response the Congress passed the Military Commissions Act (MCA) in September 2006, which provided the necessary authorisation. The MCA does criminalise the worst interrogation techniques that the administration had previously tried to argue were lawful. But, at the same time, it removes the right of detainees to invoke the Geneva Conventions in making legal challenges against their treatment, it codifies in law the use of military commissions to try civilian detainees held in Guantanamo and removes the right of detainees to challenge their detention before US courts. Human rights groups in the United States are intent on challenging the legality of the MCA. But it is clear that the Bush administration's basic position, that the law must evolve to enable civilised states to fight barbaric enemies, is one that now enjoys broad political support in the United States.[84]

Discussion questions

- What is the difference between an 'obligation *erga omnes*' and a 'peremptory norm' of international law? Give an example of each.
- What evidence can you provide that human rights operate in a positivist rule-based system? How does such a system accommodate the more liberal view that individuals have become subjects of international law?
- In what way do human rights express core liberal values?
- What role does the UN Charter play in the protection of human rights? Have the relevant UN Charter provisions been implemented (e.g., internalised)?

---

[83] United Nations Commission on Human Rights, Sixty-second session, items 10 and 11 of the provision agenda, 'Situation of detainees at Guantanamo Bay', Future E/CN.4/2006/120, 15 February 2006.

[84] Human Rights Watch, 'Q and A: Military Commissions Act of 2006,' at http://hrw.org/backgrounder/usa/qna1006/usqna1006web.pdf; Amnesty International, 'USA: Military Commissions Act of 2006 – turning bad policy into bad law', AMR 51/154/2006, 29 September 2006, at http://web.amnesty.org/library/index/ENGAMR511542006.

- What makes human rights treaties difficult, in general, to implement? What makes the ECHR system so successful in terms of compliance? Why does the refugee protection regime provide a good example of the role of self-interest in motivating states to comply with international law?
- Who are the main agents of change in international human rights law?
- How may we best explain the US redefinition of norms on the detention and treatment of foreign prisoners?

SUGGESTIONS FOR FURTHER READING

Cronin, Bruce, *Institutions for the Common Good: International Protection Regimes in International Society*, Cambridge: Cambridge University Press, 2003. A clearly written and strongly argued book on the links between international stability and the creation of international protection regimes.

Donnelly, Jack, *Universal Human Rights in Theory and Practice*, 2nd edition, Ithaca, NY: Cornell University Press, 2003. An excellent book that takes human rights into the twenty-first century with a wide range of issues being discussed, including cultural relativism, humanitarian intervention, democracy and human rights, group rights and 'Asian values'.

Forsythe, David P., *Human Rights in International Relations*, Cambridge: Cambridge University Press, 2000. An accessible and thorough treatment of the policy-making processes pertaining to human rights in the context of international relations.

Freeman, Michael, *Human Rights*, Cambridge: Polity Press, 2002. An interdisciplinary account of human rights, with particular references to the social science, philosophy and law.

Gearty, Conor, *Can Human Rights Survive?*, The Hamlyn Lectures 2005, Cambridge University Press, 2006. Most enjoyable read of 'the story of human rights' with a warning against complacency and a lucid look at the future.

Gibney, Matthew J., *The Ethics and Politics of Asylum*, Cambridge: Cambridge University Press, 2004. A well-argued work on the obligations of liberal democracies to asylum-seekers with an empirical focus on the USA, Germany, the UK and Australia.

Goodwin-Gill, Guy S., and Jane McAdam, *The Refugee in International Law*, Oxford: Oxford University Press, 2007. Probably the best substantial textbook on refugee law with a clear international focus.

Rehman, Javaid, *International Human Rights Law*, London: Longman, 2003. A comprehensive and accessible textbook.

Risse, Thomas, Stephen C. Ropp and Kathryn Sikkink (eds.), *The Power of Human Rights: International Norms and Domestic Change*, Cambridge: Cambridge University Press, 1999. An evaluation of the impact of human rights norms articulated in the Universal Declaration of Human Rights on the behaviour of national governments in five different regions of the world (i.e., Northern Africa, Sub-Saharan Africa, South-East Asia, Latin America and Eastern Europe), with a particular focus on internalisation.

Simpson, Brian, *Human Rights and the End of Empire: Britain and the Genesis of the European Convention*, Oxford: Oxford University Press, 2001. An astonishing historical account of the negotiations of the European Convention on Human Rights, with a particular focus on the role of Britain.

Steiner, Henry J., and Philip Alston, *International Human Rights in Context: Law, Politics, Morals*, Oxford: Oxford University Press, 2000. This book is unique in providing the 'big picture' of the 'human rights movement'. Highly readable, it is a masterpiece in interdisciplinary scholarship and in critical legal thinking. A third edition is on its way.

6 International crimes

International criminal law is a relatively new area of law. Traditionally and in general, the state has exercised jurisdiction over the definition and prosecution of crimes committed on its territory and/or by its subjects/citizens. Piracy has been an important exception, in that for hundreds of years it has been recognised as a crime for which all states could exercise jurisdiction, regardless of where the crime of piracy was committed and the nationality of the pirates. In the nineteenth century, states began to develop treaty law to regulate the conduct of warfare. States also began to recognise the most serious violations of these laws of armed conflict (LOAC) as incurring individual criminal liability over which extraterritorial jurisdiction might be exercised. In the twentieth century, and especially following World War II (WWII), states began to develop substantive and procedural rules on international crimes, including serious violations of LOAC, crimes against humanity and the crimes of genocide, torture and terrorism. The underlying principle is one of universal jurisdiction, exercisable by states and competent international criminal tribunals and courts, for crimes that are generally considered to be especially heinous.

International crimes cover a wide range of offences, with the spectrum running from drugs trafficking and the sex trade at the one end, to acts of terrorism, wars of aggression and genocide at the other end. This chapter focuses on the more serious end of this spectrum. As a new area of law international criminal law draws on general international law, human rights law and domestic criminal law, especially in developing procedural rules for the prosecution of international crimes. However, the substantive rules of international criminal law, concerning what constitutes a serious international crime, are most heavily influenced by the LOAC and the experience of war. Hence we pay particular attention to LOAC.

As noted in Chapter 4, LOAC (also called international humanitarian law in modern parlance) may be traced back in the just war tradition to the Christian theology, moral philosophy and military and diplomatic practice of medieval times. From this emerged a body of customary law on the conduct of warfare (*jus in bello*). Starting in the nineteenth century, states began to codify what has become the modern LOAC through a series of multilateral treaties – the 1856 Paris Declaration on Maritime War, the 1864 Geneva Convention on wounded and sick, the 1868 St Petersburg Declaration on explosive projectiles and the three Hague Conventions of 1899 (followed by another thirteen Hague Conventions in 1907).[1] These conventions, as international treaties, imposed obligations and duties upon states but they did not create criminal liability for individuals. Indeed they declare certain acts as illegal but not criminal, as such. During this time, military law also developed to regulate national military operations – most notable, in this regard, was the Lieber Code of 1863 (named after its author, Francis Lieber, Professor of Law at Columbia) which covered the conduct of the Union army during the American Civil War.[2] The Lieber Code did criminalise inhumane conduct in warfare and set penalties for serious offences. However, international rules and mechanisms for criminalising and prosecuting breaches of LOAC did not emerge until the middle of the twentieth century. The move towards developing international criminal law began in the early twentieth century. War crimes trials were provided in the peace treaties with Germany and with Turkey following World War I (WWI). However, in both cases, the crimes in question were ill-defined. Prosecutions did proceed in the German Supreme Court at Leipzig, under the terms agreed with the victorious powers, though with few convictions and light sentences; war crimes trials were never pursued in the case of Turkey because of a later amnesty inserted in the Peace Treaty of Lausanne.[3]

Following World War II, the victorious powers established International Military Tribunals (IMTs) to prosecute Nazi and Japanese officers and officials. The resulting trials at Nuremberg and Tokyo, respectively, were the first of their kind: i.e., prosecutions by international bodies for war crimes. Indeed, in the process of establishing and conducting the Nuremberg and Tokyo trials, much of the substantive and procedural law on international crimes was worked out. International tribunals to prosecute war crimes were not again convened for almost forty years. Finally, in the early 1990s, ad hoc international tribunals were set up to prosecute war crimes that occurred in the wars in the Balkans and in Rwanda. As we shall see, the case law of these tribunals has further refined, and in some

---

[1] Adam Roberts and Richard Guelff, 'Editor's Introduction', *Documents on the Laws of War*, 3rd edition (Oxford: Oxford University Press, 2000), p. 3.
[2] Richard S. Hartigan, *Lieber's Code and the Law of War* (Chicago: Precedent, 1983).
[3] William A. Schabas, *An Introduction to the International Criminal Court*, 2nd edition (Cambridge: Cambridge University Press, 2004), p. 2.

cases developed, international criminal law. Most recently a permanent International Criminal Court (ICC) has been established. The Statute of the ICC, adopted at an international conference in Rome in 1998, provides a complete and authoritative statement of international criminal law. We shall be looking at the Statute in some detail over the course of this chapter.

The first section examines the content of international criminal law. We go into some detail on the rules regarding each of the major international crimes: war crimes, crimes against humanity, genocide, the crime of aggression, torture and terrorism. We then explore human dignity as the underlying value of substantive international criminal law, and the discourse of procedural international criminal law (as derived from general international law, domestic criminal law and human rights law). The second section discusses compliance with international criminal law. In fact, the pattern appears to be more one of non-compliance. We find state consent, or lack thereof, to be the major factor in operation here. We consider the prospects of the ICC as a coercive mechanism for improving the record of compliance in this area of law. We also look closely at congruence as an important factor in explaining variation in compliance. Finally, in the third section, we examine the formal, policy and social process of change in international criminal law.

Content of international criminal law

Traditionally, individuals could not be held personally accountable for a breach of international law at the international level. However, they could be prosecuted and punished by a foreign state within the national system of that foreign state, and only if the national courts had jurisdiction and the international rule in question had been incorporated in domestic law. The rationale for this stance stems from the lack of international legal personality of individuals prior to the Nuremberg Tribunal. Thus, individuals were deemed to possess neither rights and duties under international law, nor a capacity to enforce these or have them enforced against them. The state was always the bearer of such rights and duties and hence any violations of international law were attributed solely to the state. These limiting conditions did not, however, apply to certain crimes, such as piracy and war crimes.[4] This suggests that the concept of international crimes (or crimes *jure gentium* as it used to be known) long existed in international law. The scope of these international offences has since

---

[4] Espionage and war treason had long been recognised as war crimes by customary international law.

been enlarged considerably through a process of codification of the laws and customs of war that resulted most notably in the Hague Conventions (1899 and 1907), the Geneva Conventions (1949) and the Additional Protocols to the Geneva Conventions (1977). It was also extended by international conventions dealing with specific offences such as genocide and torture. Quite crucially, as we have noted and shall explore in more detail, the jurisdiction to try and prosecute international criminals *in accordance with international law* was extended beyond states to include ad hoc international tribunals and more recently to the permanent International Criminal Court.

Prosecution of international crimes by states and competent international bodies also raises (as suggested in our introduction) the crucial question of jurisdiction. The question is actually pretty central to the world legal order. It defines the limits of the coercive power of individual states as well as the purview of their regulatory authority. Traditionally, states have applied two principles in determining jurisdiction – the principle of territoriality and the principle of nationality. These establish the sovereign authority of states to prescribe laws applicable to its territorial land, waters and skies and to its subjects or citizens. Whilst the nationality principle is more established, pre-dating the modern age, the territoriality principle is more central to the domestic legal orders of modern states. These principles prevent states from colliding with one another when exercising jurisdiction.[5] International crimes often involve the exercise of extraterritorial jurisdiction in that there may be no territorial or nationality link to the prosecuting authority (be it a state or international tribunal). Extraterritorial jurisdiction may take the form of universal jurisdiction exercised by a state or, as alluded to above, international jurisdiction conferred on a court or tribunal by a competent international authority (i.e., an international treaty or treaty-empowered body). The development of universal jurisdiction for the most serious categories of international crimes has been rooted by states and scholars alike in the customary practice whereby states exercised universal jurisdiction over the crime of piracy. In fact, the lineage is not so direct. Common *interests* led states to recognise universal jurisdiction over piracy. Because pirates usually operated beyond territorial waters with crews of mixed or uncertain nationalities, and given the demands of apprehending them, states had to accept universal jurisdiction purely on practical grounds. Common *values*, the recognition that some international crimes are especially heinous, have led states to recognise universal jurisdiction for the most

[5] Vaughan Lowe, 'Jurisdiction', in Malcolm Evans (ed.), *International Law* (Oxford: Oxford University Press, 2006), pp. 335–60.

serious war crimes, crimes against humanity and genocide.[6] Extraterritorial jurisdiction has been primarily exercised (albeit sporadically) by competent international authorities (i.e., international tribunals). At the end of the twentieth century, some states began to exercise universal jurisdiction, but this practice remains relatively rare and tentative.

The rules of international criminal law

International criminal law centres on a set of substantive rules that define the various categories of international crimes, as well as increasingly codified procedural rules on the determination and prosecution of these crimes. Putting aside piracy and slavery as international crimes that became regulated by customary international law in the nineteenth century, breaches of LOAC (i.e., war crimes) were the only crimes punishable under treaty law in the early twentieth century. Indeed, one has to wait for the adoption of the Statutes of the International Military Tribunal at Nuremberg (1945) and the International Military Tribunal for the Far East – Tokyo (1946) to see new categories of international crimes being recognised, in particular, crimes against humanity and crimes against peace. Soon after, in 1948, genocide was added to the list of international crimes (as a subcategory of crimes against humanity to start with), followed by torture in the 1980s. And more recently, the crime of aggression has once again been made punishable although a definition is still under consideration by the ICC member states. Nowadays, it is common to distinguish between so-called 'core crimes' (i.e., war crimes, crimes against humanity and genocide), which all fall within the jurisdiction of international tribunals and now of the ICC, and other crimes (i.e., aggression, torture and terrorism), which do not yet do so. Let us look in more detail at these various international crimes.

War crimes   Violations of the laws of war committed in international conflicts are of two types: grave breaches and other war crimes. The concept of grave breaches was introduced by the 1949 Geneva Conventions and encompasses the most serious and heinous violations of these conventions. Every other violation is a war crime. The main difference between the two, besides the obvious gravity element, is that while grave breaches are subject to universal jurisdiction, war crimes are not. Both types, however, are applicable when committed in the context of an armed conflict. As we noted, LOAC encompass both customary and

---

[6] Eugene Konotorovich, 'The piracy analogy: modern universal jurisdiction's hollow jurisdiction', *Harvard International Law Journal* 45 (2004), 183–238.

treaty rules – the most significant treaties being the 1907 Hague and 1949 Geneva Conventions, and the Rome Statute of the ICC. The basic rules of LOAC have been summarised by the International Committee of the Red Cross (ICRC) as being:

- Non-combatants shall in all circumstances be protected and treated humanely
- It is forbidden to kill or injure an enemy who surrenders
- Wounded and sick must be cared for
- Captured combatants and civilians must have their 'lives, dignity, personal rights, and convictions' protected
- No one shall be subject to 'physical or mental torture, corporal punishment, or cruel or degrading treatment'
- 'Parties to a conflict and members of their armed forces do not have an unlimited choice of methods of warfare of a nature to cause unnecessary losses or excessive suffering'
- Distinction must be drawn between combatants and civilians in order to spare civilians and civilian property. Attacks may only be directed against military objectives; civilians and civilian objects may never be attacked.[7]

Understandably, the treatment of wounded on the battlefield, and treatment of captured military personnel, are matters which have occupied states and their militaries in concluding treaties on LOAC. Moreover, recently there has been much controversy regarding the treatment of those captured in the course of the United States' self-proclaimed global war on terror (GWOT). Nonetheless, the last two rules listed above, concerning the limitation of excessive use of force and the protection of civilians, are the most central to the modern LOAC. Indeed, these rules flow from fundamental principles of customary law on the use of force as well as the conduct of war, namely, the principle of military necessity and the principle of proportionality.[8]

Traditionally, LOAC applied exclusively to international conflicts – that is, armed conflicts between states. It had limited application to internal conflicts – that is, an armed conflict taking place solely within the territory of a single state, between government forces and one or more non-state entities or among non-state entities, and whose intensity is higher than sporadic acts of violence or riots. Until the nineteenth century, internal conflicts were entirely a matter for the state and not subject to regulation under international law. In the nineteenth century, a typological

---

[7] Kriangsak Kittichaisaree, *International Criminal Law* (Oxford: Oxford University Press, 2001), pp. 129–30.
[8] See Chapter 4 for a detailed discussion of these principles.

understanding developed concerning the nature of internal conflicts, where they were classed as a rebellion, insurgency or belligerency. Rebellions were internal security matters outside the purview of international law. An insurgency existed when resistance to the government was sufficiently organised to present a credible threat to control of the state. On occasion, such insurgent parties were recognised as having belligerent rights. Such recognition may be extended by a third party (as was done by the United States towards Spanish American colonial insurgencies and Britain towards civil conflicts in Greece and Portugal) or indeed by the government (as by the Union government towards the Confederate side in the American Civil War). In such cases, the LOAC fully applied to the government and belligerent party. The doctrine of belligerency had become obsolete by the twentieth century (the last occasion an insurgency was granted belligerent rights was by Britain in the Boer War in 1902). Accordingly, the Hague Conventions focused on codifying LOAC as applied to international conflicts only.[9]

The 1949 Geneva Conventions and 1977 Additional Protocols do provide for a limited extension of LOAC to internal conflicts. In negotiating the Geneva Conventions, states were divided on this matter. The compromise was contained in an article common to all four of the conventions (hence it is known as 'Common Article 3'). Common Article 3 stipulates that 'in the case of armed conflict not of an international character', basic safeguards for the treatment of civilians, captured personnel and sick and wounded be provided. For most of the twentieth century, these safeguards have generally not been observed in internal conflicts. Part of the problem has to do with the lack of enforcement of Common Article 3 and the rule prohibiting interference in the domestic affairs of other states. As a result, in practice it was the state itself that rendered itself competent to recognise, or not, the existence of an armed conflict on its territory.[10] States

---

[9] It is not so surprising that the doctrine of belligerency should fall into disuse. On balance, it was more trouble than it was worth to states. Recognising belligerency permitted the government to stop and search ships on the high seas to prevent shipments of arms and other material to rebel groups. It also permitted third parties to exercise their rights as neutrals to trade freely with both sides. However, recognising belligerency was fraught with hazards for third parties. If they failed to extend such recognition where it was due, rebels would be entitled to take action in reprisal. If such recognition was not due but was extended, then the government side would be entitled to compensation for injury caused. Lindsay Moir, *The Law of Internal Armed Conflict* (Cambridge: Cambridge University Press, 2002), pp. 3–30; Stephen C. Neff, *War and the Law of Nations* (Cambridge: Cambridge University Press, 2005), pp. 258–64.

[10] It was exactly because states feared that by recognising the existence of an internal armed conflict on their territory they may be inviting a right of secession or external intervention that the drafters of Common Article 3 stipulated that the recognition of a state of armed conflict does not produce any other legal effects on the State concerned.

have generally been reluctant to extend such recognition and thereby trigger the application of Common Article 3.[11] By the early 1970s, it was realised that treaty rules on LOAC needed refinement, especially given that Common Article 3 was not really working. States came together at a diplomatic conference from 1974–7 to negotiate two Additional Protocols to the Geneva Conventions. Additional Protocol II specifically deals with non-international conflicts. This protocol elaborates on the safeguards listed in Common Article 3. However, on the key issue of how to define an internal armed conflict, Protocol II provides a narrow definition that requires the insurgent group to be organised 'under responsible command' and 'exercise such control over a part of its territory as to enable them to carry out sustained and concerted military operations and to implement this Protocol' (Art. 1.1). In effect, therefore, Protocol II kicks in only when insurgents have seized control of some territory; below this level, Common Article 3 still applies.[12]

Notwithstanding Additional Protocol II, individual criminal liability for war crimes still only existed for violations of LOAC in international armed conflicts. In negotiating this protocol, states were not prepared to recognise that there was an 'established custom' regarding use of force in non-international conflicts. This is in stark contrast, of course, to treaty law on the conduct of international armed conflicts, the principles of which are explicitly recognised to be derived from customary law. This all changed as a consequence of the case law of the International Criminal Tribunal for the former Yugoslavia (ICTY) and the International Criminal Tribunal for Rwanda (ICTR). Especially significant is the *Tadic* case (Interlocutory Appeal Decision on Jurisdiction, 1995), in which the ICTY held that serious breaches of customary and/or applicable treaty law on internal armed conflicts also incurred criminal liability of the offender under international law.[13] The Appeals Chamber of the ICTY also found in the *Tadic* case (1999) that customary international law previously applied only to international armed conflicts was also applicable to internal conflicts. This has resulted in a blurring of the traditional distinction between the highly codified law on armed conflict, and less well-developed law on internal conflict.[14] More to the point, a broad

---

[11] Moir, *Law*, p. 34.

[12] Christopher Greenwood, 'The law of war (international humanitarian law)', in Evans (ed.), *International Law*, p. 807.

[13] Antonio Cassese, 'International criminal law', in Evans (ed.), *International Law*, p. 737.

[14] Macro Saasoli and Laura M. Olson, 'Prosecutor v. Tadic (Judgment). Case No. IT-94-a-A. 38 ILM 1518 (1999)', *American Journal of International Law* 94 (2000), 576–7.

swathe of customary rules in LOAC are now applicable to all forms of armed conflict.[15]

Crimes against humanity   Crimes against humanity originally grew out of, and were linked to armed conflict and hence to war crimes.[16] Indeed, the Preamble of the 1907 Hague Convention IV Respecting the Laws and Customs of War on Land presents LOAC as serving the 'interests of humanity' and draws on the 'laws of humanity' as a source of LOAC. Thereafter, crimes against humanity develop into a specific class of international crime involving the grave abuse of civilian populations in war. As we noted, an attempt was made following WWI to prosecute Austrian, German and Turkish officials for offences against 'the laws of humanity' – these included massacre, torture, rape and deportation of civilians. This effort was blocked by American officials who argued that such offences were based on a vague notion of the principles of humanity and did not, in fact, exist in international law.[17]

This problem emerged, once again, during WWII. Allied lawyers, meeting in 1943–4 to prepare cases against German officials, realised that the most barbaric acts being committed by the Nazi regime were against their own citizens and, as such, were not illegal under LOAC. At the same time, the Allies were nervous about creating legal rules that would hinder the sovereign right of states to exercise internal control over the territory and, indeed, the right of imperial powers to control their colonies.[18] The way chosen forward is contained in Article 6(c) of the Charter of the IMT for Nuremberg, which defines crimes against humanity as

murder, extermination, enslavement, deportation, and other inhumane acts committed against any civilian population, before or during the war, or persecutions on political, racial or religious grounds in execution of or in connection with any crime within the jurisdiction of the Tribunal, whether or not in violation of the domestic law of the country where perpetrated.[19]

This definition links crimes against humanity to acts committed in war, or acts committed in connection with the other crimes covered by the IMT

[15] Theodore Meron, 'International Criminalization of Internal Atrocities', *American Journal of International Law* 89 (1995), 554–77. In its Customary International Humanitarian Law (IHL) Project, the ICRC concluded that 147 of the 161 rules it identified in customary IHL are applicable to all forms of armed conflict. See Jean-Marie Henckaerts and Louise Doswald-Beck, *Customary International Humanitarian Law*, 2 vols. (Cambridge: Cambridge University Press, 2005), vol. I: *Rules*.
[16] Crimes against humanity were also linked to crimes against peace in the statute of the Nuremburg Tribunal.
[17] Kittichaisaree, *International Criminal Law*, pp. 85–6.   [18] Schabas, *Introduction*, p. 42.
[19] Nuremberg Trial Proceedings, Vol. I, Charter of the International Military Tribunal, available at www.yale.edu/lawweb/avalon/imt/proc/imtconst.htm.

(i.e., war crimes and crimes against peace). In other words, barbaric acts of the nature listed above committed by states outside the context of war or unlawful aggression would not constitute crimes against humanity.[20] The Nuremberg Tribunal did not recognise that it was dealing with a new class of crimes. Rather it simply asserted that the Nuremberg Charter provided 'the expression of international law existing at the time of its creation'. It is true that the crimes listed in Article 6(c) closely corresponded to those for which the Axis powers were held accountable following WWI; though, as we noted, the lawfulness of such charges was disputed by the Americans at the time. In actual fact, these crimes were novel, and perhaps in sensitivity to the charge of *ex-post facto* law, in most cases the Nuremberg Tribunal found defendants to be guilty of war crimes as well as crimes against humanity.[21]

The legal force of crimes against humanity was rapidly established thereafter. It was confirmed in the Charter of the Tokyo Tribunal (Article 5(c)) and upheld in subsequent resolutions of the United Nations General Assembly (in February and December 1946). Moreover, the link between crimes against humanity and war was gradually eroded following Nuremberg, especially in the 1968 Convention on the Non-Applicability of Statutory Limitations to War Crimes and Crimes Against Humanity. Curiously, the link is restored in the ICTY Statute (Article 5), but this is because the ICTY was specifically designed to prosecute crimes committed in the context of the wars of the former Yugoslavia. Moreover, despite this, the ICTY Appeals Chamber argued in the *Tadic* case that 'there is no logical or legal basis' for such a link and moreover that 'it has been abandoned in subsequent state practice with respect to crimes against humanity'. In any case, the link is removed once again in the ICTR Statute (Article 3), and also in Article 7 of the ICC Statute. The ICTY relied on customary international law in interpreting the crimes against humanity provision in its Statute, deeming the following elements to be generally required: (a) an attack against any civilian population; (b) the attack must be widespread or systematic (a requirement that was not mentioned in the ICTY Statute); and (c) the intention of the perpetrator must be to carry out a widespread or systematic attack. The ICC Statute also expands the list of crimes against humanity, most notably in elaborating a range of sexual offences, and suggests that such crimes may be committed by non-state actors, which is something that had already

---

[20] Antonio Cassese, *International Criminal Law*, (Oxford: Oxford University Press, 2003), pp. 68–9.
[21] As it happens, the Tribunal had some leeway here as the rule prohibiting *ex-post facto* law whilst existing in most domestic legal traditions had not yet been established in international law. Cassese, *International Criminal Law*, p. 72.

been declared by the ICTY in relation to paramilitary groups and rebel entities.[22]

Genocide   Genocide was prosecuted as a species of crimes against humanity at Nuremberg. It became an autonomous crime in 1948 following the adoption of the Genocide Convention by the UN General Assembly. Genocide is defined in the 1948 Convention as an act (such as killing, causing serious harm, physical destruction, measures intended to prevent birth or the forcible transfer of children) with the intent to destroy, in whole or in part, a national, ethnical, racial or religious group as such (Art II). The main element of the offence is the special intention (*dolus specialis*) of the perpetrator to destroy the group in whole or in part, and it is that which distinguishes it from crimes against humanity. Equally, although the victim(s) are chosen because of their membership of a particular group, it is the group 'as such' that the perpetrator is intent on destroying and not the individuals. This definition is replicated in the statutes of the ICTY (Art. 4(2)), ICTR (Art. 2(2)) and ICC (Art. 6).

The crime of genocide quickly became a peremptory norm of customary international law. As the International Court of Justice (ICJ) concluded in its 1951 advisory opinion on *Reservations to the Convention on the Prevention and Punishment of the Crime of Genocide*, 'the principles underlying the Convention are principles which are recognised by civilised nations as binding on States, even without any conventional obligations'.[23] The 1948 Convention recognises that genocide may be perpetrated in time of war or peace, and that conspiracy, incitement, attempts and complicity connected with genocide are equally punishable. The 1948 Convention further provides that genocide entails the responsibility of the perpetrator (or other accomplice) of the crime (i.e., individual criminal responsibility) as well as responsibility of the state whose authorities engage or participate in the commission of the genocide (i.e., state responsibility). The ICTR also found in the *Kambanda* case (1998) that officials may be guilty of genocide if they fail to take remedial action. Some states have tried, without success, to expand the scope of this crime to include social and political groups as protected groups under the crime of genocide. This wider definition was not adopted at the Rome conference on the ICC because the ICC Statute is meant to codify existing international law and not create new law.[24]

---

[22] Schabas, *Introduction*, pp. 43–4; Kittichaisaree, *International Criminal Law*, pp. 89–90.
[23] ICJ Reports 1951, at p. 24.
[24] Kittichaisaree, *International Criminal Law*, pp. 67–73. For a contrary view of the Rome Statute arguing that it actually legislated, see L. N. Sadat, *International Criminal Court and the Transformation of International Law* (Ardsley, NY: Transnational Publishers, 2002).

The crime of aggression The crime of aggression was introduced for the first time in Article 6(a) of the Nuremberg Charter, at least in so far as it entailed the criminal liability of the offender. In fact the drafters of the Charter recognised that Nazi plans to commit a war of aggression commenced well before the start of WWII, most likely around 1933, and thus the Charter made it clear that crimes against peace may be prosecuted even at their planning stages. In order to justify and defend the non-retroactivity of crimes against peace the Nuremberg Tribunal argued that pre-existing treaties dealing with the prohibition of the use of force, particularly the 1928 General Treaty for the Renunciation of War (Kellogg–Briand Pact) were directed not only to states but also to individuals, the violation of which incurred personal liability. The Tribunal concluded that this rule made 'resort to a war of aggression not merely illegal but criminal'.[25]

Successive attempts to define the crime of aggression in a multilateral treaty since the Nuremberg Charter have failed. The major powers have preferred to invest interpretive flexibility on this matter in the United Nations Security Council (UNSC; Article 39 of the UN Charter) to respond as it sees fit to threats to international peace and security, but this has always been in the context of state responsibility. The UN General Assembly did adopt a resolution (3314) in December 1974 on the Definition of Aggression. Whatever the value of this resolution, its primary purpose was the elaboration of existing rules on the regulation of force between states and was not directly concerned with individual responsibility. In any event, the UN General Assembly recognised the authority of the UNSC to decide on the matter. The ICC does have jurisdiction over the crime of aggression. But Article 5(2) of the ICC Statute makes the exercise of this jurisdiction conditional on an agreed definition of the crime of aggression being incorporated into the ICC Statute. The Assembly of States Parties to the ICC has established a working group with a view to adopting an acceptable definition but there is no indication that a broad consensus exists.[26] Article 5(2) also requires that ICC jurisdiction over this crime must be consistent with the UN Charter, including Article 39 which gives the UNSC responsibility for matters pertaining to international peace and security. In essence, then, it remains to be seen whether the ICC can prosecute this crime without the full co-operation of the UNSC.[27]

---

[25] Judgment of the International Military Tribunal at Nuremberg, 1 October 1946, p. 220, as cited in Quincy Wright, 'The Law of the Nuremberg Trial', *American Journal of International Law* 41 (1947), 54.
[26] www.icc-cpi.int/asp/aspaggression.html.
[27] Kittichaisaree, *International Criminal Law*, pp. 206–20.

Torture   Torture may fall into three categories of international crime. First, torture may constitute a crime against humanity if it is part of a widespread or systematic practice. In such cases, the person committing the crime may either be a private individual (with some 'passive involvement' from the authorities) or a state official, but s/he must know that the act is part of a widespread or systematic practice. Second, torture may constitute a war crime if it is committed in time of armed conflict. Third, torture may constitute a 'discrete crime' under Article 1(1) of the 1984 UN Convention Against Torture (CAT) provided it is 'inflicted by or at the instigation of or with the consent or acquiescence of a public official or other person acting in an official capacity'. Whichever category of international crime the act of torture falls into, the purpose of the crime need not necessarily be 'the extraction of a confession or information from the victim'; torture may also be for the purpose of punishment, intimidation, humiliation, discrimination and so forth. The ban on torture has evolved into a general rule of international law. Citing the 'existence of [the] corpus of general and treaty rules proscribing torture', the ICTY concluded in the *Furundzija* case (1998) that 'no legal loopholes have been left'. Nonetheless, torture may constitute an international crime only if criminal intent can be shown; recklessness or culpable negligence are not sufficient *mens rea* standards (i.e., mental element that establishes criminal responsibility). Moreover, as we noted in Chapter 5, states may still disagree as to whether specific interrogation practices constitute torture.[28]

Terrorism   The criminalisation of terrorism has been achieved through the adoption of discrete conventions pertaining to particular facets of terrorist activity (the thematic method), such treaties on the safety of civil aviation, hostage-taking, crimes against internationally protected persons, terrorist financing, terrorist bombings and more recently nuclear terrorism and maritime terrorism. Acts of terrorism have been defined in the 1999 Convention for the Suppression of the Financing of Terrorism as follows:

(1) acts prohibited by nine other treaties (e.g., the Convention on Unlawful Seizure of Aircraft (1970), the Convention on the Suppression of Terrorist Bombing (1997), and so forth);

(2) 'Any . . . act intended to cause death or serious bodily injury to a civilian, or to any other person not taking an active part in the hostilities in a situation of armed conflict, when the purpose of such act, by its nature or context, is to intimidate a population, or to compel

---

[28] Cassese, *International Criminal Law*, pp. 117–20.

a government or an international organisation to do or to abstain from doing an act.'[29]
A similar definition of terrorism is adopted in a number of regional conventions to combat terrorism.[30] Thus, broad consensus exists on a general treaty definition of terrorism, in spite of remaining disagreement concerning 'freedom fighters' preventing states from agreeing at the UN level on a comprehensive Convention on Terrorism. For this as well as other reasons (e.g., prosecution at the national level might be better suited and the risk of politicising the ICC) terrorism was not included among the international crimes over which the ICC would have jurisdiction in the Statute of ICC. The lack of ICC jurisdiction over the crimes of terrorism should not, however, overshadow the fact that they are and remain international crimes.

Liberal values and substantive law

The evolution of international criminal law has involved a contest between two values, both of which we have identified as liberal values–namely, human dignity and strategic stability. At the heart of international criminal law is the protection of human dignity. Procedurally, international criminal law promotes human dignity in protecting the rights of the accused, and providing for a fair trial (as discussed below). Substantially, the promotion of human dignity may be located in the LOAC in its earliest forms. Ancient Greek, Roman, Islamic, Indian and Chinese societies all had laws to moderate the excesses of warfare, especially in terms of protecting non-combatants.[31] In the modern period, it finds expression in the famous Martens clause. This was a declaration added to the preamble of the 1899 Hague Convention, proposed by the Russian delegate to the Hague Peace Conference, the noted jurist F. F. de Martens. Recognising that the LOAC was incomplete, the Martens clause provided for all military practice, including that not covered in codified law, to be consistent with the customs of 'civilized nations', 'laws of humanity' and 'requirements of public conscience'. The Nuremberg Court was clear in the *Krupp* case (1948) that the Martens clause 'is much more than a pious declaration' but rather it provides a 'legal yardstick to be applied if and when the specific provisions of the [Hague] Convention . . . do not cover

---

[29] Article 2(a) and Article 2(1)(b) respectively.
[30] The 1998 Arab Convention for the Suppression of Terrorism, the 1999 Convention of the Organization of the Islamic Conference on Combating International Terrorism, and the 1999 OAU Convention on the Prevention and Combating of Terrorism. Cassese, 'International criminal law', p. 746.
[31] Neff, *War*, pp. 21–4, 40–5.

specific cases occurring in warfare'. The Martens clause was reproduced in the 1907 Hague Conventions and was also reformulated and reaffirmed in the 1949 Geneva Conventions and 1977 Additional Protocols. These later versions replaced 'laws of humanity' with the now more commonly used 'principles of humanity'. More recently, the Martens clause was invoked by the ICTY when declaring in the *Martic* case (1996) that 'the elementary considerations of humanity . . . constitute the foundations of the entire body of international humanitarian law applicable to all armed conflicts'.[32] Thus, while LOAC has evolved on a separate, if parallel, track to international human rights law, the two bodies of law 'share common values' with regard to controlling the (internal and external) use of force by states.[33] Human dignity is equally a value central to both the 1948 Convention on Genocide and the 1985 CAT. In proposing the Convention on Genocide, the UN General Assembly referred back to an earlier resolution from 1946 where it declared genocide to be an international crime that 'shocks the conscience of mankind' and 'results in great losses to humanity'.[34] Similarly, the preamble to CAT invokes inalienable rights that are 'inherent to the dignity of the human person'.[35]

We should note, however, that the aspiration contained within LOAC to protect human dignity is mediated by the principle of military necessity in LOAC. One of the first expressions of this principle is found in Article 14 of the Lieber Code (1863): 'Military necessity, as understood by modern civilized nations, consists of the necessity of those measures which are indispensable for securing the ends of war, and which are lawful according to the modern law and usages of war.'[36] In this early formulation, the principle of military necessity emphasised the restraints on war imposed by laws of nations and humanity. In other words, death and destruction had to be necessary for military objectives in order to

---

[32] Theodore Meron, 'The Martens Clause, principles of humanity, and dictates of public conscience', *American Journal of International Law* 94 (2000), 78–89 [citations from 80 and 82].

[33] René Provost, *International Human Rights and Humanitarian Law* (Cambridge: Cambridge University Press, 2002); Kenneth Watkin, 'Controlling the use of force: a role for human rights norms in contemporary armed conflict', *American Journal of International Law* 98 (2004), 1–34.

[34] UN General Assembly (UNGA) res. 260(III) 'Prevention and Punishment of the Crime of Genocide', 9 December 1948; UNGA res. 96(I) 'The Crime of Genocide', 11 December 1946, both at www.un.org/documents/resga.htm.

[35] United Nations, 'Convention Against Torture Other Cruel, Inhuman or Degrading Treatment or Punishment' (1985) at www.hrweb.org/legal/cat.html.

[36] US War Dept., General Order No. 100, 'Instructions for the Government of the Armies of the United States in the Field', 24 April 1863, at www.icrc.org/ihl.nsf/FULL/110?OpenDocument.

be lawful. But very quickly the principle mutated into one which operated in opposition to humanitarianism. Indeed, almost immediately the principle of military necessity was denounced by the Confederate Secretary of War as providing an apology for 'acts of atrocity' committed by the Union side in the American Civil War. Sure enough, by 1902 the principle had unquestionably evolved in German military thinking into doctrine that permitted violation of LOAC on the grounds of military necessity.[37] This position was, of course, unlawful. But it is symptomatic of the shift in the meaning of military necessity, from emphasising the limits of war imposed by humanitarian law to emphasising the limits of humanitarian law as imposed by military requirements.

The promotion of human dignity in LOAC is further hindered by the imperative to protect strategic stability. This imperative is present in the principle of military necessity which implicitly accepts that force may have to be used to prevent or reverse aggression and thereby rebalance the international system. It is also present in the non-intervention norm (as codified in Article 2(7) of the UN Charter) which, as we noted in Chapter 4, creates a default normative preference in the world legal order that raises the bar for forcible action against states on humanitarian grounds. This is most evident in the shoddy enforcement of international criminal law. This will be discussed in more detail in our section on compliance. Suffice to say at this point that up to now, states have shown some reluctance in this matter. Almost fifty years separated the establishment of the IMTs and the ICTY and ICTR. Plenty of international crimes were committed over this period, but there was no willingness among states to create international mechanisms to prosecute offenders. Indeed, states have been unwilling even to recognise many of these crimes for fear that it would require action that might be costly or destabilising. For this reason, numerous acts of genocide during the Cold War (East Biafra 1964–70, Bangladesh 1971–2, Cambodia 1975–9, Indonesia 1965 and Timor 1974–9) were not recognised as such because this could have triggered an obligation under Article 1 of the 1948 Genocide Convention 'to prevent and to punish' this crime in these cases.[38] Also noteworthy is that the international tribunals that were created to prosecute international crimes following WWII, and the Rwandan and Yugoslavian wars, delivered a form of 'victors' justice'. In other words, a partial justice that

---

[37] Burrus M. Carnahan, 'Lincoln, Lieber and the laws of war: the origins and limits of the principle of military necessity', *American Journal of International Law* 92 (1998), 217–18. On the doctrinal roots of excessive violence in German military operations of the early twentieth century, see Isabel V. Hull, *Absolute Destruction: Military Culture and the Practices of War in Imperial Germany* (Ithaca, NY: Cornell University Press, 2005).
[38] William D. Ruinstein, *Genocide* (Hallow: Pearson, 2004), pp. 257–95.

served the post-war international order. Thus, as one historian of the period notes, 'The preparation of the [Nuremberg] tribunal exposed the extent to which the trial was in effect a "political act" rather than an exercise in law.'[39] Indeed, it contained some features which violated the legal traditions of all the major allied powers (e.g., arbitrariness and retrospective justice), particularly when it came to the selection of defendants and framing of charges, but were accepted as political necessities. Whilst enforcement in this case was designed to contribute to system stability (by prosecuting the crime of aggression), this objective was somewhat undercut by the perception in Germany that the trials were delivering victors' justice. The leniency of the sentences handed out by the Nuremberg Tribunal, widely taken as a reflection of the tribunal's recognition that it had engaged in *ex-post facto* justice, served to reinforce this perception.[40] More generally, less powerful states have had good reason to see hypocrisy in an international criminal system where only the weak and defeated are brought to trial. And so we have an irony: enforcement of international criminal law has only occurred on those occasions where it serves, or at least does not threaten, international stability. But, at the same time, one must wonder whether system stability has really been served by a selective enforcement of a legal system that is widely perceived as biased towards the powerful.[41]

It remains to be seen whether or not the ICC will address this perception of inequity in the enforcement of international criminal law. In principle, it should do given that it is a permanent body (where previously only ad hoc tribunals existed) that has international jurisdiction and largely acts independently of states. But US opposition to the ICC raises concerns about whether the powerful can ever be brought to account. The United States argues that its national security interests may be compromised by the ICC Statute, especially by the inclusion of the crime of aggression (for which mischievous charges may be brought against the United States) and the possible future inclusion of terrorism and drug trafficking (which might hinder US national efforts to combat these activities). The crime of aggression was added unexpectedly at the last minute to the ICC Statute, and so US opposition to its inclusion

---

[39] Richard Overy, 'The Nuremberg trials: international law in the making', in Philippe Sands (ed.), *From Nuremberg to The Hague* (Cambridge: Cambridge University Press, 2003), p. 7.

[40] Peter Maguire, *Law and War: An American Story* (New York: Columbia University Press, 2001), pp. 283–4.

[41] Alfred P. Rubin, *Ethics and Authority in International Law* (Cambridge: Cambridge University Press, 1997), p. 99. See also Robert Cryer, *Prosecuting International Crimes: Selectivity and the International Criminal Regime* (Cambridge: Cambridge University Press, 2005).

is understandable. The United States remains unsatisfied by the compromise, which appears to recognise the authority of the UNSC when it comes to international peace and security, largely because it is not clear whether or not the actual primacy of the UNSC in such matters is recognised by the Statute.[42] If UNSC primacy is indeed recognised, then this will once again lead weaker states to wonder about the equity of the enforcement of international criminal law. Of course, as we noted, ICC jurisdiction over the crime of aggression is dormant until a definition for this crime can be agreed. Given that such a definition is unlikely to be agreed, the matter of whether or not the UNSC has primacy on this matter is most unlikely to be tested in practice.

Discourse and procedural law

International criminal law is essentially a new hybrid branch of law, combining principles and concepts from general international law, criminal law and human rights law. This provides a rich, if at times conflicting, mix of discursive resources for states and other international actors to debate and determine what constitutes criminal action in the international system. And, indeed, it should be noted that up until the ICC Statute, treaty law on the laws of war, war crimes and other international crimes has focused solely on defining prohibited actions and has not been much concerned with identifying the consequences of such actions. General rules of international law, as codified in the Vienna Convention on the Law of Treaties (1969), apply in determining the sources of international criminal law. Foremost among these sources are the London Agreement of 1945 establishing the Nuremberg Tribunal and the 1998 Rome Statute of the ICC, which provide authoritative statements of substantive and procedural law on international crime. Arguably the Chapter VII UNSC resolutions in 1993 and 1994, respectively establishing the ICTY and ICTR, are also both a form of treaty law since they are binding on all member states under Article 25 of the Charter. In addition, treaty law in this area includes the conventions outlawing various activities: the LOAC, as well as the Genocide Convention and the CAT. Courts and tribunals have also drawn on customary law, especially national criminal law. Indeed, this was especially important in fleshing out international criminal law prior to the adoption of the ICC Statute. In drawing on all this treaty and customary law, the principle of *nullum crimen* prevents a

---

[42] Christopher C. Joyner and Chistopher C. Posteraro, 'The United States and the international criminal court: rethinking the struggle between national interests and international justice', *Criminal Law Forum* 10 (1999), 359–85.

court or tribunal from applying a rule criminalising an activity that is not covered in one of the categories of crimes over which it has been given jurisdiction in its statute.[43]

In terms of the substantive rules of international criminal law, customary and treaty humanitarian law provides core principles – military necessity, proportionality and distinction – which, as we have discussed, guide state discourse about lawful force and criminal violence in war. It goes without saying that this is a politically charged discourse. States are bound to argue their corner, and equally there is often the exchange of accusations regarding war crimes. Increasingly, humanitarian and human rights organisations, which have high standards regarding restraint in armed conflict, are entering the fray in seeking to hold states and other non-state military actors to account. The Genocide Convention, CAT and various conventions on terrorism provide treaty rules to frame discourse on these international crimes. As we noted already, the crime of aggression is the only international crime to remain relatively ill-defined in state discourse.

Criminal law has been a vital source of customary procedural law for international courts and tribunals. Though, as Antonio Cassese notes, the application of criminal law is complicated by 'a real patchwork of normative standards' that is the natural product of the 'heterogeneous and composite origin' of criminal law.[44] Nevertheless, two key principles of criminal law have found general applicability at the international level. First is the principle of individual criminal responsibility. This requires, as we have already explained, that an individual incurs liability for the violation of international law only where the relevant international law addresses the particular obligation directly to individuals. This is now true for all offences under customary international law and the majority of offences under treaty law. The various contours of this principle are codified in Article 25 of the ICC Statute which recognises criminal liability for both direct and indirect perpetrators. Commission includes physical perpetration, ordering and inducing an act that is criminal as well as participation in a common plan to commit a crime within the jurisdiction of the ICC. Complicity includes consenting to aid and abet a crime with the knowledge that the act of the accomplice aids substantially the work of the principal perpetrator. A principle of liability that has crystallised since WWII is that of superior/command responsibility. This holds that a superior, whether of military or political rank, is personally responsible for crimes committed by his subordinates where the superior knows or had reason to know that crimes are taking place and fails

---

[43] Cassese, *International Criminal Law*, pp. 26–8.   [44] *Ibid.*, p. 18.

to prevent or punish the perpetrators. Command responsibility must be distinguished from the defence of superior orders, whereby the physical perpetrator of a crime may be excused completely if he was following the orders of superiors and did not know that the order was unlawful or where the order was not manifestly unlawful.[45] The second principle stemming from criminal law is that of the legality of holding particular behaviour to be an international crime. This holds that criminal rules must be as specific as possible, that they are not applied in analogy, and that they may not be applied retroactively.[46]

Human rights law also provides two key principles from which procedural rules of international criminal law are derived. First is the presumption of innocence. This principle is fundamental to criminal procedure in common law systems and indeed was cited in two cases by the Nuremberg Tribunal. But it is now generally accepted to be a basic human right (and has been so recognised by the European Court of Human Rights, the European Human Rights Commission, and the UN Human Rights Committee). The presumption of innocence is formally recognised in Article 66 of the ICC Statute. The other principle is the rights of the accused (which provides the right to a fair trial). This principle is enshrined in the Universal Declaration of Human Rights (1948), in the International Covenant on Civil and Political Rights (1966), in American, European and African human rights conventions, as well as in the 1949 Geneva Conventions. It is expressed in Article 67 of the ICC Statute.[47]

The final principle we must note, because it defines the remit of the ICC, is the principle of complementarity. The 1998 Rome Statute (para. 10 of the Preamble, as well as Articles 1, 17 and 18) gives primacy to national courts for the prosecution and punishment of international crimes. So unless a state in question is unable or unwilling to investigate and subsequently prosecute for one of the crimes listed in the Rome Statute, the ICC will not exercise jurisdiction. This state of affairs denotes quite a change from the previous Tribunals (e.g., Nuremberg, Tokyo, Yugoslavia and Rwanda) where the relevant instruments conferred primacy of jurisdiction to the international tribunals.[48]

---

[45] Kittichaisaree, *International*, pp. 233–57. See also William A. Schabas, 'Enforcing international humanitarian law: catching the accomplices', *Review of the International Committee of the Red Cross* 83 (2001), 439–59.

[46] Cassese, *International Criminal Law*, pp. 136–53.

[47] Schabas, *Introduction*, pp. 95–100.

[48] Andrew Clapman, 'Issues of complexity, complicity, and complementarity: from the Nuremberg Trials to the dawn of the new International Criminal Court,' in Sands (ed.), *From Nuremberg to The Hague*, p. 63.

A recent innovation which, in a sense, circumvents the principle of complementarity are hybrid international tribunals (also called 'internationalised' or mixed criminal courts or tribunals). These are judicial organs endowed with some international elements (e.g. statutes encompassing international crimes, appointment of some foreign judges). However, they are not truly international tribunals because they have no power or jurisdiction extending beyond the territory in which they are based. Hybrid courts have been established in Kosovo (1999), Sierra Leone (2000) and Cambodia (2004), and also in East Timor (2002) and Burundi (2005) as part of national truth and reconciliation processes. Hybrid courts may be either part of the judiciary of a state (e.g., in Kosovo, and in East Timor) or free-standing (e.g., in Sierra Leone). Hybrid courts may be established to assist in post-conflict peace-building, to bolster a weak national judiciary, or to get round a lack of political and financial will to establish an international court.[49] Against this, we should note, some critics have argued that the kind of retributive justice provided by hybrid and international courts can hinder reconciliation, and may reignite inter-communal tensions and even violence; sometimes amnesty is the price for stabilising post-conflict societies.[50]

Compliance with international criminal law

Of all the areas of law examined in this book, international criminal law is perhaps the one with the worst record of compliance. The impressive growth of law in this area has not been matched by increasing restraint in war. Indeed arguably war increasingly 'degenerated' as the twentieth century wore on, with deliberative destruction of homelands and civilian populations. Thus, genocide continued in practice (even if unrecognised so by states) following WWII.[51] Many of the worst atrocities in war and against civilian populations have occurred outside what has been called the Western liberal democratic 'zone of peace': in Africa, the Middle East, Asia and Latin America.[52] To be sure, liberal democracies have been generally law-biding when it comes to the treatment of civilians within their own territories. However, liberal democracies have a less impressive

---

[49] Philippe Sands, *Lawless World: America and the Making and Breaking of Global Rules* (London: Allen Lane, 2005), p. 52; Cassese, 'International criminal law', pp. 731–2.

[50] Jack Snyder and Leslie Vinjamuri, 'Trials and errors: principle and pragmatism in strategies of international justice', *International Security* 28 (2003–4), 5–44; Mark R. Amstutz, *The Healing of Nations: The Promise and Limits of Political Forgiveness* (Oxford: Rowan and Littlefield, 2005).

[51] Martin Shaw, *War and Genocide* (Cambridge: Polity, 2003).

[52] Max Singer and Aaron Wildavsky, *The Real World Order: Zones of Peace, Zones of Turmoil*, rev. edition (New York: Chatham House, 1996).

record when it comes to exercising restraint in armed conflict, especially in the context of attempting to maintain imperial orders. Post-WWII Dutch operations in the East Indies, French operations in Indochina and Algeria, British operations in Ireland and Kenya, and US operations in Vietnam and Central America were all characterised by activities which broke the spirit, if not the letter, of Common Article 3 of the Geneva Conventions.[53]

State consent has been central to compliance with international criminal law, and in large part explains the lack thereof. State consent has been of obvious importance in creating treaty law in this area. However, as we shall see in the next section, states are not the sole law-creating agents: courts and tribunals have played a crucial role here in providing authoritative interpretations of treaty and customary law and thereby expanding the scope of international criminal law. Moreover, not all states must consent to international criminal law to be bound by it. The core rules of the LOAC – the prohibitions against attacking civilians and civilian objects, and the requirements to tend to the wounded and treat detainees humanely – are norms of customary international law and so applicable to all states. Moreover, some rules of international criminal law, including the prohibitions against attacking civilians, genocide and torture, are pre-emptory norms of international law, which means that derogation from them by any state, for whatever reason, is strictly forbidden. However, the lack of an independent international enforcement mechanism up until the creation of the ICC has meant that states have been left to police themselves. Basically, consent has been so important because coercion has not been a compelling motivating factor for states' compliance with international criminal law. In this sense, the 'domestic analogy' so commonly applied in this area of law breaks down. In domestic systems, courts and police provide the mechanisms to prevent and punish crimes. But in the international system, these mechanisms have been absent.[54]

Obviously, there is some question as to whether or not the ICC will change all this. The ICC has jurisdiction over nationals, or over crimes committed on the territory, of states parties to the Rome Statute. Article 13(a) of the Rome Statute also gives the ICC universal jurisdiction in any

---

[53] 'Strategic culture and American empire', *SAIS Review of International Affairs* 25 (2005), 3–18. Brutal use of force against rebel groups and rising civilian populations occurred in the context of a shifting normative order that increasingly favoured the right of self-discrimination over rights of empire. See Neta C. Crawford, *Argument and Change in World Politics: Ethics, Decolonization, and Humanitarian Intervention* (Cambridge: Cambridge University Press, 2002).

[54] Immi Tallgren, 'The sensibility and sense of international criminal law', *European Journal of International Law* 13 (2002), 565–7.

case referred to it by the UNSC. Thus, the ICC has begun to investigate the commission of international crimes against civilians in the Sudanese region of Darfur following referral of this case by the UNSC in March 2005.[55] The point here being that the crimes in question have been committed by Sudanese (government and government-backed forces) in the territory of Sudan, and Sudan is not a party to the ICC. The Rome Statute does provide considerable powers to the Independent Prosecutor, i.e., s/he can conduct actual prosecutions in full independence, and also s/he has the authority to investigate suspected international crimes that fall within the jurisdiction of the ICC without seeking prior consent from states (Article 15(1), ICC Statute). But under the principle of complementarity, jurisdiction may be exercised only where states fail to conduct their own prosecutions for international crimes. This may leave open some possibility for states of bad faith to stage trials guaranteed to produce the desired verdicts.[56] Moreover, Article 18(1) allows for third parties (i.e., states not party to the Statute) to claim jurisdiction under the principle of complementarity and thereby ensure that their nationals do not face international justice.[57] In addition, Article 124 allows states parties to the Statute to exclude war crimes committed on their territory or by their nationals from the ICC's jurisdiction for a period of seven years. Finally, as noted already, Article 5(2) excludes the jurisdiction of the ICC over the crime of aggression until this crime has been defined. So there is considerable limitation to the ICC as a coercive mechanism for ensuring compliance with international criminal law.

This limitation is especially present when it comes to the most powerful state in the world system: the United States. The Clinton administration signed the final version of the Rome Statute (albeit with some hesitation) only to have the Bush administration 'unsign' it, in an action unprecedented in US foreign relations.[58] Formally speaking, the United States took issue with the ICC's jurisdiction over the nationals of non-states parties, even though such jurisdiction is perfectly in accordance with international law.[59] Probably more important for the United States was

---

[55] International Criminal Court, 'The Prosecutor of the ICC opens investigation in Darfur', ICC-OTP-0606–104-En, 6 June 2005, at www.icc-cpi.int/pressrelease_details&id=107&l=en.html.

[56] Though it should also be noted that Article 18(3) gives the ICC Prosecutor the authority to check that a pursuit of criminal proceedings by a state have been 'genuine'.

[57] Antonio Cassese, 'The statute of the International Criminal Court: some preliminary reflections', *European Journal of International Law* 10 (1999),159.

[58] Richard J. Goldstone and Janine Simpson, 'Evaluating the role of the International Criminal Court as a legal response to terrorism', *Harvard Human Rights Journal* 16 (2003), 24.

[59] Dapo Akande, 'The jurisdiction of the International Criminal Court over nationals of non-parties: legal basis and limits', *Journal of International Criminal Justice* (2003), 618–50.

the ambiguous relationship between the ICC and the UNSC: if the ICC had depended on UNSC authorisation to act, then the United States could block any threatening ICC action using their veto on the Security Council.[60] As it happens, the 1994 draft of the ICC Statute, the International Law Commission had in mind a permanent tribunal that would be very much subordinate to the Security Council and interlocked with the Charter of the United Nations. However, the final version of the Rome Statute provided quite a different picture of this relationship: one where the ICC had gained significant independence from the UNSC, most importantly with regard to the triggering of prosecutions and the deferral of cases (see Article 13). Thus, under Article 14, a case may be referred to the ICC by a state party to the Rome Statute and at the initiative of the ICC Prosecutor, as well as by the UNSC. All the Security Council can do to obstruct a case being investigated is to instruct the ICC to defer an investigation for a renewable period of twelve months (Article 16). It follows that a single member of the Security Council is not able to use its right of veto to prevent an investigation taking place. From this perspective, the ICC does have considerable potential to be an independent coercive mechanism and hence US opposition to the ICC may be understood. The United States went so far as to threaten to pull all its forces out of UN peace-keeping missions to avoid any possibility that they may be subject to ICC prosecution for actions in the course of their peace missions. The UNSC responded with a quite extraordinary practical measure, passing a controversial resolution (1422) specifically requiring the ICC to defer any potential prosecutions of non-state party peace-keepers for a twelve-month period.[61]

This highlights, then, the responsibility of states for prosecuting international crimes. Crimes against humanity and genocide have rarely been the subject of national trials; a notable exceptions being the Eichmann trial in Israel in 1961[62] and Barbie trial in France in 1987.[63] The Eichmann trial is especially significant because the 'principle of the universality of jurisdiction' was invoked by the Israeli Supreme Court in this

[60] William A. Schabas, 'United States' hostility to the International Criminal Court; it's all about the Security Council', *European Journal of International Law* 15 (2004), 704–20.
[61] Carsten Stahn, 'The ambiguities of Security Council 1422 (2002)', *European Journal of International Law* 14 (2003), 85–104.
[62] Otto Adolf Eichmann was a former Lt Colonel in the SS and had played an important role in managing the logistics of the Nazi death camps in Eastern Europe. He was captured by Israeli agents in a covert operation in Argentina in 1960 and flown back to Israel for trial. He was indicted on fifteen criminal charges, including war crimes, found guilty and executed in 1962.
[63] Klaus Barbie was a former Captain in the SS and had been in charge of the Gestapo in Lyon during World War II. He was arrested by the Bolivian government in 1984 and deported to France where he stood trial for war crimes in 1987. He was found guilty and sentenced to life imprisonment. He died four years later aged 77.

case, as there was no territorial or nationality[64] link to establish Israeli jurisdiction to prosecute this case.[65] The record is slightly better, but only ever so slightly, when it comes to national prosecution of war crimes. As David Forsythe notes, 'Only national trials for war crimes have occurred with any regularity, and these – mostly in liberal democracies – have been frequently undermined by the continuing strength of nationalism.' Simply put: it is very hard for a country to convict its own troops for misconduct in military operations that are commonly perceived to be in the service of the country.[66] This seems to be also the conclusion reached by Human Rights Watch concerning the work so far done by the Special (National) Criminal Court on the Events in Darfur (SCCED), established on 7 June 2005:

> In short, the cases brought before the SCCED to date have not begun to address issues of accountability in the region. The cases have dealt with individual abuses, which are marginally related to the serious and widespread violations committed in Darfur, and have failed to seek to bring to justice those most responsible for these extensive violations. This is the result of a lack of political will, which is reflected both in the cases chosen and in the laws governing the courts.[67]

Even when it comes to the ICC, the principle of complementarity will require many states to adopt new legislation to enable them to exercise jurisdiction over the full range of international crimes defined in the ICC Statute, as well as to enable the surrendering of suspects to the ICC when required.[68] This implicit duty of effective implementation following a state's ratification of the Rome Statute is an important part of a state's obligation of compliance with the ICC in matters that necessitate co-operation between the domestic and the international level, such as in acting on an international arrest warrant issued by the ICC or in assisting the ICC in locating witnesses. And so any lack of effective national implementing legislation could indeed impede the deliverance of international justice in cases where the ICC is to issue a request for co-operation.[69]

---

[64] The nationality link was not present as Eichmann's victims were not Israeli citizens at the time of the crimes. Indeed, Israel did not exist as a state.
[65] Covey Oliver, 'The Attorney-General of the Govement of Israel v. Eichmann', *American Journal of International Law* 56 (1962), 805–45.
[66] David P. Forsythe, *Human Rights in International Relations* (Cambridge: Cambridge University Press, 2000), p. 90.
[67] Report of June 2006 available at hrw.org/backgrounder/ij/sudan0606/2.htm#_ftn12.
[68] See, for instance, the International Criminal Court Act 2001 and the International Criminal Court (Scotland) 2001 in the UK. See also Amnesty International checklist and guidelines for effective implementation, available at www.amnesty.org/pages/icc-implementation-eng.
[69] See Philippe Sands, 'After Pinochet: the role of national courts', in Sands (ed.), *From Nuremberg to The Hague*, pp. 68–108.

State consent is crucial therefore to the prosecution of international crimes both through national courts and the ICC. Indeed, consent lies at the heart of the Rome Statute by which the ICC parts company from the ICTY and ICTR, both of which were established by UNSC resolutions. As Ruth Wedgwood notes:

> The proffered reason for creating a permanent criminal court by treaty, rather than through the exercise of the Security Council's Chapter VII powers, was that an institution of fundamental importance should have the solid grounding of direct state agreement. To be sure, states have consented to the United Nations Charter which empowers the Council, but it was felt (philosophically and politically) that a framework institution like the ICC should ground its legitimacy on the immediate consent of participating states.[70]

Such direct consent is arguably crucial in order to remove the claim that the ICC is an affront to state sovereignty. The counter-argument to this, expressed some time ago, is that states are merely exercising a sovereign right to delegate jurisdiction to a supranational court.[71]

Interest and fairness are present, but to a far lesser extent, as motivating factors when it comes to international criminal law. Both lie at the heart of the LOAC dealing with the treatment of prisoners of war (POWs). Most states have a general interest in reassuring their combatants that they will be treated humanely if captured by the enemy. Of course there are exceptions, such as Japan in the Pacific War and Germany on the Eastern front during WWII, where states have indoctrinated their soldiers not to expect or give any quarter in combat. One might think that states also have an interest in preserving the lives and wellbeing of nationals in foreign captivity as future sources of military manpower. However, in reality, former POWs that do return home are usually physically and/or psychologically incapable of going back to war.[72] The POWs were provided with a range of rights under the 1929 Geneva Convention. This provided for a decentralised system of enforcement, where states were responsible for ensuring self-compliance (with provision for voluntary submission to monitoring by the ICRC). Fairness is built into the logic of reciprocity on which this POW regime is based; hence, parties to the 1929 Geneva

---

[70] Ruth Wedgwood, 'The International Criminal Court: an American view', *European Journal of International Law* 10 (1999), 10.

[71] John W. Bridge, 'The case for an international court of criminal justice and the formulation of international criminal law', *International and Comparative Law Quarterly* 13 (1964), 1273.

[72] This argument is made in Martha Finnemore, 'Rules of war and war of rules: the International Red Cross and the restraint of state violence', in John Boli and George M. Thomas (eds.), *Constructing World Culture* (Stanford, CA: Stanford University Press, 1999), pp. 149–68.

Convention signed up to a common code of conduct whereby they guaranteed certain basic rights to POWs from each other's militaries. WWII demonstrated the limitations of this system – some states used POWs for slave labour and treated them brutally in other ways, resulting in some staggering death rates: 27 per cent for allied POWs held by Japan, up to 33 per cent for German POWs held in the Soviet Union, and up to 60 per cent for Soviet POWs held in Germany. This system of self-regulation is essentially unchanged under the Third Geneva Convention of 1949. However, this convention does increase the gravity and criminal consequence of committing an international crime against POWs. POWs are one of three classes of 'protected persons' (the other three classes being the wounded, shipwrecked and civilians) against whom it is a grave breach of the 1949 Geneva Conventions to kill, torture or treat inhumanely. Moreover, the logic of reciprocity is no longer central – POW rights are now protected under customary international law. All states, regardless of whether or not they are party to the 1949 Geneva Conventions, are bound by these rules.[73]

One might think that mutual interest and the logic of reciprocity had been at play to some extent in most aspects of LOAC. States must surely have an interest in restraining the worst excesses of war in order to protect their civilians and, indeed, spare their combatants unnecessary suffering. And yet, what we find is that national interests often underpin state attraction to and hence compliance with particular restrictions in war. Thus, LOAC happens to outlaw the kinds of warfare that powerful, developed states have no interest in waging, namely, low-technology campaigns involving direct attacks against foreign civilian populations of the kind seen in Yugoslavia and central Africa in the 1990s. However, the LOAC does not outlaw use of nuclear weapons which by their very nature are likely to cause excessive loss of civilian life and damage to civilian structures. Furthermore (as we discuss below), there is sufficient ambiguity on aspects of LOAC concerning things like the targeting of dual-use structures (i.e., civilian structures which may have military uses), for developed states to be able to exploit for the purpose of waging high-tech air war.[74]

[73] James D. Morrow, 'The institutional features of the prisoners of war treaties', *International Organization* 55 (2001), 971–91.

[74] Thomas W. Smith, 'The new law of war: legitimizing hi-tech and infrastructure violence', *International Studies Quarterly* 46 (2002), 355–74. In its controversial 1996 opinion on the legality of the threat or use of nuclear weapons, the ICJ was unable to find that nuclear use would in every circumstance be illegal. It noted that any use of nuclear weapons must be consistent with the principles of proportionality and military necessity. Such principles would be met in the case of a nuclear weapon being used against a

Congruence should go some way to explaining the compliance with LOAC. After all much of this law was developed simultaneously, if not in advance, in the military codes of the North American and European powers in the nineteenth and twentieth centuries (the Lieber Code being the most notable example). These states have had centuries to discuss, agree and internalise shared rules concerning the limits of warfare. However, the European powers during both world wars failed in their responsibilities to protect the injured, sick and civilians in war. To be sure, the liberal democracies have generally fared better than dictatorships of the twentieth century in complying with international criminal law. Thus, the justice meted out to the Nazis and Japanese at the end of WWII was not simply victor's justice. It is true that German bombing of population centres was removed from the list of offences to avoid the Allies' incriminating themselves for their strategic bombing of German and Japanese cities.[75] But the allied bombing campaigns, pursued out of a perception (misguided or not) of strategic necessity, are not comparable to the atrocities committed by the Axis powers which resulted in the murder of tens of millions of civilians under the control of German and Japanese authorities during the war.[76] Still, as we noted earlier, democracies failed to abide by Common Article 3 of the Geneva Conventions when it came to using force to bolster their crumbling empires.[77] Thus congruence is not simply a matter of crudely contrasting law-abiding democracies with atrocity-committing autocracies. Rather congruence needs to be considered in three, more precise, ways.

First is variation in congruence between specific rules of the LOAC and the military doctrines of the established powers. This variation helps account, for example, for British compliance and German non-compliance with rules prohibiting submarine attacks on civilian shipping, and British preparedness and German reluctance to engage in strategic bombing of civilian targets; the Royal Navy was uninterested in submarine warfare whereas it was central to the German Navy, and likewise the Royal Air Force was keen on strategic bombing whereas the

---

military target in an isolated area (i.e., the so-called 'clean nuclear use scenario'). See Theo Farrell and Hélène Lambert, 'Courting controversy: international law, national norms, and American nuclear use', *Review of International Studies* 27 (2001), 309–26.

[75] Overy, 'The Nuremberg trials', p. 10.
[76] One may still find that the allied bombing campaigns were immoral if not illegal. See A. C. Grayling, *Among the Dead Cities: Was the Allied Bombing of Civilians in WWII a Necessity or a Crime?* (London: Bloomsbury, 2006).
[77] Rita Maran, *Torture: The Role of Ideology in the French-Algerian War* (New York: Praeger Publishers, 1989); David Anderson, *Histories of the Hanged: The Dirty War in Kenya and the End of Empire* (New York: W. W. Norton and Co., 2005).

German Air Force was not.[78] A more recent example includes variation in the preparedness to use force by the US and British armies engaged in stability and counterinsurgency (COIN) operations. British officers have complained that the US Army is overly 'kinetic' (i.e., too quick to use lethal force) in operations that are essentially directed towards winning the hearts and minds of the local populace.[79] This disposition towards a firepower-orientated approach to stability and COIN operations may be explained in terms of an American 'way of battle' that emphasises tactical victory over campaign success.[80] In contrast, the British Army's reluctance to use lethal force in such operations may be rooted in a 'minimum force philosophy', itself the product of the Army's experience of imperial policing and more recently of policy in Northern Ireland.[81]

Second, congruence needs to be considered in terms of how states embed LOAC in their national military systems. There is enormous variation here between the largest and most developed states and the less-developed, as well as the smaller, states. Thus China decided only a few years ago to provide lawyers for military commands; more to the point, this was to ensure that commanders had access to legal advice on construction projects and not on matters concerning LOAC.[82] The comparison with the United States is striking. The United States takes the lead in terms of military structure: Judge Advocate General (JAG) officers are embedded at all levels of command right down to battalion level. This is meant to ensure that military operations conform to the applicable law, crucially by enabling JAG officers to be involved in decisions concerning military targeting.[83] Embedding LOAC in national military systems also, crucially, involves generic targeting doctrine as well as campaign rules of engagement (ROE). In terms of targeting doctrine, there is a gap emerging between the US and European militaries. Most European militaries adhere to a strict reading of Additional Protocol I

---

[78] Jeffrey W. Legro, *Restraint Under Fire: Anglo-German Restraint During World War II* (Ithaca, NY: Cornell University Press, 1995).

[79] Brigadier Nigel Aylwin-Foster, 'Changing the army for counterinsurgency operations', *Military Review* (November–December 2005), 2–15.

[80] Antulio J. Echevarria II, *Toward an American Way of War* (Carlisle, PA: Strategic Studies Institute, US Army War College, 2004).

[81] Rod Thornton, 'The British Army and the origins of the minimum force philosophy', *Small Wars and Insurgencies* 15, 1 (2004), 83–106.

[82] 'Chinese Military to Have Lawyers', *People's Daily*, 8 June 2000, at www.english.people. com.cn/english/200006/08/eng20000608_42468.html.

[83] Michael W. Lewis, 'The law of aerial bombardment in the 1991 Gulf War', *American Journal of International Law* 97 (2003), 481–509.

(Article 52(2)) which prohibits the targeting of dual-use structures (that is civilian structures which have military application, such as roads, railways and bridges) unless such structures are making an 'effective' contribution to enemy action and their neutralisation or destruction 'offers a definite military advantage'.[84] The latest US targeting doctrine removes the 'effective contribution' requirement and permits attacks on structures 'whose total or partial destruction, capture, or neutralization offer a military advantage'.[85] This doctrinal difference produced variation in how the US and European militaries interpreted the lawful range of action during the 1999 Kosovo War. The US military was perfectly satisfied in the lawfulness of extending NATO's bombing campaign to include civilian structures in and around Belgrade (including the civilian power grid), whereas the European allies were most uncertain as to the lawfulness of such military escalation.[86]

Finally, congruence may be conflict-specific. Essentially, LOAC may be interpreted in light of the nature of the enemy. Compliance is more likely where the enemy is considered similar in nature – in other words, to be a 'civilised' foe. Compliance is less likely where the enemy is considered very different in nature – be that difference defined by race, religion or ideology – or otherwise somehow 'barbaric'.[87] This is certainly evident in the late nineteenth and early twentieth centuries, when the civilised ways of conducting warfare were deemed to be inapplicable in wars against savages. Thus, whilst some European military opposed the introduction of certain uncivilised weapons (such as machineguns and poison gas) on European battlefields, they were perfectly content to use them against non-White opponents.[88] These discourses of difference also produced two different forms of warfare during WWII. Warfare between the Western allies and the Germans was conducted, for the most part, within the bounds of LOAC. However, the war in the Pacific between the Allies and the Japanese was savage and unrestrained. Each side saw the other

---

[84] Marco Roscini, 'Targeting and contemporary aerial bombardment', *International and Comparative Law Quarterly* 54 (2005), 442.

[85] US Joint Chiefs of Staff, *Joint Doctrine for Targeting* JP 3–60, 17 January 2002, A-2, 4 (b), at www.dtic.mil/doctrine/jel/new_pubs/jp3_60.pdf.

[86] Theo Farrell, 'World culture and military power', *Security Studies* 14 (2005), 484–5.

[87] Philip K. Lawrence, *Modernity and War: The Creed of Absolute Violence* (New York: St Martin's, 1997), pp. 6–34.

[88] Richard M. Price, *The Chemical Weapons Taboo* (Ithaca, NY: Cornell University Press, 1997); Trutz von Trotha, '"The fellows can just starve": on wars of "pacification" in the African colonies of imperial Germany and the concept of "Total War"', in Manfred F. Boemeke, Roger Chickering and Stig Forster (eds.), *Anticipating Total War* (Cambridge: Cambridge University Press, 1999), pp. 415–36.

as racially inferior and undeserving of humanity in war.[89] Equally, Germany's war in the East was a truly savage affair directed at an enemy considered to be subhuman; without mercy for wounded and captured combatants, and designed to exterminate or enslave the civilian population in occupied lands.[90] More recently, a discourse of difference has informed US application of the Third Geneva Convention (1949) in its treatment of detainees in the GWOT: this is the convention providing POW rights and prohibiting cruel and inhumane treatment of those captured in battle. The Bush administration started out by claiming that al-Qaeda and Taliban captured in the 2001–2 Afghanistan War were unlawful combatants and so not entitled to protection under the Geneva Conventions. In February 2002, it modified this position and said that the Third Geneva Convention would be applied to the treatment of Taliban, but not to captured al-Qaeda. Claims at the time by President George W. Bush that all detainees in US custody would be treated humanely were shown to be false with mounting evidence in 2003 of mistreatment and even torture in the interrogation of detainees. As we discussed in Chapter 5, the US Congress has since passed the 2006 Military Commissions Act (MCA) which criminalises the worst interrogation techniques. However, as we also noted, the MCA also denies detainees the right to challenge their detention in the US courts and fails to protect their rights to a fair trial. It could be argued that the United States was taking the expedient route in denying rights to those it wanted to detain and interrogate for its GWOT. This is a bit puzzling however since up to this point the United States had an exemplary record in the treatment of POWs. The US refusal to fully comply with LOAC in this case may be seen in the context of war against barbarians. Al-Qaeda (and its allies like the Taliban) is perceived to be unusually dangerous in its ideological hatred of the United States, its ability to project power worldwide, and to attack Western homelands and kill large numbers of innocent civilians. For Bush, the GWOT is about the very fight for civilisation. Harking back to the turn of the twentieth century, the Bush administration came to believe (and has attempted to argue) that laws designed to regulate conflict between civilised foe are not really applicable to a war against a barbaric enemy.[91]

---

[89] John W. Dower, *War Without Mercy: Race and Power in the Pacific War* (New York: Pantheon, 1986).

[90] Omer Bartov, *Germany's War and the Holocaust* (Ithaca, NY: Cornell University Press, 2003).

[91] Helen M. Kinsella, 'Discourses of difference: civilians, combatants, and compliance with the laws of war', in David Armstrong, Theo Farrell and Bice Maiguashca (eds.), *Force and Legitimacy in World Politics* (Cambridge: Cambridge University Press, 2005), pp. 163–86.

Change in international criminal law

All three processes of change – formal, policy and social – are involved in this area of international law. Central has been the formal process of change resting on state consent, as clearly shown in the increasing codification of international criminal law. Most notable here has been the conclusion of a succession of multilateral treaties on LOAC from the middle of the nineteenth century on. Some of these treaties were limited to particular areas, problems and/or practices of warfare, such as the Paris Declaration on Maritime War (1856), the Geneva Convention on wounded and sick (1864), and the St Petersburg Declaration on explosive projectiles (1868) noted earlier. But states gathered also for successive large peace conferences in The Hague to conclude two sets of conventions – four conventions in 1899 and thirteen conventions in 1907. These conventions also provided for very specific prohibitions in warfare, such as the Convention Prohibiting Launching of Projectiles and Explosives from Balloons (1899) and the Convention Against the Laying of Automatic Submarine Contact Mines (1907).[92] But in addition they provided more general rules concerning the conduct of warfare, such as Convention II (1899) and Convention IV (1907), both on the Laws and Customs of War on Land. General rules on warfare were further elaborated in the four Geneva Conventions (1949). The first and second convention deal with the treatment of sick and wounded in war on, respectively, the land and the sea. The third convention concerns the treatment of POWs, and the fourth deals with the treatment of civilians in war. Two additional protocols to the Geneva Conventions on, respectively, the treatment of victims of international and non-international armed conflict were concluded in 1977. Finally, a third additional protocol on the adoption of an additional emblem for the ICRC (a red cross) was recently agreed in 2005. The Geneva Conventions have become customary law because they enjoy such wide state acceptance; indeed, all 194 states in the world are party to the Geneva Convention. Over 160 states are party to the first two Additional Protocols (1977), and, as of 2006, 74 states had signed the third Additional Protocol (2005).[93] We also noted a series of treaties on other aspects of international criminal law. States have concluded treaties outlawing both genocide and torture; 140 states are party to the Genocide Convention, and 142 states are party to the

---

[92] As we noted in Chapter 4, states have also more recently concluded treaties to outlaw certain means of warfare, including chemical and biological weapons, as well as some forms of conventional weapons.

[93] The Hague and Geneva Conventions are available from the ICRC website at www.icrc.org/ihl.nsf.

CAT.[94] This degree of state support for this body of treaty law on international crime is further evidence of the central importance of the formal process of change in international criminal law.

Change as a policy process is evident in international criminal law in terms of the role of courts and of transnational activist networks in affecting legal change. As noted already, the statutes of the post-war IMTs, the ICTY and ICTR, and the ICC are all crucial sources of substantive and procedural law on international crime. However, this falls under the realist lens and the notion of a formal process of change. The statute of the IMT was negotiated between the allied powers of WWII, and the ICC Statute is a formal treaty. Most states have not directly consented to the statutes of the ICTY and ICTR, for as we noted, both were established under UNSC resolutions; however, by consenting to the UN Charter, states consented to give the UNSC broad discretion to exercise authority in matters of international peace and security. But beyond the formal law-making process surrounding their establishment, international courts and tribunals have played a vital role as authoritative decision-making bodies in developing international criminal law. Much of the content of treaty law on international crime is either ill-defined or otherwise open to interpretation. Thus, there is no clear definition of what constitutes armed conflict. And, as we discussed above, even clarification in Additional Protocol I on the targeting of dual-use structures has not prevented a major difference of interpretation between the US and European allies. As Antonio Cassese notes: 'the relative indeterminacy and "malleability" of international criminal rules heightens the significance of the role of national or international courts, which have to throw light on and give legal precision to rules of customary law as well as spelling out and elaborating upon frequently terse treaty provisions'.[95] Courts thus play a crucial role in clarifying treaty law. In addition, courts have drawn on legal principles of general international, criminal and human rights law, to elaborate customary and treaty law on international crimes. In this manner, they can be a mechanism for rapid and even quite profound change in this area of law. For instance, in rejecting the defence's argument that international law only applied to states, the Nuremberg Tribunal established the notion of individual criminal liability in international law. The Tribunal reasoned that since crimes were 'committed by men, not abstract entities', individuals had to be held to account in order to enforce international law. As Andrew Clapham notes, this was nothing less than a 'paradigm

---

[94] Data from the Office of the High Commissioner for Human Rights (updated 1 November 2006), at www.ohchr.org/english/countries/ratification/index.htm.

[95] Cassese, 'International criminal law', 723.

shift' in international law, in 'going beyond obligations on states and attaching duties to individuals involving criminal responsibility'.[96] More recently, judgments by the ad hoc tribunals for Yugoslavia and Rwanda have also established important new precedents in international criminal law, precedents that have been embraced and codified in the Rome Statute of the ICC. For instance, in the case *Prosecutor v. Tadic* decided by the Appeals Chamber of the ICTY, the Tribunal offered a progressive view of war crimes in concluding that prohibitions contained in treaty law on international armed conflict (Hague and Geneva) were also applicable to internal armed conflict under customary international law.[97] In the same case, the Tribunal also finally buried the link, originally established at Nuremberg, between crimes against humanity and armed conflict. The Appeals Chamber concluded that '[i]t is now a settled rule of customary international law that crimes against humanity do not require a connection to international armed conflict'.[98] This position was also codified in the Rome Statute (Article 7).

Domestic courts also play a modest role here. As we noted earlier, domestic courts may exercise universal jurisdiction over grave breaches of the Geneva Conventions, as well as crimes against humanity and genocide. However, up to the 1990s, states showed little interest in exercising universal jurisdiction for these crimes. The prosecution and conviction of Eichmann on charges of crimes against humanity and war crimes by the District Court of Jerusalem in 1961 is much noted precisely because it was exceptional in this regard. In recent years, domestic courts have increasingly shown a willingness to prosecute grave international crimes. Among those states that are taking the lead here, most, such as Austria, France, Germany and Switzerland, recognise a conditionality that requires the accused to be in custody before jurisdiction is exercised (thereby ensuring a fair trial). Spain and, for a while, Belgium required no such condition to exist.[99] In 2001, a Belgian court convicted four Rwandans of complicity in genocide. However, under pressure from the United States (which intensified following a series of war-crimes lawsuits against senior US officials privately filed in Belgian courts), the Belgian parliament revised the law in line with the conditionality more widely practised by states.[100]

---

[96] Clapham, 'Issues', pp. 32–3.
[97] *Prosecutor v. Tadic*, case no IT-94-1-AR72, Appeal on Jurisdiction (2 October 1995), paras. 86–137.
[98] *Ibid.*, para.141.   [99] Cassese, *International*, pp. 284–95.
[100] Yann Tessier, 'Belgian files war crimes suit against US general', Reuters, 14 May 2003; John Chalmers and Tabassum Zakaria, 'Rumsfeld Threatens NATO HQ Over Belgian Crimes Law', Reuters, 12 June 2003; Antonio Cassese, 'Is the bell tolling for universality? A plea for a sensible notion of universal jurisdiction', *Journal of International*

Even this conditional universal jurisdiction enables domestic courts to be important agents of change in international criminal law. An important example is the ruling by the British House of Lords in 1999, that the former President of Chile, General Augusto Pinochet, was not entitled to claim immunity from the jurisdiction of the English courts for acts of torture committed by the Chilean state under his rule. This case raised the issue of immunity for heads of state. This is provided in customary international law and codified in the 1961 Vienna Convention on Diplomatic Relations (Art. 39). Immunity for heads of state, government ministers and diplomats is obviously important to facilitate interstate relations. At the same time, it is problematic in the context of the growing body of international criminal law. In an inventive interpretation of international law, the House of Lords found that Pinochet was not immune from prosecution for torture. The Lords reasoned that because Chile was a party to the CAT, it had by implication waived state immunity concerning prosecution for grave violations of this convention. Otherwise, the Lords reasoned, the whole CAT is rendered meaningless. The ruling gave a fresh interpretation on the rules regarding state immunity such that former heads of state could be prosecuted for grave international crimes. However, it must be admitted that the persuasive authority of this ruling was somewhat blunted by the failure of the Lords to agree on whether Pinochet had acted in an official capacity in committing his crimes.[101] And indeed, three years later the ICJ revisited the issue in *Congo* v. *Belgium* (2002). In this case, Belgium had issued an international arrest warrant for the Congolese Foreign Minister for inciting racial hatred, violence and murder. Congo took the case to the ICJ claiming state immunity for their minister. The ICJ did not follow the House of Lords line and instead adopted a far more restrictive interpretation of the law. It ruled that former government ministers were immune from prosecution unless immunity was waived or the acts concerned were carried out in a private capacity after the minister in question had left government.[102] However, *Congo* v. *Belgium* does not necessarily provide a more authoritative interpretation than the House of Lords judgment of the law on this issue.

Criminal Justice 1 (2003), 589–95. The requirement for the accused to be physically present is also recognised as a fundamental condition for the exercise of universal jurisdiction by the Princeton Project on Universal Jurisdiction. See the project report, *The Princeton Principles on Universal Jurisdiction* (Princeton, NJ: Program on Law and Public Affairs, 2001), p. 28, at www.princeton.edu/~lapa/unive_jur.pdf.

[101] J. Craig Barker, 'The Future of Former Head of State Immunity after *ex parte Pinochet*', *International and Comparative Law Quarterly* 48 (1999), 937–49.

[102] Campbell McLachlan, '*Pinochet* Revisited', *International and Comparative Law Quarterly* 51 (2002), 959–66.

Indeed, the ICJ's judgment in this case has been heavily criticised for not reflecting the current state of customary international law.[103]

We noted in Chapter 4 the importance of national and transnational activist groups in mobilising popular and state support for the criminalisation of slavery and torture. Quite unusually for what is essentially an area of international law, an international non-governmental organisation occupies a central position in LOAC – this is the International Committee for the Red Cross.[104] The ICRC has its origins in one man's horror at the slaughter on the battlefields of Lombardy in 1859. Henri Dunant, a Swiss banker, was appalled at the lack of medical support for sick and wounded civilians and combatants. With the assistance of a small group of influential Swiss citizens (including the commander of the Swiss army), he mobilised support for a transnational network of national charities (the ICRC name was adopted in 1880) to be established to care for the sick and wounded in war. Crucially, this group of activists persuaded states to agree a treaty to recognise the rights of sick and wounded from battle as well as the neutrality of medical facilities and personnel; i.e., the Geneva Convention of 1864.[105] Thereafter, the Red Cross movement evolved along two lines. A league of national Red Cross and Red Crescent societies developed to organise local charitable work. Over time these national Red Cross societies have grown close to their respective national governments, and increasingly came to include former and serving government officials on their staffs. The league was renamed the International Federation of Red Cross and Red Crescent Societies (IFRC) in 1991, and now its activities focus on responding to natural disasters and supporting national health-care systems.[106] The ICRC remained an international non-governmental organisation, run by an all-Swiss Committee up to 1975. Most of its funds come from the Swiss government, but still the ICRC has been able to preserve its image of strict neutrality (aided, no doubt, by Swiss neutrality). The ICRC's work has concentrated on persuading states to abide by their responsibilities under LOAC. Central to

---

[103] Antonio Cassese, 'When may senior state officials be tried for international crimes? Some comments on the *Congo* v. *Belgium* case', *European Journal of International Law* 13 (2002), 853–75; Steffen Wirth, 'Immunity for core crimes? The ICJ's judgment in the *Congo* v. *Belgium* case', *European Journal of International Law* 13 (2002), 877–93.

[104] David P. Forsythe, 'The Red Cross as transnational movement: conserving and changing the nation-state system', *International Organization* 30 (1976), 607–30; David P. Forsythe, *The Humanitarians: The International Committee of the Red Cross* (Cambridge; Cambridge University Press, 2005).

[105] Martha Finnemore, *National Interests in International Society* (Ithaca, NY: Cornell University Press, 1996), pp. 73–84.

[106] The IFRC is a massive transnational network covering just about every state, with 97 million members, and some 300,000 employees. Data at www.ifrc.org/.

this work is the ICRC's extensive programme of prison visits to audit states of their compliance: e.g., by 1982 the ICRC had visited 300,000 prisoners held in seventy-five states.[107] The ICRC must negotiate access to prisoners; states are under no obligation to admit ICRC inspectors. But usually states do admit them. What is remarkable then is broad state acceptance of intrusive monitoring by an international non-governmental organisation (INGO). The ICRC recognises itself that its effectiveness rests on the 'power of persuasion'. The ICRC credits this to its 'discreet approach', whereby 'its findings are reported only to the authority concerned, [which] combined with its professional expertise and neutrality, form the key elements in persuading those in power to adopt, where necessary, more humanitarian measures'.[108] Transnational human rights organisations, most notably Amnesty International and Human Rights Watch (HRW), are also beginning to become involved in matters involving the LOAC. But their mode of operation is very different. Instead of discretely drawing states' attention to their own non-compliance with LOAC, human rights INGOs draw public attention to what they consider to be non-compliance. Where ICRC seeks to persuade states to change their ways for the better, Amnesty and HRW seek to pressure them. It is not clear that the approach of human rights organisations is any more successful; states are less likely to listen to them precisely because such organisations are perceived to be overly critical and biased. In contrast, the very restraint and discretion exercised by the ICRC makes states more inclined to take seriously ICRC reports. Of course, some states governed by murderous regimes are completely immune to persuasion or pressure.[109] NGOs also played a role in pushing for the creation of the ICC. A transnational NGO network – the Coalition for an International Criminal Court (CICC) – was formed in 1995 to encourage and even cajole states into agreeing to an independent ICC. The CICC was able to exercise some influence by targeting technical advice to developing states, and by engaging in naming and shaming of obstructionist developed states. They also benefited from the increasing willingness of states to accept NGO involvement in multilateral treaty negotiations.[110]

---

[107] J. D. Armstrong, 'The International Committee of the Red Cross and political prisoners,' *International Organization* 39 (1985), 615.

[108] 'ICRC doesn't publish its reports on prison visits – how can working confidentially be effective in preventing torture?' ICRC Brief, 15 November 2002, at www.icrc.org/Web/eng/siteeng0.nsf/html/5FMFN8.

[109] David Weissbrodt, 'Humanitarian law in armed conflict: the role of international non-governmental organizations', *Journal of Peace Research* 24 (1987), 297–306.

[110] Caroline Fehl, 'Explaining the International Criminal Court: a 'practice test' for rationalist and constructivist approaches', *European Journal of International Relations* 10 (2004), 381–2. See also CICC website at www.iccnow.org/.

Harder to gauge is the social process of change in international criminal law. It is not clear how deeply states are socialised in this area of law. We have suggested that socialisation involves a process that moves from shallow elite learning (often motivated by self/national interest), to institutionalisation of international rules in national discourse, policy and law, and finally over time to internalisation where the international rules are accepted as legitimate, even natural, and are therefore habitually followed.[111] The conclusion of a succession of treaties on international crimes (e.g., Geneva Conventions and Additional Protocols, Genocide Convention, CAT and ICC), and breadth of state consent for each, is indicative of elite learning in this area of law. It is also clear that there has been some institutionalisation by states of international criminal law. This is particularly true of LOAC, which has been incorporated into national legal systems by all states except Sudan.[112] Institutionalisation has taken a number of forms: in the state constitution (e.g., Cambodia, Croatia, Guinea, Japan, Peru, Malaysia, the Philippines and Samoa) or in a constitutional amendment (e.g., Argentina, Burkina Faso, Ireland and South Africa), in legislative acts (e.g., Cook Islands, Hungary, India, Venezuela, Rwanda, Spain, Yemen and Zimbabwe), and/or in military penal codes (e.g., Ivory coast, Republic of Korea, Mali, Mexico, Norway and Switzerland). Usually states have adopted some combination of these instruments – especially states with well-developed legal systems (e.g., Australia, Britain, France, Germany and the United States). Some states, especially former Soviet republics, have also established national committees to oversee implementation of humanitarian law (e.g., Azerbaijan, Belarus, Georgia, Kyrgyzstan, Moldova, Tajikistan and Ukraine).[113] In addition, several Western states have run training programmes for some time, the largest of which is run by the United States, to help foreign officers and defence officials develop the expertise and procedures to comply with LOAC.[114]

Shocking events have been important in pushing forward developments in international criminal law. The sheer brutality of the Nazi and Japanese regimes and their respective styles of warfare demanded attention in the post-WWII trials. It is true that the Soviet Union was not held to account

---

[111] Martha Finnemore and Kathryn Sikkink, 'International norm dynamics and political change', *International Organization* 52 (1998), 887–917.

[112] Sudan has only established, by Presidential decree, a national commission on implementing humanitarian law.

[113] Data from the ICRC database on national implementation of humanitarian law, at www.icrc.org/ihl-nat.

[114] The US programme is discussed in Major D. J. Riley, 'Seminars in Central and Eastern Europe: Spotlight Rule of Law, Military Justice', *US Foreign Policy Agenda* 4 (1999), at www.usinfo.state.gov/journals/itps/1299/ijpe/riley.htm.

for its own brutality against its own citizens, and German combatants and civilians. But, nonetheless, the excesses of the Nazi war machine, in particular, shocked the world conscience and spurred on a number of important post-war developments: the formation and jurisprudence of the Nuremberg Court, the Genocide Convention and the Geneva Conventions. Equally, the establishment of the ICTY and ICTR were entirely understandable reactions to, respectively, the atrocities in the Yugoslav wars (1992–5) and the genocide in Rwanda (1994); and, as we noted, both tribunals produced important case law on international crimes.[115]

In sum, there is considerable evidence of elite learning and domestic institutionalisation of international criminal law. Less in evidence is internalisation. Some states, to be sure, habitually act in compliance with international criminal law. Western European states are thoroughly socialised in LOAC and the prohibition against torture. At the other end of the spectrum are states in West and East Africa where wars among and involving the population are endemic and where the LOAC is ignored if even known. Genocide has also reared its ugly head in recent years in a number of African states: Rwanda, probably Burundi and most recently Sudan. In between are developed states and democracies, like Russia and Israel, whose militaries often violate LOAC with government consent (though in the case of Israel such violations have been challenged by the Israeli judiciary). Torture is also still practised in at least sixteen states: China, Egypt, Indonesia, Iran, Iraq, Israel, Malaysia, Morocco, Nepal, North Korea, Pakistan, Russia, Syria, Turkey, Uganda and Uzbekistan.[116] The process of socialisation in international criminal law, much like human rights law (as discussed in Chapter 5), is therefore patchy and incomplete.

Conclusion

The realist lens, with its focus on states and state consent, is central to our understanding of the content of, compliance with and change in international criminal law. Almost all of the major categories of international crime are covered by multilateral treaties. War crimes are codified in numerous treaties, the most important being the Hague Conventions (1899, 1907), Geneva Conventions (1949) and Additional Protocols (1977). Crimes against humanity were codified in the London Charter of the IMT Nuremberg to which the United States, Soviet Union, Britain and France were party; they were subsequently adopted in the Charter

---

[115] Christopher Rudolph, 'Constructing an atrocities regime: the politics of war crimes tribunals', *International Organization* 55 (2001), 644–91.
[116] Human Rights Watch briefing, 'Torture Worldwide' (2006), at www.hrw.org/english/docs/2005/04/27/china10549.htm.

of the International Military Tribunal for the Far East (IMTFE). The crimes of genocide and torture are codified respectively in the Genocide Convention (1948) and CAT (1984). All of the above categories of international crime are also all codified in the Rome Statute of the ICC. The crime of terrorism is defined in numerous regional conventions. The one crime that is not properly codified in treaty law is the crime of aggression. As we noted, the UN General Assembly did pass a resolution (res. 3314) in 1974 condemning it but then forwarded the matter promptly onto the UNSC. It has conditional codification in Article 5(2) of the Rome Statute – conditional in that this crime cannot be prosecuted until states have agreed a definition of aggression. In addition, war crimes, crimes against humanity and the crimes of genocide and torture all have force in customary international law. However, in the absence of an effective international mechanism to enforce these rules, compliance has rested, and still rests, on state consent. Thus, in this important respect, international criminal law is very different from domestic criminal law: states police themselves. The very poor record in prosecuting international crimes suggests the limitations of self-regulation in this area of law. It remains to be seen whether or not the ICC will be effective in being an independent international mechanism to hold all states to account for international crimes. This emphasis on the importance of consent also underlines the importance of the formal process of change in international criminal law. To be sure, the LOAC has its roots in customary law. But from the late nineteenth century on, states developed and codified in a series of conventions, rules outlawing excesses in the conduct of war. As we have seen, to this were added treaties outlawing genocide, torture and terrorism (in its particular forms) from the middle of the twentieth century on. Also indicative of the importance of the formal process of change is the breadth of state support for these various treaties.

The liberal lens directs our attention to the values that underpin international criminal law. What we find is a tension between the values of human dignity and strategic stability. Human dignity, the core liberal value, is very much present in this area of law. The 'principles of humanity', as famously expressed in the Martens clause, lie at the heart of the LOAC. Moreover, it is clear that such principles are core to the conventions outlawing genocide and torture. We also noted the core principle of military necessity which, commonly understood as opposed to its original formulation, exists in tension with humanitarianism in war. We further pointed to the poor record in enforcing international criminal law, in particular, in terms of prosecutions for violations as creating further obstacles to the effective functioning of LOAC. It also leads us to our next conclusion, namely that the liberal lens is of limited use in explaining state compliance in this area of law. The record of compliance is patchy at best. In part, this is because states do not have a compelling self-interest in compliance – indeed, often as not they are driven by narrow self-interests in proposing or opposing certain restraints in war. Fairness should also operate in the context of POW regimes. But here too, we find that, in practice, states do not necessarily reciprocate in the treatment of POWs; thus, as we noted, the Western Allies treated Axis POWs far better than the Axis powers treated Western POWs during WWII. The liberal lens is far more useful when it comes to accounting for change in this area of law. Authoritative decision-making bodies, in the form of international (and to lesser extent national) courts and tribunals, and transnational actors are both crucial in shaping change in international criminal law. We noted how much of the content of treaty law in this area is open to interpretation, often because it is ill-defined. Accordingly, courts are able to affect rapid and sometimes profound change by offering authoritative interpretations of the content and/or application of legal rules on international crimes. The important role of transnational actors is vividly illustrated by the central position occupied by the ICRC in LOAC. A number of other human rights organizations are becoming increasingly active in this policy process of legal change. We also find transnational activist networks pushing states to agree multilateral treaties, from land-mine bans to the creation of the ICC.

The constructivist lens reminds us that international criminal law also involves a discourse between states concerning what is criminal in world politics. This discourse is drawn from a number of areas of law – criminal, human rights and general international law – when it comes to procedural rules concerning matters such as the scope of criminal liability, protecting the rights of the accused and complementarity between international and national judicial bodies. Constructivism also enriches our understanding of state compliance in terms of congruence with international criminal law. At a general level, greater compliance by liberal democracies may be put down to a general congruence between international rules and national political and legal systems that abhor gross violations of human rights. However, liberal democracies do not have an unblemished record when it comes to the conduct of warfare. Accordingly, we suggest that it would be better to consider congruence more precisely in terms of specific rules of LOAC and national military doctrines, how those rules are embedded in national military systems, and in the context of specific conflicts where one or the other side perceives the enemy to be 'uncivilised'. The constructivist lens is less persuasive when it comes to explaining legal change. The succession of major multilateral treaties on various aspects of international criminal law does suggest a worldwide process of elite learning. Institutionalisation is also evident in the LOAC, with all states in the world (except Sudan) embedding LOAC rules in their national legal systems through one means or another. Furthermore, the impact of the Holocaust and of the Rwanda genocide in spurning developments in international criminal law is consistent with the constructivist emphasis on the role of shocking events in affecting legal change. However, much harder to ascertain is the degree of true internalisation by states. The widespread breaches of LOAC in conflicts around the world, and the fact that sixteen states still practise torture (and the US attempt to capitalise on this through its rendition programme,)[117] all suggest an international socialisation process that is far from complete.

Discussion questions

* How is the question of jurisdiction relevant to the prosecution of international crimes? What is the commonly cited customary basis for universal jurisdiction of international crimes? Is international criminal law anything more than 'victor's justice'?
* What are the basic rules of LOAC? What principles of customary international law underpin these rules? How are grave breaches of the Geneva Conventions distinct from war crimes? Do the rules of LOAC apply equally to international and non-international armed conflicts? Why is the *Tadic* case especially significant?
* What are crimes against humanity, and how are these crimes linked to war? How does the treatment of crimes against humanity under the ICC Statute differ from that taken by the Nuremberg Tribunal?
* How is the crime of genocide distinct from crimes against humanity? Does a state have to be a party to the 1948 Genocide Convention to be bound by the prohibition against genocide? Does the ICC have jurisdiction over the crime of aggression? Is torture a discrete crime or a subcategory of some other international crime? How can terrorism be an international crime if it does not fall under the jurisdiction of the ICC?
* How does international criminal law seek to promote human dignity? What military and strategic imperatives hinder the promotion of human dignity in LOAC? Is there inequality in the enforcement of international criminal law?
* What procedural aspects of domestic criminal law and human rights law are incorporated in international criminal law? What is the principle of

---

[117] Jane Mayer, 'Outsourcing torture: the secret history of America's "extraordinary rendition" program', *New Yorker*, 14 February 2005.

complementarity and what does it mean for the ICC? What purpose do hybrid courts serve, and are they still needed now that there is the ICC?

- Why is the 'domestic analogy' not really applicable to international criminal law? Why is state consent so crucial to making the ICC effective? Is the ICC wholly independent from the UNSC? What does the POW regime reveal about the role of mutual interest and fairness in LOAC? How does congruence explain state compliance with LOAC?
- Has international criminal law developed largely via a formal treaty-based process? In what way have international courts and tribunals acted as agents of change in this area of law? To what extent have domestic courts exercised universal jurisdiction in prosecuting international crimes? What role do transnational non-governmental actors play in promoting LOAC? How deeply socialised are states in international criminal law?

FURTHER READING

Bantekas, Ilias, and Susan Nash, *International Criminal Law*, 3rd edition, London: Routledge-Cavendish, 2007. A detailed examination of substantive, enforcement and procedural aspects of international criminal law, under both treaty and customary law.

Carnahan, Burrus M., 'Lincoln, Lieber and the laws of war: the origins and limits of the principle of military necessity', *American Journal of International Law* 92 (1998), 213–31. A fascinating article that explores the historical context of this crucial principle of LOAC.

Cassese, Antonio, *International Criminal Law*, Oxford: Oxford University Press, 2003. A good introductory textbook on the subject by a former judge and President of the ICTY.

Dinstein, Yoram, *The Conduct of Hostilities Under the Law of International Armed Conflict*, Cambridge: Cambridge University Press, 2004. An authoritative treatment of LOAC as it applies to international armed conflicts.

Fournet, Caroline, *International Crimes: Theories, Practice and Evolution*, London: Cameron May, 2006. A comprehensive treatment of the definitional aspects of international crimes that also explores possibilities for change and for improving effectiveness in this area of law.

Gardam, Judith, *Necessity, Proportionality and the Use of Force by States*, Cambridge: Cambridge University Press, 2004. A thorough and long overdue study of these two key principles on LOAC.

Konotorovich, Eugene, 'The piracy analogy: modern universal jurisdiction's hollow jurisdiction', *Harvard International Law Journal* 45 (2004), 183–238. A provocative essay on the misapplication of state custom on piracy in the evolution of modern international criminal law.

Maguire, Peter, *Law and War: An American Story* (New York: Columbia University Press, 2001). A highly original study, combining historical analysis and personal critique, on the US role in the Nuremberg trials.

Meron, Theodore, 'International Criminalization of Internal Atrocities', *American Journal of International Law* 89 (1995), 554–77. An important article on the expansion of the international regulation of internal conflict.

'The Martens Clause, principles of humanity, and dictates of public conscience', *American Journal of International Law* 94 (2000), 78–89. An excellent essay on the role of the principles of humanity in LOAC.

Moir, Lindsay, *The Law of Internal Armed Conflict*, Cambridge: Cambridge University Press, 2002. An authoritative treatment of LOAC as it applies to non-international armed conflicts.

Ralph, Jason, *Defending the Society of States: Why America Opposes the International Criminal Court and Its Vision of a World Society*, Oxford: Oxford University Press, 2007. The best account yet, combining international relations theory and international legal analysis, of US opposition to the ICC.

Rudolph, Christopher, 'Constructing an atrocities regime: the politics of war crimes tribunals', *International Organization* 55 (2001), 644–91. A really good institutional analysis of the formation and functioning of international criminal tribunals.

Sands, Philippe (ed.), *From Nuremberg to the Hague: The Future of International Criminal Justice*, Cambridge: Cambridge University Press, 2003. A fascinating set of essays that cover the path from Nuremberg to the ICC.

Schabas, William A., 'Enforcing International Humanitarian Law: Catching the Accomplices', *Review of the International Committee of the Red Cross* 83 (2001), 439–59. A useful analysis of the provisions in international criminal law for enforcing LOAC.

Tallgren, Immi, 'The sensibility and sense of international criminal law', *European Journal of International Law* 13 (2002), 561–96. A thought-providing essay on the meaning and purpose of international criminal law. Especially good on the misuse of the domestic analogy in conceptualising international criminal law.

7   International trade

The fact that most states, most of the time, observe a wide range of rules relating to international economic activities, and that they have, in recent years, been able to agree to a major expansion of the regime governing world trade in the form of the World Trade Organization (WTO) is among the clearest pieces of evidence that international law does exercise a real influence on state practice. Other important areas of economic activity that are significantly affected by rules and formal regulation include international finance, intellectual property, sea and air travel, information technology, exploitation of the resources of the sea, nationalisation of foreign owned property and much more. However, the fact that there are many generally recognised rules does not mean that this area is free from controversy. Tensions range from such fundamental issues as the Third World call for the right to development and economic redistribution, to numerous trade disputes and difficult questions arising out of intellectual property law (such as the right of Third World countries to produce cheaper versions of various anti-AIDS medicines, the patents for which are owned by Western pharmaceutical companies). Hence international economic law, both as specific rules and in terms of the more profound issues it raises, is at the heart of the contemporary world order.

However, until quite recently, the legal regulation of economic affairs did not enjoy the same 'glamour' or 'media attention' as other fields of public international law, such as use of force or human rights. Hence, in 1995, John Jackson described international economic law as the 'Boiler-room' of international relations.[1] That same year the WTO was established, and thereafter trade law moved very much into the limelight of world politics. There is also growing realisation among public opinion, informed by an explosion of activism by non-governmental organisations (NGOs) in trade matters, of the significance of this highly technical and

[1] John Jackson, 'International economic law: reflections of the "boilerroom" of international relations', *American University Journal of International Law and Policy* 6 (1995), 596.

almost arcane area of law. Anti-globalisation riots at the 1999 Ministerial Conference of the WTO in Seattle dramatically illustrated the new public engagement with trade law. The establishment of a permanent organisation to deal with trade is also indicative of the growing importance of trade regulation for states. International trade has increased by well over 15,000 per cent since the end of World War II (WWII): from US$58 billion in 1948 to US$8,907 billion in 2004.[2] Indeed, for most developed states, trade wars have replaced real wars in prospect and hence importance. The United States and European Union (EU) have nearly fought two 'trade wars' this past decade, over the EU ban on imports of American hormone-enhanced beef and of genetically modified (GM) foods from the United States. Arguably, then, the high politics of economic law concerns trade and, accordingly, it is the focus of this chapter.

The first section briefly discusses the origins of the WTO system. The second section then considers WTO law in terms of the core substantive and procedural rules of the WTO, the liberal values that underpin the organisation, and the discourses that are expressed through WTO practices. In the third section we apply our three lenses to explain state compliance with WTO law: consent, coercion, and fairness all emerge as crucial factors in our account. In the final section, the formal, policy and social processes of change in international trade law are considered; all three lenses are applied in exploring how the WTO has evolved to accommodate the concerns of developed and developing states.

The origins of the WTO

The WTO has its origins in the spate of US-led institutional building that followed WWII. Just as the post-war security order was to be anchored in the United Nations, so the post-war economic order rested on a number of economic institutions. This amounted to nothing less than 'a deep and abiding "paradigm" shift' in the legal regulation of international relations, resulting in 'a degree of institutional "constitution making" probably never seen before'.[3] Led by the United States, forty-four allied nations agreed the framework for the post-war economic order at Bretton Woods, New Hampshire, in July 1944. Central to this framework were two institutions to regulate international development and finance – the International Bank for Reconstruction and Development (more commonly referred to as the World Bank) and the International Monetary

---

[2] WTO, *International Trade Statistics 2005* (Geneva: WTO, 2005), p. 32, at www.wto.org/english/res_e/statis_e/its2005_e/its2005_e.pdf.

[3] John H. Jackson, 'Part I: the state of international economic law – 2005', *Journal of International Economic Law* 8 (2005), 9.

Table 7.1 *The GATT trade rounds*

Round	Dates	State parties
Geneva	1947	23
Annecy	1949	13
Torquay	1950	38
Geneva	1956	26
Dillon	1960–61	26
Kennedy	1964–67	62
Tokyo	1973–79	102
Uruguay	1986–94	123

Source: WTO, *Understanding the WTO*, p. 16.

Fund. The United States also proposed a third institution: the International Trade Organization (ITO). The essential purpose of the ITO was to help states to realise the benefits from reducing barriers to international trade – barriers in the form of bans, quotas and customs duties on foreign imports. As we discuss in the next section, proponents saw trade liberalisation as promising increased peace and prosperity for all. The two years of negotiations over the ITO were concluded at a UN conference in Havana in 1948. The Havana Charter was ambitious, covering employment policy, economic development and business practices, in addition to international trade. In hindsight, it was too ambitious and fell foul of the US Congress which refused to ratify it. In December 1950, the United States announced that it could not get the ITO past Congress; given that the US economy dominated the world, there was no point in continuing without the US on board.

As part of the ITO, twenty-three states agreed measures to reduce trade barriers under the General Agreement on Tariffs and Trade (GATT) concluded at Geneva in 1947. A year later, eight states agreed to apply GATT provisionally. The US administration had more flexibility in pushing forward with GATT (which was an international agreement, not a treaty) under authority granted to it by Congress under the 1945 Reciprocal Trade Agreements Act. GATT provided the structure and forum for seven additional 'rounds' of negotiations on trade liberalisation, named variously after where the negotiations took place, where they were launched, and after US Secretary of State C. Douglas Dillon and US President John F. Kennedy (see table 7.1). All the rounds up to and including Dillon dealt with further reducing tariffs (i.e., customs duties). The last three rounds involved ever-larger numbers of member states and ever-expanding agendas. The Kennedy Round sought to develop anti-dumping measures: dumping is said to exist when a company exports a product at below its home-market price. Further dramatic cuts in tariff barriers were made in the Tokyo Round: customs duties were cut by one-third in the nine main industrial markets. With the average tariff on industrial products down to 4.7 per cent, greater attention was also given in this round to non-tariff barriers (NTBs), which include unnecessary customs red-tape, and restrictive health and safety regulations. As GATT became more and more complex, so tensions and contradictions came to the fore, and consensus became increasingly elusive. Hence, a number of the agreements reached in the Tokyo Round were plurilateral codes voluntarily undertaken by some states, rather than multilateral rules binding on all.

Uruguay proved the most drawn-out and complex of the GATT rounds. There was an ambitious agenda for the Uruguay Round, covering trade in agricultural products and in textiles (both of which had enjoyed numerous exceptions under GATT) as well as, for the first time, trade in services, trade-related intellectual property rights and investment measures. The Tokyo Round showed that GATT was straining under the weight of its expanded membership and scope, so institutional reform was also on the agenda – though the creation of a new international organisation to deal with trade was not! However, in 1990, proposals were made by Italy, Canada and the European Community (EC) for a multilateral trade organisation to replace GATT. That same year, negotiations stalled in the Uruguay Round, principally over agriculture. In 1991, the EC, Canada and Mexico drafted a joint proposal for a trade organisation. In November 1992, the United States and European Union finally resolved their differences over agriculture, enabling a deal on this to be concluded under GATT. With gathering international support for a trade organisation, the new Clinton administration finally dropped US opposition to it in 1993. At last, the way was cleared for the conclusion of the *Agreement Establishing the World Trade Organization* in Marrakech in April 1994 (hereafter *WTO Agreement*).[4]

Content of international trade law

The WTO is commonly described as a 'rules-based' system. These rules are laid out in the *WTO Agreement*. This is a massive document running to some 30,000 pages and resulting in a complex structure (see

---

[4] This section draws on Peter Van den Bossche, *The Law and Policy of the World Trade Organization* (Cambridge: Cambridge University Press, 2005), pp. 78–85; and WTO, *Understanding the WTO*, 3rd edition (Geneva: WTO, 2005), pp. 16–19, at www.wto.org/english/thewto_e/whatis_e/whatis_e.htm.

Table 7.2 *The structure of the WTO agreements*

Umbrella	Goods (Annex 1a)	Services (Annex 1b)	Intellectual property (Annex 1c)
	Agreement establishing the WTO		
Basic principles	GATT	GATS	TRIPS
Additional details	Other goods, agreements and annexes	Services annexes	
Market access commitments	Countries' schedule of commitments	Countries schedule of commitments	
Dispute settlement	Dispute settlement (Annex 2)		
Transparency	Trade Policy Reviews (Annex 3)		
Plurilateral agreements	Trade in civil aircraft		
	Government procurement Dairy products Bovine meat		

Source: Narlikar, *World Trade Organization*, p. 61.

table 7.2). Under an umbrella agreement establishing the WTO are four annexes that detail organisation rules, member commitments and compliance mechanisms. Annex 1 lays out the substantive rules on trade, services and intellectual property. These are contained under three Basic Principles agreements: the GATT, the General Agreement on Trade in Services (GATS), and the Trade-Related Aspects of Intellectual Property Rights (TRIPS). Additional agreements and schedules of commitments for individual countries to provide access to markets for goods and services are provided under GATT and GATS (in Annex 1); these have yet to be agreed for TRIPS. Exceptions to these rules are specified in four plurilateral agreements on trade in civil aircraft, government procurement, dairy products and bovine meat (contained in Annex 4). Governments have also agreed the mechanisms for enforcing compliance with these rules. These are contained in procedural rules in Annexes 2 and 3 which provide, respectively, a dispute settlement mechanism and a compliance monitoring mechanism through regular Trade Policy Reviews.[5] In signing up for the *WTO Agreement*, members have agreed to be bound by all these substantive and procedural rules as a 'Single Undertaking': in

[5] Amrita Narlikar, *The World Trade Organization: A Very Short Introduction* (Oxford: Oxford University Press, 2005), pp. 60–1. Quote from WTO, *Understanding*, p. 23.

other words, members are not allowed to pick and chose between rules. In this regard, WTO differs significantly from GATT, which by the Tokyo Round had evolved to an incoherent mass of over 180 agreements (many inconsistent with one another).

The substantive rules of the WTO tackle market access and unfair trade. Market access is covered in rules on quantitative restrictions, tariffs, and NTBs. As a general rule, WTO members are forbidden to ban or impose quotas on the trade of goods; a similar prohibition applies in principle to the trade in services, though exceptions are permitted in practice under some Members Schedules of Specific Commitments. Members Schedules of Specific Commitments also contain negotiated tariff bindings – these are agreed tariff ceilings for specified goods. Rules on NTBs are covered in specific agreements. Most significant of these are the Agreement on the Application of Sanitary and Phytosanitary Measures (the SPS Agreement), which regulates the application of food safety and pest/disease control measures on trade, and the Agreement on Technical Barriers to Trade (the TBT Agreement), which regulates the application of technical regulations and standards on trade. As yet, there are no general WTO rules on unfair trade. Instead there are a number of highly technical rules that regulate specific forms of unfair trade, most important of which are dumping and subsidised trade. WTO rules permit a member to impose anti-dumping duties on products dumped in their markets in order to restore the market price of such goods. The rules on subsidies are even more complex. Subsidies are, in general, permitted. Some forms of subsidy – such as export subsidies – are prohibited. In addition, where subsidies for home industry results in an unfair trade advantage, they must be stopped or the unfair advantage negated through other steps. Where such remedial action is not taken, the injured state may be authorised to take countermeasures, including the imposition of countervailing duties.[6]

Underpinning these rules is a set of distinctly liberal values concerning the virtuous impact of free trade on wealth creation, international peace and human dignity. In his classic book, *The Wealth of Nations* (1776), Adam Smith espoused the virtues of free trade: by allowing the free exchange of goods, commerce and industry would flourish to the benefit of all. Elaborating Smith's line, David Ricardo argued that free trade enabled countries to expand trade in those areas where they had a comparative advantage; since every country had a comparative advantage in some area of trade, none would lose out.[7] The doctrine of free trade caught on in North America and Europe in the nineteenth century. The

[6] Van den Bossche, *Law and Policy*, pp. 41–2; 376–593.   [7] Ibid., pp. 19–20.

conventional story is that Britain led the way, with the dramatic reform of its system of tariffs from the 1830s on, and that other European states were spurred on to follow Britain's example and open their markets. New historical scholarship suggests that French tariff barriers may have been far lower (lower even than Britain's) than previously thought. An additional facilitating factor was the rise of the manufacturing sector, with industrialisation of European economies, which produced domestic pressure in several states for lower tariffs on agricultural goods (to make life easier for urban workers). One way or another, the doctrine of free trade came to be widely accepted across Europe, and by the mid-1800s European states were busy concluding trade treaties with one another.[8] Tariff barriers were raised across the Western world during World War I, and these remained in place following the war. When the US stock market crashed in 1929, the Congress responded by hiking up tariffs to protect the US economy. Other states retaliated with tariff rises of their own, and this fuelled the downward spiral of world economic decline. Far from protecting fragile national economics of the interwar period, trade barriers finished them off. GATT was very much born of the lessons learned from the 1930s, and a recovery of free trade doctrine.[9] Not surprisingly, therefore, the law of comparative advantage is orthodoxy in the WTO. Hence this is used to explain the 'definite statistical link between freer trade and economic growth'. In *Understating the WTO*, it is argued that: 'Simply put, the principle of "comparative advantage" says that countries prosper first by taking advantage of their assets in order to concentrate on what they can produce best, and then by trading these products for products that other countries produce best.'[10]

Liberal proponents of the WTO would argue that in addition to increasing wealth for all, trade liberalisation also promises to contribute to world peace and human dignity. Indeed, in sponsoring the International Monetary Fund (IMF), World Bank and ITO, the United States sought to fashion a liberal economic order that would prevent yet another world war.[11] The world economic crisis that preceded WWII was caused by a heady mix of financial instability and economic ruin, exacerbated by protectionism. Thus, for US policy-makers, free trade was identified as

---

[8] C. P. Kindleberger, 'The rise of free trade in Western Europe, 1820–1875', *Journal of Economic History* 35 (1975), 20–55; John Vincent Nye, 'The myth of free-trade Britain and fortress France: tariffs and trade in the nineteenth century', *Journal of Economic History* 51 (1991), 23–46.

[9] Robert A. Pollard, *Economic Security and the Origins of the Cold War, 1945–1950* (New York: Columbia University Press, 1985), pp. 11–12.

[10] WTO, *Understanding*, p. 13.

[11] Richard Gardner, *Sterling-Dollar Diplomacy: Anglo-American Collaboration in the Reconstruction of Multilateral Trade* (Oxford: Clarendon Press, 1956).

an essential facilitator of stable and peaceful relations between states. An important proponent of this view was Cordell Hull, who as a member of Congress was a long-standing advocate of trade liberalisation, and as US Secretary of State from 1933 to 1944, had concluded a number of trade agreements with foreign states. In a book entitled *Economic Barriers to Peace* (1937), Hull expressed his firm belief 'that the enduring peace and the welfare of nations are indissolubly connected with friendliness, fairness, equality and the maximum practicable degree of freedom in international trade'.[12] This view echoed, of course, the republican liberalism of Smith and Richard Cobden, and John Stuart Mill before them (as discussed in Chapter 3).

Free trade promised peace by making states more interdependent on one another, but also by increasing prosperity. In so doing, liberals argue, it contributes not only to wealth creation but also to improving the lives of ordinary people (and hence human dignity). This objective is noted in the preamble of the 1947 GATT where the parties recognise that their relations in the field of trade and economic endeavour should be conducted with a view to raising standards of living [and] ensuring full employment'.[13] This same wording reappears in the preamble to the *WTO Agreement*.[14] Free trade can benefit the poorest countries and poorest people. That is why some of the smallest and least developed countries in the world have joined the WTO. The benefits of free trade for poverty reduction have been noted in WTO research reports. One report noted the positive role of trade in producing income convergence between rich and poor states, especially between states engaged in economic liberalisation. The same study also explored how trade liberalisation contributes to poverty alleviation, by stimulating economic growth and discouraging arbitrary government intervention in home markets.[15] Another WTO study, citing World Bank figures, claims that 'abolishing all trade barriers could increase global income by US$2.8 trillion and lift 320 million people out of poverty by 2015'. This study does note the public unease with job cuts that are associated with opening home markets to foreign goods and services. However, it finds that trade liberalisation 'does not lead to drastic changes in a country's production structure', that the adjustment

---

[12] Cited in Narlikar, *World*, p. 10.
[13] *Text of the General Agreement on Tariffs and Trade*, p. 1, at www.wto.org/english/docs_e/legal_e/gatt47_e.pdf.
[14] *Agreement Establishing the World Trade Organization*, p. 9, at www.wto.org/english/docs_e/legal_e/04-wto.pdf.
[15] Dan Ben-David, Hakan Nordstrom and L. Alan Winters, *Trade, Income Disparity and Poverty* (Geneva: WTO, 1999), at www.wto.org/english/res_e/reser_e/special_studies_e.htm.

costs (i.e., job losses) of trade liberalisation are 'typically smaller, sometimes far smaller than the gains from trade', and that such adjustment costs can be offset by targeted government support.[16]

However, developing states have argued for some time that there is a disparity in the WTO rules that replicates rather than resolves the equities in the global economy. The opportunities are indeed great. Developing states could raise US$350 billion (seven times the amount they receive in aid) by increasing their share of world trade by just 5 per cent. Instead, unbalanced trade rules and the massive volume of trade within companies (amounting to 20 per cent of world trade) has resulted in increased concentration of benefits amongst developing states from the growth in global trade. Moreover, the theory that increased trade would reduce poverty and improve living standards is not matched by the reality on the ground: dramatic growth in exports has been accompanied by rising unemployment in Latin America, whilst growing textile exports from Asia is dependent on exploited labour.[17] Indeed, some would take issue with the claim that there is a causal link between trade liberalisation and economic growth. Arguably, the causal link is too complex to be validated (not in the least because we do not have accurate comparative measures of trade liberalisation). Also the theory is contradicted by spectacular economic growth by China and India some ten years *before* either country began to undertake trade reform. If anything, these cases suggest the benefits of gradual liberalisation as opposed to the WTO preference for rapid trade reform.[18] In response to growing pressure from developing states, NGOs and domestic public opinion for fairer trade, the WTO adopted, to much fan-fair, a development agenda at the Ministerial Conference in Doha in 2001. This agenda included additional concessions to developing and least-developed countries, including some flexibility in implementation of trade liberalisation commitments.

In addition to disagreement over the effectiveness of the WTO in supporting development, there is also a debate between Western and non-Western states, and between proponents and opponents of globalisation (or, more accurately, economic liberalisation), over values. Enlightened liberalism saw free trade as an expression of economic values based on economic rationality. Obviously, this vision has continued and remains relevant today; indeed, it underpins the WTO. However, trade rules have

---

[16] Marc Bacchetta and Marrion Jansen, *Adjusting to Trade Liberalisation* (Geneva: WTO, 2003), pp. 5–6, at www.wto.org/english/res_e/reser_e/special_studies_e.htm.
[17] Oxfam, *Rigged Rules and Double Standards: Trade, Globalisation and the Fight Against Poverty* (2002), pp. 8, 10, at www.maketradefair.com/assets/english/report_english.pdf.
[18] Kamal Malhotra, *Making Trade Reform Work* (New York: UN Development Programme, 2003), pp. 28–31, at www.rbf.org/publications/globaltrade.html.

never been value-neutral. GATT was an expression of Western values during the Cold War, and the process of globalisation driven forward by trade liberalisation was a process that excluded the communist bloc. In this sense, globalisation was not a truly global phenomenon before 1990. Some developing countries, as well as trade unions, environmentalists and human rights activists also see a North–South divide in values and warn against WTO (and GATT before it) becoming an instrument of neo-imperialism; an instrument that would allow the most powerful states to impose their values (social, environmental and cultural) onto other states. Hence, Philippe Sands correctly notes: 'global trade rules necessitate discourse and debate on cultural and social values. The GATT rules come under scrutiny when they are seen to impose – inappropriately – one set of values to the detriment of another. Free trade is not socially or culturally neutral.'[19] It would seem that most developing states have accepted the necessity, if not desirability, of adopting Western norms of economic liberalisation. To be sure, these norms are materially empowered by international institutions – by accession conditions to the WTO, and conditions on aid and assistance from the World Bank and IMF. Such strong material support also confers legitimacy on these norms. Nonetheless, debate over values continues, with some states still resisting Western-style liberalism of their economies.

In addition to codifying rules and expressing values, the WTO provides the discursive resources for states to deliberate and decide what is appropriate in their trade relations. Even though it was provisional, GATT operated for over forty years (1947–94) to enable states to develop the normative framework for international trade. GATT not only gave states the forum for deliberation, it also encoded the rules of the game which, in turn, were practised in eight rounds of talks. Through these norm-bound talks, states were able to agree substantive rules on trade policy. These rules of trade talks and trade policy are embodied in the WTO (as are new rules on services and intellectual property), and indeed reinforced by the permanency, organisational structure and stronger enforcement mechanisms provided in the *WTO Agreement*.

The on-going debate over values indicates both the importance of state discourse over trade, and the fact that this discourse ranges over many controversies. Contained within this discourse are a number of assumptions (e.g., freer trade through progressive liberalisation, and a general prohibition against quantitative restrictions on trade through quotas and bans) and aspirations (e.g., increasing market stability and predictability

---

[19] Philippe Sands, *Lawless World: America and the Making and Breaking of Global Rules* (London: Allen Lane, 2005), p. 104.

through controls on trade barriers, and encouraging economic development through liberalisation and trade concessions). Three principles also lie at the heart of the WTO discourse on trade liberalisation.

First is the principle of reciprocity. This principle provides the underlying logic of all treaty law (except in the area of human rights).[20] In the context of GATT/WTO, states negotiated the principle that trade concessions by one member will be reciprocated by other members. Note that the implication of this principle does not actually mean that concessions will be precisely matched. For starters, as we note below, reciprocity is calibrated to allow for the peculiar needs of developing and least-developed countries. Moreover, multilateral permanent institutions allow for diffused reciprocity to develop, with more scope for mutual gain through repeated interactions in multiple actors. This also creates more slack for disparity in trade concessions between members to alleviate structural inequities in the global economy.[21] Nonetheless, the general principle stands that no state is allowed to 'free ride' within the WTO. Reciprocity is also inherent in the substantive rules of the WTO. The bilateral obligation of these rules is evident in the dispute settlement process: where the defendant loses and fails to comply with the outcome, the winning side is usually authorised to impose countermeasures directly against the losing side. As Joost Pauwelyn notes: 'this exclusively bilateral modality in enforcement of WTO rules is an important indication that most WTO obligations are reciprocal in nature'.[22]

Second is the principle of non-discrimination, both in the treatment of trading partners and in the treatment of foreign goods, services and intellectual property protection in home markets. Traditionally, states have been able to offer more advantageous trading terms to some states over others (through bilateral treaties and so forth). Hence, such advantaged trading partners were accorded 'most-favoured nation' (MFN) status. But GATT/WTO requires members to be treated equally: all must be accorded MFN treatment. Universal MFN is expressed as a rule in GATT (Article 1), and is recognised as a priority in GATS (Article 2) and TRIPS (Article 4). Equally, imported goods, services and intellectual property rights must not be discriminated against in domestic markets. Once foreign-produced goods enter domestic markets, they must be treated equally as local goods. The same applies to foreign services, and foreign trademarks, copyrights and patents. These rules are also

[20] Malcolm N. Shaw, *International Law*, 5th edition (Cambridge: Cambridge University Press, 2003), p. 7.
[21] Robert Axelrod, *The Evolution of Cooperation* (New York: Basic Books, 1984).
[22] Joost Pauwelyn, *The Nature of WTO Obligations*, Jean Monnet Working Paper 1/02 (New York: New York University School of Law, 2002), p. 19.

codified respectively in GATT (Article 3), GATS (Article 17) and TRIPS (Article 3).[23]

Third is the principle of special and differential treatment for developing and least-developed countries. GATT originally functioned to regulate trade between developed states, and as such was derided as a 'rich man's club'. With the establishment of the United Nations Conference on Trade and Development in 1964, GATT came under increasing pressure to broaden its remit to include the concerns of developing states. Attempts were made in the 1970s to incorporate these concerns into the GATT framework. Eventually, recognition was given to the need to 'bring about further liberalization and expansion of world trade to the benefit of all countries, especially less-developed contracting parties'.[24] There is also explicit provision in WTO rules for additional concessions to developing countries, including flexibility in the implementation of their obligations.[25] Thus, this principle of special and differential treatment modifies the application of the principle of reciprocity when it comes to developing countries and less-developed countries (LDCs). Indeed, the principle of 'less than full reciprocity in reduction commitments' is deemed to apply in such cases.[26]

As we shall see, these principles of reciprocity and non-discrimination are central to how states understand the WTO and appreciate the advantages of complying with its rules. Obviously, the principle of special and differential treatment is especially important to the perceptions and aspirations of developing countries.

Compliance with WTO law

There is a powerful logic to lowering trade barriers as all stand to gain from it. Thus, self-interest is a driving motive for compliance with WTO law. But perhaps even more important are consent, coercion and fairness. Unlike GATT, the WTO has powerful enforcement mechanisms to which states have consented. For a variety of reasons, states do not have equal ability to avail themselves of these mechanisms. But, nonetheless, the WTO is considered to be more or less fair by all members. When the WTO has got into trouble, such as at public demonstrations at the Ministerial

---

[23] WTO, *Understanding*, pp. 10–11.
[24] Surya P. Subedi, 'The road from Doha: the issues for the development round of the WTO and the future of international trade', *International and Comparative Law Quarterly* 52 (2003), 426.
[25] 'Ministerial decision on measures in favour of least developed countries', at www.wto.org/english/docs_e/legal_e/31-dlldc.pdf.
[26] Doha Ministerial Declaration, WT/MIN(01)/DEC/1, 14 November 2001, para. 16, at www.wto.org/english/thewto_e/minist_e/min01_e/mindecl_e.htm.

Conference in Seattle (1999) or the emergence of a blocking coalition of developing states at the Ministerial Conference at Cancun (2003), it is because its fairness was called into question. On both occasions, the WTO acted to restore this sense of fairness.

Consent is important in so far as the WTO is treaty law. Members of the organisation have given their consent to be bound by the substantial and procedural rules of the WTO. As of January 2007, there are 150 members of the WTO: most are states; a handful are custom territories (e.g., the EC, Hong Kong, Macao). Of these, 123 are 'original members', which is to say that they joined at the founding of the organisation pursuant Article XI of the *WTO Agreement*. The rest went through a lengthy and laborious accession process (set out in Article XII). The shortest accession took three years; the longest is on-going since 1987 (GATT accession talks for several countries were converted into WTO accession talks in 1995). The most difficult accession, but also most important given the size of its market, was China's in 2001. Vietnam is the most recent entrant to the WTO, having joined in January 2007.[27] The terms of accession will be negotiated between the candidate state (or customs territory) and the existing members of the WTO, and this will concern the schedule of commitments for the candidate state (in terms of opening up its market and so forth) and any concessions that they may expect if they are a developing country. Obviously, this can drag out the process considerably; for example, progress in Russia's accession has been delayed over Russian reluctance to stop state subsidies for the energy sector, and to open up its meat and services markets. The bottom line, however, is that the candidate state must accept the 'acquis' (to borrow a term familiar to European lawyers), i.e., the terms of the *WTO Agreement* and the Multilateral Trade Agreements (GATT and GATS). Article XIV(5) clearly stipulates that 'No reservations may be made in respect of any provision of this Agreement' and that 'Reservations in respect of any of the provisions of the Multilateral Trade Agreements may only be made to the extent provided for in those Agreements.' A member may request to waive a 'problematic' obligation, but this will only be granted in 'exceptional circumstances' (by the Ministerial Conference); moreover, the waiver is temporary and, if lasting beyond a year, is subject to annual review. For example, several states have been granted a waiver to control the importation of diamonds from conflict zones (as part of an international effort to stop the trade in 'blood diamonds').[28] However,

---

[27] Membership data as of 11 January 2007, at www.wto.org/english/thewto_e/whatis_e/tif_e/org6_e.htm.
[28] Van den Bossche, *Law and Policy*, pp. 109–15.

the point to note is that the WTO rules have been agreed between states – as the WTO puts it: 'the rules are actually agreements that governments negotiated'[29] – and when new members join they must consent to these rules.

We have already discussed the notion that free trade is in every state's interest: as expressed in the 'law of comparative advantage'. Given this logic of self-interest, one might question the need for an enforcement mechanism in the WTO system. As Steve Charnovitz notes: 'Why governments need to require themselves to perform what is in their own interest is the puzzle of the trading system.'[30] However, Christopher Joyner sums up the common wisdom on this: 'a rules-based commercial system would mean little if the rules could not be enforced'.[31] Because GATT remained a provisional agreement without the means to enforce its rules, its members could always claim that national sovereignty was not affected and that the GATT decisions were not legally binding. This cannot be said of the WTO. With good reason, Amrita Narlikar describes the dispute settlement mechanism as 'the jewel in the crown' of the WTO.[32]

Under GATT, dispute settlement was referred to as 'conciliation', thereby highlighting the strong diplomatic elements of this process, in particular regarding its origins, aims and the panellists themselves who for the most part were trade diplomats with little knowledge of general international law.[33] Disputes were usually heard by so-called panels of three to five independent experts from GATT members not involved in the dispute. These panels would then be reporting to the GATT Council, composed of all members, and panel reports (recommendations and rulings) would only become legally binding on the parties to the dispute if adopted by consensus. This meant that a losing party in any given dispute could 'block' the adoption of an adverse report. It could even refuse to agree to a panel being established, thereby preventing any possible embarrassment of a panel findings. For instance, in 1989, the United States blocked the establishment of a panel which had been requested by the EC to decide on an EC ban of meat from the United States produced with the use of hormones. Thus, in April 1989, the members agreed to adopt new rules (known as the 'Montreal Rules') design to reduce any

---

[29] WTO, *Understanding*, p. 23.
[30] Steve Charnovitz, 'Triangulating the World Trade Organization', *American Journal of International Law* 96 (2002), 35.
[31] Christopher C. Joyner, *International Law in the 21ˢᵗ Century* (Oxford: Rowman and Littlefield Publishers, 2005), p. 259.
[32] Narlikar, *World*, p. 85.
[33] David Palmeter and Petros C. Mavroidis, *Dispute Settlement in the World Trade Organization: Practice and Procedure*, 2nd edition (Cambridge: Cambridge University Press, 2004), pp. 6–7.

further blockage in the establishment of panels.[34] These rules changed the requirement of positive consensus to establish a panel into a requirement of negative consensus – whereby consensus is required to prevent the establishment of a panel. However, the panellists' lack of knowledge of other areas of international law beyond the remit of trade remained a major weakness of the system as illustrated in the *Tuna–Dolphin* case. In 1991, the United States sought to ban imports of tuna products caught by Mexican fishing boats, on the grounds that these products had been made in an environmental harmful way (i.e., it was not 'dolphin friendly'). Mexico challenged this attempt as no international rules protecting dolphins or regulating tuna fisheries off the Mexico coast existed. A GATT panel ruled on the matter and reached a decision strongly in favour of Mexico. The panel report was strongly criticised for going 'too far in promoting free trade values, and not far enough in recognising the importance of environmental and other values'.[35]

Since 1995, the task of resolving trade disputes between members of the WTO belongs to the Dispute Settlement Body (DSB), in accordance with the provisions of the *Understanding on Rules and Procedures Governing the Settlement of Disputes* (also known as the Dispute Settlement Understanding or DSU).[36] According to the DSU, the DSB is 'a central element in providing security and predictability to the multilateral trade system' (Article 3.2) and it has compulsory jurisdiction for the purpose of resolving trade disputes. The DSB is composed of representatives from every WTO member. Dispute settlement panels of three members are generated by and from the DSB. A judgment by a panel may be appealed on a matter of law (rather than the facts of the case) to a standing Appellate Body (of seven members). The important point to note is that whereas GATT panels were staffed mostly by trade diplomats, the WTO panels and the Appellate Body are mostly international lawyers.

This change in the professional background of those charged with adjudicating trade disputes quickly brought about very different results. In

---

[34] *Improvements to the GATT Dispute Settlement Rules and Procedures*, Decision of 12 April 1989, BISD 36S/61.

[35] Sands, *Lawless World*, p. 109.

[36] The DSU is attached to the WTO Agreement in Annex 2. Annex 3 contains the Trade Policy Review Mechanism by which the Trade Policy Review Body undertakes periodic review of the trade policies of the WTO members. The EC, the USA, Japan and Canada are all subject to review every two years. The next sixteen less-large trade entities are subject to review every four years, and other members are being reviewed every six years or even longer in the case of least-developed country members. This mechanism, which is clearly separate from the dispute settlement system, is designed to make public instances of inconsistencies with WTO law, and by this process of 'naming and shaming' to improve compliance. Van den Bossche, *Law and Policy*, pp. 94–7.

1996, the Appellate Body of the WTO gave its very first ruling in a dispute between Venezuela and Brazil against the United States on standards for reformulated and conventional gasoline. The Appellate Body also ruled in *US-Reformulation Gasoline* (1996) that the WTO rules are not to be interpreted in 'clinical isolation from public international law'; a view it reiterated in *Korea-Government Procurement* (2000). The Appellate Body thus rejected the view previously held by the GATT panel in the *Tuna-Dolphin* case that free trade rules created a self-contained regime in total exclusion from other rules of international law.[37]

The establishment of dispute settlement panels follows the negative consensus rule in use since 1989 whereby a panel will be established unless there is a consensus to the contrary. It is also the task of the DSB to adopt panel and Appellate Body reports (again following the negative consensus rule), to monitor compliance with its rulings and recommendations, and to authorise the suspension of concessions and other obligations if its rulings and recommendations are not being complied with. Thus, there has been a shift from power-related negotiations (mostly reliant on diplomacy) in the GATT conciliation system, to legal adjudication by panels and the Appellate Body around clear and precise rules in the WTO dispute settlement system. And even though in theory, WTO members remain free to continue to use 'good offices, conciliation and mediation' offered by the DSB, in practice, the panels and especially the Appellate Body have acted as quasi-courts and have gained considerable legitimacy. The jurisdiction of the Appellate Body is indeed limited to issues of law raised in a panel report and to legal interpretations developed by a panel. Moreover, its findings (whether it decides to uphold, modify or reverse the legal findings of a panel) are final. It is for these reasons that Jackson has described the WTO appellate procedure as 'unique in international law and international relations'.[38]

The DSB gives coercive force to the WTO system. However, larger and wealthier members – especially the United States and EU – are better able to take advantage of the dispute settlement process. Litigation under the DSB is an enormously expensive undertaking, involving the hiring of large legal teams. The United States and EU can benefit from economies of scale given that their stakes in the trading system are invariably high. Both can also raise the costs of litigation for other members by dragging

---

[37] However, it remains to be seen whether this will open the door for international laws on human rights, the environment and employment, to impact on the rules of trade. Anja Lindroos and Michael Mehling, 'Dispelling the chimera of "self-contained regimes": international law and the WTO', *European Journal of International Law* 16 (2006), 857–77.

[38] Jackson, 'Part I', 5.

out cases, and the mere threat of this tends to discourage litigation by developing states. For the same reason, US and EU threats to invoke litigation in trade rows are far more credibile than threats from developing states. US and EU participation rates in fully litigated WTO cases (97 and 82 per cent respectively) reflect the advantages these members enjoy over others in the dispute settlement process.[39]

Notwithstanding the material advantages enjoyed by the US, and EU within the WTO system, the *idea* of fairness is incredibly important to the operation, development and longevity of the trade regime. As we noted in Chapter 3, fairness may be conceived (and perceived) in terms of legitimacy of process and in terms of just distributive outcomes. In the early years of GATT, fairness was claimed, and perceived to operate, in terms of even-handed and efficient procedural rules. However, the expansion of the free trade regime, taking in developing states and their concerns, has led to a major shift in the fairness discourse towards the notion of fairness as distributive justice. To be sure this fairness discourse suits most developing states, but it is also invoked by many developed and (quite wealthy) developing states that have little material interest in making special concessions to the worse off.[40] Of course, there may well be a gap between rhetoric and reality in terms of how fair the WTO actually *is* – both in terms of how the dispute settlement mechanism actually operates (process), and more generally in terms of the treatment of LDCs (outcomes). Still, the WTO can use its considerable material and social power to '"lock-in" a given fairness discourse' and thereby define what constitutes fair and unfair trade practice.[41] Notwithstanding the shift in the outlines of this fairness discourse towards distributive justice, what is still a WTO-sponsored discourse may have blinded many developing states to the true social, political and economic costs of buying into the free trade regime.[42]

Arguably, the WTO is founded on a central fairness discourse – on a 'Grand Bargain' between developed and developing states. Developed states got the things they wanted included in the *WTO Agreement*: the replacement of GATT with a trade organisation, the Single Undertaking, the inclusion of new agreements on services (GATS) and intellectual

---

[39] Gregory Shaffer, 'Power, governance, and the WTO: a comparative institutional approach', in Michael Barnett and Raymond Duvall (eds.), *Power in Global Governance* (Cambridge: Cambridge University Press, 2005), pp. 136–7.

[40] Amrita Narlikar, 'Fairness in international trade negotiations', *World Economy* 29 (2006), 1005–28.

[41] Ethan B. Kapstein, 'Power, fairness, and the global economy', in Barnett and Duvall (eds.), *Power*, p. 82.

[42] Graham Dunkley, *The Free Trade Adventure*, 2nd edition (London: Zed Books, 2001).

property protection (TRIPS) and a stronger dispute settlement mechanism. In exchange, the developing states got what they wanted: the inclusion of agriculture and textiles in GATT, special treatment on some commitments and some flexibility in implementing the new agreements.[43]

The inclusion of services in the GATT was first suggested by the United States at the Ministerial Conference in 1982, but it met with strong resistance (largely from developing countries) on the grounds that it was an area substantively different from goods, that it constituted a threat to sovereignty and that it was a distraction from the crucial issues. Following the proposal from the United States, over sixty developing countries formed a blocking coalition and progress was made through reaching a series of 'compromises'. The inclusion of trade-related intellectual property rights in the GATT followed a similar pattern. First suggested by the United States the idea for inclusion was rejected by developing countries who preferred to see the World Intellectual Property Organisation (WIPO) dealing with the issues. However, US unilateral trade sanctions on developing countries for violating US patent law, combined with various concessions being offered in other areas, and the fact that some developing countries believed (wrongly) that the TRIPS agreement would be limited to counterfeit goods, resulted in the adoption of the TRIPS agreement at the end of the Uruguay Round. This agreement covers copyrights, trademarks, geographical indications, industrial designs, patents, lay-out designs of integrated circuits and undisclosed information including trade secrets. The agreement is based on the same principles of transparency and non-discrimination as the GATT, but further it establishes minimum standards that the member states must abide by in all the seven areas. As in the case of the minimum standards set under GATT, the minimum standards relating to intellectual property rights are clearly based on the interests of developed countries.

When it comes to implementation of the rules in new trade areas (such as services, SPS, TBT, TRIPs), developing countries were granted some concessions in the form of longer periods for implementation. However, these concessions have proved to be inadequate, given the challenges and costs of implementation for some developing countries, especially LDCs. In addition, insufficient progress has been made by developed states in lowering barriers to trade in agriculture and textiles. These problems were brought to the fore by developing countries and NGOs in the run-up to the Ministerial Conference in Doha, Qatar, in November 2001. The result was a package of measures designed to further support the poorest members of the WTO – these included, making accession for

[43] Narlikar, *World*, p. 25.

LDCs faster and easier, establishing the objective of 'duty-free, quota-free' market access for products originating from LDCs, and recognition that TRIPS 'should not prevent members from taking measures to protect public health'.[44] It remains to be seen whether these promised benefits for developing states under the Doha Development Agenda will actually materialise. In some areas there has been progress. There have been major reductions in NTBs in the past ten years, although the difficulties in quantifying NTBs make it difficult to assess accurately progress on this.[45] However, critics argue that they amount to 'more spin than substance', that developed states have yet to make genuine cuts in tariffs and NTBs on agriculture, that effective action has yet to be taken to deal with the dumping of goods from developed states, and that developing states should not be pushed to open services markets without safeguard measures (e.g., for public services).[46] The figures also suggest that far more progress is needed. Developed countries still provide around US$1 billion a day in subsidies for agriculture. Tariffs on textile products from LDCs is still very high (the United States imposes an average tariff of 14 per cent on textiles from Bangladesh as against only 1 per cent from textiles from France). Implementation of TRIPS promises to result in massive transfers of wealth from developing to developed countries (the United States stands to gain an estimated US$5.8 billion per year).[47] The continued vitality of the fairness discourse will depend on further progress in the Doha Development Agenda. The UN Development Programme observed that progress on this agenda 'has been sluggish' up to the Hong Kong Ministerial Conference in December 2005.[48] Major differences, as it happens between the US and EU, over how far to reduce tariffs on imported agriculture and subsidies for domestic agriculture, and how much priority to give to opening services markets' have delayed progress on the Doha Development Agenda.[49]

The constructivist lens – which emphasises congruence, persuasion and habit – is less able to explain compliance in multilateral trade

---

[44] Doha Ministerial Declaration, paras 3, 6, 13, 42–4. See also Doha Development Agenda, at www.wto.org/english/tratop_e/dda_e/dohaexplained_e.htm.

[45] OECD, *Looking Beyond Tariffs: The Role of Non-Tariff Barriers in World Trade* (Paris: OECD, 2005).

[46] Oxfam Briefing Paper 87, *A Recipe for Disaster: Will the Doha Round Fail to Deliver for Development?* (April 2006), at www.oxfam.org/en/policy/briefingpapers/bp87_recipefordisaster_060427.

[47] Shaffer, 'Power', p. 134.

[48] 'Statement circulated by the United Nations Development Programme Administrator (as an Observer)', 15 December 2005, WT/MIN(05)/ST/54, p. 1, at www.undp.org/poverty/economic.htm.

[49] 'WTO to miss key trade-deal date', *BBC News*, 24 April 2006, at www.news.bbc.co.uk/1/hi/business/4940292.stm.

law. Congruence has some relevance for developed states with capitalist economics; though, even among the Western capitalist economies,
elite opinion has varied considerably across countries and over time as
to the role of the state in the national economy. Obviously, congruence
does not exist for those states that have a tradition of mercantilism, or for
developing states where state intervention in the economy is the norm.
For developing states, there is some element of persuasion at play, in that
developed states do sell the virtues of trade liberalisation. In this enterprise, developed states enjoy considerable social resources, including the
'social science of economics', large staffs of trade and legal experts, and
legitimacy conferred by the WTO discourse of fairness. Far less likely is
compliance with trade rules out of habit. As we discuss in the section on
legal change, there is some internalisation of WTO rules. But internalisation only occurs at a shallow level. The rules on tariffs involve carefully
negotiated state-specific concessions. Tariffs per se are permitted and
widely accepted. Thus these rules do not develop the same normative
traction with policy-makers, politicians and publics as do legal rules that
are more absolute in nature, such as the prohibition against military targeting of civilians. Even the WTO prohibition on quotas is contingent in
that a wide range of 'exceptions' are permitted, especially in agriculture
and textiles. The contingent nature of WTO rules is also indicated by the
use of preferential trading arrangements (PTAs), where particular grouping of states agrees to preferential trade liberalisation between them. Such
activity ought to be restricted under the principle of non-discrimination.
But just about every member of the WTO belongs to some kind of PTA.
However, WTO rules on PTAs contain so many loopholes that 'almost
anything goes'. Differences of opinion within the WTO and (before it)
GATT bodies charged with regulating PTAs have meant that in all but
one of 118 cases, no judgment was reached on whether the PTA under
scrutiny complied with WTO rules. Essentially PTAs are so popular with
states because they provide a way to create bargaining leverage on international trade in the context of a multilateral regime that is removing the
traditional tools of leverage: tariffs and NTBs.[50] The use of PTAs, and
indeed the many exceptions to rules within the WTO, suggested a degree
of conditionality in state compliance with WTO law. To the extent that
states do comply with WTO rules, such compliance is mostly due to consent, a degree of coercion (through the WTO enforcement mechanisms)
and a perception that the rules are mostly fair.

[50] Edward D. Mansfield and Eric Reinhardt, 'Multilateral determinants of regionalism: the
effects of GATT/WTO on the formation of preferential trading arrangements', *International Organization* 57 (2003), 831–3.

Change in international trade law

International trade law has clearly changed through a formal process of negotiation between states. WTO rules have been negotiated over the seven rounds of GATT and six WTO Ministerial Conferences (Singapore 1996, Seattle 1999, Doha 2001, Cancun 2003, Geneva 2004 and Hong Kong 2005). Consistent with the positivist lens, this suggested the primacy of state action in shaping this area of law. All states (and custom territories) are equal in the eyes of the WTO: on the principle of one member, one vote. But, of course, they are not equal in reality. GATT was founded on US hegemony in the post-WWII world.[51] And the United States and the EU have had far more influence than any other members in shaping the WTO. Developing states are at a particular disadvantage. Gregory Shaffer notes that '[m]ost developing countries are able to post only one or a few representatives in Geneva to follow WTO matters before the WTO's numerous councils, committees, and working groups'. With up to ten meetings per day in the WTO, these small delegations are invariably overwhelmed. Switzerland's provision of subsidised office accommodation for delegations from LDCs, while commendable, does little to address this problem. As Shaffer concludes: 'WTO members with greater resources, such as the United States and EU, thus drive WTO agendas.'[52] As we have noted, the United States and the EU also have disproportionate resources to pursue litigation (which can result in change through treaty interpretation), and to threaten punitive unilateral measures against other states that oppose them.

Developing states have responded by forming a number of coalitions. Indeed, four significant coalitions emerged at Cancun in 2003 (see table 7.3). A Core Group of developing countries joined voices to prevent the EU from closing down debate on unresolved issues from the Singapore Ministerial Conference (1996). Another group, the G20,[53] formed to resist EU efforts to include new issues (investment and competition) in the trade talks, and to push for further concessions from the United States and the EU on agriculture. A third group, the G33 (previously known as the Alliance on Strategic Products and Special Safeguard Mechanism), sought special measures to protect particular products and

---

[51] Robert O. Keohane, *After Hegemony: Cooperation and Discord in the World Political Economy* (Princeton, NJ: Princeton University Press, 1984); G. John Ikenberry and Charles A. Kupchan, 'Socialization and hegemonic power', *International Organization* 44 (1990), 283–315.

[52] Shaffer, 'Power', p. 134.

[53] This group is not to be confused with the G20 group of finance ministers and central bank governors.

Table 7.3 *Developing country coalitions formed at Cancun*

Coalition	Members
Core Group	Bangladesh, Cuba, Egypt, India, Indonesia, Kenya, Malaysia, Nigeria, Pakistan, Venezuela, Zambia and Zimbabwe
G20	Argentina, Bolivia, Brazil, Chile, China, Cuba, Egypt, Guatemala, India, Indonesia, Mexico, Nigeria, Pakistan, Paraguay, Philippines, South Africa, Thailand, Tanzania, Uruguay, Venezuela and Zimbabwe
G33	33 countries from Central and Southern America, South Asia, South-East Asia and Africa
G90	Comprising the Africa Group, ACP and LDCs

domestic markets. Finally, several coalitions came together on the last day of the Cancun Ministerial Conference to form an umbrella coalition (G90) to hammer home the demand for debate on the Singapore issues.

Narlikar finds that these coalitions 'were striking in their ability to endure pressures and remain united in the endgame at Cancun, but also their durability thereafter'. Not only were they resilient in defending their interests, they were also effective in advancing detailed proposals. Moreover, the coalitions 'also made a conscious effort to coordinate their positions' through joint meetings at the Ministerial Conference.[54] The success of these broad-based coalitions contrasts with the failure of issue-based coalitions, such as the Cairns Group of sixteen agriculture-producing nations (including, a number of Latin American states, South-East Asian states, as well as Australia, New Zealand, Canada and South Africa) to advance their special interests.

Change in international trade law has also occurred via a policy process, involving transnational networks of trade specialists and international lawyers. Indeed, the liberal lens offers an important layer of explanation for the foundations of the post-war liberal economic order. The realist account that emphasises US hegemony does not explain why a previously isolationist United States became so stridently internationalist, nor why a Britain concerned about the future of its own imperial trade bloc should support trade liberalisation. The answer lies in the emergence of a powerful trans-governmental network, comprised of monetary and trade specialists on both sides of the Atlantic, favouring liberalisation of the world economy. Notably, many of the US policy officials in this network were Harvard-trained economists imbued with the new British doctrine of

---

[54] Narlikar, *World*, p. 113. See also Amrita Narlikar, *International Trade and Developing Countries: Bargaining Coalitions in the GATT and WTO* (London: Routledge, 2003).

Keynesianism.[55] Equally, driving GATT forward, and especially important in the development of its procedural rules, was a transnational trade policy elite comprised of current and former trade officials, officials in the GATT secretariat, independent trade 'experts' and GATT-friendly academics, trade lawyers and trade consultants of various ilk. This elite strived to isolate trade matters from the everyday mess of world politics: in effect, to create 'a regime grounded in the insights of economic "science", and not vulnerable to the open-ended normative controversies and conflicts that plagued most international institutions and regimes, most notably, the United Nations'.[56] This insider-network has lost control of the agenda under the WTO with the impact of normative concerns on the environment, human rights and especially with distributive justice on trade rules. This expanded agenda is supported by a growing 'critical mass of noninsiders' in global civil society (especially NGOs such as Oxfam) who have developed 'a high level of expertise about trade law and policy'. These outsiders are increasingly being brought into the WTO negotiating process by those states (mostly developing states) seeking to widen the WTO agenda. As Robert Howse observes: 'just as the outsiders are no longer completely outsiders, the impermeability and homogeneity of the *insider* network are beginning to be compromised' by young idealist staff in the WTO secretariat trained in law, environment or development studies, rather than economics, and, accordingly, who see 'beyond the narrow economic outlook that traditionally unified the insider network'.[57]

The liberal lens also highlights the role of authoritative decision-making bodies – i.e., policy bodies that are legally empowered. Such bodies can produce legal change when their decisions have some force in law. We noted in Chapter 4 that the United Nations Security Council has this capacity. The comparison between the UN and WTO is instructive here. Supporting the work of the UN is a large secretariat, larger by far than the secretariat supporting the WTO. In this sense, the WTO is much more of a member-led organisation (in that state officials do most of the 'staff work'). But as we noted earlier, the WTO has in the Appellate Body a body whose decisions are binding on the members of the organisation (at least those states involved in the dispute), and from which there is no appeal. Hence the Appellate Body has been compared to bodies that essentially sit in judgment on states and whose interpretation of the law is authoritative (e.g., the International Court of Justice (ICJ), the European

[55] G. John Ikenberry, 'A world economy restored: expert consensus and the Anglo-American postwar settlement', *International Organization* 46 (1992), 289–322.

[56] Robert Howse, 'From politics to technology – and back again: the fate of the multilateral trading regime', *American Journal of International Law* 96 (2002), 94–5.

[57] Howse, 'From politics', p. 117.

Court of Justice (ECJ) and the European Court of Human Rights).[58] As discussed earlier, the Appellate Body has further asserted its independence and assured its authority through its determination to overrule the previous practice of treating GATT as a self-contained regime and instead to interpret WTO rules in the context of general international law. Technically speaking, Appellate Body reports (and dispute settlement panel reports) are only binding on the parties to a particular dispute. However, in *Japan –Alcoholic Beverages II* (1996), the Appellate Body considered that prior GATT panel reports formed 'an important part of the GATT *acquis*' in that they create 'legitimate expectations' among WTO members. Thus, any previous report that is directly relevant to solving an issue should be taken into account by panels. This position is fully consistent with the practice of the ICJ. This reasoning applies even more so to WTO panel reports and Appellate Body reports because 'adopted reports have strong persuasive power and may be viewed as a form of non-binding precedent'.[59]

Less significant is the social process of change in international trade law. As suggested by the evolution of the transnational insider network supporting the traditional WTO agenda, and growing outsider network championing a broader social agenda, change in this area of law does involve learning by policy elites and pressure groups in civil society. It also involves some internationalisation. However, as noted earlier, internalisation occurs at a shallow level (given the nature of the rules). Moreover, it is an uneven process. For developed states, it is a matter of bureaucrats specialising in trade reform pushing the cause in national policy-making. Of course, countervailing pressure will come from domestic economic groups seeking to maintain tariffs, subsidies and the like that protect their interests. Also, political appointees to trade bureaus (such as the US Trade Representative) will seek to shape and use WTO rules strategically to maximise national advantage. For developing states, internalisation appears to be contingent on the position and influence of trade specialists in internal policy debates. Within the EU, for instance, trade specialists in the European Commission (in DG1(trade)) are particularly important in affecting change in EU policy to make it compliant with WTO rules. Empirical evidence from both the EU and Japan suggests that trade officials will exert most influence in ensuring compliance by heading off measures that will be non-compliant with WTO rules;

---

[58] Anne-Marie Slaughter, *A New World Order* (Princeton, NJ: Princeton University Press, 2004), p. 163.
[59] David Palmeter and Petros Mavroidis, 'The WTO legal system: sources of law', *American Journal of International Law* 92 (1998), 401.

once such measures have been adopted, support for them grows among domestic constituencies, and withdrawal of such measures may involve a politically costly 'climb-down'.[60]

Internalisation is complicated in the case of the EU by the relative standing of international and EC law. Articles 26 and 27 of the Vienna Convention on the Law of Treaties require states to honour their international obligations (*pacta sunt servanda*). In the European legal order, this principle is expressed through the 'doctrine of consistent interpretation' (established by the ECJ), which requires that EC legislation ought to be construed in a manner consistent with the international agreement concerned. However, given the complexity of WTO and EC law, there are plenty of opportunities for clear incompatibility. In such cases, the ECJ has not permitted individuals (including interest groups and corporations) to appeal directly to WTO rules over EC legislation (unless the legislation makes direct reference to the WTO rule concerned).[61] Obviously, this unresolved issue of the hierarchy of international and European law has important implications not only for internalisation of WTO rules by the EU, but also for compliance with those rules by one of the two major trading blocs in the world.

Internalisation by developing states has involved more profound normative change. It has also involved developed states – especially the United States and the EU – using their material and social power to affect socialisation by developing states into WTO rules. Through negotiation, litigation and the provision of 'technical assistance', the United States and the EU have manipulated the material incentives and reconstituted the substantive beliefs of developing states in favour of trade liberalisation. This is well illustrated in the area of intellectual property rights. US officials and corporations have co-operated in promoting the virtues of TRIPS and in providing WTO-sponsored training on intellectual property protection. (Overall, the WTO organises some 500 'technical cooperation activities' each year for developing countries.) Developing states that fail to provide effective regimes for the protection of intellectual property are marginalised as 'pirates' in the trade world. Moreover, corporations have also used US domestic law (section 301 of the 1974

---

[60] Leonard J. Schoppa, 'Two-level games and bargaining outcomes: why *Gaiatsu* succeeds in Japan in some cases but not others, *International Organization* 47 (1993), 354–86; Sebastiaan Princen, 'EC compliance with WTO law: the interplay of law and politics', *European Journal of International Law* 15 (2004), 555–74.

[61] Thomas Cottier and Krista Nadakavukaren Schefer, 'The relationship between World Trade Organization law, national and regional law', *Journal of International Economic Law* 83 (1998), 83–122; Mario Mendez, 'The impact of WTO rulings in the Community legal order', *European Law Review* 29 (2004), 517–29.

Trade Act) to require the US government to withdraw special tariff concessions to such 'pirate' states. Similar use of extra-legal tools is made by the EU to force developing states to accept and comply with the new TRIPS regime.[62]

Violation of WTO rules does not trigger legal change. By their very nature, with so many exceptions to substantive trade rules, often it is unclear that violation has occurred until this has been determined by a WTO panel. The point is that in such cases states do not set out to challenge (let alone violate) the law; such cases are not about the ethics or efficiency of trade rules, but rather the extent of state commitments under agreed schedules of commitments. States will also push the limits of what is permissible under WTO rules. In some areas, such as PTAs, there is much mutual rule-bending and exploitation of loopholes in the law. But again, such activity is not rule-challenging in intention or effect.

However, external shock – in the form of economic collapse – has played a role in change in international trade law. We saw how the lessons of the economic crash of the 1930s spurred the United States to create a free trade regime following WWII. Shock can also shape legal change at a state level. The bursting of the economic 'bubble' in Japan in the early 1990s led to a major government drive to lower tariff and non-tariff barriers to trade. Of course, prior internalisation of WTO rules (particularly in the Ministry of International Trade and Industry) was crucial in ensuring that further trade reform was identified as the 'solution' to looming recession in the 1990s. But equally, the search of this solution was triggered by government recognition in 1993 that the economy was in 'dire straits'.[63]

Conclusion

The realist lens provides the starting point for viewing international trade law: its content, why states comply with it and how it changes. The international trade regime is clearly a rules-based one. The substantive rules are codified in the *WTO Agreement*, and in three major Basic Principles agreements on trade in products, services and intellectual property rights. Procedural rules that provide dispute resolution and compliance-monitoring mechanisms are also codified in annexes to the *WTO Agreement*. Since international trade law is treaty law, consent is obviously central to state compliance. When the *WTO Agreement* was concluded,

---

[62] Shaffer, 'Power', pp. 136, 138; Ikenberry and Kupchan, 'Socialization', p. 283.
[63] Andrew P. Cortell and James W. Davis, 'When norms clash: international norms, domestic practices, and Japan's internalization of the GATT/WTO', *Review of International Studies* 31 (2005), 3–26.

123 states (and custom territories) gave their consent. Moreover, under the Single Agreement, states agreed to be bound by all the rules of the WTO. In the following eleven years, another twenty-six states acceded to the WTO. Under the terms of accession, these new members also had to consent to all the rules of the trade regime. Given the scope and complexity of the trade regime, and the domestic politics of trade reform, consent is not enough to ensure state compliance. The GATT lacked the means to coerce compliance, as states were able to block the work, and even the creation, of GATT dispute settlement panels. In contrast, the WTO panels cannot be vetoed by states, and so the WTO does have the capacity to coerce states into complying with WTO rules. The manner in which the GATT evolved through seven negotiating rounds, and the six major trade conferences under the WTO, point to the formal process of change in international trade law. This is a process dominated by states. The GATT regime owes its origins to the work of a handful of developed states, led by the United States. Two major trading powers – the United States and EC – exert most influence over change in the WTO (especially in developing GATS and TRIPS). At the same time, developing states are proving increasingly effective at forming coalitions to advance alternative agendas for change.

The liberal lens enriches our perspective by providing insight into the values and policy processes that underpin this rules-based system. Wealth creation is obviously the primary value, but also important are system stability and human dignity. The United States took the lead in creating the post-war liberal economic order so as to avoid a third world war. Human dignity has assumed increasing importance in the WTO, as developing states and NGOs seek to advance trade rules that will alleviate world poverty. The liberal lens also reveals much about the motives for state compliance. Self-interest is certainly present. Trade liberalisation promises to increase wealth for all. This is certainly true of developed states, which will clearly benefit from trade reform. The law of comparative advantage suggests that developing states, even LDCs, also stand to benefit. The experience of developing states suggests a more troubling picture. Some states, such as Haiti, that rapidly removed trade barriers have suffered economic collapse. Also, increased exports from some developing states has done little to improve the lives of the poor in those countries. The picture is clouded by the lack of reliable comparative measures of trade liberalisation, and the sheer complexity of causation between trade and development. Inequities in the global economy give added importance to the perception of fairness in motivating states to comply with trade rules. Fairness in terms of legitimate process is provided in procedural rules of the WTO: in the 'one-member-one vote' rule, and in the trade policy review and dispute settlement mechanisms. In reality, the material inequalities between the very rich and very poor states blunt the fairness of these procedures as they really operate: very well-resourced states are far more able to control the agenda of negotiations (whatever the voting rule), and to undertake the costs of pursuing cases through dispute settlement process. However, the substantive rules of the WTO do sustain a fairness discourse that appeals to all states. The Grand Bargain promised something for everyone – inclusion of GATS and TRIPS for developed states, action on agriculture and textiles for developing states. However, developed states have failed to deliver their side of this bargain. Frustration at this boiled over in angry public demonstrations at Seattle in 1999. The Development Agenda agreed at Doha (2001) expresses a renewed promise by developed states to make further concessions to the poorest states and to reduce barriers to free trade in agriculture and textiles. With slow progress in implementing the Doha Development Agenda, it remains to be seen if it will revitalise the fairness discourse of the WTO. International trade law has changed profoundly since the end of WWII. It has evolved from a provisional regime with 23 members focused on trade in products, to a permanent organisation with 149 members and covering products, services and intellectual property. Within and alongside the formal process of states negotiating these changes, has been a policy process of legal change. This policy process has involved a transgovernmental elite of trade specialists that have worked within states to advance the cause of free trade. Increasingly, it also involves a transnational network of NGOs and other activists concerned about the impact of trade liberalisation on development. There is also some blurring of the boundaries between these insider and outsider networks, as trade specialists are becoming alert to the social consequences of trade reform, and NGO expertise is being used by developing states in the WTO. Also potentially of great significance to legal change is the WTO Appellate Body, whose judgments have the capacity to offer authoritative interpretations of WTO rules.

When it comes to the content of international trade law, the constructivist lens is crucial to explaining what the WTO is about. In addition to rules and values, the WTO regime is a discourse between states about trade. This discourse centres on the principles of reciprocity, non-discrimination and special and differential treatment. These principles are embodied in key rules of the WTO regime (such as those on MFN and dispute settlement) and expressed in the fairness discourse. However, the constructivist lens has less to offer in explaining why states comply with WTO rules. There is such variation among developed states in terms of the role of the government in national economic affairs to suggest that congruence is not an important factor here; and for developing states it certainly is not a factor. Persuasion emerges as a second-order explanation, really as a function of the fairness discourse – which enables developed states and the WTO to persuade the developing countries that trade liberalisation will serve their economic interest. Habit is even less in evidence as a mechanism of compliance; states just do not take trade rules to heart, in the way that they do with rules on human rights and use of force. The constructivist lens is also of limited use when it comes to explaining change. Change in international trade law is a social process only in so far as developing states clearly are being socialised into the WTO regime. This socialisation is backed by EU and US material power (i.e., the size of their trade delegations and size of their economies) which enables these actors to push trade liberalisation on weak states. However, internalisation only occurs at the shallow level – developed states still seek to exploit the trade regime to their advantage (e.g., through the use of PTAs), and developing states do not entirely buy into the Western vision of a free trade world. Thus, the on-going battle over the Doha Development Agenda is, in part, a battle over competing visions for further trade liberalisation – one that seeks aggressively to move on into new areas (services and intellectual property rights) versus one that seeks to adapt further the WTO regime to address structural inequalities in the global economy.

Discussion questions

- What was the International Trade Organization, and how did it lead to the General Agreement on Tariffs and Trade (GATT)? Why did the GATT rounds become increasingly complex?
- What is the basic structure of the WTO agreements? What is the 'Single Undertaking'? What are the basic WTO rules on import bans, tariff barriers, dumping and subsidised trade?
- What is the law of comparative advantage? How is freer trade supposed to contribute to system stability and to human dignity? To what extent is there a North–South divide in trade values?
- How do the principles of reciprocity and non-discrimination operate in the context of the WTO regime? Are these principles consistent with the principle of special and differential treatment, and why is this latter principle important to the sustainability of the WTO?
- What were the weaknesses in the GATT dispute settlement process as a mechanism for enforcing compliance with trade rules? How does the WTO dispute settlement process remedy these weaknesses? How does this process still favour larger and wealthier WTO members? How

much enforcement and persuasive power does the WTO Appellate Body wield?

- Why is the idea of fairness central to the WTO regime, and how has this fairness discourse changed over time? What is the 'Grand Bargain' at the heart of WTO, and to what extent have developed states kept their side of the bargain? How have developing countries sought to improve their bargaining power in WTO negotiations?
- To what extent have states internalised WTO rules? What complicates internalisation by EU member states? How have developed states sought to socialise developing states into WTO rules?
- How has the transnational policy network sustaining the free trade regime evolved in recent decades?

SUGGESTIONS FOR FURTHER READING

Grieco, Joseph M., and G. John Ikenberry, *State Power and Global Markets: The International Political Economy*, New York: W. W. Norton, 2003. An accessible text providing a realist perspective on the global economy.

Hoekman, Bernard, and Michael Kostecki, *The Political Economy of the World Trading System*, 2nd edition, Oxford: Oxford University Press, 2001. A comprehensive and accessible introduction to the institutional mechanics, economics and politics of the global trading networks.

Howse, Robert, 'From politics to technology – and back again: the fate of the multilateral trading regime', *American Journal of International Law* 96, (2002), 94–117. An insightful analysis of the evolving transnational policy network supporting the WTO system.

Ikenberry, G. John, 'A world economy restored: expert consensus and the Anglo-American postwar settlement', *International Organization* 46, 1 (1992), 289–321. An interesting account of the origins of the free trade regime emphasising the role of a transatlantic policy network.

Narlikar, Amrita, *The World Trade Organization: A Very Short Introduction*, Oxford: Oxford University Press, 2005. The best available introduction to the WTO.
International Trade and Developing Countries: Bargaining Coalitions in the GATT and WTO, London: Routledge, 2003. An impressive study on the dynamics of developing country coalitions from the Uruguay Round up to the Doha Ministerial Conference.

Odell, John (ed.), *Negotiating Trade: Developing Countries in WTO and NAFTA*, Cambridge: Cambridge University Press, 2006. A recent volume exploring how developing countries operate within the WTO.

Oxfam, *Rigged Rules and Double Standards: Trade, Globalisation and the Fight Against Poverty* 2002 at www.maketradefair.com/assets/english/report_english.pdf. A strident critique of the continued inequalities in the world trade system.

Shaffer, Gregory, 'Power, governance, and the WTO: a comparative institutional approach', in Michael Barnett and Raymond Duvall (eds.), *Power in Global*

Governance, Cambridge: Cambridge University Press, 2005, pp. 130–60. An analysis of institutional rules, processes and power in the WTO.

Van den Bossche, Peter, *The Law and Policy of the World Trade Organization*, Cambridge: Cambridge University Press, 2005. A comprehensive text on the institutional and substantive law of the WTO.

World Trade Organization, *Understanding the WTO*, 3rd edition, Geneva: WTO, 2005, at www.wto.org/english/thewto_e/whatis_e/whatis_e.htm. A concise official introduction to the WTO.

8   The environment

Although environmental issues have become increasingly prominent in international law and politics since 1945, the actual term 'environment' eludes an easy definition on which all can agree, and indeed very few international legal conventions relating to the environment have attempted to define it.[1] One succinct dictionary definition, 'the conditions or influences under which any person or thing lives or is developed',[2] probably encompasses most of the specific areas that have been addressed by the many international environmental conferences that have taken place, but it lacks the kind of precision lawyers seek when framing would-be binding agreements. This is not mere pedantry because one of the many controversies in environmental politics revolves around different understandings of the term: some stressing human needs and requirements, others seeing biodiversity and preserving the ecosystem as values in themselves, independent of their utility to human beings.[3] Similarly, varying economic, cultural, social, political and scientific approaches to environmental problems may lead to significantly different emphases.[4] For example, population control, which some see as central to an effective long-term environmental policy, is viewed differently by different religions and cultures.

Here we consider, first, some of the conflicts and tensions that are inherent in environmental issues. Next we provide a brief historical overview of the evolution of international environmental law with the aim of illustrating how such problems impacted upon specific environmental questions. Finally we look at different theoretical perspectives on

---

[1] Patricia Birnie and Alan Boyle, *International Law and the Environment*, 2nd edition (Oxford: Oxford University Press, 2002), p. 3.
[2] *Shorter Oxford English Dictionary*, (Oxford: Oxford University Press, 1987), Vol. I, p. 667.
[3] For a detailed discussion of the underlying values of 'anthropocentric' and 'non-anthropocentric' perspectives on the environment, see Alexander Gillespie, *International Environmental Law, Policy and Ethics*, Oxford: Oxford University Press, 1997).
[4] See also the discussion in Philippe Sands, *Principles of International Environmental Law*, 2nd edition (Cambridge: Cambridge University Press, 2003).

the environment with a view to reaching some tentative conclusions about the future development of environmental law.

The international politics of the environment: some fundamental controversies

International environmental negotiations have been marked by intense and sometimes bitter confrontations, especially as states have sought to move from broad affirmations of principle to clear and precise commitments. Sometimes these have essentially been reflections of wider conflicts of interest between specific states or groups of states but they also derive from certain fundamental and, in some cases, intractable tensions and dichotomies that lie at the heart of environmental issues, of which the most important are discussed below.

The state system versus global governance

The foundation stone of the contemporary politico-legal international order is the principle of sovereignty, with its key corollaries of state control over natural resources and non-intervention in a state's internal affairs. One political outcome of this, at least in 'realist' perspectives on International Relations (IR), is the competitive pursuit by states of their separate national interests, with a further consequence that international co-operation tends to be limited and short term at best, with frequent incentives to defect from, cheat or be a free-rider in international agreements. Many environmental questions, in contrast, are global, or at least regional, in their nature and impact and their solution requires close and enduring co-operation. In some cases, such as climate change, environmentalists argue that a crisis of catastrophic proportions is unfolding which requires nothing less than a fundamental restructuring of the international system with a view to creating effective global institutions with the power to impose restrictions on states and punish lawbreakers. However, as Hurrell and Kingsbury point out, there are five standard objections to such a course of action: people remain strongly attached to the nation state; sovereignty has its own moral validity while many states both embody and protect distinct national values; environmental problems are not the only important global issues, nor, necessarily, the ones with the greatest capacity to cause serious harm to human beings; there is no guarantee that a supranational authority would necessarily be effective, particularly in view of all the additional conflict it would produce; and finally there is the 'basic paradox' that all such schemes must confront: if the unity of purpose required to bring about a world government could be found, the reason for it would have disappeared.[5]

A further challenge to the classical state system stems from the fact that, more than any other issue-area, developments in international environmental law-making have been strongly influenced, if not actually driven, by non-state actors. These have come from all sides of the various arguments involved, including commercial interest groups, scientists and 'epistemic communities', green political parties, non-governmental organisations (NGOs) and other activists. Over time this has brought such actors into an ever closer involvement with environmental law, not simply as lobbyists but sometimes as negotiators or even, in some countries, law-makers. Amongst other consequences, this has produced a highly complex politico-legal context for environmental law, in which international conventions need to be considered alongside regional (especially in the case of the European Union), national, and even sub-national (especially in the case of the United States) laws and decision-making processes for the full picture to become clear.[6]

Liberal versus regulated economic order

Ever since the Reagan–Thatcher era in the 1980s, economic thinking has been dominated by neoliberal principles that favour deregulation, privatisation and trade-led growth. In the view of many environmentalists, all three policies carry unacceptable environmental risks. In recent years this conflict of fundamental principles has tended to focus in particular upon the world trade regime, with environmental concerns amongst the issues raised by 'anti-globalisation' protestors at World Trade Organization (WTO) meetings. This issue was brought into sharp relief by the 1991 and 1994 Tuna–Dolphin cases when, as we noted in Chapter 7, a General Agreement on Tariffs and Trade (GATT) disputes panel found US import restrictions on tuna caught without sufficient regard for the incidental killing or injuring of dolphins to be incompatible with GATT regulations on free trade. However, later WTO cases on similar matters tended to take more account of environmental concerns.[7]

---

[5] Andrew Hurrell and Benedict Kingsbury (eds.), *The International Politics of the Environment* (Oxford: Oxford University Press, 1992), pp. 7–8.
[6] Dana R. Fisher, *National Governance and the Global Climate Change Regime* (Lanham Rowman and Littlefield, 2004), pp. 1–20. See also Jon Burchell, *The Evolution of Green Politics* (London: Earthscan Publications, 2002).
[7] Sands, *Principles*, pp. 953–77.

The issues involved here are, in reality, more multifaceted than this simple dichotomy might suggest. For example, while some environmentalists work from broadly anti-capitalist ideologies, others are more concerned that unregulated trade might favour those trading nations with the more lax environmental standards. Similarly, there may be some force in free traders' arguments that restrictive rules regarding imports that have been introduced ostensibly for environmental reasons, such as those relating to product standards, in reality derive from protectionist motivations. Moreover, even where there may be some agreement on the adverse environmental consequences of free trade in certain cases, there is still a deep chasm between those who believe the only effective response to be a complete restructuring of the global politico-economic order, as against those who argue that these problems can be managed within the existing structure. On balance the WTO, although more responsive to environmental concerns than its predecessor, the GATT, still gives the greatest weight to its essential mission to liberalise trade. For example, the Ministerial Declaration at the WTO's 2001 Doha Conference, while calling for negotiations on the trade–environment relationship, was firm in asserting that the outcome of such negotiations 'shall be compatible with the open and non-discriminatory nature of the multilateral trading system'.[8]

Just as some environmentalists tend to see capitalism and market-based economic systems as the fundamental enemy of their cause, so some economists counter with highly sceptical views of the apocalyptic scenarios portrayed by environmentalists. They point out, for example, that economic growth – which freer trade promotes – invariably leads to increased spending on environmental matters, so, by this argument, trade and growth should be encouraged, not discouraged, by environmentalists.[9] Similarly, they argue that climate change will produce economic benefits as well as costs and, more generally, that the economic impacts of global warming 'hardly justify the alarm and calls for dramatic action that characterise much public discussion of this issue'.[10] Inevitably, however, not all economists adopt this position: some point to hidden costs of environmental damage of which conventional techniques of economic analysis and measurement fail to take account.[11]

---

[8] Paragraph 32, Doha WTO Ministerial Declaration, WT/MIN(01)DEC/1, 14 November 2001.

[9] Daniel C. Esty, 'Economic integration and environmental protection', in Regina S. Axelrod, David l. Dounie and Norman J. Vig (eds.), *The Global Environment: Institutions, Law and Policy* (Washington: CQ Press, 2005), p. 152.

[10] Wilfred Beckerman, 'Global warming and international action: an economic perspective', in Hurrell and Kingsbury (eds.), *International Politics*, p. 260.

[11] Thomas F. Franck, *Fairness in International Law and Institutions* (Oxford: Oxford University Press, 1995), pp. 365–6.

Development versus environmental protection

The most difficult and complex aspect of the debate over the economics of environmentalism concerns the needs of the developing countries. As we shall see, this has also been an on-going issue in the major environmental law-making conferences. The underlying problem is that if all of the – steadily growing – world population is to achieve the same level of prosperity as its richest third, it may only be able to do so at some significant cost to the environment through resource depletion, increasing pollution and production of greenhouse gases and deforestation. Developing nations have been particularly insistent on their absolute sovereignty over their own natural resources and also that they should not be expected to bear the full costs of implementing globally agreed environmental standards.

Several key principles have emerged from the international environmental discourse of the last twenty years in an attempt to address the issues arising in this debate. A number of key environmental Conventions and Declarations acknowledge the 'right to development', notably the 1992 Rio Declaration on Environment and Development. The Rio Conference also enshrined the principle of 'sustainable development' that had been made a central feature of the 1987 Brundtland Report. This somewhat vague principle constituted an attempt to reconcile the conflicting imperatives of development and environmental protection by calling for development to take place in a manner that would not seriously affect the lives of later generations. The third principle endorsed by the conference was that states had 'common but differentiated responsibilities' – i.e., while all shared the same interest in protecting the environment, richer countries had greater responsibilities, including the need to transfer relevant technologies and provide other kinds of aid to developing countries. Notwithstanding the Rio Declaration's bland language, the negotiations leading up to it were intense and sometimes angry.

Precaution versus certainty

While the broad categories of environmental risk are reasonably clear, it is impossible to achieve absolute scientific certainty about such key factors as precise timescales, degrees of damage, economic and human costs, relative levels of hazard between different countries and possible negative consequences of proposed solutions. Although these observations are valid for all environmental questions, they have been posed particularly acutely in regard to the issue of climate change. In that case, although scientists are increasingly certain that global warming is occurring, there is far less consensus about the relative human and natural contributions to this, given that the earth has previously experienced periods of both global warming and cooling and that greenhouse gases are produced by natural as well as human causes. There is further disagreement about the costs and benefits of various courses of action that have been proposed to deal with the problem and also about the differential consequences of global warming, given that some regions might actually benefit from it.

All international environmental negotiations have given rise to divisions between different interest groups, and global warming has been particularly susceptible to this. On the one hand, environmental activists have, with some success, urged the adoption of the so-called 'precautionary principle' elaborated in Principle 15 of the Rio Declaration:

In order to protect the environment, the precautionary approach shall be widely applied by states according to their capabilities. Where there are threats of serious or irreversible damage, lack of full scientific certainty shall not be used as a reason for postponing cost-effective measures to prevent environmental degradation.

The principle has appeared in numerous international agreements, albeit, as one writer has noted, in at least fourteen different formulations, suggesting a lack of agreement about its meaning or application in specific circumstances.[12] The principle starts from a 'better safe than sorry' assumption that if some human activity – or proposed activity – has the potential to cause serious and irreversible damage, steps should be taken to control or prevent it, even where scientific certainty is lacking.

The precautionary principle has been subjected to constant criticism since it first began to be frequently used in the 1980s. In some cases, this came from commercial interest groups, such as the Australian coal and OPEC (Organization of the Petroleum Exporting Countries) oil lobbies.[13] In other cases, objections tended to be broader based, including general critiques of the human tendency to respond irrationally to perceived risks[14] as well as arguments that very little scientific progress would have been made if human beings had always erred on the side of caution.[15] Inevitably, such disagreements feed into the complex

---

[12] David VanderZwaag, 'The precautionary principle in environmental law and policy: elusive rhetoric and first embrace', *Journal of Environmental Law and Practice* 8, 3 (Oct. 1999), 355–75, cited in Elizabeth R. DeSombre, *The Global Environment and World Politics*, (London and New York: Continuum, 2002), p. 57.

[13] Philippe H. Martin, '"If you don't know how to fix it, please stop breaking it": the precautionary principle and climate change', *Foundations of Science* 2 (1997), 282.

[14] C. R. Sunstein, *Risk and Reason: Safety, Law and the Environment* (Cambridge: Cambridge University Press, 2002), pp. 102–5.

[15] E.g., Helene Guldberg, 'Challenging the precautionary principle', *Spiked Online*, 1 July 2003.

international politics of climate change law-making, with, for example, oil-producing nations and the United States, which stand to lose considerably from a stringent greenhouse gas regime, leading a 'sceptical' lobby, while small island countries, who are potentially the most threatened by global warming, being the strongest supporters of the precautionary principle.[16] However, negotiations did not merely reveal conflicting interests but also underlying differences between politico-legal cultures, with Americans seeing the principle as involving not a precise commitment but a vague and open-ended obligation that, in the American legal context, could lead to endless litigation.[17]

The evolution of international environmental law

This section is divided into four subsections. In the first, we examine the evolution of international law on the environment up to the United Nations Stockholm Conference on the Human Environment in 1972. In the second, we discuss developments following on from Stockholm. In the final two subsections we focus, respectively, on the law on ozone protection and climate change.

To the Stockholm Conference

The period since the 1972 Stockholm Conference has witnessed a constantly accelerating growth in national, regional and international initiatives relating to the environment. Before then, although environmental issues of various kinds – deforestation, pollution of air, seas and rivers and threats to birds, animals and fish – have occurred since ancient times, relatively little international attention was paid to such problems. Two arbitration cases are often cited as marking important turning points: one, the Pacific Fur Seals case in 1893 between Britain and the United States over seal hunting, the other, the Trail Smelter case between Canada and the United States in 1941 over sulphur fumes from a Canadian smelter that were causing damage in the United States. In the latter case, the tribunal declared, as a general norm of international law, that 'no state has the right to use or permit the use of its territory in such a manner as to cause injury by fumes in or to the territory of another or the properties or persons therein'.[18] During the interwar period a number of environmental issues were also addressed by the League of Nations,

---

[16] For an excellent discussion of the politics of climate change negotiations by an international lawyer who was present at some of them, see Philippe Sands, *Lawless World: America and the Making and Breaking of Global Rules* (London: Allen Lane, 2005), pp. 69–94.
[17] *Ibid.*, pp. 83–4.   [18] Sands, *Principles*, p. 30.

including the regulation of whaling and controlling the pollution of the seas by oil, although its efforts, including a 1931 convention on whaling, had little impact.[19]

The first twenty-five years after World War II witnessed a steady increase in international interest in environmental matters. Growing concern with atmospheric nuclear tests led eventually to the 1963 Test Ban Treaty. The problems of oil pollution produced a global convention in 1954 together with more detailed and binding treaties relating to oil pollution in the North Sea (1969 and 1983 Bonn Agreements), following the 1967 oil spill when the Torrey Canyon ran aground in the English Channel, and on liability and compensation for oil spillage in the event of accidents like that disaster (1969, 1971 and 1992 Conventions).[20] This period also saw an extension of the limited earlier interest that had been shown in protecting various forms of wildlife to broader issues of conservation, as in the 1949 UN Conference on the Conservation and Utilisation of Living Resources (UNCCUR). However, the environment remained a matter of relatively marginal concern to the international community, with conferences and (more rarely) agreements taking place on a random and ad hoc basis, rather than within the context of a coherent overall environmental strategy that was co-ordinated, implemented and regulated by a central agency.

Stockholm and after

A number of developments in the 1960s brought about a gradual change in this situation, culminating in the 1972 Stockholm Conference. These included books like Rachel Carson's *Silent Spring*, Paul Ehrlich's *The Population Bomb* and the Club of Rome's *The Limits to Growth*, together with disquiet over the environmental damage being caused by Agent Orange and other American weapons in the Vietnam War, the massive oil spill from the Torrey Canyon, the 'acid rain' issue and a more general cultural shift in Western countries as increasing affluence was accompanied by a growing interest in 'quality of life' issues.[21] Although the Stockholm Conference's specific achievements were relatively few, it did mark a clear

---

[19] Denise K. DeGarmo, *International Environmental Treaties and State Behavior: Factors Influencing Cooperation* (New York and London: Routledge, 2005), p. 33.

[20] Sands, *Principles*, pp. 33, 452–3, 913–15.

[21] This involved clear evidence that acidification in Scandinavian countries originated in coal burning in Britain and elsewhere. M. S. Sooros, 'Global Institutions and the Environment: an Evolutionary Perspective', in Axelrod, Dounie and Vig (eds.), *Global Environment*, p. 24.

shift towards a more concerted and systematic international concern with the environment.

It was also clear that comprehensive negotiations about the environment would be accompanied by sharp political divisions of the kind already mentioned. The Soviet bloc did not attend in protest at the non-representation of East Germany but, given that its collective view tended to be framed in terms of environmental problems being a by-product of capitalism, the conference was at least spared the kind of Cold War animosities that prevailed in most international gatherings of that period. However, all of the North–South issues that were to prove so contentious in later conferences did make themselves felt in 1972. There were fundamental differences of opinion over the need to reduce population and indeed whether the environment could be a major priority at all for developing nations, given their need to achieve high levels of economic growth. The principle of 'additionality' – the insistence by poorer states that the costs of any environmental measures on their part should be funded by additional economic aid – was resisted by the United States, among others. Brazil maintained that the principle of states' sovereignty over their own resources gave it the sole right to determine the future of its forests.[22] France was criticised over its nuclear tests, the United States over the Vietnam War, the developed world as a whole for its protectionist trade policies and certain Western multinationals for their environmentally damaging practices.

Despite these divisions, the 113 delegations were able to achieve consensus on a Declaration comprising 26 principles, an Action Plan, including 109 recommendations and a Resolution on Institutional and Financial Arrangements. The principles and recommendations did not have binding force and in reality represented a set of fairly anodyne sentiments that clearly sought to give something to everybody, especially the developing countries who managed to obtain condemnation of racial discrimination and colonialism as well as principles advocating 'transfer of substantial quantities of financial and technological assistance', price stability and adequate earnings for primary commodity producers and an acceptance that 'standards which are valid for the most advanced countries' might be inappropriate for developing countries. Principle 22 was watered down from an earlier version making states liable for environmental damage resulting from activities within their territory to a much softer call on states to 'cooperate to develop further the international law regarding liability and compensation for the victims of pollution and other environmental damage caused by activities within the jurisdiction or control

---

[22] DeGarmo, *International Environmental Treaties*, p. 39.

of such states to areas beyond their jurisdiction'.[23] The frequently cited Principle 21 in reality confirmed two distinct and potentially incompatible principles: the sovereign right of states over their own resources and their responsibility to ensure that they did not cause environmental damage beyond their borders.

Nonetheless, Stockholm may still be regarded as a turning point–because it was the first conference to consider environmental issues as a whole, because it created the United Nations Environment Programme (UNEP) as the first central co-ordinating agency for the environment and also because of the participation of a substantial number of NGOs. Indeed Stockholm's innovation of a parallel forum for non-state actors, running alongside the official conference, established a template for many later world gatherings.[24]

Stockholm was followed by steadily increasing numbers of multilateral instruments on various aspects of the environment and the creation of intergovernmental and non-governmental institutions. The UN Law of the Sea Conference (1973–82) commenced in the immediate aftermath of Stockholm, resulting in a comprehensive legal regime encompassing marine pollution, dumping at sea and conservation and management of living resources, together with provisions for research, monitoring, compliance and liability among its many environmental provisions. There were also numerous statements of general principle, of which the most important was probably the 1987 Brundtland Report, which was itself an outcome of the UNGA's establishment of the World Commission on Environment and Development in 1983.[25] The Brundtland Report popularised the concept of sustainable development, emphasised the increasing interdependence of both states and issue-areas and called for a considerably strengthened institutional and legal regime that would have a source of funding independent of governmental contributions (such as a tax on trade). It also advanced twenty-two general principles that were to guide the proposed new regime, including the notion that a clean environment was a fundamental human right and the norm of 'intergenerational equity' (rights possessed by future generations) together with more specific guidelines for state conduct in environmental matters, such as obligations to carry out assessments of the impact on the environment of proposed industrial or other developments, to notify other states, to prevent

---

[23] Sands, *Principles*, p. 38. Text of Principle in UNEP *Declaration of the UN Conference on the Human Environment*, Stockholm 1972.
[24] Sakato Mori, 'Institutionalisation of NGO involvement in policy functions for global environmental governance', in Norichika Kanie and Peter M. Haas (eds.), *Emerging Forces in Environmental Governance* (Tokyo: UN University Press, 2004), pp. 157–75.
[25] UN General Assembly A/47/427, 4 August 1987.

damage where possible, to provide compensation to other affected states and to settle disputes peaceably.

The ozone layer

To paint a comprehensive picture of the current state of international environmental law would be an impossible task in a single chapter, not least because such an account would need to encompass not just the many international conventions on an increasing range of environmental issues and the numerous legal institutions associated with these but also a great deal of national legislation. Account would also have to be taken of the rapidly evolving concerns, perceptions and priorities relating to the environment, as the quickening pace of scientific change gives rise to new possibilities and risks. For example, developments in biotechnology have produced a whole new array of environmental issues, each involving complex regulatory issues. In some cases, where the potential risks were unclear, the precautionary principle has been invoked with some success. For example, the treaty governing biosafety and trade in biotechnology adopted in Cartagena in 2000 was a relatively speedy response to the dangers some perceived in the growing trade in genetically modified organisms (GMOs). Given the extensive disagreement amongst scientists about the risks posed by genetic modification, and the deep political divisions between the USA and Europe and between North and South on the question, Cartagena was a remarkable achievement for the precautionary principle.[26]

Hence we confine ourselves to two of the most important issues to have dominated international environmental discourse since the early 1980s: the depletion of the ozone layer and climate change. These encapsulate both the possibilities and the problems associated with environmental law-making. So far as attempts to regulate them are concerned, the international ozone layer regime has been by far the most successful, in part because it lacked some of the controversial aspects of climate change. Briefly, the ozone present in the stratosphere, by absorbing some of the Sun's ultraviolet radiation, reduces the harmful effects of the Sun in causing skin cancer, damaging plant life and affecting certain human immunities. In the mid-1970s scientists found that certain manufactured chemicals, notably chlorofluorocarbons (CFCs) that were used in refrigeration, fire extinguishing, air conditioning and for other purposes, were

---

[26] For a comprehensive discussion of Cartagena, see C. Ball, R. Falkner and H. Marquard (eds.), *The Cartagena Protocol on Biosafety: Reconciling Trade in Biotechnology with Environment and Development* (London: Earthscan Publications, 2002).

depleting the ozone layer. The first UNEP discussion of this took place in 1976[27] and from the early 1980s the United States, Canada and some Scandinavian states instituted national measures to limit production of CFCs in various areas deemed non-essential, such as aerosols.[28] When the first major international meeting on the issue took place in Vienna in 1985, there was at first disagreement between the USA, on the one hand, and the European Community, whose members included some major producers of the relevant goods, and developing nations, who were concerned about possible implications for their economic growth, on the other hand.[29] However a relatively anodyne Convention was eventually agreed. This was quickly superseded by the 1987 Montreal Protocol on Substances that Deplete the Ozone Layer, which was itself amended by meetings in London in 1990, Copenhagen in 1992, Montreal in 1997 and Beijing in 1999. The Montreal Protocol set out a timetable for reducing production of harmful substances and provided support for developing countries. The later amendments added to the list of regulated substances, substantially improved the financial assistance available for developing countries and brought back the target dates for reducing production of the named substances.

The Ozone regime is significant in five key respects so far as the larger context of environmental law and politics is concerned:

- The shift from the fairly cautious commitments of 1985 to the more rigorous obligations of the Protocol and its amendments demonstrated the importance of (relative) scientific certainty. What were essentially theoretical hypotheses in the 1970s had become demonstrable facts by the 1990s.[30]
- The Protocol essentially established a 'framework' agreement, in which the basic principles were set out but with a built-in expectation that they would be elaborated and solidified in future negotiations.[31]
- There was a clear acceptance of the need to provide financial and technical assistance to developing countries, as well as a longer timescale to enable them to meet their obligations. Specific provisions ranged from the establishment of a multilateral fund to enable transfer of technology and other assistance to novel provisions allowing parties to trade their rights to produce controlled substances so long as total combined production did not exceed the limits set out in the Protocol.

---

[27] UNEP Ozone Secretariat website, www.ozone.unep.org/.
[28] United States Environmental Protection Agency website, www.epa.gov/.
[29] Birnie and Boyle, *International Law*, pp. 517–19.
[30] DeSombre, *Global Environment*, pp. 102–5.
[31] For a discussion of the value of the 'framework' approach, see J. Sebenius, 'Designing negotiations toward a new regime: the case of global warming', *International Security* 15, 4 (1991), 110–48.

• The regime (and subsequent legislation in the USA, the EU and elsewhere) incorporated novel regulatory mechanisms, including market-based incentive schemes to encourage the industrial sector to develop less harmful alternatives.[32]

• Under Article 2, in the event of a failure to achieve consensus over proposed amendments, they could still 'as a last resort' be adopted by a two-thirds majority, so long as that included a majority of both developed and developing nations. Once adopted, amendments were binding on all parties, including those who had not consented to them.

One of the many issues in the complex interaction between politics, economics and environmental regulation concerns the long time frames involved before the success or failure of a particular course of action can be reliably assessed. In the case of the ozone layer, after a period in the mid-1990s, when there was some concern about a burgeoning black market in the proscribed products,[33] there was growing optimism that genuine progress was being made towards reducing and eventually reversing the depletion of the ozone layer. However a possible setback occurred in 2005, when it was reported that a serious depletion had been observed in the ozone layer over the Arctic.[34] This was particularly significant since it had been the discovery of an ozone 'hole' over Antarctica that had given an added urgency to the pursuit of an effective regime.

Climate change

Far greater controversy has accompanied negotiations over a climate change regime from the outset. The reasons for this are not hard to find since the issue raises in its sharpest form all four of the fundamental dichotomies discussed earlier in this chapter. While there is increasing consensus over the reality and seriousness of global warming, there are still disagreements about the precise dimensions of the human contribution to it as well as other questions, such as its exact impact. But it is in the other three areas that the greatest tensions are in evidence. The global regime that some believe will be required would create a degree of external control over many aspects of internal state policies and practices – from transport to taxation – that is currently unimaginable in a sovereign state system. The same is true of the levels of state (and indeed global) intervention in national economies that some environmentalists

[32] DeSombre, *Global Environment*, pp. 106–7.
[33] O. Greene, 'The system for implementation review in the ozone regime', in D. G. Victor, K. Raustalia and E. B. Skolnikoff (eds.), *The Implementation and Effectiveness of International Environmental Commitments: Theory and Practice* (Cambridge, MA: MIT Press, 1998), p. 91.
[34] www.europa.eu.int/comm./environment (this is the EU's environment website).

urge. But the greatest controversies to date have stemmed from the development versus environment issue. Rapidly developing countries such as India and China which have the potential to become major producers of greenhouse gases – even rivalling the US contribution of 25 per cent, let alone the EU's 14 per cent share – have resisted American and other arguments that they should not be placed in the same category as other developing nations but should be subject to an agreed regime from the start.

The so-called 'greenhouse gases', such as carbon dioxide and methane, play a key role in maintaining the earth's temperature at a level some 30°C warmer than it would otherwise be if the gases did not prevent solar radiation from escaping the earth's surface. If, however, the current balance were altered, climate changes would become inevitable. Current estimates are that carbon dioxide levels have risen by around 30 per cent in the last 300 years, with most of the increase accounted for by the use of fossil fuels and deforestation.[35] Since the impact of global warming is greatest at the poles, one consequence of this has been the gradual melting of the icecaps. This in turn is liable to lead to a significant raising of sea levels, with numerous consequences, including flooding – to the extent that some island states might even disappear altogether, along with London and New York – and a cooling of the Gulf Stream, which keeps northern Europe at a significantly higher temperature than would normally be the case. Action to reduce global warming needs to address problems relating to 'sinks' and 'reservoirs' (natural means of absorbing greenhouse gases, such as forests and oceans) as well as 'sources', such as fossil fumes. As Birnie and Boyle point out, the problem is so multifaceted and touches upon so many political, social and economic issues that 'the sectoral approach, which has traditionally dominated international regulation of the environment is inappropriate to the interconnected and global character of climate change'.[36]

Speculation about the human impact on the climate goes back nearly 200 years, but the issue only began to be taken very seriously in the 1980s, particularly since the formation of the Intergovernmental Panel on Climate Change (IPCC) in 1988. This international body of scientists has taken the lead in investigating all aspects, including socioeconomic ones, of climate change.[37] Although in no doubt about the seriousness of the problem, it has recently focused on mitigation strategies less harmful

[35] Lorraine Elliott, *The Global Politics of the Environment*, 2nd edition (Houndmills: Palgrave, 2004), p. 79.
[36] Birnie and Boyle, *International Law*, p. 523.
[37] DeSombre, *Global Environment*, pp. 100–1.

to economic growth than a simple reduction in industrial activity, notably through the most 'hi-tech' option: capture and storage of carbon dioxide.[38] Other mitigation approaches, such as the use of renewable energy sources like wind power, have attracted some scepticism about their true potential, while one proposal – a shift to nuclear power – has aroused considerable controversy.

The first significant international negotiations over the issue led to the 1992 United Nations Framework Convention on Climate Change, signed at Rio. This is, perhaps, most useful as evidence of the deep divisions to which the issue had already given rise, especially between developed and developing nations but also within each of those two camps (with the United States taking a notably harder line than its OECD partners), and the small island states, major oil producers like Saudi Arabia and the largest developing countries all representing their own distinctive positions. Like the 1987 Montreal Protocol on the ozone layer, the Rio Convention was a framework agreement, without real legal force, other than perhaps as an instrument of 'soft law'. So far as its specific provisions are concerned, it calls for stabilising the level of greenhouse gases in the atmosphere, rather than reducing it and repeats the broad principles elaborated at earlier meetings. These include intergenerational equity, sustainable development, the precautionary principle and the need to take account of the 'specific needs and special circumstances' of developing countries through the principle of 'common but differentiated responsibilities'. However, it also stresses the need for a 'supportive and open' economic system, in which measures to combat climate change were not in reality attempts to restrict trade.[39] It sets out in Article 4 a detailed list of responsibilities for both developed and developing countries, albeit cast in fairly general terms; sets up institutions, notably the Conference of the Parties (COP) and a Secretariat; and, most concretely, also establishes a financial mechanism, to be controlled by the Global Environmental Facility of the World Bank and UN Development Programme (UNDP) through which financial assistance and transfer of technology to developing nations may be co-ordinated.

The Framework Convention did not attempt to prescribe specific targets for individual states, nor did it lay down any enforcement provisions. These were to be left to later negotiations, of which the most important was the meeting in December 1997 that led to the Kyoto Protocol. This

[38] The full text of the 2005 report, *Carbon Dioxide Capture and Storage* is available on the IPCC website, www.ipcc.ch/.
[39] For the principles, see Article 3, UNFCCC, available on the official site for the UN Climate Secretariat, www.unfccc.int/2860.php.

entered into force as a binding legal document on 16 February 2005, after it had received the requisite number of ratifications. At the heart of the Protocol is a commitment by the developed countries to reduce their collective emissions of greenhouse gases by 5.2 per cent from their 1990 levels by 2008–2012, of which the major shares are reductions of 8 per cent by the EU, 7 per cent by the USA and 6 per cent by Japan. One controversial feature of Kyoto (which also appeared in a more elementary form in the ozone regime) was a provision under which countries whose emission levels were below their prescribed levels, such as Russia, could 'trade' their surplus emission quota to enable purchasing states to achieve their required levels through that means. The Protocol also envisages the possibility of states grouping together to work out means of jointly implementing their overall requirements. Article 11 confirms the Rio provisions for a financial mechanism to assist developing countries. Under Article 17, further meetings of the COP were to work out procedures and mechanisms in the event of non-compliance, including 'the development of an indicative list of consequences'.

American hostility to Kyoto pre-dates the George W. Bush administration: for example a Senate meeting in July 1997 decided unanimously that the United States should not be a party to an agreement that did not bind developing nations or that might cause serious harm to the United States. Although the Clinton administration did formally sign the agreement, its successors, while accepting that climate change was a serious problem, adopted a fairly hard line on the need for the rapidly developing economies of China and India, in particular, to be obliged to accept emission constraints. However, some American states and cities have begun to address the possibility of their taking individual actions to reduce emissions. The Bush administration's position has been opposed by the European Union, which has tended to represent itself as the most 'virtuous' of the developed countries, with an extensive regional regime backing up such claims, including financial penalties for non-compliance. Things are not quite so simple, however: several EU countries had already begun to shift from coal, with its high emission levels, to other fuels before 1990, so that their actual required reduction from 1997 (rather than the stipulated 1990) levels was much less than the 30 per cent reduction that would have been required from the United States. The EU target was also aided by the fact that the collapse of communism in 1989 in what were to be its newest entrants had been accompanied by a sharp fall in emission levels in the following years, so that 1990 marked a relative high point for European emissions.

In December 2005 the first session of the governing body of the Kyoto Protocol, Conference of the Parties serving as Meeting of the Parties to the Kyoto Protocol (COP/MOP) was held in Montreal. Against the expectations of many, this did not collapse in the face of widespread disagreements, as a 2000 meeting in The Hague had done, but was able to achieve consensus on all of its main issues, including the 'Marrakech Accords', which had elaborated the 'principles, nature and scope of the mechanisms' relating to key provisions of Kyoto at a meeting in 2001.[40] Crucially, these included procedures designed to ensure compliance, including verification measures and 'binding consequences' in the event of non-compliance. These were relatively mild, such as a deduction in a state's permitted emission in the next period greater than the amount by which it had exceeded its permitted emission in the previous period and restrictions on its emissions trading rights, but the aim was in part to promote confidence in the market mechanisms that were an important part of the regime. Calls from the group of least-developed countries for more stringent penalties, including 'compensation for damages due to unavoidable adverse impacts of climate change', were resisted but this issue will clearly remain on the agenda.[41] Perhaps of equal significance was the fact that the United States, after an initial show of aggression, including walking out of the meeting, agreed to further dialogue on the future of Kyoto after 2012, so long as this was not seen as involving binding commitments. Given that a more intransigent American position might, in effect, have condemned Kyoto to the waste bin, even this fairly grudging concession was important in enabling the process of environmental law-making to edge tentatively forward. It is possible that the US delegation, aware that many states, including what it saw as the sanctimoniously hypocritical Europeans, were failing to meet their targets, was content to let matters take what it believed to be their inevitable course towards a gradual collapse of Kyoto rather than play the part of villain that it had been allotted in previous negotiations. However, the fact that the United States opted to remain engaged in the Kyoto process meant that Kyoto remained the principal framework within which climate change discourse took place.

Theoretical lenses

Environmental law-making does not fit easily into a single theoretical perspective, not least because the many specific environmental issues differ from each other in the problems they pose and the kinds of regulatory

---

[40] Marrakech Accords, 21 January 2002 (FCCC/CP/2001/Add.2).
[41] Benito Müller, *Montreal 2005: What Happened and What it Means* (Oxford: Oxford Institute for Energy Studies, February 2006).

solutions they require: pollution of rivers may involve precise levels of damage inflicted by one state upon another, with the possibility of a conventional bilateral International Court of Justice (ICJ) hearing, while the consequences of global warming cannot be handled within a purely legal framework but require political and economic mechanisms as well as juridical ones. It may be easier to agree regimes in relatively narrow issue areas, like the protection of whales or endangered wildlife, than over the broad range of interests affected by global warming. Nonetheless, the conceptual and theoretical structure we developed in Chapter 3 still provides a useful preliminary framework for evaluating environmental law.

Content

Realism provides some key insights into state behaviour in environmental negotiations and their outcomes. States clearly seek to shape the content of agreements in ways that reflect their specific interests: for example, their developing or developed status, their relative positions as producers of carbon fuels or ozone pollutants or as contributors to or recipients of financial assistance; and they are careful to avoid entering into far-reaching binding commitments, preferring looser and more flexible 'framework' agreements. Similarly, even where potentially calamitous consequences are threatened, as in the case of climate change, states have proven incapable of yielding any significant part of their sovereign powers to a new global authority. Hence, the classic realist explanatory forces of power and state-centrism still provide the broad parameters within which any kind of environmental regime can emerge. The neoliberal institutionalist variant on realism might add that the proposed regime for global change has insufficient incentives built in to attract the United States to participate, still less to act as global environmental hegemon.[42] The most that can be said for institutionalist perspectives (like regime theory) on environmental law-making is not that their predictions that institutions provide structures that encourage states to seek co-operative solutions to collective problems are valid, but that the jury is still out on that question: the United States remains involved in the Kyoto process.

Within those parameters, however, more complex developments are discernible and here both liberal and constructivist perspectives have greater explanatory potential. Although some would argue that democracies actually tend to have more harmful environmental policies because

---

[42] Robyn Eckersley, 'Soft law, hard politics and the Climate Change Treaty', in Christian Reus-Smit (ed.), *The Politics of International Law*, (Cambridge: Cambridge University Press, 2004), pp. 80–105.

they find it harder to impose the requisite costs on their electorates, the consensus is that environmentalist norms have emerged most emphatically in democracies, under the influence of non-state actors like Greenpeace.[43] Similarly, transnational epistemic communities are seen by some as having, in effect, helped to bring about what amounts to a normative paradigm shift over issues ranging from the moral rights of animals to the obligations of the rich to the poor.[44] Certainly, the role of scientists in raising environmental consciousness has been central, not least those contributing to the IPCC, and may even have contributed to the gradual emergence of a new concept of international legitimacy incorporating environmentally responsible behaviour. If so, that development might lend weight to the liberal perspective on international law, with its emphasis on the role of law in promoting values and performing functions other than the strictly 'legal' ones, including providing modes of communication, reassurance and co-operation in international politics.

Constructivism, including its critical variant, may shed most light upon what is really going on in the international politics of environmental lawmaking.[45] This is particularly the case of the newest and most controversial environmental issues, such as GMOs and global warming. In those cases, which were barely on the horizon forty years ago and where many uncertainties still abound, we have witnessed an on-going discursive process in which scientific knowledge has developed and entered the public domain, in part through the activities of NGOs. Eventually, discourse has reached a level where politicians try to argue through and possibly reconcile their different interests and agree to meaningful, if initially broad and loose, commitments. In later stages of this process, lawyers have sought to make these commitments more precise and indeed 'law-like'. As we suggested in Chapter 1, 'in the course of any discourse, the arguments engaged in by the participants will lead them towards shared understandings of the facts (the "external world"), the normative issues involved (the "social world") and their own subjective responses (the "inner world")'. In every sense of the term a process of 'social construction of reality',[46] embracing all aspects of 'reality' from factual knowledge to normative

---

[43] DeGarmo, *International Environmental Treaties*, pp. 24–6. But see also the arguments of environmental sociologists to the effect that it is the commitment to ever greater economic growth that is an inescapable facet of capitalist democracies that will inevitably lead to increasing environmental degradation. Fisher, *National Governance*, pp. 9–11.

[44] Gillespie, *International Environmental Law*.

[45] For a strong argument in favour of a critical constructivist approach, see Eckersley, 'Soft law'.

[46] The term is of course borrowed from Peter L. Berger and Thomas Luckmann, *The Social Construction of Reality: A Treatise in the Sociology of Knowledge* (New York: Dobleday, 1966).

structures, and from demarcation of political boundaries to rule-making has been going on in the context of these major environmental questions.

Compliance

The classic 1968 article 'The Tragedy of the Commons' pointed to the difficulties with securing compliance with environmental regimes, even when it is in everybody's interest to comply.[47] Incentives to cheat are strong, given fears that others will be gaining from one individual's forbearance by cheating themselves, with the outcome – ecological destruction – inevitable in any case. A further problem in the environmental context is that, whereas in a formal sense it is states who comply with international obligations, in reality – especially in the case of global warming – compliance requires appropriate behaviour on the part of every individual and collective member of the state, which in turn requires comprehensive and expensive national monitoring and enforcement mechanisms. If a powerful state chooses to ignore its obligations, not only will it not institute such mechanisms, it may actually assist non-compliers: the Soviet Union colluded with its whalers in vastly exceeding their allotted limits in the 1980s, including reporting whale catches to the International Whaling Commission that were well below the actual hauls and also permitting its military to dump oil and nuclear waste at sea.[48] Partly in recognition of the complexities and costs involved with creating an effective system to enforce compliance, the international community has, for the most part, avoided coercive approaches to this issue. Even in the case of the ozone layer regime, which has the most fully developed set of provisions for dealing with non-compliance, the main emphasis is on building in incentives for states to comply and on non-confrontational discussions, although financial penalties, such as withdrawing financial assistance from the Protocol's Multilateral Fund and the World Bank's Global Environment Facility (GEF) have occasionally been employed, to some effect, as has the threat of trade sanctions against non-members.[49]

Yet it is clear that a purely game-theoretical perspective, with its assumptions about 'rational', self-interested actors and its emphasis on incentives to cheat or be a free-rider, does not tell anything like the whole

---

[47] Garrett Hardin, 'The tragedy of the commons', *Science* 162 (1968), 1243–8.

[48] DeSombre, *Global Environment*, pp. 23, 132–3.

[49] The GEF was established in 1990 by the World Bank, UNDP and UNEP to fund research, training and transfer of technology relating to the environment. For a detailed account of the Protocol's non-compliance system, see David G. Victor, 'The Montreal Protocol's non-compliance procedure', in Victor, Raustalia and Skolnikoff (eds.), *Implementation and Effectiveness* pp. 137–76.

story. Explanations based on self-interest, particularly different degrees of vulnerability to a specific problem and relative levels of economic costs in implementing solutions, may well be necessary elements in any approach to theorising the different responses of states to compliance issues,[50] but they are not sufficient, as the case of the United States and global warming suggests. Here again liberal and constructivist accounts have more to offer. Three other factors have been especially significant in the development of effective environmental regimes. First, science has played an increasingly crucial role in raising public awareness of the relevant issues, formulating policy at the national and international levels and monitoring and implementing agreed regimes. One may even postulate a direct correlation between the degree of scientific certainty about a specific issue and the effectiveness of the international regime relating to that issue, based on the experience with the ozone layer. Second, public opinion, especially in its organised and activist forms, has been of great importance in pushing governments to play an increasingly active role in environmental affairs. The neorealist notion of the state as a unitary actor, whose international behaviour is determined mainly by its relative power position in the international system, is woefully inadequate in the environmental context. For example, one factor in the American shift from a hardline posture in the December 2005 negotiations was a speech in Montreal strongly supportive of a climate change regime by former President Clinton. This was seen by some as helping to 'shame' the US delegation over its earlier intransigence: the domestic context of American politics thus playing a key role in shaping American policy.[51] In terms of the theoretical framework developed in Chapter 3, environmental policy, including willingness to comply with international obligations, may be seen, especially in the Western democracies, as in part an outcome of persuasion by NGOs and other actors. Although there are of course also powerful lobbies, such as oil companies, promoting very different positions from those of the NGOs, the question of relative degrees of congruence with the overall normative system of the state in question also enters into the picture. As states have grown wealthier, so has public attention increasingly come to focus on 'lifestyle' issues and on international justice: both of which point to the need for greater environmental protection. Third, there is some suggestive evidence that international institutions may help to enmesh states in a framework where, because they are obliged to interact with other states in an on-going manner, they are more likely to tend

[50] Detlef Sprinz and Tapani Vaahtoranta, 'The interest-based explanation of international environment policy', *International Organization* 48, 1 (Winter 1994), 77–105.
[51] Benito Müller, *Montreal 2005*.

towards conformity with the behavioural norms of such institutions.[52] The fact that states will interact in many different kinds of institutions helps to create the possibility of linkage between separate issues, so that states will be more likely to compromise over one in order to achieve concessions over another. Over time states get into the habit of co-operating in institutions and value the stability and predictability that ensues.

None of this is to say that state compliance with their environmental obligations is at a high level. Few states will reach their Kyoto targets and, even where a major compliance requirement is simply providing regular data to a regime's reporting system, several states fail to do this, often because they lack the necessary administrative capacity effectively to monitor their compliance with their commitments. A recent major study of factors affecting a state's compliance with environmental accords found that

A country's physical conditions, its history, and its culture establish basic parameters that affect implementation and compliance. The economy, political institutions, and public opinion have an effect but it is generally indirect. These factors operate through proximate variables. In our view, the most important proximate variables are administrative capacity, leadership, NGOs, knowledge and information. All these factors, of course, are shaped by the country's preexisting traditions, legislation and regulations in the area involved.[53]

The same study found that there was a gradual trend towards greater compliance with environmental obligations.

Change

Much the same kinds of theoretical observations apply for the questions of how and why change occurs in relation to environmental law-making and where environmental regimes may be heading in the future. The world is still a considerable distance from the major paradigm shift that would be required for the kind of global governance that some call for in relation to climate change, so the system of sovereign states will continue to set the broad parameters within which environmental regimes

---

[52] The work of Robert O. Keohane, John G. Ruggie and Oran R. Young has been particularly influential here. See, for example, Keohane's *International Institutions and State Power*, (Boulder: CO: Westview, 1989), Ruggie's *Multilateralism Matters* (New York: Columbia University Press, 1993) and Young's *International Cooperation: Building Regimes for Natural Resources and the Environment* (Ithaca, NY: Cornell University Press, 1989).

[53] Harold K. Jacobson and Edith Brown Weiss, 'Stengthening compliance with international environmental accords', in Paul F. Diehl (ed.), *The Politics of Global Governance: International Organizations in an Interdependent World* (Boulder, CO: Lynne Rienner, 2001), pp. 406–35.

develop. The 'tragedy of the commons' is likely to be repeated in many contexts, from fish stocks to global warming. Nonetheless, concern with environmental issues has grown enormously since Stockholm, with many hundreds of international instruments now in existence, compared with around twenty in 1972. At the very least, a global environmental discourse about the environment has become a permanent feature of international politics, from which more agreements will emerge – however imperfect – and from which no state of any significance will be able to abstain. In this discourse, different national and commercial interests will play an important part, but so will many normative considerations, including issues of justice relating to the rights of poorer countries, indigenous peoples and indeed animals. Agreed rules will reflect the wishes of the most powerful states but also changing conceptions of international legitimacy, which will, in turn, be affected by normative developments, especially in the more democratic states.

Market mechanisms designed to encourage commercial interests and individuals to adopt environmentally friendly procedures are likely to remain more prominent than coercive measures, such as financial penalties and trade sanctions, although the latter may well gradually increase in significance. Scientific findings, an array of domestic factors and also international institutions will continue to be key influences on international bargaining. Technological changes that provide the possibility of effective environmental protection without substantial economic damage will be sought with increasing urgency and, when discovered, will tend to determine, or at least be a major factor in, future environmental regimes.

In terms of our theoretical framework outlined in Chapter 3, formal legal structures establishing, through consent, binding obligations with built-in penalties are likely to be the exception rather than the rule. This is essentially for three reasons: states have too many separate interests to protect for a comprehensive regime to be possible, especially in areas like climate change or GMOs which carry far-reaching economic and political implications; the combination of continuing scientific uncertainty alongside new discoveries and technological developments emphasises the need for agreements to build in the maximum possible flexibility, as in the various Framework Agreements; an effective sanctions regime would create more problems than it would solve, quite apart from its enormous cost. Change in this area is far more likely to resemble the liberal and constructivist perspectives with, on the one hand, a comprehensive but complex process of decision-making embracing many actors – state, non-state and interstate – and, on the other hand, a social process incorporating interaction at elite levels (leaders, epistemic communities and norm entrepreneurs), on-going learning by both elites and communities as a whole and the development and internalisation of new norms.

Discussion questions

- Why has it proved so difficult for states to reach agreement on environmental issues?
- Does effective environmental regulation require a major step towards world government or can it be accommodated within the contemporary international system?
- Is effective environmental regulation compatible with a free-market world economy?
- How have states attempted to reconcile development with the need for environmental regulation?
- Is the precautionary principle a valid approach to the prevention of environmental damage? Can such a principle be properly incorporated into international law?
- Why were states able to achieve relatively speedy agreement on an ozone layer regime? How would you evaluate the significance of the Montreal Protocol and its later amendments?
- Has the concept of a 'framework agreement' in environmental regulation proved a useful innovation or merely a way of postponing difficult decisions?
- Why has the United States resisted climate change regulations so strongly?
- How useful are the realist, liberal and constructivist lenses for understanding environmental issues?

SUGGESTIONS FOR FURTHER READING

Axelrod, R. S., D. L. Downie and N. J. Vig (eds.), *The Global Environment. Institutions, Law and Policy*, 2nd edition, Washington: CQ Press, 2005. A useful collection of essays from leading American and European scholars from several disciplinary backgrounds examining both broad conceptual and theoretical questions and specific issues ranging from compliance problems to the implementation of environmental agreements in the USA, Europe, China and the Third World.

Birnie, Patricia, and Alan Boyle, *International Law and the Environment*, 2nd edition, Oxford: Oxford University Press, 2002. One of the best of a large number of substantial textbooks on environmental law. Clear and comprehensive presentation of the major issues.

De Garno, Denise, *International Environmental Treaties and State Behavior: Factors Influencing Cooperation*, New York and London: Routledge, 2005. A brief study of the applicability of international relations theory to environmental problems, using quantitative data and case studies. No particularly surprising findings but although constructivism and realism both receive some backing, the strongest case is made for supporting economic growth and political liberalisation in poor countries as conditions most likely to give rise to environmentalist policies.

DeSombre, Elizabeth, *The Global Environment and World Politics*, London and New York: Continuum Press, 2002. A relatively short but clearly written and well-constructed discussion of some of the theoretical questions in the context of four key environmental issue-areas: ozone depletion and climate change, whaling, Amazonian biodiversity and acid rain.

Elliott, L. M., *The Global Politics of the Environment* 2nd edition, Houndmills: Palgrave, 2004. A well-constructed and researched survey of all the main issues.

Fisher, Dana R., *National Governance and the Global Climate Change Regime*, Oxford: Rowman and Littlefield, 2004. An environmental sociologist's study, based on interviews with Japanese, Dutch and American officials and activists, that highlights the importance of domestic interests in environmental policy-making.

Gillespie, Alexander, *International Environmental Law, Policy and Ethics*, Oxford: Oxford University Press, 1997. An interesting if slightly dated discussion of these key questions.

Hurrell, A. and B. Kingsbury (eds.), *The International Politics of the Environment*, Oxford: Clarendon Press, 1992. Dated but still well worth reading for the introductory chapter by the editors and some of the theoretical discussions, not least the robust economic perspective offered by Wilfred Beckerman.

Kütting, G., *Environment, Society and International Relations: Towards More Effective International Environmental Agreements*, London: Routledge, 2000. An unusual take on the subject, examining the impact of social organisation on the environment and criticising standard neoliberal institutionalist regime-based approaches.

Globalization and the Environment: Greening Global Political Economy, Albany: State University of New York Press, 2004. Seeks to develop an 'eco-holistic' conceptualisation, bringing together social, political, economic and environmental perspectives with a view to providing a more comprehensive analytical framework than other approaches. This is then applied to the garment trade and West Africa.

Liftin, K. T. (ed.), *The Greening of Sovereignty in World Politics*, Cambridge, MA: MIT Press, 1998. Essays on the key question of whether sovereignty and environmental management are irreconcileable principles. Thorough and interesting.

Sands, Philippe, *Principles of International Environmental Law*, 2nd edition, Cambridge: Cambridge University Press, 2003. A comprehensive survey by a leading authority.

Victor, D. G., K. Raustiala and E. B. Skolnikoff (eds.) *The Implementation and Effectiveness of International Environmental Commitments: Theory and Practice*, Cambridge, MA: MIT Press, 1998. A very thorough survey of the key issue of implementation of agreements in fourteen case studies. Slightly dated but still invaluable for its methodology, findings and policy recommendations.

Weiss, E. B., and H. K. Jacobson (eds.), *Engaging Countries: Strengthening Compliance with International Environmental Accords*, Cambridge MA: MIT Press, 1989. A comparative study of compliance with environmental accords by several disparate countries.

Part III

Conclusions

9 International law in a unipolar age

In our introduction to this book, we asserted that international law matters more now than ever before. On the face of it, the rise of US power at the turn of the third millennium appears to challenge this assertion. The collapse of the Soviet Union in 1991 left the world with only one superpower. What was quickly recognised to be a 'unipolar moment' in world history has turned into a unipolar age. The concentration of economic, military and political power in the United States is so great that no rival power will rise, nor counterbalancing alliance emerge, for the foreseeable future.[1] Indeed, it is now common to speak of US hegemony in imperial terms. Hence Joseph Nye noted in 2003: 'the world "empire" has come out of the closet. Respected analysts on both the left and the right are beginning to refer to "American empire" approvingly as the dominant narrative of the 21st century.'[2] This view of the United States is shared across the world. As one Russian specialist observed, 'whether or not the United States now views itself as an empire, for many foreigners it increasingly looks, walks and talks like one, and they respond to Washington accordingly'.[3]

In recent years, this hegemonic United States has appeared to show scant regard for international law. It has opposed major multilateral treaties on nuclear testing, land-mines, climate change, biological diversity, law on the sea and the International Criminal Court (ICC), all of which are supported by most other states. To be sure, the United States is legally entitled not to consent to these treaties. But a certain lawless spirit has been read in the US refusal to work within these multilateral regimes. More dramatically still, the controversial US invasion of Iraq in 2003 without a clear mandate from the United Nations Security Council

---

[1] Charles Krauthammer, 'The unipolar moment', *Foreign Affairs* 70 (1990/1), 22–3; William C. Wohlforth, 'The stability of a unipolar world', *International Security* 24 (1999), 5–41.

[2] Joseph S. Nye, Jr., 'American power and strategy after Iraq', *Foreign Affairs* 82 (2003), 60.

[3] Dimitri K. Simes, 'America's imperial dilemma', *Foreign Affairs* 82 (2003), 93.

(UNSC) is widely pointed to as evidence of actual US lawlessness. The picture that emerges is one of an unbound United States pushing its weight around the world.

For realists in IR, this is all to be expected. Power defines national interest. The powerful do as they want, and the weak must endure. Realists see little reason to expect the United States, from its dominating global position, to bother much with international law. Once again, from a realist perspective, power politics trumps international law as the real mechanism for world order. And indeed, it would seem that US hegemony presents a challenge to the positivist perspective of an apolitical rule-governed legal order, one where states consent to such rules on the basis of sovereign equality. Sovereignty has always been more of an ideal than a reality, never more so than in the contemporary world characterised, as it is, by increasing globalisation.[4] More to the point, clearly this is not a world of equals. Power plays a role in how states shape legal regimes on human rights, international crimes, trade, the environment, and how states operate within them. And politics imbues the formation processes, functions, and purposes of such legal regimes. Indeed, power and law interact in defining the very meaning of sovereignty, in that the great powers have worked through multilateral institutions (such as the UNSC and the Nuclear Non-proliferation Regime) to brand some states as outlaws and so push them to the margins of the world order.[5]

In this book, we have situated international law in its historical context and approached it from a number of theoretical perspectives. Viewed across the sweep of history, recurring themes in the politics of international law are revealed. Chief among these is the role of Western power and norms in shaping the world legal order. But this is not a straightforward matter of might makes right. Power, politics and law have interacted in complex ways across history in shaping the current world order. Our theoretical lenses also reveal the differing functions of international law, the different ways it takes effect and the different processes whereby it evolves. They further show that the dominant approaches to International Relations (IR) and International Law (IL) – realism and positivism – cannot tell us all we need to know about international law in world politics. The liberal and constructivist lenses complete our picture of the impact of US unipolarity on the world legal order.

---

[4] Stephen D. Krasner, *Sovereignty: Organized Hypocrisy* (Princeton, NJ: Princeton University Press, 1999).
[5] Gerry Simpson, *Great Powers and Outlaw States: Unequal Sovereigns in the International Legal Order* (Cambridge: Cambridge University Press, 2004).

International law in historical context

Any legal system, we have suggested here, is both the product and the servant of a particular political association. The nature of that association, the requirements of its constituents, the power relations among them and the way in which they organise themselves institutionally will determine the essential character of the legal order to which the association gives rise. Sovereign states possessing very uneven power and existing in an overall context of anarchy have produced an international legal system without a centralised source of legitimate authority, and the rules of which have tended to reflect principles like state consent and non-intervention. Institutional structures charged with upholding and enforcing international law, like the United Nations, also incorporate such principles, while the jurisdiction of the International Court of Justice (ICJ) is likewise dependent on state consent.

Although the idea of the rule of law is founded on principles like impartiality and fairness, the content of any legal system will in practice inevitably tend to reflect the interests and assumptions of those most able to make their voices heard in the law-making process. These, in turn, will tend to be the more powerful members of the community to which the legal system applies. Similarly, while those charged with applying the law will, ideally, seek to perform their task in as neutral and objective a manner as possible, the ability of the wealthier members of a community to afford the best available legal advice and representation may help them to secure favourable judgments.

Within states, such potential inequities may be mitigated to some degree by various means: poorer and less powerful individuals strengthen their legal position by combining in trade unions and other means of collective representation, democratic pressures promote rules and procedures designed to redress imbalances and the mass media highlight individual cases of injustice. Some would argue that, not only are such remedies absent in the international legal system, but that it systematically promotes the interests and values of the wealthier and more powerful states, especially the West. From this perspective, international law should be seen, not as a means of bringing order through ever more sophisticated and comprehensive rules, combined with reasoned argument, to the interaction among states but as a means of legitimising past rapaciousness and present structures of domination and exploitation.

Such a perspective derives from three key sets of argument. The first rests on a particular interpretation of the history of international law, especially in the crucial periods following Columbus's voyage to America and in the nineteenth century.[6] In the earlier period, would-be authoritative legal pronouncements by the Vatican were employed to justify European seizure of the 'New World', while the writings of jurists, notably Vitoria, provided a more sophisticated legal rationale for privileging the rights of the conquistadores over those of the indigenous Americans.[7] In the nineteenth century, the same alliance of European imperialist powers and international lawyers developed an interrelated conceptual framework revolving around social Darwinism, racism and distinctions between 'civilised' and 'uncivilised' nations to explain and justify European expansion and the unequal relationships with non-Western countries, even where these were not directly colonised, as in the most notable case of China.

A second line of argument asserts that, notwithstanding the formal end of European colonial empires, various forms of neo-imperialism have emerged, with international law, once again, playing an important role in rationalising and legitimising the new structure of domination and exploitation. Illustrations offered to support this perspective range from specific areas of international law, such as those relating to intellectual property rights[8] or the requirement of 'prompt, adequate and effective compensation' for the expropriation of foreign-owned assets,[9] to the fact that many international organisations, including the UNSC, the World Bank and the International Monetary Fund (IMF) are structured in ways that favour the major Western powers. More subtle inequities may derive from the fact that wealthier nations are better able to maintain highly qualified and experienced legal staff to ensure their interests are protected, both in drafting international regulations and in subsequent legal procedures where disputes arise.

Even on the occasions where international courts find against major powers, the latter may find it easier to ignore such findings, as the United States did when the ICJ ruled against it over its support for the Nicaraguan Contras and when the State of Virginia went ahead with the execution

---

[6] For a Marxist perspective on the history of international law in these terms, see China Miéville, *Between Equal Rights: A Marxist Theory of International Law* (London: Pluto Press, 2005), pp. 154–293.

[7] A. Anghie, 'Francisco de Vitoria and the colonial origins of international law', *Social and Legal Studies* 5 (1996), 321–36 and Anghie, *Imperialism, Sovereignty and the Making of International Law* (Cambridge: Cambridge University Press, 2004).

[8] Ikechi Mgbeoji, 'The juridical origins of the international patent system: toward a historiography of the role of patents in industrialization', *Journal of the History of International Law* 5 (2003), 399–418. See also Mgbeoji, *Global Biopiracy: Patents, Plants and Indigenous Knowledge* (Ithaca, NY: Cornell University Press, 2006).

[9] The phrase was used by American Secretary of State Cordell Hull in respect of a dispute with Mexico in 1938.

of a Paraguayan national in 1998, despite the ICJ's calling for a stay of execution on the grounds that he had not been given consular access, as agreed in the 1963 Vienna Convention on Consular Relations, to which the USA was a party. As we have noted, the United States has taken an increasingly assertive attitude in recent years where it has believed international legal developments might conflict with important national interests, as in its opposition to the International Criminal Court (ICC), its rejection of the Kyoto Protocol on climate change and its dismissal of criticism of the legality of its detention of prisoners in Guantanamo Bay and its war in Iraq. The leading international lawyer, Philippe Sands, goes so far as to describe such conduct as comprising a 'war on law'.[10]

The third set of arguments focuses on the norms, implicit and explicit, that underpin international law. These are seen as reflecting essentially Western values and, as such, helping to confirm and legitimise Western, especially American, dominance. In this perspective, the more overt and direct use of the 'standard of civilisation' to confirm European power in the nineteenth century has been overtaken by more subtle uses of essentially similar devices. For example, in the post-war period, legal instruments like the 1948 Universal Declaration of Human Rights and the 1951 Refugee Convention were sometimes used as valuable tools in the West's ideological struggle against the Soviet Union during the Cold War, while numerous developing countries have argued that the human rights enshrined in the Declaration and subsequent Covenants on Civil and Political Rights and Economic and Social Rights reflect primarily Western values. More recently, major Western powers, together with agencies they effectively control, like the World Bank and the IMF, have brought various forms of pressure, including making aid conditional on Third World states agreeing to restructure their governing institutions and processes along Western models of 'good governance', while also liberalising their economies. It is also worth noting that the great majority of litigators representing states (including developing countries) in cases brought before the ICJ have come from a few major Western states. This is, essentially, a consequence of the fact that lawyers from those states will tend to have the requisite training, qualifications and experience, but it does raise the question whether they also, albeit unintentionally, reflect a narrow set of Western norms in their arguments.

Many counter-arguments may, of course, be made to these three sets of assertions. Nineteenth-century critics of European imperialism and the notion of a 'civilising mission' included several French international

---

[10] Philippe Sands, *Lawless World: America and the Making and Breaking of Global Rules* (London: Allen Lane, 2005), pp. xii.

lawyers.[11] Indeed Vitoria had attempted to defend the legal rights of indigenous peoples, even while also advancing arguments that could be used to legitimise imperial conquest. A number of contemporary legal instruments, like the Kyoto Protocol, contain provisions for the richest states to bear the greatest share of the cost. World Trade Organization (WTO) rulings have often found in favour of developing countries, while the latter have shown, in the WTO and elsewhere, that they can enhance their influence through forming bargaining coalitions.[12] While the United States seemed determined, in the first years after 9/11, to show its contempt for any rules or institutions that might purport to constrain it, its more recent behaviour has shown a partial retreat from the more extreme versions of this stance. Finally, the argument about the imposition of Western human rights values can be countered by the fact that these are also – formally at least – subscribed to by the overwhelming majority of UN members, and Western pressure may help to bring about some genuine improvements in the internal governance of states. The argument that the freedom of a dictator to murder, oppress and steal from his fellow citizens is his legal right under a strict application of the principle of non-intervention is no less a part of the normative framework of 'old' international law than the right of imperial conquest or the mission to 'civilise'. In short, history reveals the interplay of power and politics to operate in complex and contingent ways in shaping and working through international law.

Three perspectives on international law

We have argued in this book that there is much common ground between the dominant theoretical approaches to IR and IL, as there is between their challengers. From these points in common we have suggested three interdisciplinary lenses through which to view the nature and function of international law in world politics.

The realist lens

Realism and positivism both seek to describe the world as they see it. Both see no place for values in their respective visions of the world – as a jungle for realists, and as a closed legal system for positivists. Both offer an essentially structural view of things, where the balance of power

---

[11] Martti Koskenniemi, *The Gentle Civilizer of Nations: The Rise and Fall of International Law 1870–1960* (Cambridge: Cambridge University Press, 2001), pp. 105–8.

[12] Amrita Narlikar, *International Trade and Developing Countries. Bargaining Coalitions in the GATT and WTO* (London and New York: Routledge, 2003).

and international law delimit the choices available for states to advance their self-interests. Combined into a unified realist lens, international law is reduced to rules to which states have consented. The realist perspective does reveal much about modern international law which is, indeed, increasingly treaty-based. This is certainly evident in all of the areas of law examined in this book. In some areas, such as human rights and international crimes, legal rules are codified in a tapestry of treaties. In other areas, such as use of force and trade, there are keystone treaties (the UN Charter and WTO Treaty respectively) that provide the core rules.

In this rules-based system, consent is the major driver for state compliance. We see this in international criminal law where, in the absence of an effective international mechanism, compliance has depended on self-regulation. In this area of law, there is generally a poor record of compliance, suggesting the conditionality of state consent. The importance of consent is also evident in the continued vibrancy of Charter law notwithstanding repeated non-compliance by states; the non-use of force norm has survived because states continue to recognise its legal force. The realist lens also points to coercion as an important inducer of state compliance. This is evident in trade law, in the beefed up dispute settlement body of the WTO which can force states to comply with WTO rules.

This emphasis on states and consent also points to a formal process of legal change, primarily through treaty law. Again, the international trade regime provides a very good example of this, developed, as it was, through a succession of multilateral negotiations (seven General Agreement on Tariffs and Trade (GATT) rounds and six WTO trade conferences to date). In addition, more than in other areas of treaty law – such as human rights, the law of armed conflict (LOAC) and international crimes – GATT/WTO law has been dominated by states with non-state actors playing minor outsider roles (with the exception of the European Union which is a party to the WTO). This formal process based on state consent may also explain the form of an evolving legal regime. In the case of the environment, we find that states have sought to avoid far-reaching binding commitments in favour of more flexible 'framework' agreements.

The liberal lens

Liberals in IR and IL offer a prescriptive theory for a better world. Progressive values are core to liberal visions of the world. This is a more agent-centred perspective, one that recognises a plurality of actors working with, alongside and against states in world politics. Liberal values are most in evidence in human rights and international crimes. Underlying both is the promotion of human dignity. This value is present in international trade law in so far as freer trade promises, in principle, to alleviate world poverty; though, in practice, trade liberalisation often threatens the fragile economies of the least-developed states. World peace via system stability is also an underlying value of trade law, in that liberals argue that free trade increases the incentives for peaceful relations between states. Furthermore, this value is fundamental to law on the use of force. The concern with system stability led to the gradual abandonment of the just war tradition in the eighteenth and nineteenth centuries in favour of a more secular 'law of nations'. This then turned into a focus on world peace in twentieth-century positivist law, with the general prohibition on the use of force being codified in a number of multilateral treaties, most important of which is the UN Charter. System stability does conflict with human dignity in this area of law when it comes to the evolving practice of humanitarian intervention. The prioritisation of the former over the latter exists in state reluctance to recognise the legality of humanitarian intervention.

The liberal lens puts state compliance down to self-interest and fairness. Both motivating factors are certainly evident in trade law. Trade liberalisation clearly benefits the developed economies of the world. 'Law of comparative advantage' suggests that it will also benefit the less-developed economies. Sustaining the WTO regime is a central fairness discourse based on a grand bargain between the developed and developing states: liberalisation of the trade in services and protection of intellectual property rights for developed states, removal of non-tariff barriers to trade in agriculture and textiles for developing states. However, the continued viability of this fairness discourse will depend on the implementation of the 2001 Doha development agenda, which was launched in response to widespread recognition that the developed states have failed to keep their side of this bargain.

Through the liberal lens, change in international law is viewed as a policy process involving actors operating below and above the level of the state. Included here are authoritative decision-making bodies such as international courts and tribunals. These have indeed played an important role in affecting change in international criminal law by providing authoritative interpretations of (often ambiguous) customary and treaty law in this area. Also significant are quasi-legal bodies such as the UNSC and WTO Appellate Body, whose decisions are binding on states and may therefore create new legal obligations. Transnational advocacy groups further play an active role in advancing both human rights and international criminal law. Such non-governmental organisations use 'naming and shaming' tactics to get states to fall in line with existing legal regimes and provide expert knowledge to support progressive campaigns for the creation of new legal rules. Non-governmental organisations also mobilise public support and expert knowledge but to less effect in seeking to develop legal rules on fairer trade and on environmental protection.

The constructivist lens

Constructivists seek to explain the world that we have got. Values, recast as norms, become explanatory variables – norms and identities condition the possibilities for meaningful action. This is a mostly structural account of the world, but with a difference; contrary to realism, which conceives of structure in material terms (i.e., the balance of power), constructivists conceive of it in social terms. Hence, the world legal order not only expresses the distribution of power, it contains the script for power to be purposively (if not legitimately) exercised. Furthermore, international law not only provides modes of co-operation and legitimation, it also provides the discursive resources for states to engage in argumentation and through this to 'learn' and internalise new norms. Viewed thus, as a discourse, law serves a much broader function than mere rules for rational action. In human rights, law provides the discourse for constituting the relationship between states and individuals, as well as the moral vocabulary for judging state action. Customary and treaty law on use of force expresses a discourse centred on the principles of necessity and proportionality. Similarly the discourse at the heart of WTO law revolves around the principles of reciprocity, non-discrimination and special and differentiated treatment for developing states. Indeed, the grand bargain at the heart of the WTO is in trouble precisely because developed states are not abiding by these principles in their treatment of developing states. International criminal law further shows how principles may be imported from other areas of law – in this case, general international law, human rights law and domestic criminal law – into discourse on procedural and/or substantive norms. Finally, the tendency in environmental law-making to reach 'framework agreements' which lay down broad principles rather than 'hard law' is designed to encourage continuing discourse in this complex area where so many different interests are in contention.

The constructivist lens points to persuasion, congruence and habit as crucial factors in producing state compliance with international law. Persuasion does play an important role in environmental law in that regime effectiveness appears to be greatly enhanced by improved scientific certainty about specific environmental issues. Congruence is evident in international law on human rights and use of force in so far as liberal democracies are generally better at meeting their obligations under human rights treaties and are disinclined to resort to force in their external relations with each other. Indeed, generally and for the most part, compliance with international human rights law is habitually practised in liberal democracies. However, a caveat is in order: the record on this is complicated by the leeway available in *how* states, including liberal democracies, comply with their obligations under international human rights law. This involves both rule definition (such as US and European differences over the definition of torture when it comes to interrogation techniques), and the mode of incorporation and effect of international rules in domestic law. Moreover, when it comes to the use of force, liberal democracies have shown an increasing tendency in the post-Cold War period to engage (albeit selectively) in war for liberal ends and especially against illiberal regimes.[13] Congruence also plays a part when it comes to war crimes. It is suggested in the generally better record of liberal democracies in abiding by LOAC. However, the record on this is hardly unblemished for liberal democracies. This leads us to suggest that congruence be considered more precisely in terms of how specific rules of LOAC fit with national military doctrine and are embedded in national military systems. We also suggest that the LOAC may operate differently in the context of specific conflicts where, as in the case of the US war on al-Qaeda, one or the other side perceives the enemy to be 'uncivilised'.

Finally, constructivism presents legal change as a social process involving state learning and internalisation of new norms. Moreover, constructivism suggests that this socialisation may be aided by norm entrepreneurs (in the form of world leaders and leading states) and can be pushed along by big shocks (especially the trauma of major wars). Such socialisation processes are evident in international law on use of force, international crimes and trade. The emergence of an international law profession in the twentieth century, and the increasing placement of lawyers in state diplomatic and military services were central to the growing legalisation of state activity in all three areas. This professional network of international lawyers operated both transnationally at multilateral forums, and nationally within states, to frame problems and related solutions in the conduct of war and trade in terms of law. The networks sustaining these legal regimes have themselves evolved over time with greater state attention to public concerns, and the increasing inclusion of non-government actors in national policy formation and even multilateral negotiations on issues from land-mines to fair trade. This has had the effect of blurring the

---

[13] Lawrence Freedman, 'The age of liberal wars', in David Armstrong, Theo Farrell and Bice Maiguashca (eds.), *Force and Legitimacy in World Politics* (Cambridge: Cambridge University Press, 2005), pp. 93–107.

boundary between 'insider' policy experts and 'outsider' advocacy groups in the transnational legal networks working on human rights, LOAC and trade. A succession of wars, shocking in their scale of destructiveness, mobilised support among states for the outlawing of war. The devastation wrought by World War II (WWII) also gave added purpose to a legal regime to promote more trade and thereby, it was hoped, peace between nations. Similarly, the shocking atrocities committed against civilians during WWII, as well as the wars in the former Yugoslavia and Rwanda, spurred the development of international criminal law. Even so, in some areas of international law, most notably trade and the environment, socialisation has only occurred at a shallow level. Developed states still seek to exploit the WTO regime to their advantage and developing states are understandably unsure about the Western vision of a free trade world. And whilst social learning is occurring among states and policy elites regarding the need for co-ordinated international responses to environmental challenges, they have yet to learn to put environment concerns before national economic interests and so remain reluctant to enter into enforceable binding agreements.

American power, liberal ideology and international law

The three lenses help us to appreciate why international law will remain vibrant in this new unipolar age. The rise of US power may, in the long term, challenge the development and purpose of international law. Classical realists and positivists originally both accepted that international law required a balance of power to function. Equally, it could be argued that international law may need to adjust to the new polarity if it is to remain functional. In this context, the US attempt to claim special rights concerning preventive use of force may be read as an attempt to adjust international law to fit the new global power structure. The United States would be probably better advised to push for such adjustments by working within the framework of international law.[14] But sometimes it is necessary to break international law to remake it – indeed, norm violation is a usual procedure for affecting legal change, especially in areas where customary law is prevalent like use of force.[15] Regardless of whether such

---

[14] Edward Kwakwa, 'The international community, international law, and the United States: three in one, two against one, or one and the same?', in Michael Byers and Georg Nolte (eds.), *United States Hegemony and the Foundations of International Law* (Cambridge: Cambridge University Press, 2003), pp. 25–56.
[15] Oscar Schachter, 'Self-defense and the rule of law', *American Journal of International Law* 83 (1989), 267; Michael Bothe, 'Terrorism and the legality of pre-emptive use of force', *European Journal of International Law* 14 (2003), 16.

an adjustment is taking, and will, take place, international law remains a vital instrument of statecraft for all great powers, including the dominant one. Indeed, as Shirley Scott reasonably argues, international law is 'integral' to the power struggle between states.[16]

The liberal and constructivist lenses complete, rather than compete with, this realist account. Both help explain why even an all-powerful United States has good reason to work through international institutions whenever possible. Liberal IR scholars point out that by binding itself to international law, the United States will reassure states that are nervous about the concentration of US power and so be able to wield it without triggering resistance.[17] Similarly, constructivists point to the crucial role of international law and institutions in legitimating and thereby enabling US leadership. Here Christian Reus-Smit highlights the 'central paradox of hegemony: that stable, enduring leadership requires power to be socially embedded, and that unilateral action can be socially corrosive, with implications for both the preponderant power and world order'.[18] And, indeed, the United States is able and does wield its power through many of these institutions which it played the leading role in founding – such as the United Nations, WTO, and international financial institutions.[19] Thus, the United States' main problem with the ICC was not the fact of the court itself. After all, the United States was behind the establishment of the Nuremberg and Tokyo courts, and has been supportive since of the development of international criminal law. Rather, what alarmed US policy-makers was the proposal that the ICC be able to operate independently of the UNSC. The United States is ideologically hostile to the idea of judicial bodies being able to hold states to account (hence it has had a troubled relationships with the ICJ and the WTO Appellate Body), and moreover has a national interest in preventing the creation of international institutions through which it cannot exercise power.[20]

---

[16] Shirley V. Scott, 'Is there room for international law in realpolitik? Accounting for the US "attitude" towards international law', *Review of International Studies* 30 (2004), 88.

[17] G. John Ikenberry, *After Victory: Institutes, Strategic Restraint, and the Rebuilding of Order After Major Wars* (Princeton, NJ: Princeton University Press, 2001).

[18] Christian Reus-Smit, *American Power and World Order* (Cambridge: Polity, 2004), p. 6; on this point, see also Bruce Cronin, 'The paradox of hegemony: America's ambiguous relationship with the United Nations', *European Journal of International Relations* 7 (2001), 103–30.

[19] Nico Krisch, 'More equal than the rest? Hierarchy, equality and US predominance in international law', in Byers and Nolte, (eds.), *United States*, pp. 56–9.

[20] John F. Murphy, *The United States and the Rule of Law in International Affairs* (Cambridge: Cambridge University Press, 2004); Jason Ralph, 'International Society, the International Criminal Court and American foreign policy', *Review of International Studies* 31 (2005), 27–44.

The liberal and constructivist lenses also round out our understanding of how the United States sees and uses international law. Liberal values underpin US purpose in the world – a purpose once aimed at defeating fascist and communist peer powers, now directed towards promoting human dignity and spreading democracy.[21] Critics would suggest that US foreign policy is really about advancing the interests of 'corporate America' and that this requires suppressing human dignity and real democracy so as to reduce labour costs and remove barriers to foreign resource extraction.[22] There is sufficient evidence to suggest that economic interests exercised through US foreign policy can produce these effects. Indeed, we noted how the United States was operating through the WTO to cajole, pressurise and socialise the least-developed states into opening their fragile markets to US goods and services. However, it is also abundantly clear that the dominant narrative of US foreign policy, one that gives purpose to US leadership in the world, is a narrative of human rights and democracy promotion. To be sure, the United States is also preoccupied with its current 'global war on terror'. But realism cannot explain the 2003 Iraq War. There is no doubting now that US policy-makers realised that Iraq was not an immediate threat to US national security. Liberalism better explains this case, as an example of an 'offensive liberal war' (albeit not a terribly successful one) – that is to say, a war waged to protect human rights or/and promote regional peace through regime change.[23] Arguably this offensive liberalism is deeply ingrained in US strategic culture.[24] Indeed, it may be traced back to the nation's foundation, in the marriage of ideological exceptionalism and aggressive expansionism that characterised the American colonies as they fought off their imperial masters, wiped out native populations and spread out across the continent.[25] The same aggressive liberal purpose, renewed in post-Civil War America, may be found in the rise of US naval power and its projection into the Pacific at the turn of the twentieth century.[26] Viewed thus, as a liberal hegemon, it is understandable that the United

---

[21] Tony Smith, *America's Mission: the United States and the Worldwide Struggle for Democracy in the Twentieth Century* (Princeton, NJ: Princeton University Press, 1994).

[22] William I. Robinson, *Promoting Polyarchy: Globalization, Intervention and US Hegemony* (Cambridge: Cambridge University Press, 1996); Noam Chomsky, *Deterring Democracy* (London: Vintage, 1992).

[23] Lawrence Freedman, 'Iraq, liberal wars, and illiberal containment', *Survival* 48 (2006–7), 51–66.

[24] Theo Farrell, 'Strategic culture and American empire', *SAIS Review of International Affairs* 25 (2005), 3–18.

[25] Robert Kagan, *Dangerous Nation: American and the World, 1600–1898* (New York: Alfred A. Knopf, 2006).

[26] Edward Rhodes, 'Constructing power: cultural transformation and strategic adjustment in the 1890s', in Peter Trubowitz, Emily O. Goldman and Edward Rhodes (eds.), *The*

States would seek to create a world legal order that advances liberal values. This liberal imprint is clear in the legal regimes on human rights, international crimes and trade.

Constructivism directs our attention to how the United States views its role in the world, and the norms that shape US foreign policy. The irony is that as a liberal hegemon, the United States is ideologically inclined towards a rule-governed international order. However, crusading liberalism and the mantle of leadership often push and pull the United States into projecting power, sometimes in contradiction of international law, as occurred in the liberal wars in Kosovo in 1999 and Iraq in 2003.[27] This further suggests that in addition to the discourses on international law shared by states in general (and as expressed in the principles of customary and treaty law examined in this book), individual states also read international law through the prisms of national legal cultures. For the United States, this is a legal culture in which the US Constitution takes centre stage. Hence, the United States always attaches reservations to international human rights treaties whereby obligations are undertaken on condition that they do not contradict the US Constitution.[28] From a constructivist perspective, the US refusal to recognise the superiority of international rules over domestic law as many European states do, is not about the assertion of US power so much as the expression of US exceptionalism. Equally, it is understandable that there should be a growing preference in the United States for reading international law purposively through liberal eyes, rather than adopt the approach generally accepted by most states, which is to adopt a common-sense interpretation of the rule in question. This preference is informed by the progressive agenda for international law proposed by the New Haven School during the Cold War and has been revived by the new liberalism in American international law (in work by scholars such as Anne-Marie Slaughter, Thomas Franck and Fernando Tesón).[29] In short, even in this unipolar age, international law as read through American liberal ideology will continue to provide a central mode for the expression of US identity and exercise of US power.

Politics of Strategic Adjustment: Ideas, Institutions, and Interests (New York: Columbia University Pres, 1999), pp. 29–78.

[27] Colin Dueck, *Reluctant Crusaders: Power, Culture and Change in American Grand Strategy* (Princeton, NJ: Princeton University Press, 2006).

[28] Scott, 'American realpolitk', p. 85; Krisch, 'Hierarchy', pp. 163–7.

[29] Michael Byers and Simon Chesterman, 'Changing the rules about rules? Unilateral humanitarian intervention and the future of international law', in J. L. Holzgrefe and Robert O. Keohane (eds.), *Humanitarian Intervention: Ethical, Legal and Political Dilemmas* (Cambridge: Cambridge University Press, 2003), pp. 184–7.

Index

Acheson, Dean, 15, 78
Afghanistan
  pre-emptive action, 131
  US and LOAC, 2, 208
  US bombings (1998), 124, 126
  US invasion, 125–6
African Charter on Human and Peoples'
  Rights, 153, 162, 163, 197
aggression
  definition, 200
  international law, 189
AIRE Centre, 168
al-Qaeda, 208
Alexandrowicz, C. H., 66
Alsace, 56, 58
Alston, Philip, 177
American Convention on Human Rights,
  153, 155, 161, 162, 167, 197
American Declaration of the Rights and
  Duties of Man, 161
Amnesty International, 157, 214
Amphyctionic Council, 41
Anand, R. P., 66
Ancient Egypt, 38
Ancient Greece, 39, 40–2, 44, 72
Ancient Rome. *See* Rome
Anghie, Anthony, 66
Annan, Kofi, 146
anti-globalisation protests, 2, 223, 234,
  249, 255
Aquinas, Thomas, 44, 45, 52, 120
Arab League, 130, 163
arbitration
  Ancient Greece, 41–2
  Jay Treaty (1794), 57
  Permanent Court of Arbitration, 58
Arend, Anthony Clark, 31, 77–8, 110, 113
Argentina, 164, 215
Armstrong, David, 3, 113, 149
Asian Human Rights Charter, 163
Asian values, 65
Assyrians, 37

asylum, 165–6, 171
Augsberg, Treaty of (1555), 56
Augustine, Saint, 44, 45, 120
Austin, John, 9, 10–11, 12, 75–6, 77, 79
Australia, 129, 215, 243
Austria, WWI crimes, 186
Avignon, 58
Axelrod, R.S., 276
Azerbaijan, 215
Aztecs, 37

Baldus, 48
Bangladesh, 193, 240
Bantekas, Ilias, 220
Barbie, Klaus, 201
Beck, Robert, 31, 113
Bederman, David, 67
Belarus, 215
Belgium, universal jurisdiction, 211,
  212–13
Bentham, Jeremy, 43, 75–6, 79
Berlin Crisis, 15
Best, Geoffrey, 67
Biafra, 193
Biersteker, Thomas, 113
biological weapons, 141–2
  Biological Weapons Convention (BWC),
  141, 142, 146
biotechnology, 263, 271–2, 275
Birnie, Patricia, 266, 276
Blair, Tony, 146
blood diamonds, 234
Boer War, 184
Bosnia, 133
Boyle, Alan, 266, 276
Boyle, Francis, 92
Brazil, 164, 261
Brownlie, Ian, 152–3
Brundtland Report, 257, 262–3
Bull, Hedley, 18, 19, 31
Burkina Fasso, 215
Burundi, 198, 216

Bush, George H., 124
Bush, George W., 126, 128, 130, 139, 140,
    173, 175, 200, 268
Byers, Michael, 32, 113, 149
Byzantium, 45, 47

Cairns Group, 243
Cambodia, 132–3, 140, 193, 198, 215
Canada, 135, 225, 243, 259
Carnahan, Burrus, 220
Caroline case, 126–7, 128
Carr, E. H., 2, 16, 72, 78, 79, 80, 81–2,
    85, 89
Carson, Rachel, 260
Cartagena Convention (2000), 263
Carthage, 40
Cassese, Antonio, 133, 155, 196, 210, 220
Central African Republic, 132–3
CFCs, 263–4
Charles III, Emperor, 48
Charnovitz, Steve, 235
Chayes, Abram, 90
chemical weapons, 141–2
    Chemical Weapons Convention
        (CWC), 141, 142, 146
Chile, 164, 212
China
    ancient civilisation, 40
    environmental politics, 266, 268
    growth, 230
    human rights, 171
    Iraq War and, 130
    Kosovo and, 135
    LOAC and, 206
    nuclear weapons, 142
    origins of international law, 35
    torture, 216
    tribute system, 45
    UN veto right, 139
    Western perspective, 284
    WTO accession, 234
chivalric orders, 45, 51
chivalry, 45
Christianity
    ethical doctrines, 46
    just war, 120–1
    medieval concept of international order,
        47
Cicero, Marcus Tullius, 39, 43–4
civil wars, LOAC and, 183–6
civilians, 204–6
CIS (Commonwealth of Independent
    States), 134
Clapham, Andrew, 210
climate change. *See* global warming

Clinton, Bill, 200, 225, 268, 273
Club of Rome, 260
Cobden, Richard, 84, 229
coercion
    compliance with IL, 108–9
    positivism, 11
Cohen, Raymond, 67
Cold War
    1980s renewal, 85
    bipolarity, 80
    Cuban Missile Crisis, 89
    GATT and, 231
    human rights discourse, 157
    liberalism and, 89
Colombia, 164
colonialism
    colonial wars, 198–9
    mandates, 61
    neo-imperialism, 284–6
    New World, 50–1
    warfare methods, 207–8
common law
    evolution, 10
    precedents, 28
communication
    Habermas theory, 29–30
    states, 29
Comprehensive Test Ban Treaty (CTBT),
    139
Congo, 212–13
Constance, Council of (1414–18), 48
Constantinople, sack of (1204), 45
constructivism
    agency, 99–100, 104
    emergence, 70, 95
    environment and, 271–2, 273, 275
    generally, 95–105
    human rights, 172
    international law, 101–5, 289–91
        compliance, 109–10
    international relations, 95–101
    legal change and, 111–12
    liberal democracies and war, 140
    LOAC and, 218–19
    norms, 97–8, 102–3
    structures, 98–9, 103–4
    US hegemony and, 292–4
    use of force and, 147–8
    WTO and, 240–1, 249–50, 289
consuls, 48
Convention Against Torture (CAT), 160,
    164, 167, 168, 175, 190, 192, 195,
    196, 210, 212, 215, 217
Convention for the Suppression of the
    Financing of Terrorism, 190

Convention on Certain Conventional
    Weapons (CCW), 142, 144, 146
Convention on the Elimination of All
    Forms of Racial Discrimination,
    160
Convention on the Elimination of All
    Forms of Discrimination Against
    Women, 160
Convention on the Rights of the Child,
    160
Cook Islands, 215
cosmopolitanism, 64–5
Council of Europe, 157, 161, 163, 164,
    168
counter-terrorism
    rule of law and, 19
    self-defence, 123–6
    US and LOAC, 2, 183, 206–7, 208, 215
Crimean War, 58
crimes against humanity, 186–8
critical theory, 69, 70, 100
Croatia, 215
Cronin, Bruce, 166, 176
crusades, 45
Cuba, human rights, 159, 164
Cuban Missile Crisis, 15, 89, 90
cultural relativism, 154
customary international law
    constructivism, 103
    Geneva Conventions and, 199–201, 209
    genocide, 188
    human rights law, 153
    Kelsen, 13, 14
    scope, 16, 185, 195, 211
    self-defence, 122
    state objections, 108
    use of force, 119

D'Amato, Anthony, 17
Danzig, 61
Darfur, 200, 202
Darwinism, 284
De Garno, Denise, 276
DeSombre, Elizabeth, 277
democracy
    liberal democracies. See liberal
        democracies
    right to democracy, 155
Desch, Michael, 149
developing countries
    environmental protection
        additionality principle, 261
        environment v development, 257, 264
    good governance, 285
    neo-imperialism and, 284–6

right to development, 257
special and differentiated
    responsibilities, 233, 257
and WTO, 230, 239, 246–7
    Cancun coalitions, 243
    Development Round, 239–40
    disputes, 286
    representation, 242–3
    TRIPS, 239, 246–7
Diehl, Paul, 32
dignity. See human dignity
Dillon, Douglas, 224
Dinstein, Yoram, 149, 220
diplomacy
    ancient times, 40
    common culture, 28–9
    consuls, 48
    development, 56
    diplomatic immunity, 212
    Middle Ages, 47–8
    origins, 37–8
    Vattel, 55
distributive justice, 109
Donnelly, Jack, 155, 158, 161, 176
Downie, D. L., 276
drugs trafficking, 178
Dunant, Henri, 213
Durkheim, Émile, 95–6, 100
Dworkin, Ronald, 20

East Timor, 133–5, 193, 198
East Timor case, 154
ECOWAS (Economic Community of West
    African States), 134
Egypt, 216
Ehrlich, Paul, 260
Eichmann, Adolf, 201, 211
El Salvador, 164
Elliott, L. M., 277
environment
    compliance with international law,
        272–4
    constructivist perspective, 271–2, 273,
        275
    controversies, 254–9
    definition, 253
    development and, 257, 264
    development of international law,
        259–69
    global warming. See global warming
    Intergovernmental Panel on Climate
        Change (IPCC), 266, 271
    Kyoto Protocol, 267, 268, 269
    legal change, 274–6
    liberal perspective, 270–1, 273, 275

environment (*cont.*)
  liberal v. regulated economic order,
    255–6
  non-state actors, 255
  ozone layer, 263–5, 272
  precautionary principle, 257–9, 263
  realist perspective, 270, 272–3
  state v. global governance, 254–5
  sustainable development, 257
  theoretical perspectives, 269–76
  WTO rules and, 236, 255, 256
erga omnes obligations, 154
Eritrea, 138
Ethiopia, 138
European Convention on Human Rights,
    153, 154, 155, 160, 162, 163, 167,
    197
European Court of Human Rights
  authority, 62, 64
  global jurisprudence, 169–70
  torture, 169
European Court of Justice, 2, 62
European Union
  asylum regime, 166, 168, 171
  environmental protection, 264
  human rights, 165
  Kyoto Protocol, 268
  WTO and
    beef hormones, 235
    origins, 225, 245–6
    power, 248
    Singapore issues, 242
    US disputes, 223, 242

Falk, Richard, 89–90, 91
Farrell, Theo, 3, 113, 149
Finnemore, Martha, 103, 113, 145, 149
Fisher, Dana, 277
Forsythe, David, 155, 164–5, 176, 202
Fournet, Caroline, 220
France
  1930s balance of power, 23
  Barbie trial, 201
  colonial wars, 199
  human rights, 165
  intervention in Central African Empire,
    132–3
  intervention in Lebanon (1861), 156
  Iraq War and, 129, 130
  Kosovo intervention, 135
  LOAC and, 215
  nuclear tests, 261
  nuclear weapons, 142
  Revolution, 58–9, 74
  sovereignty, 48

tariff barriers, 228
UN veto right, 139
US Libyan bombing and, 124
Vienna Convention and, 15
Franck, Thomas, 30, 32, 91, 92, 109, 110,
    149, 294
Freeman, Michael, 176

G20, 242
G33, 242
G77, 135
G90, 243
game theory, 272–3
Gardam, Judith, 149, 220
GATS, 226, 238
GATT, 224–5, 226–7, 228, 229, 231,
    232–3, 235–7, 244, 248
Gearty, Conor, 176
Geneva Conventions, 145, 175, 181, 182,
    183, 184–5, 192, 197, 203, 208,
    209–10, 211, 215, 216
  additional protocols, 181, 184, 185,
    206, 209, 215, 216
  Common Article 3, 184, 185, 199, 205
genocide
  episodes, 193, 216
Genocide Convention, 188, 192, 193, 195,
    196, 209, 215, 216, 217
  international criminal law, 188
Gentili, Alberico, 39, 53
Georgia, 134, 215
Germany
  anti-militarist culture, 99
  human rights, 165
  LOAC and, 215
  Nazi period, 72, 85, 216
  positivism, 76
  prisoners of war, 203, 204
  unification wars, 136
  WWI crimes, 179, 186
  WWII warfare methods, 205, 208
Gibney, Matthew, 176
Gillespie, Alexander, 277
Global Environmental Facility, 267, 272
Global War on Terror, 167, 174, 184, 208
global warming
  compliance with international law, 272
  constructivist perspective, 271
  debate, 2
  depletion of ozone layer, 263–4
  greenhouse gases, 266
  international law, 265–9
globalisation
  anti-globalisation protests, 2, 223, 234,
    249, 255

cosmopolitanism, 64–5
global governance and liberal values,
    92–5
international society, 63–4
GMOs, 263, 271, 275
Goldsmith, Peter, 19
good governance, 27–8, 65, 285
Goodwin-Gill, Guy, 176
Gray, Christine, 149
Greco, Joseph, 251
Greece, 64
    See also Ancient Greece
greenhouse gases, 266
Greenpeace, 271
Grewe, Wilhelm, 15, 36, 67
Grotius, Hugo, 50, 53, 59, 74, 121
Guantanamo Bay, 19, 173, 174–5,
    285
Guatemala, 164
Guinea, 215
Guinea-Bissau, 125

Habermas, Jürgen, 29–30
Hague Convention (1899), 57, 181, 191,
    216
Hague Convention (1907), 58, 137, 141,
    145, 183, 216
Haiti, 248
Hall, Stephen, 74, 75
Hanseatic League, 45, 51
Harris, E. M., 67
Hart, H. L. A., 11, 19, 75, 76–7, 79, 110
Hathaway, Oona, 113
Havana Charter, 224
Held, David, 65
Henkin, Louis, 14, 90, 92, 109
Henry I, King of Saxony, 48
Herz, John, 17–18
Higgins, Rosalyn, 88, 109, 127, 154
Hilpod, Peter, 132
history of international law
    ancient times, 37–44
    emergence of positive law (1500–1800),
        50–6, 74
    European invention, 34
    French Revolution to League of
        Nations, 57–61
    generally, 34–65
    Middle Ages, 44–50
    origins, 34–6
    post-war era, 61–5
    Rome, 40–4
Hitler, Adolf, 85
Hittites, 37, 38
Hobbes, Thomas, 72, 78, 81

Hoekman, Bernard, 251
Hoffman, Stanley, 81
Holy Roman Emperor, 45
Hong Kong, 234
Hopf, Ted, 96
Howse, Robert, 244, 251
Hull, Cordell, 229
human dignity
    core liberal value, 92, 93, 154
    international crimes and, 191, 192–4
    WTO and, 248
human rights
    abuses, 171–2
    Afghanistan operations, 2
    African instruments, 162–3
    American conventions, 161–2
    Asian instruments, 163
    change in international law, 166–72
    compliance with international law,
        157–66
    constructivist perspective, 155–7,
        163–5, 170–2
    core liberal values, 154–5
    cultural relativism, 154
    discourse, 285
    emergence, 23
    erga omnes obligations, 154
    European conventions, 160–1
    internalisation, 170–1
    international case law, 168–70
    international criminal law and, 192
    international institutions, 64, 167–8
    international law, 152–7
    Iraq, 2
    liberal perspective, 153–5, 158–63,
        167–70, 172
    NGOs, 168
    realist perspective, 152–3, 157–8,
        166–7, 172
    regional treaties, 160–3
    UN institutions, 158–60
    UN instruments, 64, 160
    United States and, 162, 173–5, 294
Human Rights Watch, 157, 202, 214
humanitarian interventions
    Cold War period, 132–3
    emergence of principle, 24
    legality, 131–6, 146
    necessity, 122
    sovereignty and, 64
    state practice, 121–2
    UN Charter and, 121, 193
humanitarian law. See LOAC
Hungary, 215
Hurrell, Andrew, 254, 277

Ikenberry, John, 251
IMF, 64, 223, 228, 231, 284
immunities, heads of state, 212
imperialism, neo-imperialism, 284–6
India, 35, 40, 132–3, 142, 215, 230, 266,
    268
Indonesia, 19, 193, 216
Inter-American Commission on Human
    Rights, 162
Inter-American Court on Human Rights,
    161, 169
inter-disciplinary approaches, 70, 83,
    88–9, 106–12
International Campaign to Ban Landmines
    (ICBL), 144
International Committee for the Red
    Cross. See Red Cross
International Covenant on Civil and
    Political Rights, 153, 155, 159, 167,
    175, 197, 285
International Covenant on Economic,
    Social and Cultural Rights, 153,
    160, 167, 285
International Court of Justice
    jurisdiction, 62
    and jus cogens, 15
    precedents, 28
    role, 2
International Criminal Court
    aggression, 189
    CICC, 214
    complementarity principle, 197, 200,
        202–3
    creation, 180
    crimes against humanity, 187
    genocide, 188
    jurisdiction, 199
    new actor, 3
    power balance, 194–5
    presumption of innocence, 197
    Rome Statute, 195
    US rejection, 17, 62, 194, 200–1, 285,
        293
international crimes
    aggression, 189
    change, 209–16
    complementarity principle, 197, 200,
        201–2
    compliance with, 198–208
    constructivist perspective, 195–8,
        205–8, 213–16, 218–19
    content, 180–98
    crimes against humanity, 186–8
    discourse and procedures, 195–8
    domestic prosecutions, 201–2, 211–13

genocide, 188
history, 178–80
hybrid courts, 198
individual liability, 180–1, 196–7
internalisation, 215–16
jurisdiction, 181–2, 211–13
liberal perspective, 191–5, 203–4,
    210–13, 217–18
liberal values, 191–5
presumption of innocence, 197
realist perspective, 182–91, 199, 204,
    209–10, 216–17
rules, 182
terrorism, 190–1
torture, 190
tribunals, 62
victors' justice, 193, 205
war crimes, 182–6
International Criminal Tribunal for
    Rwanda (ICTR)
    case law, 185
    crimes against humanity, 187
    genocide, 188
    precedents, 211
    UNSC treaty, 195, 210
International Criminal Tribunal for the
    Former Yugoslavia (ICTY)
    case law, 185–6
    crimes against humanity, 187–8
    genocide, 188
    Martens clause and, 192
    precedents, 211
    torture, 190
    UNSC treaty, 195, 210
international humanitarian law. See LOAC
International Labour Organization, 61
international law
    change, 26, 110–12
    compliance with
        coercion, 108–9
        consent, 108
        constructivism, 109–10
        fairness, 109
        perspectives, 108–10
        persuasion, 109–10
        self-interest, 109
    constructivist perspective, 101–5,
        289–91
    emergence of profession, 290
    evolution. See history of international
        law
    foundations, 10–15
    functions, 24–6
    historical context, 283–6
    international relations and, 69

interpretation, 10
liberal perspective, 287–9
nature, 9–31
positivism. *See* positivism
power and politics, 15–18
realist perspective, 15–18, 286–7
rules and norms, 18–24, 35–6, 39
scope, 4, 107–8
theories. *See* theories
US power and, 17, 65, 291–4
international relations
constructivism. *See* constructivism
debate, 2–3
English school, 31, 82–3
founding of discipline, 72
international law and, 69
liberalism. *See* liberalism
power and politics, 15–18
realism. *See* realism
international sensibility, 102
international society
English School, 82
globalisation and, 63–4
great community concept, 52–3
historical concepts, 51–2
nature, 24–31
society of states, 52, 53–5
universal society, 51–2, 55
Vattel, 53–5
international trade. *See* trade; WTO
International Trade Organization, 224, 228
Iran, 29, 216
Iraq
2003 war. *See* Iraq War
invasion of Kuwait, 129, 138
Israeli bombing (1981), 127
torture, 216
US Baghdad bombing (1993), 124
US intervention in Kurdish territory (1991), 134
Iraq War
debate, 30
illegality, 2, 17, 281, 285
LOAC and, 2
pre-emptive action, 129–31
realist perspective, 293
US justification, 140
WMDs and, 147
Ireland, 165, 215
Isidore of Seville, 45
Islam
emergence, 45
ethical doctrines, 46
human rights and, 65

injunctions on war, 120
umma, 45
Israel
Eichmann trial, 201, 211
invasion of Lebanon, 125
LOAC and, 216
nuclear weapons, 142
pre-emptive actions, 127, 129
Strasbourg jurisprudence and, 169
torture, 216
use of force, 124
Israelites, 37
Italy, 131, 225
Ivory Coast, 215

Jackson, John, 222
Jacobson, Harold, 274, 278
Jamaica, 169
Janis, Mark, 67
Japan
1990s economic crisis, 247
anti-militarist culture, 99
constitutional rights, 215
human rights, 171
Kyoto Protocol, 268
prisoners of war, 203, 204
rise, 58
WTO and, 245
Jay Treaty (1794), 57
Jellinek, Georg, 76
John, King of England, 47
Johnson, James Turner, 150
Joyner, Christopher, 32, 113, 235
jus ad bellum, 119
jus cogens, 14–15
jus gentium, 43, 50
jus in bello, 119, 179
just war, 42, 44, 45, 46, 59, 119–21

Kant, Immanuel, 84
Kellogg–Briand Pact, 118, 119, 189
Kelsen, Hans, 11–13, 14, 16, 17, 18, 19, 76
Kennan, George, 16–17, 78
Kennedy, David, 101–2
Kennedy, John F., 15, 224
Keohane, Robert, 25, 32
Keynesianism, 244
Kingsbury, Benedict, 82, 254, 277
Koh, Harold Hongju, 110, 113
Kohn, Harold, 105
Konotorovich, Eugene, 220
Koskenniemi, Martin, 32, 67, 101, 102
Kosovo
hybrid court, 198

Kosovo (*cont.*)
    NATO intervention, 130, 133, 135–6,
        144, 294
    US warfare methods, 207
Kostecki, Michael, 251
Kratochwil, Friedrich, 32
Kritsiotis, Dino, 150
Ku, Charlotte, 32
Kurdistan, 125
Kütting, G., 277
Kuwait, Iraqi invasion, 129, 138
Kyoto Protocol, 2, 267–9, 270–1, 285,
        286
Kyrgystan, 215

Lambert, Hélène, 3
land-mines, 144
Lasswell, Harold, 88–9, 90, 109, 111
law of nations, 121
law of the sea, 50, 62, 262
League of Nations, 2, 58, 59–61, 62, 85,
        137, 145, 259
Lebanon, 125, 156
Lesaffer, Randall, 67
liberal democracies
    colonial wars, 198–9
    core liberal value, 92, 93, 154
    environmental politics, 270–1
    human rights and, 163–4
    international law and, 91
    liberal democratic peace, 140
    war and, 86–7, 140–1
liberalism
    agent-centric approach, 94
    challenge, 69
    core values, 92, 93, 154–5
    environment and, 270–1, 273,
        275
    generally, 83–95
    global governance and, 92–5
    human rights and, 153, 172
    institutions and, 94–5
    international crimes and, 191–5
    international law perspective, 287–9
    IR theory, 83–7
    legal change and, 111
    legal process theory, 88–92
    liberal economics and environment,
        255–6
    LOAC and, 217–18
    non-state actors
    soft law and, 95
    US hegemony and, 291–4
    use of force, 146–7
    utopianism, 72
    war and, 84, 86–7

WTO and, 227–30, 243–6, 248–9,
        288–9
Liberia, 134
Libya, 124, 138–41
Lieber Code (1863), 179, 192, 205
Liftin, K. T., 277
Lithuania, 49
LOAC (Law of armed conflict)
    application, 183–6
    basic rules, 183, 196, 199–201
    belligerency, doctrine of
    civilians, 204–6
    constructivist perspective, 218–19
    contents, 180–98
    development, 178–80
    internal conflicts, 183–6
    internalisation, 215–16
    liberalist perspective, 217–18
    Lieber Code, 179, 192, 205
    Martens clause, 191–2, 217
    NGOs, 213–14
    prisoners of war, 203–4
    racialisation, 207–8
    realist perspective, 216–17
    targeting doctrine, 206–7
    US counter-terrorism and, 2, 183,
        206–7, 208, 215
Locke, John, 84
Loriaux, Michael, 32
Lynch, Cecilia, 32

McAdam, Jane, 176
Macao, 234
McDougal, Myres, 88–9, 90, 109
Machiavelli, Niccolò, 72
Maguire, Peter, 220
Maiguashca, Bice, 113
Malaysia, 215, 216
Mali, 215
Marxism, 21
Meron, Theodore, 220, 221
Mesoamericans, 37
Mesopotamians, 38
methodological formalism, 19
Mexico, 215, 225, 236
Middle Ages
    Christian concept of international order,
        47
    diplomacy, 47–8
    ethical doctrines, 46
    generally, 44–50
    just war, 46
    legal culture, 49–50
    origins of sovereignty, 48–9
    state practice, 46–7
    treaties, 49

Mine Ban Treaty (MBT), 144, 146
Military Commissions Act (US), 175, 208
Mill, John Stuart, 84, 229
Milosevic, Slobodan, 138
Moir, Lindsay, 221
Moldavia, 215
Monroe Doctrine, 58
Montesquieu, Charles-Louise de, 34
Montreal Protocol (1987), 264–5
morality
    liberalism, 88–92
    positivism, 77, 78–9, 88
    realism, 78–9
Morgenthau, Hans, 2, 16, 72–3, 78, 79,
    80, 81, 85, 89
Morocco, 216

Namibia, 135
Narlikar, Amrita, 226, 235, 251
Nash, Susan, 220
national security, state business, 27
NATO, intervention in Kosovo, 130,
    135–6
natural law, 14, 43–4, 52–4, 57, 58, 74–5,
    81, 119, 121
necessity
    military necessity, 192–3
    self-defence, 122
Neff, Stephen, 67, 150
neo-imperialism, 284–6
Nepal, 216
Netherlands, 135, 199
New Stream scholarship, 69, 101
New Zealand, 243
NGOs
    environment, 255
    human rights, 168
    LOAC and, 213–14
    role, 3, 26
    United Nations and, 64
Nicaragua, 164
Nicaragua case, 143, 284
Nigeria, 19
norms
    basic norms, 13, 76
    constructivism, 97–8, 102–3
    good governance, 27–8
    international law, 18–24, 35–6, 39
    Kelsen, 11–12, 13
North Korea, 216
Norway, 215
nuclear weapons
    civilian killing, 204
    legality, 143
    Nuclear Non-proliferation Treaty
        (NPT), 142

treaties, 142
Nuremberg trials, 179, 182, 186–7, 188,
    189, 191, 194, 195, 210
Nussbaum, Arthur, 68
Nye, Joseph, 281

Odell, John, 251
Onuma, Yasuaki, 113
opinio juris, 103
Oppenheim, Lassa, 82
Organization of American States (OAS),
    161, 162, 163
OSCE, 157, 170
Ottoman Empire, 58
Oxfam, 251
ozone layer, 263–5, 272

pacta sunt servanda, 16, 246
Pakistan, 19, 124, 132–3, 142, 216
papacy, 45, 47, 48, 51, 52, 58, 284
Partial Test Ban Treaty, 142, 260
Paulus Vladimiri, 49
Pauwelyn, Joost, 232
Peloponnesian War, 72
Permanent Court of International Justice,
    60
Peru, 164, 215
Philippines, 215
Pinochet, Augusto, 212
piracy, 39, 178, 180, 181
Poland, 49, 131, 165
politics, and international law, 15–18
positivism
    coercion, 11
    definition of law, 94–5
    emergence, 50–6, 74
    international law and, 9, 11–15, 77–8,
        286
    Kelsen, 17
    legal positivism, 74
    meaning, 9
    morality and, 77, 78–9, 88
    realism and, 69–70, 71, 78–83
    rules and norms, 18–24
power
    international law and, 15–18
    law and power, 21
    realist theory, 72, 74
    Rome, 42
    structural approaches, 80–3
    theories, 70
pre-emptive actions
    Iraq War, 129–31
    legality, 123, 126–31
precautionary principle, 257–9, 263
presumption of innocence, 197

primitive legal systems, 12–13, 19
prisoners of war, 203–4
proportionality, use of force, 119, 123, 126
Publicists, 43–4, 50, 51–3, 74
Pufendorf, Samuel von, 53

Ralph, Jason, 221
Rasmusen, Hjalte, 169
Raustiala, K., 277
Reagan, Ronald, 255
realism
    English School, 31, 82–3
    environmental law and, 270, 272–3
    generally, 71–83
    human rights, 172
    international law perspective, 15–18, 286–7
    IR theory, 9, 15, 71–4
    Iraq War and, 293
    legal positivism and, 69–70, 71, 77
    LOAC and, 216–17
    meaning, 9
    morality and, 78–9
    power focus, 29
    rules and norms, 18–24
    state system, 254
    unipolar world, 282
    WTO and, 247–8, 287
Red Cross (ICRC), 144, 183, 203, 213–14
Refugee Convention, 164, 166, 167, 171, 285
refugees, 165–6, 171, 172
Rehman, Javaid, 176
renewable energy, 267
reprisals, 125
Reus-Smit, Christian, 31, 32, 103–4, 105, 113, 292
rhetoric, 42, 44
Rhodes, 41
Ricardo, David, 227
Rio Declaration (1992), 257, 258, 267
Risse, Thomas, 176
Roelofsen, C.G., 68
rogue states, 101
Rome
    division of empire, 45
    jus gentium, , 43
    just war, 119–20
    natural law, 43–4
    revival of Roman law, 49
    Roman law, 40–4
Roosevelt, Franklin, 145
Root, Elihu, 145
Ropp, Stephen, 176

Rubinstein, L., 67
Rudolph, Christopher, 221
rule of law, 18–19, 28, 283, 285
Russia
    See also Soviet Union
    1905 defeat by Japan, 58
    democracy, 170
    Iraq War and, 129, 130
    Kosovo and, 135
    Kyoto Protocol, 268
    LOAC and, 216
    nuclear weapons, 142
    pre-emptive action, 129
    torture, 216
    UN veto right, 139
    US Baghdad bombing (1993) and, 124
    US bombings in Afghanistan (1998) and, 124
    WTO accession, 234
Rwanda, 145, 179, 215, 216, 219, 291

Saar, 61
Saddam Hussein, 2
Saladin, 45
Samoa, 215
Sands, Philippe, 221, 231, 277, 285
Sardinia, 58
Saudi Arabia, 159, 267
savages, 52
Savigny, Friedrich Carl von, 22
Savoy, 58
Schabas, William, 221
Schachter, Oscar, 169
science, 75, 78
Scott, Shirley, 101, 113
Seattle protests, 2, 223, 234, 249
Selden, John, 50
self-defence
    international law, 123–31
    necessity, 122
    pre-emptive actions, 123, 126–31
    proportionality, 123, 126
    terrorism, 123–6
self-help, 12, 13, 74
Senegal, 125
September 11 attacks, responses, 125, 146, 174
sex trade, 178
Shaffer, Gregory, 242, 251
Sierra Leone, 198
Sikkink, Kathryn, 176
Simes, Dimitri, 281
Simpson, Brian, 176
Simpson, Gerry, 71, 113
Skolnikoff, E.B., 277

Slaughter, Anne-Marie, 91–2, 94, 101,
    113, 169–70, 294
slavery, 168
Smith, Adam, 84, 227, 229
social Darwinism, 284
Somalia, 133
South Africa, 169, 215, 243
South Korea, 215, 237
sovereignty
    emergence of concept, 45
    global governance and, 254
    ideal, 282
    origins, 48–9
    Peace of Westphalia (1648), 56
    sovereign equality, 16
    UN Charter, 131
    Vattel, 53–5
Soviet Union
    See also Russia
    collapse, 281
    human rights, 170, 215
    prisoners of war, 204
    whaling, 272
Spain, 131, 165, 211, 215
SPS Agreement, 227
state immunitiy, 212
state practice
    customary international law, 103
    Middle Ages, 46–7
    pre-emptive actions, 127
states
    communications, 29
    environmental governance, 254–5
    evolution, 26–9
    exercice of power, 72
    legal positivism, 75
    liberal theory, 87
    positivism, 79–80
    realist theory, 73, 79–80
    reputation, 30
    Western redefinition, 27–8
Steiner, Henry, 177
Stockholm Conference (1972), 260–2
Stoics, 43
structures, constructivism, 98–9, 103–4
Suarez, Francisco, 52–3, 74
Sudan, 124, 126, 159, 200, 202, 215, 216
Suez invasion, 140
sustainable development, 257
Sweden, 96
Switzerland, 56, 213, 215, 242
Syria, 216

Tadic case, 185, 187, 211
Tajikistan, 125, 134, 215

Tallgren, Immi, 221
Tanzania, 132–3
TBT Agreement, 227
Templars, 45
terrorism
    See also counter-terrorism
    definitions, 190–1
    international law, 190–1
Tesón, Fernando, 90–1, 92, 294
Teutonic Knights, 45, 49
Thatcher, Margaret, 15, 255
theories
    constructivism. See constructivism
    critical theory, 69, 70, 100
    generally, 69–112
    interdisciplinary approaches, 70,
        106–12
    liberalism. See liberalism
    New Stream scholarship, 69
    positivism. See positivism
    realism. See realism
Thirty Years' War, 96
Thucydides, 39, 72, 78
Tokyo trials, 179, 182, 187
Torrey Canyon, 260
torture
    See also Convention Against Torture
    ECHR jurisprudence, 169
    human dignity and, 192
    international law, 190
    state practice, 216
    universal jurisdiction, 212
trade
    See also WTO
    change of WTO rules, 242–7
    compliance with WTO rules, 233–41
    constructivist perspective, 231–3,
        240–1, 245–7, 249–50
    GATT trade rounds, 224
    international rules, 225–33
    liberal perspective, 227–31, 235–40,
        243–6
    liberal values, 227–30
    Most-Favoured Nation status, 232,
        249
    realist perspective, 225–7, 233–5,
        242–3, 247–8
tragedy of the commons, 272, 275
Trail Smelter case, 259
treaties See entries for specific treaties
    ancient times, 40
    Middle Ages, 49
    origins, 38
    Peace of Westphalia (1648), 56
    validity, threat of force, 108

Triepel, Heinrich, 76, 77
TRIPS, 226, 232–3, 239, 240, 246–7
Troope, Stephen, 104
Tulumello, Andrew, 113
Turkey, 125, 179, 186, 216

ubu societas ibi lex, 20
Uganda, 132–3, 216
Ukraine, 215
UNCLOS, 262
UNDP, 240, 267
UNEP, 262, 264
unipolarity, 80, 281–2
United Kingdom
    1930s balance of power, 23
    abolition of slavery, 168
    Boer War, 184
    Caroline case, 126–7
    colonial wars, 199
    free trade, 228
    human rights, 165
    Iraq War. *See* Iraq War
    Jay Treaty (1794), 57
    Kosovo intervention, 135
    LOAC and, 215
    nuclear weapons, 142
    Pinochet case, 212
    post-Napoleonic world, 59
    rule of law and, 19
    Suez invasion, 140
    United Nations and, 139
    US, support of, 124
    warfare methods, 206
    WWII strategies, 205–6
United Nations
    1970 Declaration on Friendly Relations,
        118–19, 124
    aggression and, 189
    anti-terror conventions, 123–6
    establishment, 61
    General Assembly resolutions, 63
    great powers, 58
    human rights institutions, 158–60
    human rights instruments, 64, 156–7,
        160
    and Israel, 124
    Security Council. *See* United Nations
        Security Council
United Nations Charter
    American critique, 17
    Articles
    2(4), 118, 121, 124, 131, 133, 138, 141
    2(7), 121, 131, 133, 193
    51 (as in Article 51), 118, 119, 121,
        123, 126

    55 (as in Article 55), 155, 156
    56 (as in Article 56), 156
    Chapter VII, 118, 124, 133, 134, 137,
        143, 195
    humanitarian interventions and, 121,
        193
    NGOs and, 64
    realist perspective, 287
    state sovereignty, 131
    use of force, 118
    United Nations High Commissioner for
        Human Rights (UNHCHR), 158,
        160
    United Nations High Commissioner for
        Refugees (UNHCR), 144, 171
United Nations Security Council
    compliance mechanisms, 137–9
    humanitarian interventions and, 133–5
    ICC powers, 201
    Iraq War and, 129–31
    Israel and, 127
    power balance, 195, 284
    reprisals and, 125
    resolutions: 678, 687, 688, 1160, 1199,
        1296, 1373, 1422, 1441, 129, 130,
        134, 135, 143, 146, 201
    role, 2
    terrorism and, 125
    use of force, 142–4
United Provinces, 56
United States
    1930s isolationism, 23
    African embassy bombings, 124
    Aghanistan and. *See* Afghanistan
    Berlin Crisis, 15
    Bretton Woods institutions and, 228–9
    Cambodian bombing, 140
    Caroline case, 126–7
    Civil War, 136, 184, 193
    Cold War, 73
    colonial wars, 199
    counter-terrorism and LOAC, 2, 183,
        206–7, 208, 215
    Cuban Crisis, 15
    development aid, 261
    empire, 281
    environment, 264
        international politics, 267, 270, 273
        Kyoto Protocol, 268–9, 270–1, 285
        precautionary principle, 259
        Trail Smelter case, 259
    free trade, 228–9
    Guantanamo Bay, 19, 173, 174–5, 285
    hegemony, 243, 281–2
    human rights and, 162, 173–5, 294

humanitarian interventions, 24, 135
ICC and, 62, 194, 200–1, 285, 293
international law and, 17, 65, 291–4
Iranian airliner shooting (1988), 127
Iraq, interventions in, 124, 134
Iraq War. *See* Iraq War
Israel and, 124
Jay Treaty (1794), 57
lawlessness, 284–5
liberalism, 90
Libyan bombing, 124
Military Commissions Act, 175, 208
Monroe Doctrine, 58
Nicaragua case, 17
North Korea and, 99
nuclear weapons, 142
pre-emptive actions, 128–31
rule of law and, 19
September 11 attacks, 125, 146, 174
stock market crash (1929), 228
tariff barriers, 240
unilateralism, 139, 281–2
unipolarity, 80, 281–2, 291–4
United Nations and, 139
and Vienna Convention, 15
Vietnam War, 73, 261
warfare methods, 206
WTO and, 293
  beef hormones, 235
  disputes, 223, 242
  gasoline, 237
  IPRs, 239, 246
  origins, 223–5
  power, 248
  services, 239
  tuna–dolphin, 236, 237
Universal Declaration of Human Rights
  (UDHR), 65, 155, 156, 170, 197,
  285
universal jurisdiction, 181–2, 211–13
use of force
  ancient rules, 40
  chivalric codes, 45
  compliance with law on, 136–41
  constructivist perspective, 122–3,
    144–8
  humanitarian interventions. *See*
    humanitarian interventions
  international law, 118–136
    customary law, 119
    UN Charter, 118, 121
  jus cogens, 15
  just war, 42, 44, 45, 46, 59, 119–21
  legal change, 141–6
  liberal democracies and, 86–7, 140–1

liberal perspective, 119–22, 142–4,
  146–7
Locke on, 84
meaning of armed attack, 123
proportionality, 119, 123, 126
realist perspective, 72, 118–19, 141–2,
  146
reprisals, 125
Roman rules, 42, 44
self-defence. *See* self-defence
state business, 27
threat, and validity of treaties, 108
utilitarianism, 75–6
utopianism, 72
Utrecht, Treaty of (1713), 56
Uzbekistan, 216

Van den Bossche, Peter, 252
Vander Lugt, Robert, 31, 113
Vattel, Emerich de, 53–5, 74
Venezuela, 215
Venice, 47, 48
Verzijl, J. H. W., 68
Victor, D.G., 277
victors' justice, 193, 205
Vienna Convention on Diplomatic
  Relations, 212, 285
Vienna Convention on the Law of Treaties,
  108, 195, 246
Vietnam, 132–3
Vietnam War, 73, 260, 261
Vig, N. J., 276
Vitoria, Francisco de, 52, 74, 286
Vladimiri, Paulus, 49

Waltz, Kenneth, 73, 74, 78, 79, 80, 82
war. *See* use of force
wars
  Afghanistan, 126, 131, 208
  American Civil War, 136
  Balkan Wars, 138
  Bosnian War, 133
  Ethiopian-Eritrean War, 138
  Cold War, 122, 132, 133, 134, 135, 137,
    138, 155, 156, 157, 193, 231, 285
  Kosovo War, 130, 133, 135, 147, 207,
    294
  Iraq War, 128, 129, 130, 134, 138, 140,
    141, 147, 293, 294
  Wars of German Unification, 136
  World War I (*see* World War I)
  World War II (*see* World War II)
war crimes
  individual liability, 180
  international law, 182–6

weapons of mass destruction, 91, 123, 147
Weber, Max, 96, 100
Webster, Daniel, 126
Wedgwood, Ruth, 203
Weiss, Edith Brown, 274, 278
Welch, David, 72
welfare states, 27
Wendt, Alexander, 98–9, 103
Westbrook, Raymond, 67
Westphalia, Treaty of (1648), 34, 56, 59, 121
whaling, 272
Wheeler, Nicholas, 150
Wilson, Woodrow, 72, 145
Wolff, Christian, 52, 74
Wood, Stepan, 113
World Bank, 64, 223, 228, 229, 231, 267, 272, 284
World Health Organization, 143
World Order Models (WOM), 89, 90
World War I, 85, 137, 179, 186, 187, 228
World War II, 85, 99, 118, 119, 136, 137, 139, 147, 153, 154, 178, 186–7, 189, 196, 198, 203, 205, 207, 210, 215, 218, 223, 228, 242, 247, 249, 260, 291
WTO
    agreements, 226
    anti-globalisation protests, 2, 223, 234, 249, 255
    change, 242–7
    coalitions, 242–3
    compliance with rules, 233–41
    constructivist perspective, 240–1, 249–50, 289

developing countries. *See* developing countries
Development Round, 239–40, 249, 250
dispute settlement, 2, 62, 235–8
environment and, 236, 255, 256
fairness discourse, 238–9, 241, 248–9, 288
foundation, 222
institutions, 244–5
intellectual property, 239
liberal perspective, 248–9, 288–9
liberal values, 227–30
Montreal rules, 235
non-discrimination principle, 232–3, 241; *see also* Post-Favoured Nation status (under Trade heading)
North-South value conflict, 230–2
origins, 223–5
preferential trading arrangements, 241, 250
principles, 232–3
realist perspective, 247–8, 287
reciprocity principle, 232
rules, 225–33
services, 239
Singapore issues, 242
technical assistance, 246
unbalanced rules, 230

Yemen, 215
Yugoslavia, 138–9, 171, 179, 291

Zimbabwe, 169, 215